Democracy for the Few

Second Edition

Democracy for the Few

SECOND EDITION

Michael Parenti

St. Martin's Press
New York

JK
271
. P29
1977

Library of Congress Catalog Card Number: 76-41932
Copyright © 1977 by St. Martin's Press, Inc.
All Rights Reserved.
Manufactured in the United States of America.
0987
fedcba
For information, write: St. Martin's Press, Inc.,
175 Fifth Avenue, New York, N. Y. 10010

cover design, cover art, and interior art by Warren Linn

cloth ISBN: 0-312-19320-3
paper ISBN: 0-312-19355-6

To Samuel Hendel and Clara Hendel

Preface to Second Edition

Democracy for the Few attempts to bring together and analyze the major aspects of the American political system. This second edition preserves the basic structure of the first, along with many of the original materials, but it also contains much updated information and, I think, a more developed interpretation. Added attention has been given to the dynamics of the political economy, the abuses of state power at home and the role of U.S. power abroad. The hope is that this updated edition retains whatever virtues were found in the original, while adding a few of its own.

More than a dozen years ago, Theodore Lowi wrote a lively and insightful critique of existing American government textbooks. Among other things, he said most texts lack an analytic perspective and tend to be inventorial, overly comprehensive and therefore dull. The superior book would be one that "is hardly half the size of the typical leading texts, yet certainly more than half the usual nuts and bolts are contained somewhere within its pages. . . . In place of coverage, it offers analysis, good middle level theory and, therefore, incitement to controversy and inquiry."[1]

Whether Lowi would agree or not, I believe this is an apt description of the kind of book I have tried to write: one that is packed with information about the substance, performance, output and structure of the political system, but information which, rather than cataloguing the obvious and the trivial, draws the reader to an inquiry, an analysis and an overall synthesis of American political reality.

Democracy for the Few is more concerned with being relevant than topical, more concerned with scrutinizing than sustaining the established myths of the existing politico-economic system. My hope is that it will do its small part in developing an informed citizenry dedicated to principles of equality, self-rule and socio-economic justice.

---

1. Theodore Lowi, "American Government, 1933–1963: Fission and Confusion in Theory and Research," *American Political Science Review*, 58, September 1964, p. 599.

For the present edition I once more enjoyed the expert editorial support of Thomas Broadbent of St. Martin's Press. The efforts of Carolyn Eggleston, also of St. Martin's, are also appreciated. I am indebted to David Danelski, Azriel Bibliowicz Goldstein and Douglas Rosenberg for their guidance and assistance. Those persons who worked directly on the manuscript of the first edition ought to have their names preserved herein, specifically, Peter Bachrach, Philip Meranto, Peter Schwab, Catherine MacKinnon, the late Richard Warner, the late Lyman Jay Gould, Barry Rossinoff and most of all Cheryl Smalley.

The personal inscription remains the same: To Clara and Samuel Hendel, one of the very nicest and best teams in the academic world. Their friendship and support, extending back over many years, have helped me in ways that go beyond the confines of scholarship. In return they have my lasting appreciation and the dedication of this book.

Michael Parenti

Contents

Democracy for the Few

Second Edition

The Study of Politics

1

WHO GOVERNS IN THE UNITED STATES? Whose interests are served by the American political system? Who gets what, when, how and why? Who pays and in what ways? These are the questions investigated in this book. American government as portrayed in most textbooks bears little resemblance to actual practice. What many of us were taught in school might be summarized as follows:

(a) The United States was founded by persons dedicated to building a nation for the good of all its citizens. A Constitution was fashioned to limit authority and check abuses of power. Over the generations it has proven to be a "living document" which, through reinterpretation and amendment, has served us well.

(b) The nation's political leaders, the President and the Congress, are for the most part responsive to the popular will. The people's desires are registered through periodic elections, political parties and a free press. Decisions are made by small groups of persons within the various circles of government, but these decision-makers are kept in check by each other's power and by their need to satisfy the electorate in order to remain in office. The people do not rule but they select those who do. Thus government decisions are grounded in majority rule—subject to the restraints imposed by the Constitution for the protection of minority rights.

(c) The United States is a nation of many different social, economic, ethnic and regional groups, which make varied and competing demands on public officeholders. The role of

1

government is to act as a mediator of these conflicting demands, attempting to formulate policies that benefit the public. Most decisions are compromises that seldom satisfy all interested parties but usually allow for a working consensus; hence every group has a say and no one chronically dominates.

(d) These institutional arrangements have given us a government of laws and not of men which, while far from perfect, allows for a fairly high degree of popular participation and a slow but steady advance toward a more prosperous and equitable society.

Up from Innocence

Recently many Americans have begun to question whether the political system works as described above. With the persistence of poverty, unemployment, inflation, overseas interventions, gargantuan military budgets, crises in our transportation, health, educational and welfare systems, environmental devastation, deficient consumer and worker protection, increasing taxes, a growing national debt, municipal bankruptcies, urban decay, widespread crime in the streets and in high public places—many persons find it difficult to believe that the best interests of the American people are being served by the existing political process.

The central theme of this book is that our government represents the privileged few rather than the needy many, and that elections, political parties and the right to speak out are seldom effective measures against the influences of corporate wealth. The laws of our polity operate chiefly with undemocratic effect because they are written principally to advance the interests of the haves at the expense of the have-nots and because even if equitable in appearance, they usually are enforced in highly discriminatory ways. Furthermore, it will be argued that this "democracy for the few" is not a product of the venality of officeholders as such but a reflection of how the resources of power are distributed within the entire politico-economic system. The chapters ahead treat such topics as America's dominant value system, the structure of the corporate economy, the outputs of public policy, the role of the mass media, the uses of law and order and the functions of voting, elections, political parties, pressure groups, the Constitution, Congress, the presidency, the courts and the federal bureaucracy.

The Inescapability of Politics

The "political system," as the term is used here, refers to the executive, legislative and judicial institutions of government along with the political parties, elections, laws, lobbyists and private-interest groups that affect public policy. One of my conclusions is that the distinction between "public" and "private" is often an artificial one. Public agencies are heavily under the influence of private-interest groups, and there are private interests, like some defense companies, that depend completely on the public treasure for their profits and survival.

The decisions made by government are called "policy" decisons. One characteristic of policy decisions is that they are seldom, if ever, neutral. They almost always benefit some interests more than others, entailing social costs that are rarely equally distributed. The shaping of a budget, the passage of a piece of legislation and the development of an administrative program are all policy decisions, all *political* decisions, and there is no way to execute them with neutral effect. If the wants of all persons could be automatically satisfied, there would be no need to set priorities and give some interests precedence over others, indeed, no need for policies or politics as the words have just been used.

"Politics" herein refers to the play of forces bearing upon the public decision-making process and the interplay of public and private power, group demands and class interests. The way prisons and mental institutions are run, for instance, is not only an administrative matter but a political one, involving the application of a particular ideology about normality, authority and social control which is protective of certain interests and values and suppressive of others.[1]

"Politics" can be used in something other than the interest-group sense. Among socialists, for instance, "politics" signifies not only the competition among groups within the present system but also the struggle to change the entire politico-economic structure, not only the desire to achieve predefined ends but the struggle to redefine ends by exposing the injustices of the capitalist system and posing alternatives to it.[2]

1. See the section in Chapter Nine entitled "Psycho-controls for Law and Order."

2. However, socialists frequently will engage in political struggles for immediate goals, such as agitating against government oppression and U.S. militarism at home and abroad, and supporting progressive causes like environmental protection and lettuce and grape boycotts led by the United Farm

Politics today covers every kind of issue from abortion to school prayers, but the bulk of public policy is concerned with economic matters. The most important document the government produces each year is the budget. Probably the two most vital functions of government are taxing and spending. Certainly they are necessary conditions for everything else it does, whether it be delivering the mail or making war. The very organization of the federal government reflects the close involvement the state has with the economy: thus one finds the Departments of Commerce, Labor, Agriculture, Interior, Transportation and Treasury, and the Federal Trade Commission, the National Labor Relations Board, the Interstate Commerce Commission, the Federal Communications Commission, the Securities and Exchange Commission, etc. Most of the committees in Congress can be identified according to their economic functions, the most important having to do with taxation and appropriations.

If so much of this study of American government seems concerned with economic matters, it is because that's what government is mostly about. Nor should this relationship be surprising. Politics and economics are but two sides of the same coin. Economics is concerned with the allocation of scarce resources for competing ends, involving conflicts between social classes, and among groups and individuals within classes. Much of politics is a carry-over of this same struggle. Both politics and economics deal with questions affecting the material survival, prosperity and well-being of millions of people; both deal with the first conditions of social life itself.

One of the central propositions of this book is that there exists a close relationship between political power and economic wealth. As the sociologist Robert Lynd once noted, power is no less political because it is economic. By "power" I mean the ability to get what one wants, either by having one's interests prevail in conflicts with others or by preventing others from raising conflicting demands. Power presumes the ability to control the actions and choices of others either through favor, fear, fraud or force and to

---

Workers. They do so because they are interested in alleviating the plight of oppressed people even if only in marginal ways and they wish to contain the ruling powers of the center-right forces as much as possible. Also, through such struggles they seek to heighten political consciousness and develop ways of fighting the abuses of capitalism. Even when running their own candidates, most socialists see election campaigns primarily as a way of alerting voters to the evasive and deceptive qualities of the major candidates and creating a dialogue that goes beyond mainstream politics.

manipulate the social environment to one's advantage. Power belongs to those who possess the resources which enable them to control the behavior of others, such resources as jobs, organization, technology, publicity, media communication, social legitimacy, expertise, essential goods and services and—the ingredient that often determines the availability of these things—money.

Many political scientists have managed to ignore the relationship between power and wealth, treating the corporate giants, if at all, as if they were but one of a number of interest groups. Most often this evasion is accomplished by labeling any approach which links class, wealth and capitalism to politics as "Marxist." To be sure, Marx saw such a relationship, but so did more conservative theorists like Hobbes, Locke, John Harrington, Adam Smith and, in America, Hamilton, Adams and Madison. Indeed, just about every theorist and practictioner of politics in the seventeenth, eighteenth and early nineteenth centuries saw the linkage between political organization and economic interest, and between state and class, as not only important but *desirable* and essential to the well-being of the polity. "Those who own the country ought to govern it," declared John Jay. A permanent check over the populace should be exercised by "the rich and the well-born," urged Alexander Hamilton.

Unlike most of the theorists before him, Marx was one of the first in the modern era to see the existing relationship between property and power as *un*desirable, and this was his unforgiveable sin. Marx wrote during the mid-to-late nineteenth century, when people were becoming increasingly critical of the abuses of industrial capitalism and when those who owned the wealth of society preferred to draw attention away from the relationship between private wealth and public power and toward more "respectable" subjects. The tendency to avoid critical analysis of American capitalism persists to this day among business people, journalists, lawyers and academics.[3]

Politics remains very much a part of our lives, whether we want it that way or not. The government plays a crucial role in determining the condition of our communities, our housing,

3. See William Appleman Williams, *The Great Evasion* (Chicago: Quadrangle Books, 1964) for an analysis of the way Marxist thought has been stigmatized or ignored by American intellectuals and those who pay their salaries. See also Sidney Fine, *Laissez-Faire and the General-Welfare State* (Ann Arbor: University of Michigan Press, 1964) for a description of capitalist, anti-Marxist orthodoxy in the United States in the late nineteenth century and its control over business, law, economics, university teaching and religion.

education, medical care, work, recreation, transportation and natural environment. As a protector of privilege and purveyor of power, the state can bestow favors on a select few while sending many off to fight wars halfway around the world. In ostrich-like fashion readers might go "do their own thing," pretending that they have removed themselves from the world of politics and power. They can leave political life alone but it will not leave them alone. They can escape its noise and its pretensions but not some of its worst effects. One ignores the doings of the state only at one's own risk—and at the risk of one's fellow citizens, many of whom are less fortunately situated and more adversely affected by what government does and does not do.[4]

Rather than evade controversial questions in the pages ahead, I will pursue certain of them. But my intent is not to provoke controversy for its own sake. Rather I wish to offer a realistic and neglected analysis of what is happening in the American polity, even at the risk of courting some heretical ideas about the political life of our nation.

---

4. It should be added that "politics" extends beyond the actions of state and government. Decisions that leave certain matters within "private" systems of power (e.g., leaving rental costs or health care to the private market) are highly political. Private power often is even more inequitable and more difficult to evade. However, in this book we will focus on government and on how private power bears upon and is served by it.

Wealth and Want in the United States

2

IF POLITICS IS CONCERNED WITH WHO gets what, then we might begin by considering who's already got what. How is wealth distributed and used in the United States? What we discover will tell us something important about the capitalist system.[1]

Who Owns America?

About one-fifth of one percent of the population, the "super rich," own almost 60 percent of the corporate wealth in this country. Approximately 1.6 percent of the population own 80 percent of all stock, 100 percent of all state and municipal bonds, and 88.5 percent of corporate bonds.[2] There are sixty billionaire families in the United States and over 100,000 millionaires. In just about every major industry, be it steel, oil,

1. By "capitalism" I mean that system of production, ownership and consumption found in most Western and Third World countries and Japan which manifests two essential conditions: (1) the means of production, specifically the factories, land, mines, utilities, offices, banks, etc., are under private ownership; (2) their primary function is to make money for those who own them. Terms like "corporate capitalism," "corporatism" and "corporate system" refer herein to modern-day capitalism, a system in which economic power is embodied in a relatively small number of large corporations.

2. Ferdinand Lundberg, *The Rich and the Super Rich* (New York: Lyle Stuart, 1968), pp. 144 ff. Also Robert Lampman, *The Share of Top Wealth-Holders in National Wealth* (Princeton, N.J.: Princeton University Press, 1962).

aluminum or automotive, a few giant companies do from 60 to 98 percent of the business. Some two hundred companies account for about 80 percent of all resources used in manufacturing. In 1975 Exxon alone had net assets of over $32 billion; General Motors had assets of $21 billion, and American Telephone and Telegraph was worth $65 billion. Five New York banks[3] managed stock portfolios valued at $84.5 billion in 1972 and held a controlling share of the stock in three-fourths of the top 324 corporations. Chase Manhattan Bank, controlled by the Rockefellers, is the largest stockholder in CBS, NBC, Union Carbide, General Electric, United Airlines, Safeway Supermarkets and AT&T—to name only a few of its holdings. The wealth of America is not in the hands of a broadly based "middle-class ownership." If anything, the trend continues to be toward ever greater concentrations of economic power.

Yet the public is still taught that the economy consists of a wide array of independent producers. We refer to "farmers" as an interest apart from businessmen and bankers, at a time when the Bank of America has a mulitmillion-dollar stake in California farmlands; the Southern Pacific Railroad is a shipper to "agribusiness" and an owner of vast land acreage; Cal Pak, the world's largest canner of fruits and vegetables, operates at every level from the field to the supermarket with annual sales of over $400 million; and Hunt Foods and Industries, also with sales of over $400 million, has holdings in steel, matches and glass containers.

A notion enjoying popularity today is that the control of wealth has passed into the hands of corporation managers who themselves own but a small segment of the assets they command, while the corporation's actual owners, the stockholders, exercise little of the power their wealth would normally confer and have little say about the management of their own holdings. Since Berle and Means first portrayed the giant firms as developing "into a purely neutral technocracy," controlled by disinterested managers who allocated resources "on the basis of public policy rather than private cupidity,"[4] many observers have come to treat this fantasy as a reality.

Supposedly the separation of ownership from management has created a benign, service-minded corporation. In fact, the separation of ownership from management is far from complete. Almost one-third of the top 500 corporations in the United States are con-

3. Chase Manhattan, Morgan Guaranty Trust, First National City, Bankers Trust and the Bank of New York.
4. A. A. Berle, Jr., and Gardner C. Means, *The Modern Corporation and Private Property* (New York: Harcourt, Brace, 1932), p. 356.

trolled by one individual or family. Furthermore, many of the "smaller" companies are controlled by the wealthy class in America, including "more than 25,000 family-owned or closely held corporations with assets of more than $1 million which have grown and prospered. . . ."[5]: The decline of family capitalism has not led to widespread ownership among the general public. *The diffusion of stock ownership has not cut across class lines but has occurred within the upper class itself.* In an earlier day three families might have owned companies A, B and C respectively, whereas today all three have holdings in all three companies, thereby giving "the upper class an even greater community of interest than they had in the past when they were bitterly involved in protecting their standing by maintaining their individual companies."[6] The common myth is that stock ownership is widespread. This is true in that many people hold a few shares each. But the concentration of ownership is such that a very few people hold the bulk of it.

Some "family enterprises" are of colossal size. For example, the DuPont family controls eight of the forty largest defense contractors and grossed over $15 billion in defense contracts during the Vietnam war. The DuPonts control ten corporations, each with over $1 billion in assets, including Penn Central, General Motors, Coca Cola, Boeing and United Brands, along with numerous smaller firms. Over a million people work for DuPont-controlled firms. The DuPonts serve as trustees in scores of colleges including some of the country's elite schools. They own about forty manorial estates and private museums in Delaware alone, and, in an attempt to keep the money in the family, have set up thirty-one tax-exempt foundations. The family is frequently the largest contributor to Republican presidential campaigns and has financed and provided leadership for right-wing and antilabor organizations such as the proto-fascist American Liberty League and the American Conservative Union.[7] And in 1976 Pierre DuPont won the governorship of Delaware.

An even more powerful family enterprise is that of the Rockefellers. They hold over $300 billion in corporate wealth, extending into just about every industry, in every state of the Union

5. F. G. Clark and S. Ramonaczy, *Where the Money Comes From* (New York: Van Nostrand, 1961), p. 42; quoted in G. William Domhoff, *Who Rules America?* (Englewood Cliffs, N.J.: Prentice-Hall, 1967), p. 38.

6. Domhoff, *Who Rules America?*, p. 40.

7. Gerald C. Zilg, *DuPont: Behind the Nylon Curtain* (Englewood Cliffs, N.J.: Prentice-Hall, 1974).

and every nation in the nonsocialist world. The Rockefellers control five of the twelve largest oil companies and four of the largest banks in the world. They have holdings in chemicals, steel, insurance, sugar, coal, copper, tin, computers, utilities, television, radio, publishing, electronics, agribusiness, automobiles, airlines—indeed, in just about every known natural resource or manufactured commodity and service. The Rockefellers finance universities, seminaries, churches, "cultural centers," museums and youth organizations. At one time or another, they or their close associates have occupied the offices of the President, Vice-President, Secretaries of State, Commerce, Defense and other cabinet posts, the Federal Reserve Board, the governorships of several states, key positions in the CIA, the U.S. Senate and House, and the Council of Foreign Relations.[8]

In those firms not directly under family control, the supposedly public-minded managers are themselves large investors in corporate America. Managers award themselves stupendous salaries, stock options, bonuses and other benefits. The managerial elite of the top corporations are almost always wealthy men. One need only think of names like Thomas Watson, George Humphrey, David Packard, Charles Wilson and Robert McNamara (the last four also having been presidential cabinet appointees). As president of General Motors, Wilson owned GM stock worth $2.5 million; as Ford president, McNamara owned Ford stock worth $1.6 million and held stock options valued at $270,000. The interest that managers have in the corporation's profits is a direct one. Far from being technocrats whose first dedication is to advance the public welfare, they represent the more active and powerful element of a self-interested owning class.[9] Their power does not rest in their individual holdings but in their corporate positions. "Not great fortunes, but great corporations are the important units of wealth, to which individuals of property are variously attached," C. Wright Mills reminds us. "The corporation is the source of, and the basis of, the continued power and privilege of wealth."[10]

8. See Peter Collier and David Horowitz, *Rockefellers: An American Dynasty* (New York: Holt, Rinehart and Winston, 1976).

9. For lucid discussions of these points see Ralph Miliband, *The State in Capitalist Society* (New York: Basic Books, 1969), pp. 28–36, and Paul Baran and Paul Sweezy, *Monopoly Capital* (New York: Monthly Review Press, 1968).

10. C. Wright Mills, *The Power Elite* (New York: Oxford University Press, 1956), p. 116.

The Pursuit of Corporate Profit

In their book *Monopoly Capital,* Baran and Sweezy write: "The primary objectives of corporate policy—which are at the same time and inevitably the personal objectives of the corporate managers —are . . . strength, rate of growth and size. . . . Profits provide the internal funds for expansion. Profits are the sinew and muscle of strength. . . . As such they become the immediate, unique, unifying, quantitative aim of corporate success."[11] The function of the corporation, as corporation leaders themselves announce in their more candid moments, is not to perform public services or engage in philanthropy but to make as large a profit as possible.

The social uses of the product, its effects upon communal life, personal safety, human well-being and the natural environment, win consideration in capitalist production, if at all, only to the extent that they do not violate the pecuniary interests of the producer.

This relentless pursuit of profit results from something more than just the greed of businessmen. It is an unavoidable fact of capitalist life that enterprises must expand in order to survive. To stand still amidst growth is to decline, not only relatively but absolutely. Robert Theobald concludes that business firms

have a special interest in the fastest possible rate of growth, which may not be compatible in the long run with the interests of society. . . . The corporation's profits depend essentially on economic growth and . . . any slowing down in the rate of increase in production tends to cut into the profits of the firm. The corporation must therefore press for policies that will cause the most rapid rate of growth.[12]

Profits are made by getting workers to produce more in value than they receive in wages. Profits are accumulated in the form of savings which produce interest, or capital investments which produce further profits. Corporate profits are themselves surplus wealth which must either be distributed to the rich as dividends for their private consumption or reinvestment, or reinvested by the corporation for more profit. Capital must always be realizing itself through investment, through its actualization and expansion in labor and production. Ironically then, those with great wealth face the problem of constantly having to devise ways of making more money, of finding profitable areas into which they can invest their profits.

11. Baran and Sweezy, *Monopoly Capital,* pp. 39–40.
12. Robert Theobald, *The Challenge of Abundance* (New York: American Library, 1962), p. 111.

WARREN LINN

Corporations draw subsidies from the public treasure, rig prices at artificially high levels, impose speedups, layoffs and wage cuts, and move to cheaper labor markets in other countries. In these ways they are often able to increase profits amidst widespread want and unemployment. Business does fine but the people suffer. The economy booms but the people bust. In the first quarter of 1975, for instance, corporate after-tax profits totaled $62.3 billion while unemployment increased by one million, bringing the official total to 8.2 million, or almost 9 percent of the labor force.

By cutting labor costs in order to increase profits, corporations also cut into the buying power of the very public that is supposed to buy their commodities. This is one of the contradictions of capitalist economics:

Every capitalist's ideal would undoubtedly be to pay his workers as little as possible, while selling products to better-paid workers from other businesses. For the system as a whole, no such solution is possible; the dilemma is basic to capitalism. Wages, a cost of production, must be kept down; wages a source of consumer spending, must be kept up.[13]

It is often claimed by businessmen that wage increases are the cause of inflation. In fact, wages have not kept pace with profit growth. In 1974, to take one industry, coal profits rose 181 percent, coal prices increased 61 percent, but unemployment in the mines increased drastically and miners' wages rose only 8 percent.[14] It is not wage demands that determine the upward direction of prices. *The "wage-price spiral" has really been a profit-price spiral, and the worker is more the victim than the cause of inflation.*

The tendency in a capitalist economy is toward the kind of chronic instability caused by overproduction, overinvestment, underconsumption, misuse of productive capacities and labor resources, distorted growth patterns, social dislocation, a glut of nonessential consumer goods and services and a shortage of essential ones. Production is sometimes cut back, sometimes intensified, in order to maintain profits; prices are raised to compensate for diminished sales; and layoffs and wage cuts are imposed whenever possible. Demand decreases; markets shrink still further; prices are rigged still higher; inventories accumulate; investment opportunities disappear; capital—much of it nothing more than an elaborate web

13. "Economy in Review," *Dollars and Sense,* March 1976, p. 3.
14. *Boston Globe,* November 29, 1974; also Peter Kihss, "Factory Workers in Suburbs are Reported on Treadmill," *New York Times,* July 29, 1969.

of credit—begins to "shrink away," and the country moves toward a recession. This instability is endemic to the system, there having been at least sixteen business cycles within the last hundred years.[15]

Recessions function to keep labor from getting "too aggressive," as well as weeding out the weaker capitalists. In boom times, with nearly full employment, workers are more ready to strike and press for better contracts. Other jobs are easy to get, and business finds it too costly to remain idle while markets are expanding. Wages are able to cut into profits during good times, but a recession reverses the trend. Business is better able to resist labor demands. A reserve army of unemployed helps to deflate wages. Unions are weakened and often broken; labor contracts offer little in the way of gains and benefits, and profits rise far faster than wages. A review of the U.S. economy for the recession year of 1975 shows big business "coming out ahead of the workers in most areas. The general pattern reveals increased profits, decreased real wages, increased unemployment, higher labor productivity and decreased strike activity."[16]

During recessions, real hardship is experienced by millions, especially those in the lower-income brackets. But the very rich, enjoying vast reserves, suffer no deprivations to speak of in their personal lives. Indeed, during the recession years of 1974 and 1975, sales of jewelry, antiques, executive apartments, mansions, yachts and Rolls-Royces were booming among upper-class customers.[17] And in business affairs, the economically strong are able to turn the adversity of others into gain for themselves. In the depression of 1875, Morgan, Rockefeller, Gould, Carnegie, Vanderbilt, Frick and others found ample opportunity to press their advantages without stint, gathering control over the broken holdings of smaller competitors, cutting wages, breaking strikes and increasing profits. In more recent depressions, the fortunes of such men as Joseph Kennedy, Howard Hughes and John Paul Getty grew, as did the wealth of the Morgans, Mellons, DuPonts and Rockefellers.

During good times and bad, giant firms rarely go bankrupt. As the steel companies have shown, they can be inefficient and still make profits. While operating at less than full capacity, at a

15. David M. Gordon, "Recession Is Capitalism as Usual," *New York Times Magazine*, April 27, 1975.

16. Ben Bedell, "Workers Lost Out in 1975," *Guardian*, January 14, 1976, p. 4.

17. See the *New York Times*, February 2, 1975, and the *New York Post*, March 5, 1975. U.S. sales of Rolls-Royce automobiles were up 25 percent in the first quarter of 1976; see *Dollars and Sense*, April 1976, p. 9.

time of high unemployment and price squeeze, U.S. Steel showed a profit increase of 62 percent in the first quarter of 1973. For the various giants, their position in the industry and their share of the market may change slightly over the years, "but mergers and reorganizations keep the assets and production facilities intact."[18] Even if it is assumed that great profits are the just reward for great risks, in truth there is seldom much risk for the super rich.

One explanation as to why our nation's economic problems remain unsolved or actually worsen is that most of the resources of our society are devoted to other things, to the production of goods and services for private profit. Those who insist that private enterprise can answer our needs seem to overlook the fact that private enterprise has no such interest, at least not in those areas where no profit is to be had. The poor may *need* shoes but they offer no market for shoes; there is a market only when need (or want) is coupled with *buying power* to become *demand*. The shoe manufacturer responds to market demand—that is, to a situation in which he can make money—and not to human need no matter how dire it be. When asked by the Citizens' Board what they were doing about the widespread hunger in the United States, numerous food manufacturers responded that the hungry poor were not their responsibility. As one company noted: "If we saw evidence of profitability, we might look into this."[19]

The difference between *need* and *demand* shows up on the international market also. When buying power rather than human need determines how resources are used, then poor nations feed rich ones. Much of the beef, fish and other protein products consumed by North Americans (and their livestock and domestic pets) comes from Peru, Mexico, Panama, India, Costa Rica and other countries where grave protein shortages exist. These foods find their way to profitable U.S. markets rather than being used to feed the children in these countries who suffer from protein deficiencies. In Guatemala alone, 55,000 children die before the age of five each year because of illnesses connected to malnutrition. Yet the dairy farmers of countries like Guatemala and Costa Rica are converting to more profitable beef cattle for the U.S. market. The children *need* milk, but they lack the pesos, hence there is no market. Under capitalism, money is invested only where money is to be made.

18. Andrew Hacker, *The End of the American Era* (New York: Atheneum, 1970), p. 44.
19. Quoted in *Hunger, U.S.A.*, a report by the Citizens' Board of Inquiry into Hunger and Malnutrition in the United States (Boston: Beacon Press, 1968), p. 46.

Some defenders of the established system contend that the pursuit of profit is ultimately beneficial to all since the productivity of the corporations creates mass prosperity. This argument overlooks several things: high productivity frequently *detracts* from the common prosperity even while making fortunes for the few, and it not only fails to answer to certain social needs but may create new ones. The coal mining companies in Appalachia, for example, not only failed to mitigate the miseries of the people in that area; they *created* many miseries, swindling the Appalachians out of their land, underpaying them, forcing them to work under inhumane conditions, destroying their countryside and refusing to pay for any social costs resulting from corporate exploits.

Furthermore, an increasing productivity, as measured by a growing Gross National Product (GNP), may mean less efficient use of social resources and more waste. As the environmentalist Barry Commoner pointed out: in the last two decades production techniques have been developed which sharply decrease the efficiency of energy use for the sake of profits. Thus the use of leather and steel, which require $.97 and $1.50 worth of oil respectively for the production of $100 worth of goods, has been replaced by plastics requiring $8.72 worth of oil to produce the same amount of goods. Fossil fuel and nuclear energy systems may be socially wasteful and dangerous compared to solar and tital energy, yet they are highly profitable for those who have capital investments in them.

The *human* value of productivity rests in the social purpose to which it is directed. Is the purpose to plunder the environment without regard to present and future ecological needs, fabricate endless consumer desires, produce shoddy goods that are designed to fall apart quickly, create wasteful high-priced forms of production and service, pander to snobbism and acquisitiveness, squeeze as much compulsive toil out of workers while paying them as little as possible—all in order to grab as big a profit as one can? Or is productivity geared to satisfying the communal needs of the populace in an equitable and rational manner? Is it organized to serve essential needs first and superfluous wants last, to care for the natural environment and the health and safety of citizens and workers? Is it organized to maximize the capabilities, responsibilities and participation of its people? Capitalist productivity-for-profit gives little consideration to the latter set of goals. Indeed, what is called productivity, as measured by *quantitative* indices, may actually represent a decline in the *quality* of life—hence the relationship between the increasing quantity of automobiles and the deceasing quality of the air we breathe. Such measurements of "prosperity" offer, at best, a most haphazard accounting of many qualities of social life.

The apologists for capitalism argue that the accumulation of great fortunes is a necessary condition for economic growth, for only the wealthy can provide the huge sums needed for the capitalization of new enterprises. Yet a closer look at many important industries, from railroads to atomic energy, would suggest that much of the funding has come from the public treasury—that is, from the taxpayer—and that most of the growth has come from increased sales to the public—from the pockets of consumers. It is one thing to say that large-scale production requires capital accumulation but something else to presume that the source of accumulation must be the purses of the rich.

In areas of private research giant corporations leave a good deal of the pioneering work to smaller businesses and individual entrepreneurs, holding back their own resources until money is to be made. Referring to electric appliances one General Electric vice-president noted: "I know of no original product invention, not even electric shavers or heating pads, made by any of the giant laboratories or corporations. . . . The record of the giants is one of moving in, buying out and absorbing the small creators."[20]

Apologists for the present system insist that big production units are more efficient than smaller ones. In fact, it is highly questionable whether the huge modern firm represents the most efficient form of production. In many instances, production units tend to become less efficient and more bureaucratized with size, and after a certain point in growth there is a diminishing return in productivity.

Moreover, bigness is less representative of an increasing technological efficiency than of an increasing greed. When the same corporation has holdings in mining, manufacturing, housing, insurance, utilities, amusement parks, publishing and communications, it becomes clear that giantism is not the result of a technological necessity that supposedly brings greater efficiency but the outcome of capital concentration. The search is not for more efficient production but for new areas of investment. Thus firms like ITT, Gulf Oil, and General Motors are today buying up great tracts

---

20. Quoted in Baran and Sweezy, *Monopoly Capital*, p. 49. The record of the biggest oil companies, Exxon and Shell, is strikingly undistinguished in the field of oil exploitation. See Anthony Sampson, "How the Oil Companies Help the Arabs to Keep Prices High," *New York*, Sepetmber 22, 1975, p. 55.

of land throughout America, aware that land values have almost doubled in one decade. With control over the land, corporations are able to profit greatly in the development of residential areas. U.S. Steel constructed a town in Maryland; Gulf Oil built Reston, Virginia; and Westinghouse and ITT laid plans for "cities within a city," in the Washington, D.C., area, against the protests of local residents.

If the public welfare is at most a secondary consideration in the management of business affairs, the same may be said of the well-being of industrial production itself. One need only recall how railroads, shipping lines, mines and factories have been bought and sold like so many game pieces for the sole purpose of extracting as much profit as possible, often with little regard for maintaining the functional capacity of the firms themselves. Describing the doings of the tycoon Jay Gould, one historian noted that whenever Gould acquired a railroad: "There was never any effort to build up a strong, soundly managed group of roads. . . . The one dominant note was speculation. . . . The roads that he touched never quite recovered from his lack of knowledge and interest in sound railroading."[21] What was true then still holds today: the long-term survival and functional capacity of an office, factory, farm, mine, railroad, bus line or newspaper are of less concern to the investor than the margin of profit to be had. If railroads and aeronautic firms sometimes totter on the edge of ruin, to be rescued only by generous infusions of government funds, it is after stockholders have collected millions in high profits. Thus during the years 1967 to 1971, the "depressed" aerospace industry, plagued by climbing costs and layoffs and repeatedly rescued from the brink of insolvency by fat government subsidies, netted for its investors $3 billion in after-tax profits.

The power of the business class is not total, "but as near as it may be said of any human power in modern times, the large businessman controls the exigencies of life under which the community lives."[22] The giant corporations control the rate of technological development and the terms of production; they fix prices and determine the availability of livelihoods; they decide which

21. R. E. Riegal, *The Story of the Western Railroads* (New York: Macmillan, 1926), cited in Matthew Josephson, *The Robber Barons* (New York: Harcourt, Brace, 1934), p. 203. Josephson offers a similar observation about Daniel Drew, p. 19.
22. Thorstein Veblen, *The Theory of Business Enterprise* (New York: New American Library Edition, n.d.), p. 8. Originally published in 1904.

labor markets to explore and which to abandon; they create new standards of consumption and decide the quality of goods and services; they divide earnings among labor, management and stockholders and donate funds to those political causes they deem worthy of support; they transform the environment itself, devouring its natural resources and poisoning the land, water and air; they command an enormous surplus wealth while millions live in acute want. And they exercise trustee power over religious, recreational, cultural, medical and charitable institutions and over much of the media and the educational system. Describing Standard Oil Company of New Jersey, David Horowitz wrote:

It has a budget exceeding $15 billion, or double the Gross National Product of Cuba. More powerful than many sovereign states, it has 150,000 agents, organizers and hired hands operating 250 suborganizations in more than 50 countries. It is part of an international syndicate which controls the economic lifeblood of half a dozen strategic countries in the underdeveloped world. In itself it is a major political force in the key electoral states of New York, Pennsylvania, New Jersey and Texas, and it has close links with other syndicate members that are major political forces in California, Ohio, Louisiana, Indiana and elsewhere. Its agents and their associates occupied the cabinet post of Secretary of State in the Administrations of Eisenhower, Kennedy and Johnson, and at the same time had influence in the CIA and other foreign-policy-making organizations of government at the highest levels. It has its own intelligence and paramilitary networks, and a fleet of ships larger than the Greek Navy. It is not a secret organization, but it is run by a self-perpetuating oligarchy whose decisions and operations are secret. And these affect directly and significantly, the level of activity of the whole U.S. economy.[23]

Assessing the influence of large corporations, Theobald concludes that "in fact the actual 'political' role of business is wider than that which has been held proper for *governments* under Western [political] theory."[24]

The Distribution of Want and Misery

The United States has been portrayed as a land of prosperity and well-being. But closer scrutiny brings no great cause for celebration.

23. David Horowitz, "Social Science or Ideology?" *Social Policy*, 1, September–October 1970, p. 30.
24. Theobald, *The Challenge of Abundance*, p. 110. Italics in the original.

The life expectancy of American men is lower than in eighteen other countries. The infant mortality rate is worse than in thirteen other nations. In eleven countries women have a better chance to live through childbirth than in the United States.[25] One out of every five American adults is functionally illiterate.[26] Almost 80 million Americans live in conditions of need on incomes that have been estimated as below minimum adequacy by the Department of Labor. Of these about 26 million are designated as living in acute poverty and want. Of the poor, only 5.4 million get either food stamps or free food. Of 6 million school children from rock-bottom poverty families, most attend substandard, overcrowded schools and fewer than 2 million receive either free or reduced-price school lunches.[27]

The majority of the poor are Whites, a fact which is not surprising in a country with a White population of more than 85 percent. Yet Black people, who compose only about 13 percent of the population, make up something closer to 45 percent of those below the officially designated poverty level. (Statistics like these are usually distorted in a way that underestimates the number of poor, and of Black poor in particular, being based on a national census that drastically undercounts transients, homeless people and those living in crowded ghettos. In April 1973 the Census Bureau reported that the 1970 census had missed counting an estimated 5.3 million people, a disproportionate number being poor and Black.)

Some Americans believe that those described as "poor" in the United States would be considered fairly well-off in Third World nations.[28] However, the Citizens' Board of Inquiry into Hunger and Malnutrition discovered in 1968 that in the United States more than 12 million suffer from conditions of malnutrition and hunger comparable to those found in places like Turkey and Pakistan. These conditions, "increasing in severity and extent from year to year," exist in every state in the Union, in rural areas, small towns and large cities.[29]

The Citizens' Board reported that many American infants die

25. Samuel Shapiro et al., *Infant, Prenatal, Maternal and Childhood Mortality in the United States* (Cambridge, Mass.: Harvard University Press, 1968) and Erwin Knoll, "The Coming Struggle for National Health Insurance," *Progressive*, December 1969, p. 30.

26. According to a U.S. Office of Education survey; see *Syracuse Post-Standard*, October 30, 1975.

27. See *Hunger, U.S.A.*

28. See Michael Harrington, *The Other America: Poverty in the United States* (Baltimore: Penguin Books, 1963), p. 9.

29. See *Hunger, U.S.A.*

within the first two years of life because of starvation. Another study found that the premature-birth rate of the poor in the United States is three times that of middle-income people, and some 50 percent of children from very poor families grow to maturity with impaired learning ability, while 5 percent are born mentally retarded because of prenatal malnourishment.[30] In 1975 a group of scientists at the University of California released a study showing that over *one million* babies and young children in the nation are suffering brain damage from malnutrition caused by extreme poverty. When malnourished pregnant women are included in the findings, another million babies yet to be born are seriously imperiled.[31] One doctor found "serious malnutrition deficiencies" in almost half the children from poor families in Texas and Louisiana.[32] And a Senate select committee reported that "infectious diarrhea, dehydration, malnutrition and anemia" were typical health conditions among children of the rural poor.[33] "Mother after mother in region after region reported that the cupboard was bare, sometimes at the beginning and throughout the month, sometimes only in the last week of the month."[34] Teachers reported that children came to school too hungry to learn and sometimes in such pain that they had to be taken home. Younger children regularly went to bed hungry, never knowing the taste of milk.

Children who live in chronic hunger, according to Dr. Robert Coles, "become tired, petulant, suspicious and finally apathetic." Malnourished four- and five-year-olds, he noted, experience the aches of the body as more than just a physical fact of life. They interpret such misery as a judgment made by the outside world upon them and their families, a judgment that causes them to reflect upon their own worth.

They ask themselves and others what they have done to be kept from the food they want or what they have done to deserve the pain they seem to feel. . . .

All one has to do is ask some of these children in Appalachia who have gone north to Chicago and Detroit to draw pictures and see the way

30. Nick Kotz, *Let Them Eat Promises: The Politics of Hunger in America* (Englewood Cliffs, N.J.: Prentice-Hall, 1969).
31. *New York Times*, November 2, 1975.
32. *New York Times*, April 28, 1970.
33. "Rural Housing Famine," *Progressive*, April 1971, pp. 7–8; see also Homer Bigart, "Hunger in America: Stark Deprivation Haunts a Land of Plenty," *New York Times*, February 16, 1969.
34. *Hunger, U.S.A.*, p. 9.

they will sometimes put food in the pictures. . . . All one has to do is ask them what they want, to confirm the desires for food and for some kind of medical care for the illnesses that plague them.[35]

The well-known Field Foundation report by a team of doctors investigating rural poverty in 1967 noted:

In child after child we saw: evidence of vitamin and mineral deficiencies; serious untreated skin infestation and ulcerations; eye and ear diseases, also unattended bone diseases secondary to poor food intake; the prevalence of bacterial and parasitic disease as well as severe anemia, with resulting loss of energy and ability to live a normally active life; diseases of the heart and lungs—requiring surgery—which have gone undiagnosed and untreated; epileptic and other neurological disorders; severe kidney ailments, that in other children would warrant immediate hospitalization; and finally, in boys and girls in every county we visited, obvious evidence of severe malnutrition with injury to the body's tissues —its muscles, bones, and skin as well as an associated psychological state of fatigue, listlessness, and exhaustion.[36]

In the United States today, people living in shacks on the outskirts of cities like New Orleans scavenge the dumps, eating and surviving on the garbage they find. In some communities people band together to share the little food they have. Many, despite prolonged illness and destitution, cannot get on welfare after repeated attempts. Government food programs and private charities reach only a small portion of the poor, and often not those most in need. In areas like Detroit, hunger has reached epidemic proportions. Of that city's 1.5 million people, 200,000 are starving, according to the mayor's office. Fully one-third are eligible for food stamps but only 18 percent are receiving them.[37]

The inflation of recent years has meant additional misery for the poor. As grocery prices soar, families with somewhat higher incomes are forced to buy cheaper foods such as beans, rice, grits and flour. The prices on these commodities are raised still higher by profiteering producers and retailers. (Thus in 1974 the price of dried beans climbed 256 percent and rice over 100 percent.) Poor families, already buying the cheapest foods, are hit the hardest as a result. One last response has been an increased human consumption of dog food: an estimated one-third of all dog food sales

35. Quoted in *ibid.*, pp. 31–32.
36. Quoted in *ibid.*, p. 13.
37. *Workers World*, February 28, 1975.

in low-income area supermarkets goes for human consumption.[38] A 1976 survey found that "poor diets are increasing in the United States," with more people eating foods that are deficient in essential nutrients.[39]

Unemployment continues to plague millions of Americans. Supposedly unemployment has been about 6 to 9 percent of the work force in recent years. But this figure includes only persons collecting unemployment insurance or registered as looking for employment. It does not count many whose benefits have run out or who never qualified for benefits, nor those who have given up looking for work, nor part-time workers who need full-time work, nor the tens of thousands of youth thrown into the labor market immediately after leaving school, nor many women who need work but are classified as "housewives," nor the many who join the armed forces because they cannot find employment. "For 1975, a conservative estimate would be that 24 million people, one worker in four, were unemployed at some time during the year."[40]

The groups that have been hit hardest by unemployment are women, racial minorities, youths and unskilled workers—although in recent years even White male professionals, such as teachers, engineers, and sales managers, have faced a depressed labor market. Among those who work, a large portion cannot earn enough to support their families. "They work for a living but not for a living wage."[41] The 1970 Census Bureau survey of fifty-one urban areas discovered that more than 60 percent of all workers in the inner city could not make enough money to maintain a decent standard of living and 30 percent were earning wages below the poverty level.[42]

While many are unemployed, there are millions who are obliged to hold down more than one job in order to make a sufficient income. Millions more are compelled by their bosses to work ten and twelve hour days for extended periods. Involuntary overtime is a major complaint among automotive, postal, steel, mining, trucking and utilities workers. Owners prefer to impose overtime

38. John Cook, "Hunger: High Prices Drive Many to Dog Food," *Guardian*, July 3, 1974, p. 3.
39. Survey by the Department of Agriculture, *New York Times*, March 13, 1976.
40. *Dollars and Sense*, January 1976, p. 10.
41. William Spring, Bennett Harrison and Thomas Vietorisz, "Crisis of the *Under*employed—In Much of the Inner City 60% Don't Earn Enough for a Decent Standard of Living," *New York Times Magazine*, November 5, 1972.
42. *Ibid.*

hours rather than hire more workers, thereby saving on the benefits that must be paid to additional employees. About one out of every four workers puts in more than an eight hour day because of overtime or an extra job.

From nearly every state and in greater numbers each year, unemployed workers and their families are wandering around the country in the hope of finding work, traveling in all directions—"only to find there are no jobs when they arrive."[43] Mortgage foreclosures in many areas are ten times what they used to be. Unable to keep up payments, many jobless persons abandon their homes and take to the road.

Unemployed workers have resorted to selling their blood in order to feed their families. The father, mother and oldest son of one destitute family, homeless because they could not pay their rent, and denied welfare assistance because they had no permanent address, took to selling weekly pints of plasma until they were rejected because of the low iron content of their blood—a condition caused by malnutrition.[44] A jobless worker ran an advertisement in a Pittsburgh newspaper offering to sell one of his kidneys for $5,000. The Kidney Foundation reported one hundred such offers in early 1976 from persons who "needed money." An unemployed father of five in Georgia offered to sell an eye or a kidney for $10,000.[45]

With economic recession there comes an increase in human unhappiness and social pathology. Dr. Harvey Brenner of Johns Hopkins University observed that unemployment and recession were bringing a noticeable rise in mental illness, alcoholism and suicide.[46] In 1975 the suicide rate jumped about 25 percent. Homicide rates have been increasing steadily, 21 percent between 1970 and 1974.[47] With crime on the upswing, jails are overcrowded, about half a million persons being incarcerated in local, county, state and federal prisons. Almost two million are currently in

43. Rod Such, "In Search of Work, Jobless Workers Roam U.S.," *Guardian*, March 26, 1975, p. 3.

44. *Guardian*, April 21, 1976.

45. *New York Daily News*, March 28, 1975; *Ithaca New Times*, February 1, 1976.

46. *Buffalo Courier-Express*, December 7, 1975. According to the National Center for Health Statistics, at least 20,000 would take their lives in 1976; see *Moneysworth*, July 21, 1975. The suicide rate for young Black males is twice that for young White males. See Herbert Hendin, *Black Suicide* (New York: Basic Books, 1969).

47. U.S. Census Bureau, *Statistical Abstracts of the United States: 1974*, 95th ed. (Washington, D.C., 1974), p. 147; also *New York Times*, February 4, 1976.

mental hospitals, and millions more have received some sort of psychiatric care. Millions are addicted to drugs, mostly amphetamines, barbiturates and other stimulants and tranquillizers. The pushers are doctors; the suppliers are the drug industry; the profits are stupendous.

At least 250,000 to 300,000 children, predominantly but not exclusively from low-income families, are tortured, maimed and brutalized by adults each year. Child abuse kills more children annually than leukemia, automobile accidents or infectious diseases.[48] In areas of growing unemployment, incidents of child abuse by jobless fathers have increased dramatically. Child labor is still practiced in the United States. Almost one million children, some as young as seven years, serve as underpaid farmworkers, dishwashers, laundry workers and domestics for as long as ten hours a day. Agribusiness is increasingly using child labor in the fields. In states such as Oregon, Washington and Louisiana as much as 75 percent of the commercial farm work is done by children. In Maine 35 percent of the potato harvest is gathered by more than 15,000 children aged five and older.[49]

Economic want is a common condition among the elderly. Of the almost 30 million Americans who are 65 years or older, more than half live below the poverty level. As many as 50 percent live on diets that fail to provide adequate nutrients.[50] And 27 percent of the White and 36 percent of the Black adults aged 60 and over have a daily intake of less than 1,000 calories—amounting to a slow starvation diet.[51] "We do see regularly those [elderly] who are found dead in their homes who are almost like walking skeletons," noted Dr. John Shinner, a county medical examiner in Florida.[52] The elderly are unable to afford needed medical and home nursing care and are unable to find decent housing or transportation that would allow them to maintain normal social rela-

48. Ray Helfer and C. Henry Kempe, *The Battered Child* (Chicago: Chicago University Press, 1969); and David G. Gill, *Violence Against Children* (Cambridge, Mass.: Harvard University Press, 1970).
49. Cassandra Stockburger, "Yes, Child Labor Is Still a Problem," *New York Times*, September 4, 1972; also Rod Such, "New Growth in Use of Child Labor," *Guardian*, June 2, 1971.
50. *Hunger, U.S.A.*, pp. 9, 24.
51. The Health and Nutrition Examination Survey, 1971–1972, sponsored by the U.S. Department of Health, Education and Welfare, reported in *Workers World*, November 22, 1974. For a statement on poverty and old age, see Sharon R. Curtin, *Nobody Ever Died of Old Age* (Boston: Little, Brown, 1972).
52. *Buffalo Evening News*, October 13, 1974.

tions. They are denied jobs through arbitrary retirement rules. They face loneliness, boredom and ridicule in a market society that treats old people like used cars.[53] Many of them suffer physical abuse, beatings and neglect at the hands of their grown-up children. "With high prices and unemployment," observes one authority on the subject, "some families resent the old person living with them. They consider him just an extra mouth to feed and a nuisance to look after." The mistreatment of elderly parents is "a new social phenomenon with thousands of victims,"[54] a problem that seems to grow as economic conditions worsen.

What of the "middle class"? An amorphous category including everyone from well-paid professionals to thrifty postal employees, the "middle Americans" are said to be economically well-off, increasing in numbers and occupying the comfortable nonmanual jobs of an ever-expanding "service sector." In fact, many jobs classified as "white collar" or "service" are among the lowest-paying, menial occupations. Service workers include such occupations as janitors, typists, waiters, porters, ushers and shoeshine boys. Contrary to myths about "affluent workers," the average annual pay for employees in all occupations, union and nonunion, was $7,254 in 1972, about $4,000 less than the "moderate budget" for a family of four set by the U.S. Bureau of Labor Statistics. Even better-paid employees enjoy a tenuous "prosperity," having nothing to cushion them against loss of earning power through catastrophe, recession, layoffs, wage cuts or simply old age.[55] While they may be earning a comfortable salary, they have virtually no wealth—in a society in which wealth is the only certain measure of security. As the recession deepened in 1974, another 1.3 million "middle Americans" fell below the poverty line.[56] And in 1975 the number living in poverty grew by 10 percent (the largest increase in the seventeen years that the government has been keeping poverty statistics).

53. Millions of elderly "live" on less than $1,000 a year. See John H. Clairborne, "Old Age in Capitalism," *Monthly Review*, November 1972, p. 52.

54. Dr. Erdman Palmore of Duke University quoted in David Hughes, "Grown-up Children Who Beat Their Aging Parents," *National Enquirer*, June 17, 1975.

55. Andrew Levison, *The Working Class Majority* (New York: Penguin Books, 1974) treats this subject well. See also Arthur Shostak, *Blue Collar Life* (New York: Random House, 1969).

56. According to the U.S. Census Bureau, reported in the *New York Times*, February 2, 1976. The federal government sets the poverty level at $5,500 annual income for a family of four.

Almost all Americans, including better-income, middle-class people, are insufficiently protected by private health insurance against prolonged illness and hospitalization. If delivered from special catastrophe, middle-income people, feeling the pressures of consumerism, taxes and inflation, still live under the constant strain of money anxieties and manifest an alarming incidence of physical and mental illness. Even the better-paid professionals, the "upper-middle Americans," seem to be showing the strain. One spokesperson for the business world offers this composite picture of the male professional "who from many standpoints is better off than many of his countrymen":

He is living under such pressure that the chances are one in three that he will be hospitalized for a mental or emotional illness. . . .

The person I'm describing has a good job and yet in just two years when he is 45 he will be considered "over the hill" by most businesses. In fact he has two friends who lost their jobs who haven't been able to find work in almost a year.

He's worked hard all his life and yet in ten years the chances are 2 in 14 that he will have to depend on some form of government relief. But he may not live that long. Sometimes he drinks too much—if it keeps up he could become an alcoholic. . . . He's a prime candidate for a heart attack before he's fifty.[57]

It is said that the "prosperity" of the United States is widely shared, and incomes are becoming more equal. But recent studies find that the gap between rich and poor has widened over the last twenty-five years. The difference in the mean annual income of the richest 5 percent of U.S. families and that of the poorest 5 percent was $17,057 in 1947 but had grown to $27,605 by 1969 (weighting for inflation by using 1969 dollar value). Between 1968 and 1972 there was a marked upward shift in income distribution, with close to $10 billion being redistributed from the bottom three-fifths of American families to the richest one-fifth.[58] As of 1976 the trend toward greater inequality of income continued, with Blacks and poor Whites losing ground, and the newer regions of the country and the suburbs doing better than rural areas and

57. Donald A. MacDonald, vice-president of Dow Jones, in a newsletter mailed to private recipients during the spring of 1972. MacDonald drew his estimates from statistics gathered from the Department of Health, Education and Welfare and the American Medical Association.
58. Henry S. Reuss, "A Democrat's Critique of Nixonomics," *New York Times Magazine,* July 7, 1974, p. 11.

cities.[59] *Almost one out of every ten Whites and nearly one out of every three Blacks, Puerto Ricans and Chicanos live below the poverty level.*

Many of us have been taught that "America belongs to the people," but in fact almost all Americans are tenants, debtors, and hired hands in their own country, working for someone else, paying rent to someone else, or paying high interest rates on mortgages, loans and installment purchases to someone else. In these relationships the advantage is on the side of the employer, the landlord, the manufacturer and the bank. The boss hires us because he can make a profit from our labor; the landlord rents to us so that he can make an income on the rental; the manufacturer sells to us because he can make more wealth on his product than he put into it; and the bank or loan company extends credit so that it can get back substantially more than it lends.[60]

If many Americans enjoy all "the good things that money can buy," they also are burdened with many of the things they cannot afford to buy, being bombarded each year by multibillion-dollar advertising campaigns to induce them to purchase still more of the commodities produced by profit-oriented corporations. And each year they go deeper into debt. In 1955 the consumer debt owed by Americans on their automobiles, television sets, furniture, fixtures and other such goods and services amounted to $29 billion. In 1967 the consumer debt stood at $75 billion. By 1974 it had grown to $200 billion and the mortgage debt was $600 billion.[61] (About one in four American families "own" their homes, but the ownership

59. *New York Times,* February 25, 1976; also S. M. Miller and Pamela Roby, *The Future of Inequality* (New York: Basic Books, 1970); and Leonard Ross, "The Myth That Things Are Getting Better," *New York Review of Books,* August 12, 1971, pp. 7–9.

60. A basic distinction one might make is between those who own and control the wealth and institutions of the society—the "owning class," or "propertied class"—and those who are dependent on the owning class for their employment. The latter, the "working class," includes not only blue-collar workers but also accountants, clerks, professors and anyone who has a job or is trying to get one. The distinction is blurred somewhat by the range of wealth within both the owning and working class. Thus while "owners" include both the owners of giant corporations and the proprietors of small grocery stores, the latter control a minuscule portion of the wealth and hardly qualify as part of the *corporate* owning class. Likewise, among the working class are professionals and middle-level executives who in income and life-style tend to be identified as "middle class," apart from "ordinary workers." Then there are some stars from the entertainment and sports worlds, some lawyers and many doctors who earn such lavish incomes that they invest their surplus wealth and become in part, or eventually in whole, members of the owning class.

61. "The Debt Economy," *Business Week,* October 12, 1974.

is mostly in the hands of banks.) According to one conservative publication, mounting debts "are threatening a financial crackup in more and more families. . . . Excessive debt is engulfing thousands of families."[62] The interest rates charged on most sales (when buying on time) bring more profit to the seller than the price markup, thus constituting a kind of legal usury. As consumers, Americans are also victimized by shoddy, unsafe products, deceptive packaging, swindling sales and numerous other unscrupulous practices.[63]

In sum, the history of the great "affluence" in the United States since World War II is of people becoming increasingly entrapped as wage earners, tenants and debtors in a high-production, high-consumption, high-profit system. Millions of Americans live under starvation conditions; millions are desperate for work; millions are afflicted by one or another socioeconomic pathology. Millions live in crowded, dilapidated, poorly ventilated, ill-heated and hazardous domiciles. Millions who identify themselves as middle class live in overpriced, poorly constructed, heavily mortgaged homes or high-rent apartments that consume a large part of their incomes while providing living quarters that are far from satisfactory. Millions are immobilized by inadequate or nonexistent public transportation facilities and have no access to decent recreational areas. Millions complain about living empty, joyless, lonely lives. At the same time, environmental devastation continues unabated: our rivers are turned into open sewers by the countless tons of raw industrial waste dumped into them by industry, our air made foul, our forests and wildlife destroyed, our roadsides uglified by commercial enterprise, and our cities are showing serious signs of decay, bankruptcy and social demoralization.

Presiding over all this are the privileged few who control the enormous corporate wealth of the society who have more money than they know what to do with and who enjoy all the advantages of power and position that come with wealth.

It is not enough to denounce the inequities that exist between the few and the many; it is also necessary to understand the connection between them. For it is the way wealth is organized and used which creates most of the existing want. By its very nature,

62. *U.S. News and World Report,* June 22, 1970; also David Caplovitz, *The Poor Pay More* (New York: Free Press, 1967) for a study of how the poor are victimized as consumers and debtors.
63. See the collection of expose articles in David Sanford et al., *Hot War on the Consumer* (New York: Pitman, 1969).

the capitalist system is compelled to exploit the resources and labor of· society for the purpose of maximizing profits. It is this operational imperative of the system which perforce creates the commodity glut, the privation, wastage, scarcity, unemployment and general economic oppression which brings misery and malaise to so many. And, as we shall see in the chapters ahead, it is the concentrated power of corporatism which prevents a reordering of our priorities and a move toward a more equitable and sane society.

The American Way

3

WHAT KIND OF A NATION IS THE
United States? What are its predominant values
and modes of social organization? Although our
society is composed of over 220 million persons
of varying occupational, regional, ethnic and religious backgrounds, there are certain generalizations one can make about its beliefs and institutions—keeping in mind that these allow for
exceptions.

Who's on Top?

A remarkable but often overlooked feature of
American society is that its industrial, com-
municational, transportational, educational, recreational and cultural institutions are controlled
by rich businessmen. Industry is ruled largely by
wealthy individuals or by boards of directors
composed of successful businessmen[1]. In almost
no instance do the workers, the people who contribute the labor and skills essential for production, have any decision-making powers over
corporate methods, purposes and profits.

Business control extends into areas beyond
the business world. Most universities and colleges, publishing houses, newspapers, television
and radio stations, professional sports teams,
foundations, churches, private museums and

1. See Richard Barber, *The American Corporation*
(New York: Dutton, 1970); Richard C. Edwards, Michael
Reich and Thomas E. Weisskopf, *The Capitalist System*
(Englewood Cliffs, N.J.: Prentice-Hall, 1972); and Paul
Baran and Paul Sweezy, *Monopoly Capital* (New York:
Monthly Review Press, 1968).

hospitals are organized as corporations and ruled by self-appointed boards of trustees (or directors or regents) composed overwhelmingly of businessmen. These boards, accountable to no one for their decisions, exercise final and absolute judgment over all institutional matters.[2]

Consider the university: most institutions of higher education are public or private corporations (e.g., the Harvard Corporation, the Yale Corporation) run by boards of trustees with ultimate authority over all matters of capital funding and budget; curriculum, scholarships and tuition; hiring, firing and promotion of faculty and staff; degree awards, student fees, etc. Most of the tasks related to these activities have been delegated to administrators, but the power can be easily recalled by the trustees, and in times of controversy it usually is.[3] These trustees (one of whom is usually the university president) are not elected by students, faculty or staff, although an occasional student or professor may be allowed to sit on the board, usually in a nonvoting capacity. The board members are granted legal control of the property of the institution not because they have claim to any academic experience but because as successful bankers, industrialists, insurance persons, corporate lawyers, realtors and heirs to family wealth, they supposedly have proven themselves to be the responsible and proper leaders of the community.[4]

This, then, is a feature of real significance in any understanding of political power in America: *almost all the social institutions and*

2. My *Power and the Powerless* (forthcoming) has a more detailed discussion of power within social institutions.

3. See James Ridgeway, *The Closed Corporation* (New York: Random House, 1969) for a study of the university that differs from the "ivy-covered" image we usually have of it.

4. Even if it were true that their guidance might be needed on financial matters, it is never explained why trustees should have ultimate power. They could function as consultants without being accorded executive authority over all matters. In fact, on most technical problems, the trustees themselves rely on advisors and specialists. The argument is made that trustees take the financial risks for the university and therefore should have the authority. In fact, they seldom take on personal financial liabilities. Legal judgments made against their decisions are usually covered by insurance paid out of the university budget. If anything, trustees are likely to profit personally by awarding university contracts to their own firms or the firms of business associates. Another argument for trustee power is that students, faculty and staff compose a transient population and therefore cannot be expected to run the university. But their stay at the university is longer than that of the average trustee, who serves for three years, often does not even live in the same city as the university he presides over, and visits it for decision-making meetings, at most, once a month.

material resources existing in this society are controlled by non-elected, self-selected, self-perpetuating groups of middle-aged, White, male business people who are accountable to no one but themselves.

The rest of us make our way through these institutions as employees and clients, performing according to standards set by the ruling oligarchs or their administrative agents. The method of rule exercised over us is hierarchical and nondemocratic. These institutions determine many of our experiences as citizens, students, workers, professionals, consumers, tenants, etc., yet we have no vote, no portion of the ownership and no legal decision-making power within them.

Labor unions provide some collective voice for employees and help limit the abuses of management. Some of the more class conscious unions have supported progressive legislative measures, taken stands against the Vietnam war and criticized the privileges and powers of owners. But unions seldom can match the material resources that corporations command. Barely one in four American workers is unionized and many have no legal right to strike.

Furthermore, some union leaders begin to take on the boss's perspective, emphasizing labor's common stakes with management and stressing the necessity of maintaining high productivity. They allow their membership little voice in running the union. In the worst instances they turn the union organization into a personal bureaucratic empire, misusing funds, padding payrolls and voting munificent salaries for themselves and their cohorts. Union leaders are often described as potentates who preside over vast armies of workers. They are indeed powerful in relation to their own membership, but with management they tend to be tame junior partners.[5]

In our "democracy," the individual's opportunities for self-governance seem to be limited to those few moments spent in the polling booth—assuming that voting is an act of self-government. Many Americans do not seem terribly upset by this situation. They

5. For some of the many accounts published on the complicity of union leaders with management and their betrayal of their own rank and file, see Don Stillman, "Murder and the Mines," *New Politics*, 9, Winter 1972, pp. 22–29; Membership Party of Local 6, "Our Union Elections Are a Fraud," *ibid.*, pp. 30–39; Joseph Nabach, "The Telephone Strike: Frozen Militancy," *ibid.*, pp. 40–46; Burton Hall, "ILGWU and the Labor Department: Just a Perfect Friendship," *New Politics*, 9, Spring 1970, pp. 15–23; Paul Schrade, "Growing Bureaucratization of the UAW," *New Politics*, 10, Winter 1973, pp. 13–21; Burt Hall, "Painter's Union: Troubles of an Ex-Reformer," *ibid.*, pp. 22–29. The *Guardian* frequently carries stories about union leaders selling out their membership.

believe as they were taught, that they are a free people. This belief is held even by many who refuse to voice opinions on controversial issues for fear of jeopardizing their jobs and careers.

The power of business does not stand naked before the public; rather it is enshrouded in a mystique of its own making. In the minds of many, the "free-enterprise system" has become indelibly associated with the symbols of America, Patriotism, Freedom, Democracy, Prosperity and Progress.

Today convictions about the virtues of private enterprise and the evils of socialism and communism are widely held among Americans of all classes. Yet we should remember that such beliefs did not emerge full-blown from nowhere, nor do they circulate like disembodied spirits. Rather they have been propagated over the generations by the agencies of a capitalist society, including the media, the professions, the schools, the churches, the politicians and the policymakers.[6]

Courses designed to instill appreciation for our "free enterprise system," taught by community leaders, businessmen and economists are required in high schools in Delaware, Tennessee, Oklahoma, Arizona, Florida and other states. Criticisms of "free enterprise" often are equated with un-Americanism. Capitalism is treated as a necessary condition for political freedom, contraposed as the sole alternative to "community tyranny." The private-enterprise system, it is taught, creates equality of opportunity, rewards those who show ability and initiative, relegates the parasitic and slothful to the bottom of the ladder, provides a national prosperity that is the envy of other lands, safeguards (through unspecified means) personal civil liberties and political freedom, promises continued progress in the endless proliferation of goods and services and has made America the great, free and beautiful nation it is.

Getting More and Getting Ahead

In the United States many billions of dollars are spent each year to induce people to consume as much as they can and—through

6. See William Preston, Jr., *Aliens and Dissenters* (Cambridge, Mass.: Harvard University Press, 1963); William Appleman Williams, *The Great Evasion* (Chicago: Quadrangle Books, 1964); Michael Parenti, *The Anti-Communist Impulse* (New York: Random House, 1969); Francis X. Sutton et al., *The American Business Creed* (New York: Schocken Books, 1962); Sidney Fine, *Laissez-Faire and the General-Welfare State* (Ann Arbor: University of Michigan Press, 1964).

installment plans—more than they can afford. The inducements seem to work: Americans are a people dedicated to the piling up of goods, services and income. This consumerism is not just a habit but *a way of life,* a measure of one's accomplishment and a proof of one's worth.

For most people life is defined as a series of private goals to be attained through personal means, rather than as collective efforts in pursuit of rewards that might be communally distributed and enjoyed. One should endeavor to "get ahead." Ahead of what? Of others and of one's own present status. This "individualism" is not to be mistaken for freedom to choose moral, political and cultural alternatives of one's own making. Each person is expected to operate "individually" *but in more or less similar ways and similar directions.* Everyone competes against everyone else but for the same goals and with the same values in mind. "Individualism" in the United States refers to *privatization* and the absence of communal forms of production, consumption and recreation. You are an individualist in that you are expected to get what you can for yourself, by yourself, and not to be too troubled by the needs and problems faced by others. This attitude, considered criminal in many human societies, is labeled approvingly as "ambition" in our own and is treated as a quality of great social value.

Whether or not this "individualism" allows one to have control over one's own life is another story. The decisions about the quality of the food we eat, the goods we buy, the air we breathe, the prices we pay, the way work tasks are divided and jobs defined, the kinds of transportation, recreation and entertainment we are offered, the opinions and values fed to us by newspapers, magazines, television and radio, the kind of treatment accorded us in our schools, clinics and hospitals—the controlling decisions concerning the palpable realities of our lives—are made by people other than ourselves. Yet Americans continue to think of themselves as self-reliant individualists. What they seem to be referring to is the privatism and atomization of their social relations and the relative absence of cooperative endeavor.

Competitive privatism brings a good deal of loneliness and isolation and few occasions for meaningful community experiences with other human beings. Philip Slater argues that Americans constantly attempt to minimize or deny human interdependence. We seek a private home, a private country place, a private means of transportation, a private laundry, private recreation, private lessons, a private garden, etc. Even within the family, each member seeks a separate room and a separate telephone, television and car when it is economically possible to do so. "We seek more and more privacy," Slater notes, "and feel more and more alienated and lonely when we get it."[7]

The lack of community does not prevent Americans from identifying with larger collective entities such as a school, a town or the nation. But even this identification is expressed in terms that are competitive with other schools, towns or nations. In sports, for instance, it is said that the important thing is not who wins but how the game is played; yet whole schools and cities are gripped by joyful frenzy when their team wins a championship. The really important thing is the winning.

The need to be first and foremost extends with special intensity to the nation. We are instructed to love America because it is "the greatest country in the world," the presumption being that if it were not so great it would not be so lovable. America is great because of its laudable intentions and practices—and its military might. Greatness, then, is a matter not only of virtue but of strength. The superpatriots are usually the most militaristic. Love of country becomes associated with huge military budgets and armed intervention throughout the world. As part of our greatness we need to keep the world safe from revolutionaries who advocate a different kind of social order. The presumption that the United States has a right to police the entire globe rests on the belief that our intentions are honorable, our interests selfless and the outcomes of our actions salutary for other peoples.

In their personal and national egoisms Americans are hardly unique; but the United States is unique in the magnitude of its powers and the effects its actions have on other peoples. For many generations Americans have envisioned mankind developing as an extension of the American experience, enjoying the inspirational example of our political institutions. Our goal has been a world of "law and order" with a decided advantage going to those who define the order and enforce the law—a world respectful of mankind's best interests. That these interests also happen to be identical with the best interests of the United States, as defined by its ruling elites, is no cause for embarrassment, it being understood that less fortunate peoples, if not misled by revolutionaries and if given occasional succor from the happiest, richest, most successful nation in the world, will eventually develop orderly institutions

7. Philip Slater, *The Pursuit of Loneliness* (Boston: Beacon Press, 1970), p. 7.

like our own and achieve the blessings of peace, prosperity and property. Give or take some cultural variations, they will emerge as did America, from the howling wilderness to the machine-fed garden.

This global vision is still with us, but so is the nightmare that always lurked behind it—the fear that others might turn their backs on the American-defined world order and construct competing social systems which propagate values (especially those relating to the use and distribution of wealth) that might somehow undermine our American Way of Life, plunder our treasure and oust us from our position of preeminence. "America," President Nixon warned, "must never become a second-rate power." Only in supremacy do we hope to find security. The haves always live in fear that the have-nots will try to equalize things. President Johnson summed it up before a Junior Chamber of Commerce audience: "We own half the trucks in the world. We own almost half of the radios in the world. We own a third of all the electricity. . . ." But the rest of the world wants it for themselves, he added. "Now I would like to see them enjoy the blessings that we enjoy. But don't you help them exchange places with us, because I don't want to be where they are." For many Americans, Johnson was touching the vulgar heart of the matter: keep others from taking what we have.

From their earliest grade school days Americans are taught competitive methods of accomplishment. One's peers are potentially one's enemies; their successes can cause us envy and anxiety, and their failures bring secret feelings of relief. The ability or desire to work collectively with others is much retarded. Competitive efforts are primarily directed against those of the same class or those below, a condition that suits the interests of those at the top. Among the strongest critics of workers who get better wages through collective bargaining and collective action are workers who do not and who complain, like management itself, that their more fortunate brethren are never satisfied. Any unusual success enjoyed by a friend, co-worker or colleague can evoke more jealousy in people than the successes enjoyed by a multimillionaire on the far-off upper rungs of the social ladder.

Many feel even more competitive toward those defined as their social inferiors: the poor, Blacks, other minorities and women. To be outdone by one's peers is bad enough, but the White male, raised in a sexist, racist, class chauvinist society and taught to define his self-worth and "manliness" in terms of his superiority over Blacks, women and lower-class persons, finds it insufferable to be outdone by his "inferiors." As products of a competitive, acquisitive society, many Americans do not welcome equality; they fear and detest it and have a profound commitment to inequality.

People who have invested much psychic energy and years of toil in maintaining or furthering their positions within the social heirarchy become committed to the heirarchy's preservation. Even those perched on modest rungs of the ladder—the millions of small proprietors, lower-paid semiprofessionals and white-collar workers, often described as "middle Americans," who could have much to gain from a more egalitarian social order—fear that they might be overtaken by those below, making all their toil and sacrifice count for naught.[8]

The hostility they may feel for the welfare poor does not encompass—at least not with the same intensity—the welfare rich, those at the top who receive billions of dollars from the government in the form of subsidies, tax write-offs and other services. The middle Americans might utter a passing criticism of corporations and millionaires who do not pay taxes, but their greatest passion is reserved for the poor. If anything, the advantages enjoyed by the wealthy are seen as "earned" by their intelligence and resourcefullness and therefore deserved. Proximity to the poor is to be avoided, while wealth is something to be attained someday by oneself or one's children—something, in any case, to be admired. Hence the road upward should be kept open with no artificial impediments imposed by the government on those who can advance, while the road behind should not be provided with conveyances for those who wish to catch up effortlessly.

To be sure, Americans have their doubts about the rat race, but they canot lightly discard the years of effort and sacrifice they have invested in it and shift to another set of values. As Slater notes: "Suburbanites who philosophize over their back fence with complete sincerity about their dog-eat-dog-world, and what-is-it-all-for, and you-can't-take-it-with you, and success-doesn't-make-you-happy-it-gives-you-ulcers-and-a-heart-condition—would be enraged should their children pay serious attention to such a viewpoint."[9]

The American's competitiveness is fortified by a *scarcity psychology* that bears little relation to how much he has. There is always more to want and more to get, more to hang on to and more to lose. Thus the highly paid professional feels the pressure of "moreness" as much as the lowly paid blue-collar worker. Economi-

8. See Robert Lane, *Political Ideology* (New York: Free Press, 1962), pp. 57–81.
9. Slater, *The Pursuit of Loneliness*, pp. 6–7.

cally deprived groups like urban ghetto dwellers, sharecroppers, welfare recipients, female employees and low-income workers are seen as a nuisance and a threat because, like the rest of us, they want more, and more for them might mean less for us. The scarcity psychology, then, leaves us with the feeling that the poor and the racial minorities (our potential competitors) should be kept in their place and away from what we have and want.

A belief in the inferiority of deprived groups is functional for those possessed by a scarcity psychology. Racism, sexism and class bigotry help us exclude large numbers of people, limiting the field of competitors and justifying in our minds the inequities these groups are made to endure. Having designated them as moral inferiors, we become easily convinced that the hardships they suffer are due to their own deficiencies (lazy poor, dumb Blacks, dirty Mexicans, silly women, etc.). "Those people don't *want* to better themselves," is the comment often made by individuals who then become quite hostile when lower-status groups take actions intended to better themselves. The belief that others are lacking in natural abilities does not seem to free us of the anxiety that they might catch up and even surpass us.

In movies, on television, in grade-school textbooks and in popular fiction, the world is portrayed as a predominantly middle-class place; working-class people are often presented as uncouth, unintelligent and generally undesirable. A TV series like "All in the Family," while supposedly exposing bigotry, practices a bigotry of its own by stereotyping the working-class lead character, Archie Bunker, as a loud-mouthed ignoramus and bully, poking fun at his mispronunciations, life-style and physical appearance. Class chauvinism is one of the most widely spread forms of prejudice in American society and one of the least challenged. As one of the characters in Kurt Vonegut's *Slaughterhouse-Five* observes:

To quote the American humorist Kim Hubbard, "It ain't no disgrace to be poor, but it might as well be." It is in fact a crime for an American to be poor. . . . Every other nation has folk traditions of men who were poor but extremely wise and virtuous, and therefore more estimable than anyone with power and gold. No such tales are told by the American poor. They mock themselves and glorify their betters. The meanest eating or drinking establishment, owned by a man who is himself poor, is very likely to have a sign on its wall asking this cruel question: "If you're so smart, why ain't you rich?". . . .

Americans . . . who have no money blame and blame and blame themselves. This inward blame has been a treasure for the rich and powerful, who have had to do less for their poor, publicly and privately, than any other ruling class since, say, Napoleonic times.[10]

If material success is a measure of one's worth, then the poor are not worth much and society's resources should not be squandered on them. If rich and poor get pretty much what they deserve, then it is self-evident that the poor are not very deserving. When farm workers earn only $2,000 a year, as one prosperous, middle-class White male remarked to me, "Then that's all they must be worth." The competitive society has little room for compassion and collective social betterment; those who dream of getting ahead and making it to the top have little time for those below.

It would be easy to fault Americans who manifest the above belief patterns as people who lack some proper measure of humanity. But what must be remembered about such attitudes is that they evolve as value components of a capitalist society. The value placed on getting ahead, on moreness and material success, on putting down others in order to boost oneself is not the outcome of some inborn genetic flaw in the American character. In a society where material wealth is *the key determinant of one's life chances,* and birth, luck, corruption and individuated competition the key means of getting it, then the competitive drive and the desire for material success are not merely symptoms of greed but factors in one's economic survival, shaping the very texture of one's life. When human services are based on ability to pay, money becomes a matter of life and death. To be poor is to run a higher risk of death, illness, insufficient medical care, malnutrition and job exploitation, and to have a lesser opportunity for education, comfort, mobility, leisure, travel, etc. The desire to "make it," even at the expense of others, is not merely a wrong-headed attitude but a reflection of the actual material conditions of capitalist society wherein no one is ever really economically secure except the very affluent.

The Other America

The image of Americans as a nation of acquisitive, competitive, jingoistic admirers of big money is hardly the whole picture. Many, including millions of the more conventional minded, have serious questions about the institutions and practices of their society. Polls

10. Kurt Vonnegut, Jr., *Slaughterhouse-Five* (New York: Delta, 1969), pp. 111–112.

show that among all groups of Americans there has been a growing feeling of distrust and alienation toward the dominant economic and political elites. One survey found that between 1966 and 1976 public confidence in those who ran the major corporations declined from 55 percent to 16 percent. Confidence in other establishment elites dropped as follows: (a) leaders of organized religion: from 41 to 24 percent; (b) military leaders: from 62 to 23 percent; (c) doctors: from 73 to 42 percent.[11] During this same decade, disillusionment with government in general grew, the number of people who felt their interests were "left out" climbing from 9 to 42 percent. Those who agreed that "most people with power try to take advantage of people such as myself" increased from 33 percent in 1971 to 63 percent in 1976, with poor Whites and racial minorities feeling the most alienated.[12]

A 1975 national survey found that 33 percent of the respondents believe our capitalistic economic system is "on the decline," as against 22 percent who think it is getting better. Fifty-five percent believe both the Democratic and Republican parties favor big business over the average worker. Fifty-eight percent think that major corporations tend to dominate Washington, while 25 percent think it's the other way around. Concerning our economy: 41 percent want "sweeping changes"; 37 percent favor minor adjustments, and only 17 percent are for letting the economy straighten itself out. Forty-four percent believe public ownership of the oil industry and other natural resources would do "more good than harm," while 42 percent feel the contrary. The survey concluded that the public seemed open to new and bold experiments in economic matters. Thus a whopping 66 percent would like to work for a company that is owned and controlled by its employees.[13] At the same time, people appear skeptical of the same old New Deal type of spending programs which throw billions at problems but bring no solutions.[14]

Harris polls in January and April of 1973 found that by majorities of more than two to one citizens favored increased government efforts to (a) curb air and water pollution, (b) aid education and (c) help the poor. At the same time they were against increased spending for highways, the military and the space program. By 72 to 20 percent they judged that "too much money is going into

11. Harris survey, *Ithaca* (N.Y.) *Journal*, March 22, 1976.
12. Harris survey, *Ithaca* (N.Y.) *Journal*, March 25, 1976.
13. A Peter Hart poll reported in Mary McGrory's syndicated column, *Ithaca* (N.Y.) *Journal*, September 5, 1975.
14. Harris survey, *Chicago Tribune*, April 8, 1976.

wars and defense." By 80 to 13 percent they felt the tax system was set up to favor the rich at the expense of the average person. On almost every major policy issue, the electorate seemed to hold attitudes which were quite opposite those held by corporate and political elites.[15]

A 1974 survey noted that Americans were becoming more tolerant of cultural and political dissenters. In 1967, by majorities of 60 to 75 percent, respondents declared the following groups "dangerous or harmful to the country": atheists, Black militants, student demonstrators and homosexuals. But by 1973 no majority could be found to label these groups as harmful. However, lopsided majorities considered the following people dangerous: politicians who engage in secret wiretapping, businessmen who make illegal contributions, generals who conduct secret bombing raids.[16] A 1975 Haris survey found that substantial majorities of Americans are no longer willing to be stampeded by the kind of fear appeals that characterized past conservative campaigns—such as the "soft on communism," "soft on Blacks" and "soft on crime" issues.[17]

Despite the four to one opposition to school busing for racial purposes,[18] racist attitudes have declined somewhat in the last decade, the change being most dramatic in the South, where the number of White parents objecting to their children attending school with an equal Black and White enrollment dropped from 78 to 38 percent.[19] In the North the drop was 33 to 24 percent. Hostility toward school busing or housing integration seems most intense when Whites fear that the safety and career changes of their children or the property value of their homes are being jeopardized.

In sum, despite the propaganda of the corporations, the political parties, the media and the government—to be explored in the chapters ahead—Americans have not been completely taken in. The disparities between what the established elites profess and what they practice is becoming increasingly apparent to larger numbers of people. Americans are not as conservative, biased and unaware of their own interests as their leaders seem to think. If given more

15. The *New York Post*, January 8, 1973, and the *Burlington* (Vt.) *Free Press*, April 12, 1973. The large majority willing to "help the poor" were thinking of programs other than welfare. Increased spending for welfare, seen by many as nothing but a handout to loafers, was rejected by two to one.

16. Harris survey, *New York Times*, January 21, 1974.

17. Harris survey, *Chicago Tribune*, January 5, 1975.

18. Harris survey, *Chicago Tribune*, April 8, 1976.

19. Gallup poll, *New York Times*, October 10, 1975.

truthful information about what is happening and if they could see a way to change things, Americans would be willing to move in a progressive direction on most socioeconomic matters.

Conservatives, Liberals, Socialists and Democracy

Political opinion in the United States might be roughly categorized as conservative, liberal and socialist. A *conservative* can be described as someone holding the ideology of free enterprise and the interests of business and property. Conservatives believe that most reforms should be resisted. They may recognize that there are some real inequities in society, but these will either take care of themselves or be taken care of over a long period of time in slow and cautious ways or, as with poverty, will always be with us. Conservatives believe that people are poor usually because, as Richard Nixon once noted, they are given to a "welfare ethic rather than a work ethic." Conservatives are for strong or weak government depending on what interests are being served. They denounce as government "meddling" those policies which appear to move toward an equalization of life chances, income and class, or which attempt to make business more accountable to public authority. But they usually advocate a strong government role in the regulation of private morals, crime control, security surveillance, restrictions on dissent, suppression of leftists and the use of overseas military intervention for purposes of "national defense." They are against all government handouts except defense contracts, corporate subsidies and tax breaks for business and the well-to-do.

Conservatives say they are for "telling the government to leave the individual alone," yet for them the main component of individual rights is the enjoyment of property rights. Indeed, conservatives cherish private property quite independently of the value placed on individuals, so when the two values conflict, property is often protected in preference to individual life and sometimes at a cost to individual life.[20] In short, conservatives put their stock in individual self-advancement, a sound business market, authority, hierarchy, a strong police force, gut patriotism and American military strength. Richard Nixon, Gerald Ford and Ronald Reagan are fairly representative of American conservatism. Millions of others who witnessed the bankruptcy of liberal programs that siphoned

20. See the discussion in Dorothy James, *Poverty, Politics and Change* (Englewood Cliffs, N.J.: Prentice-Hall, 1972).

money from the middle class to the rich in the name of the poor now, not knowing what else to do, oppose big government, centralization, bureaucracy and high taxes—and *call* themselves conservatives.

A *liberal*, like a conservative, accepts the basic structure and value system of the capitalist system but believes that social problems should be rectified by a redirection of government spending and by better regulatory policies. Liberals do not usually see these problems as being interrelated and endemic to the present system. Since they assume that the ills of the politico-economic system are abberations in the workings of capitalism, they believe that the fault must be with the personages who have gained power. If the right persons finally win office, and with the right combination of will, public awareness and political push, the system will be able to take care of its many crises. Liberals generally support government intervention in the economy in the hope of curbing some of the worst abuses of the economic system and changing "our warped priorities" so that more money will be spent on needed public services and less on private privileges. Yet while liberals call for cuts in "excessive" military spending and advocate protection of individual rights against government suppression and surveillance, and assistance for the poor and needy, in the world of action many liberals vote for huge military budgets, support security and intelligence agencies, and make cuts in human services for the needy.

Some liberals are not overly fond of capitalism, but they like socialism even less. Socialism, in their minds, conjures up stereotyped images of "drabness" and "regimentation," of people waiting in line for shoddy goods wrapped in dull gray packages and of Stalinist purges and labor camps. The liberal's concern seems to be that freedom would be lost or diminished under socialism. (Many liberals believe they are free under the present poltico-economic system.) They are also worried about the diminution of their own class and professional privileges and the loss of status they might suffer with the democratization and equalization promised in a socialist society. In this respect, they often resemble conservatives.

In matters of foreign policy, liberals generally have shown themselves as willing as conservatives to contain the spread of socialism in other lands and make the world safe for American corporate investments and markets. Since Vietnam, many liberals have come to think that we should not get involved in suppressing social revolutionary movements in other countries. But whatever their feelings about revolution abroad. most liberals have little tolerance for revolutionary struggle in the United States.

A *socialist* is someone who wants to replace the capitalist system with a system of public and communal ownership and who sees capitalism as the major cause of imperialism, racism and sexism. Socialists are distinguished from liberal reformers in their belief that our social problems cannot be solved within the very system that is creating them. Socialists do not believe that *every* human problem at *every* level of existence is caused by capitalism but that many of the most important ones are and that capitalism propagates a kind of culture and social organization that destroys human potentials and guarantees the perpetuation of poverty, racism, pollution and exploitative social relations at home and abroad. Socialists even argue that much of the unhappiness suffered in what are considered purely "interpersonal" experiences relates to the false values and anxieties of an acquisitive, competitive capitalist society.

Socialists believe that American corporate and military expansionism abroad is not the result of "wrong thinking" but the natural outgrowth of profit-oriented capitalism. To the socialist, American foreign policy is not beset by folly and irrationality but has been quite successful in maintaining the status quo and the interests of multinational corporations, crushing social change in countries like Indonesia, Guatemala, the Dominican Republic, Iran, Greece, Chile, Brazil, etc., and establishing an American financial and military presence throughout most of the world.

Conservatives, liberals and socialists all profess a dedication to "democracy," but tend to mean different things by the term. As used in this book, *democracy* refers to a system of rule in which decision-makers are held accountable and responsible to the constituency that is affected by their judgments rather than allowed to operate irresponsibly and arbitrarily. Those who are ruled exercise a measure of control by picking their rulers and by subjecting them to open criticism and the periodic checks of free elections. A democratic people should be able to live without fear of oppression and fear of want. The conditions of their lives should be humane and roughly equal.

Some people think that if you are free to say what you like, you are living in a democracy. But freedom of speech is not the sum total of democracy, only one of its necessary conditions. A government is not a democracy when it leaves us free to *say* what we want but leaves others free to *do* what they want with our country, our resources, our taxes and our lives. Democracy is not a seminar but a system of power, like any other form of governance. Free speech, like freedom of assembly and freedom of political organization, is meaningful only if it keeps those in power responsible to those over whom power is exercised.

Nor are elections and political party competitions a sure test of democracy. Some two-party or multiparty systems are so thoroughly controlled by like-minded elites that they discourage broad participation and offer policies that serve establishment interests no matter who is elected. In contrast, a one-party system, especially in a newly emerging, social revolutionary country, might actually provide *more* democracy—that is, more popular participation, more meaningful policy debate within the party than occurs between the parties in the other system, and more accountability and responsiveness to the people.

In the chapters ahead, we will take a critical look at our own political system and measure it not according to its undoubted ability to hold elections but its ability to serve democratic ends. It will be argued that whether a political system is democratic or not depends not only on its procedures but on the *substantive* outputs—that is, the actual material benefits and costs of policy and the kind of social justice or injustice that is propagated. By this view, a government that pursues policies which by design or neglect are so inequitable as to deny people the very conditions of life is not democratic no matter how many competitive elections it holds.

A Constitution
for the Few

4
TO HELP US UNDERSTAND THE AMER-
ican political system, we might give attention
to its formal structure, the rules under which it
operates and the interests it represents, beginning with the Constitution and the men who
wrote it.

It is commonly taught that entrepreneurs
of earlier times preferred a government that
kept its activities to a minimum. In actuality,
capitalist theorists and practitioners of the eighteenth and nineteenth centuries were not against
a strong state but against state restrictions on
business enterprise. It was never their desire to
remove civil authority from economic affairs but
to make sure that it worked *for* rather than
against the interests of property. If they were
for laissez-faire, it was in a highly selective way:
they did not want government limiting their
trade, controlling their prices or restricting their
markets, but not for a moment did they want
a weak government as such. Rather they sought
one that was actively on their side. So they frequently advocated an *extension* rather than a
diminution of state power.

"Civil authority," wrote Adam Smith in
1776, "so far as it is instituted for the security
of property, is in reality instituted for the defense of the rich against the poor, or of
those who have some property against those
who have none at all."[1] Smith, who is above

1. Adam Smith, *An inquiry into the Nature and
Causes of the Wealth of Nations* (Chicago: Encyclopedia

suspicion in his dedication to capitalism, argued that as wealth increased in scope, a government would have to perform more extensive services on behalf of the wealthy. "The necessity of civil government," he wrote, "grows up with the acquisition of valuable property."[2] He expected government to "facilitate commerce in general" by maintaining the necessary auxiliaries of trade, transportation and communication and providing for the armed protection of commerce "carried on with barbarous and uncivilized nations."[3]

Class Power in Early America

Adam Smith's views of the importance of government were shared by men of substance in the late eighteenth century including those who lived in America. During the period between the Revolution and the Constitution, the dominant political tone in the United States was set by the rich and well-born who, far from keeping a distance between themselves and the state, were much involved in shaping its activities.

Their power was born of place, position, and fortune. They were located at or near the seats of government and they were in direct contact with legislatures and government officers. They influenced and often dominated the local newspapers which voiced the ideas and interests of commerce and identified them with the good of the whole people, the state, and the nation. The published writings of the leaders of the period are almost without exception those of merchants, of their lawyers, or of politicians sympathetic with them.[4]

The United States of 1787 has been described as an "egalitarian" society free from the extremes of want and wealth which characterized the Old World. To be sure, the opulent and corrupt kings and bishops of Europe were not to be found in North America, but there were landed estates and colonial mansions

Britannica, Inc., 1952), p. 311. A century before Smith, John Locke in his *Second Treatise of Civil Government* described one of the central purposes of government as protecting the interests of property.

2. Smith, *Wealth of Nations,* p. 309.

3. *Ibid.,* p. 315 ff.

4. Merrill Jensen, *The New Nation* (New York: Random House, 1950), p. 178.

which bespoke a munificence of their own. Although land was abundant as compared to Europe, there was no equal opportunity in acquiring it. From the earliest English settlements, men of influence had received vast grants of land from the Crown. And through their control of the provincial governments, they had gained possession of the western parts of their states. By 1700 three-fourths of the acreage in New York belonged to less than a dozen persons. In the interior of Virginia, seven persons acquired a total of 1,732,000 acres, almost a quarter million per person.[5] By 1760 fewer than 500 merchants in five colonial cities controlled most of the trade on the eastern seaboard and themselves owned much land. "The men who promoted the new banking, transportation, mining, and manufacturing companies were usually persons who had already achieved wealth and prominence as landed gentry, merchants, or professionals."[6]

Here and there could be found "middle-class" farmers, tavern keepers, distillers and shop owners who, by the standards of the day, might be judged as comfortably situated. But the great bulk of small yeomen, composing about 80 to 85 percent of the White population, were poor freeholders, tenants, squatters, indentured laborers or hired hands. The cities had their poor and their poorhouses, along with their cobblers, weavers, bakers, blacksmiths, peddlers, laborers, clerks and domestics who worked long hours for meager sums.

As of 1787 property qualifications left perhaps more than a third of the White, male population disfranchised. There were steep property qualifications for holding office, so that most voters could not qualify as candidates themselves. In addition, there was the practice of oral voting, the lack of a secret ballot and an "absence of a real choice among candidates and programs" which led to "widespread apathy."[7] The result was that the gentry, merchants and professionals monopolized the important offices. "Who do they represent," Josiah Quincy asked about the South Carolina legislature. "The laborer, the mechanic, the tradesman, the farmer, the husbandman or yeoman? No. The representatives are almost if not wholly rich planters."[8] People of modest rank could hope only for lesser posts like constable, market clerk or assessor, jobs which

5. Sidney H. Aronson, *Status and Kinship in the Higher Civil Service* (Cambridge, Mass: Harvard University Press, 1964), p. 35.
6. *Ibid.*, p. 41.
7. *Ibid.*, p. 49.
8. Quoted in *Ibid.* p. 49.

the well-to-do found burdensome. Upper-class leadership extended into other institutions. Thus the officers in Washington's army were mostly "gentlemen," as were most members of the professions.

The American Constitution was framed by financially success-ful planters, merchants, lawyers, bankers and creditors, many of them linked by kinship and marriage and by years of service in the Congress, the military or diplomacy. They congregated in Philadelphia in 1787 for the professed purpose of revising the Articles of Confederation and strengthening the powers of the central government. They were impelled by a desire to build a nation and by the explicit intent of doing something about the increasingly insurgent spirit evidenced among poorer people.

The rebellious populace of that day has been portrayed by textbook writers as irresponsible spendthrifts who never paid their debts and who believed in nothing more than timid state govern-ments and inflated paper money. Little has been said about the actual plight of the common people, the great bulk of whom lived at a subsistence level. The poorer farmers were burdened by the low prices offered for their crops by merchants, the high costs for merchandised goods and regressive taxes. They often bought land at inflated prices, only to see its value collapse and to find them-selves unable to meet their mortgage obligations. Their labor and their crops usually were theirs in name only. To survive, they fre-quently had to borrow money at high interest rates. To meet their debts they mortgaged their future crops and went still deeper into debt. Large numbers were caught in that cycle of rural indebted-ness which is the common fate of agrarian peoples in many coun-tries to this day. The underpaid and underemployed artisans and workers (or "mechanics," as they were called) in the towns were not much better off.

Among the poor there grew the feeling that the revolution against the king of England had been fought for naught. When many debtors were jailed in Massachusetts early in 1787 and others threatened with foreclosures on their farms, angry men began gathering at the county towns to prevent the courts from presiding over debtor cases. By the winter of 1787, farmers in western Massa-chusetts led by Daniel Shays had taken up arms. But their rebellion was forcibly put down by the state militia after some ragged skirmishes.

The specter of Shays' Rebellion hovered over the men who gathered in Philadelphia three months later, confirming their worst fears about the populace. They were determined that persons of birth and fortune should control the affairs of the nation and check the leveling impulses of that propertyless multitude which composed "the majority faction." "To secure the public good and private rights against the danger of such a faction," wrote James Madison, "and at the same time preserve the spirit and form of popular government is then the great object to which our inquiries are directed." The Framers of the Constitution were to agree with Madison when he wrote in *Federalist* No. 10 that "the most common and durable source of factions has been the various and unequal distribution of property. Those who hold and those who are without property have ever formed distinct interests in society." And most of them did not hesitate to construct a strong central government that would insure their victory in the struggle between these "distinct interests."

The Founding Fathers were of the opinion that things had become, in the words of one, "too democratic." They deemed the state legislatures too responsive to the people. "The evils we experience flow from the excess of democracy," complained Elbridge Gerry of Massachusetts, who noted that the people are "daily misled into the most baneful measures and opinions." Both he and Madison warned of "the danger of the leveling spirit." "The people," said Roger Sherman, "should have as little to do as may be about the Government. They want information and are constantly liable to be misled." But it remained for Alexander Hamilton to provide the memorable summation:

All communities divide themselves into the few and the many. The first are the rich and the well born, the other the mass of the people. The voice of the people has been said to be the voice of God; and however generally this maxim has been quoted and believed, it is not true in fact. The people are turbulent and changing; they seldom judge or determine right. Give therefore to the first class a distinct, permanent share in the government. They will check the unsteadiness of the second and as they cannot receive any advantage by a change, they therefore will ever maintain good government.[9]

9. The quotations by Gerry, Madison, Sherman and Hamilton are taken from Max Farrand (ed.), *Records of the Federal Convention* (New Haven: Yale University Press, 1927), vol. 1, *passim.* For further testimony by the Founding Fathers and other early leaders, see John C. Miller, *Origins of the American Revolution* (Boston: Little, Brown, 1943), pp. 491 ff., and Andrew C. McLaughlin, *A Constitutional History of the United States* (New York: Appleton-Century, 1935), pp. 141–144.

Containing the Spread of Democracy

The Framers spent many weeks debating their differences, but these were the differences of merchants, slave owners, and manufacturers, a debate of haves versus haves in which each group sought safeguards within the new Constitution for its particular regional or commercial interests. Added to this were the inevitable disagreements that arise over what are the best means of achieving agreed-upon ends. Questions of structure and authority occupied a good deal of the delegates' time: How much representation for the large and small states? How might the legislature be organized? How should the executive be selected? What length of tenure for the different officeholders? But certain questions of enormous significance, relating to the new government's ability to protect the interests of property, were agreed upon with surprisingly little debate. For on these issues there were no dirt farmers or poor artisans attending the Convention to proffer an opposing viewpoint. The debate between haves and have-nots never took place.

The portions of the Constitution giving the federal government the power to support commerce and protect property were decided upon after amiable deliberation and with remarkable dispatch considering their importance. Thus all of Article I, Section 8 was adopted within a few days.[10] This section delegated to Congress the power to (a) regulate commerce among the states and with foreign nations and Indian tribes, (b) lay and collect taxes and impose duties and tariffs on imports but not on commercial exports, (c) establish a national currency and regulate its value, (d) "borrow Money on the credit of the United States"—a measure of special interest to creditors,[11] (e) fix the standard of weights and measures necessary for trade, (f) protect the value of securities and currency against counterfeiting, (g) establish "uniform Laws on the subject

10. John Bach McMaster, "Framing the Constitution," in his *The Political Depravity of the Founding Fathers* (New York: Farrar, Straus, 1964), p. 137. Originally published in 1896. Farrand refers to the consensus for a strong national government that emerged after the small states had been given equal representation in the Senate. Much of the work that followed "was purely formal" albeit sometimes time-consuming. See Max Farrand, *The Framing of the Constitution of the United States* (New Haven: Yale University Press, 1913), pp. 134–135.

11. The original wording was "borrow money and emit bills." But the latter phrase was deleted after Gouverneur Morris warned that "The Monied interest" would oppose the constitution if paper notes were not prohibited. There was much strong feeling about this among creditors. In any case, it was assumed that the borrowing power would allow for "safe and proper" public notes should they be necessary. See Farrand, *The Framing of the Constitution*, p. 147.

of Bankruptcies throughout the United States," (h) "pay the Debts and provide for the common Defence and general Welfare of the United States." Congress was limited to powers specifically delegated to it by the Constitution or implied as "necessary and proper" for the performance of the delegated powers. Over the years, under this "implied power" clause, federal intervention in the private economy grew to an extraordinary magnitude.

Some of the delegates were land speculators who expressed a concern about western holdings; accordingly, Congress was given the "Power to dispose of and make all needful Rules and Regulations respecting the Territory or other Property belonging to the United States. . . ." Some of the delegates speculated in highly inflated and nearly worthless Confederation securities. Under Article VI, all debts incurred by the Confederation were valid against the new government, a provision that allowed speculators to make generous profits when their securities were honored at face value.[12]

In the interest of merchants and creditors, the states were prohibited from issuing paper money or imposing duties on imports and exports or interfering with the payment of debts by passing any "Law impairing the Obligation of Contracts." The Constitution guaranteed "Full Faith and Credit" in each state "to the Acts, Records, and judicial Proceedings" of other states, thus allowing creditors to pursue their debtors more effectively.

The property interests of slave owners were looked after. To give the slave-owning states a greater influence, three-fifths of the slave population were to be counted when calculating the representation deserved by each state in the lower house. The importation of slaves was allowed to continue until 1808. And under Article IV, slaves who escaped from one state to another had to be delivered up to the original owner upon claim, a provision that was unanimously adopted at the Convention.

The Framers believed the states acted with insufficient force against popular uprisings, so Congress was given the task of "organizing, arming, and disciplining the Militia" and calling it forth, among other things, to "suppress Insurrections." The federal government guaranteed every state in the Union a "Republican Form

12. The classic study of the economic interests of the Founding Fathers is Charles A. Beard, *An Economic Interpretation of the Constitution* (New York: Macmillan, 1913). Critiques of Beard have been made by Robert E. Brown, *Charles Beard and the American Constitution* (Princeton, N.J.: Princeton University Press, 1956), and Forrest McDonald, *We the People—The Economic Origins of the Constitution* (Chicago: Chicago University Press, 1958).

of Government" and protection against invasion and "against domestic Violence." Provision was also made for "the Erection of Forts, Magazines, Arsenals, dock-Yards and other needful Buildings," and for the maintenance of an army and navy for national defense and to police unsettled American territories. To protect overseas trade, Congress could take steps to "punish Piracies and Felonies committed on the high Seas, and Offences against the Law of Nations."

In keeping with their desire to contain the majority, the Founding Fathers inserted "auxiliary precautions" *designed to fragment power without democratizing it.* By separating the executive, legislative and judiciary functions and then providing a system of checks and balances among the various branches, including staggered elections, executive veto, Senate confirmation of appointments and ratification of treaties, and a two-house legislature, they hoped to dilute the impact of popular sentiments. To the extent that it existed at all, the majoritarian principle was tightly locked into a system of minority vetoes, making swift and sweeping popular actions nearly impossible.

The propertyless majority, as Madison was to point out in *Federalist* No. 10, must not be allowed to concert in common cause against the established social order.[13] First, it was necessary to prevent a unity of public sentiment by enlarging the polity and then compartmentalizing it into geographically insulated political communities. The larger the nation, the greater the "variety of parties and interests" and the more difficult it would be for a majority to find itself and act in unison. As Madison argued, "A rage for paper money, for an abolition of debts, for an equal division of property, or for any other wicked project will be less apt to pervade the whole body of the Union than a particular member of it. . . ." An uprising of impoverished farmers may threaten Massachusetts at one time and Rhode Island at another, but a national government will be large and varied enough to contain each of

---

13. *Federalist* No. 10 can be found in any of the good editions of the *Federalist Papers.* It is one of the finest essays on American politics ever written. With clarity and economy of language it explains, as do few other short works, how a government may utilize the republican principle to contain the populace and protect the propertied few from the propertyless many, and it confronts, if not solves, the essential question of how government may reconcile the tensions between liberty, authority and dominant class interest. In effect, the Tenth Federalist Paper maps out a method, relevant to this day, of preserving the existing undemocratic class structure under the legitimating cloak of democratic forms.

these and insulate the rest of the nation from the contamination of rebellion.

Second, not only must the majority be prevented from finding horizontal cohesion, but its vertical force—that is, its upward thrust upon government—should be blunted by interjecting indirect forms of representation. Thus the Senators from each state were to be elected by their respective state legislatures. The chief executive was to be selected by an electoral college voted by the people but, as anticipated by the Framers, composed of political leaders and men of substance who would gather in their various states and choose a President of their own liking. It was believed they would be unable to muster a majority for any one candidate, and the final selection would be left to the House, with each state delegation therein having only one vote.[14] The Supreme Court was to be elected by no one, its Justices being appointed to life tenure by the President and confirmed by the Senate. In time, of course, the electoral college proved to be something of a rubber stamp, and the Seventeenth Amendment, adopted in 1913, provided for the direct election of the Senate.

The only portion of government directly elected by the people was the House of Representatives. Many of the Framers would have preferred excluding the public entirely from direct representation: John Mercer observed that he found nothing in the proposed Constitution more objectionable than "the mode of election by the people. The people cannot know and judge of the characters of Candidates. The worst possible choice will be made." Others were concerned that demagogues would ride into office on a populist tide only to pillage the treasury and wreak havoc on all. "The time is not distant," warned Gouverneur Morris, "when this Country will abound with mechanics and manufacturers [industrial workers] who will receive their bread from their employers. Will such men be the secure and faithful Guardians of liberty? . . . Children do not vote. Why? Because they want prudence, because they have no will of their own. The ignorant and dependent can be as little trusted with the public interest."[15]

Several considerations softened the Framers' determination to contain democracy. First and most important, the delegates recognized that there were limits to what the states would ratify. They

14. The delegates did expect that George Washington would be overwhelmingly elected the first President, but they anticipated that in subsequent contests the electoral college would seldom be able to decide on one person.
15. Farrand, *Records of the Federal Convention*, vol. 2, pp. 200 ff.

also understood that if the federal government were to have any kind of stability, it must gain some measure of popular acceptance; hence, for all their class biases, they were inclined to "leave something for the-people," even if it were only "the *spirit* and *form* of popular government," to recall Madison's words. In addition, some of the delegates feared not only the tyranny of the many but the machinations of the few. It was Madison who reminded his colleagues that in protecting themselves from the multitude, they must not reintroduce a "cabal" or a monarchy, thus erring in the opposite direction. Finally, a few of them—notably George Mason and Benjamin Franklin—expressed a positive regard for the common folk. If they said nothing in support of extending the franchise, they did speak out against limiting it. Franklin lauded "the virtue and public spirit of our common people; of which they displayed a great deal during the war," and he commended their tendency to be loyal and faithful citizens if treated decently.

In any case, when the delegates agreed to having "the people" elect the lower house, they were referring to a somewhat select portion of the population. Property qualifications disfranchised the poorest in various states. Half the adult population was denied suffrage because they were women. About one-fourth, both men and women, had no vote because they were held in bondage, and even among Blacks who had gained their legal freedom, in both the North and the South, none was allowed to vote until the passage of the Fourteenth Amendment after the Civil War.

Plotters or Patriots?

The question of whether the Founding Fathers were motivated by financial or national interest has been debated ever since Charles Beard published *An Economic Interpretation of the Constitution* in 1913. It was Beard's view that the Founding Fathers were guided by their class interests. Arguing against Beard's thesis are those who believe that the Framers were concerned with higher things than just lining their purses and protecting their property. True, they were monied men who profited directly from policies initiated under the new Constitution, but they were motivated by a concern for nation-building that went beyond their particular class interests, the argument goes.[16] To paraphrase Justice Holmes,

16. For some typical apologistic arguments on behalf of the Founding Fathers, see Broadhus Mitchell and Louise Pearson Mitchell, *A Biography of*

these men invested their belief to make a nation; they did not make a nation because they had invested. "High-mindedness is not impossible to man," Holmes reminds us.

And that is exactly the point: high-mindedness is one of man's most common attributes even when, or especially when, he is pursuing his personal and class interest. The fallacy is to presume that there is a dichotomy between the desire to build a strong nation and the desire to protect property and that the Framers could not have been motivated by both. In fact, like most other people, they believed that what was good for themselves was ultimately good for the entire society. Their universal values and their class interests went hand in hand, and to discover the existence of the "higher" sentiment does not eliminate the self-interested one.

Most persons believe in their own virtue. The Founding Fathers never doubted the nobility of their effort and its importance for the generations to come. Just as many of them could feel dedicated to the principle of "liberty for all" and at the same time own slaves, so could they serve both their nation and their estates. The point is not that the Framers were devoid of the grander sentiments of nation-building but that *there was nothing in that concept of nation which worked against their class interest and a great deal that worked for it.*

People tend to perceive things in accordance with the position they occupy in the social structure, and that position is largely determined by their class status. Even if we deny that the Framers were motivated by the desire for personal gain that moves other successful businessmen, we cannot dismiss the existence of their class interest. The Founding Fathers may not have been solely concerned with getting their own hands in the till, although enough of them did; but they were admittedly preoccupied with defending the propertied few from the propertyless many—for the ultimate benefit of all, as they understood it. "The Constitution," as Staughton Lynd notes, "was the settlement of a revolution. What was at stake for Hamilton, Livingston, and their opponents, was more than speculative windfalls in securities; it was the question, what kind of society would emerge from the revolution when the dust

the Constitution of the United States (New York: Oxford University Press, 1964), pp. 46–51, and David G. Smith, *The Convention and the Constitution* (New York: St. Martin's Press, 1965), Chapter Three. Smith argues that the Framers had not only economic motives but "larger" political objectives, as if the political had no relation to the economic or as if the political objectives were more impelling because they were directed toward a "national interest" rather than self-interest or a class interest.

had settled, and on which class the political center of gravity would come to rest."[17]

Finally those who argue that the Founding Fathers were motivated primarily by high-minded objectives consistently overlook the fact that the delegates repeatedly stated their intention to erect a government strong enough to protect the haves from the have-nots. They gave voice to the crassest class prejudices and never found it necessary to disguise the fact—as have latter-day apologists—that their uppermost concern was to diminish popular control and resist all tendencies toward class equalization (or "leveling" as it was called). Their opposition to democracy and their dedication to the propertied and monied interests were a matter of openly avowed ideology. Their preoccupation was so pronounced that one delegate did finally complain of hearing too much about how the purpose of government was to protect property. He wanted it noted that the ultimate objective of government was the ennoblement of mankind—a fine sentiment that evoked no opposition from his colleagues as they continued about their business.

An Elitist Document

More important than conjecturing about the Framers' motives is to look at the Constitution they fashioned, for it tells us a good deal about their objectives. It was and still is largely an elitist document, more concerned with the securing of property interests than with personal liberties. Bills of attainder and ex post facto laws are expressly prohibited, and Article I, Section 9 assures us that "the Privilege of the Writ of Habeas Corpus shall not be suspended, unless when in Cases of Rebellion or Invasion the public Safety may require it," a restriction that leaves authorities with a good measure of discretion. Other than these few provisions, the Constitution that emerged from the Philadelphia Convention gave no attention to civil liberties. When Colonel Mason suggested to the Convention that a committee be formed to draft "a Bill of Rights," a task that could be accomplished "in a few hours," the representatives of the various states offered little discussion on the

17. Staughton Lynd, *Class Conflict, Slavery and the United States Constitution* (Indianapolis: Bobbs-Merrill, 1967), selection in Irwin Unger (ed.), *Beyond Liberalism: The New Left Views American History* (Waltham, Mass.: Xerox College Publishing, 1971), p. 17.

motion and voted unanimously against it. Guarantees of individual rights—including freedom of speech and religion; freedom to assemble peaceably and petition for redress of grievances; the right to keep arms; freedom from unreasonable searches and seizures, from self-incrimination, double jeopardy, cruel and unusual punishment and excessive bail and fines; and the right to a fair and impartial trial and other forms of due process—were tacked on as the first ten amendments (the Bill of Rights) only after the Constitution was ratified and the first Congress and President had been elected.

The twentieth-century concept of social justice, involving something more than procedural liberties, is afforded no place in our eighteenth-century Constitution. The Constitution says nothing about those conditions of life which have come to be treated by many people as essential human rights—for instance, freedom from hunger, the right to decent housing, medical care and education regardless of ability to pay, the right to gainful employment, safe working conditions, a clean, nontoxic environment. Under the Constitution equality is treated as a *procedural* right without a *substantive* content. Thus "equality of opportunity" means equality of opportunity to move ahead competitively and become unequal to others; it means a chance to get in the game and best others rather than enjoy an equal distribution and use of the resources needed for the maintenance of community life.

Some people have argued that democracy is simply a system of rules for playing the game which allows some measure of mass participation and government accountability, and the Constitution is a kind of rule book. One should not try to impose, as a precondition of democracy, particular class relations, economic philosophies or other substantive arrangements on this open-ended game. This argument certainly does reduce democracy to a game. It presumes that procedural rules can exist in a meaningful way independently of substantive realities. Whether procedural rights are violated or actually enjoyed, whether one is treated by the law as pariah or prince, depends largely on material realities that extend beyond a written constitution or other formal guarantees of law. The law in its majestic equality, Anatole France once observed, prohibits rich and poor alike from stealing bread and sleeping under the bridges. And in so doing the law becomes something of a farce, a fiction that allows us to speak of "the rights of all" divorced from the class conditions that place the rich above the law and the poor below it. In the absence of certain substantive conditions, legalistic and procedural rights are of little value to millions who have neither the time, money nor opportunity to make a reality of their formal rights.

Take the "right of every citizen to be heard." In its majestic equality the law allows both the rich and the poor to raise high their political voices: both are free to hire the best-placed lobbyists and Washington lawyers to pressure public officeholders; both are free to shape public opinion by owning a newspaper or television station; and both rich and poor have the right to engage in multimillion-dollar election campaigns in order to pick the right persons for office or win office themselves. But again, this formal political equality is something of a fiction, as we shall see in the pages ahead. Of what good are the rules for those millions who are excluded from the game?

The Growth
of Government

5

ALTHOUGH THE DECISIONS OF GOVERN-
ment are made in the name of the entire society,
they rarely benefit everyone. Some portion of
the populace, frequently a majority, loses out.
What is considered *national* policy is usually
the policy of dominant groups strategically located within the political system. The standard
textbook view is that American government
manifests no consistent class bias. The political
system is said to involve a give-and-take among
many different groups, "a plurality of interests."
What government supposedly does in this pluralistic interplay is act as a regulator of conflict,
trying to limit the advantages of the strong and
minimize the disadvantages of the weak.

In violation of that notion, I will argue that
the existing political system may regulate but it
does not equalize, and that its overall effect is
to deepen rather than redress the inequities of
capitalist society. The political system enjoys no
special immunity to the way power resources
are distributed in society. It responds primarily,
although not exclusively, to the powers and
needs of the corporate system. "The business
of government is business," President Calvin
Coolidge once said. In this chapter we will explore the meaning of that observation, focusing
primarily on the "reformist" periods of our
history.

Serving Business: The Early Years

The upper-class dominance of public life so characteristic of the Founding Fathers' generation

continued into the nineteenth century. The United States of the early 1800s had an informal but financially powerful aristocracy that controlled "the economic life of the great northeastern cities," and exercised a "vast influence" over the organizational life of the nation.[1] "Amid all the hullabaloo about his alleged dominance in the era, the common man appears to have gotten very little of whatever it was that counted for much," concludes one historian after a systematic study of the period.[2]

During the Jacksonian era, supposedly an "age of egalitarianism," there were more lawyers and bankers occupying top administrative posts than under the Federalist administration of John Adams. President Andrew Jackson's key appointments were drawn overwhelmingly from the ranks of the rich. Jackson cultivated his "Old Hickory" image, talked a great deal about the virtues of the frontiersmen and the common folk, and for this won their support, but he himself identified with, and in fact *was* a member of the affluent gentry, comfortable in the company of those born to positions of economic, military and political leadership. The fact that Jackson said he would change the social composition of decision-makers and would drive out the money changers, led to the mistaken belief that he had actually done so. Jackson's attack on the Bank of the United States leaves the misleading impression that he warred against the entire monied class. As Aronson notes: "Jackson's followers, who hoped he would democratize the administration, interpreted the small changes that actually took place as major reforms; Jackson's enemies, who feared that he would turn the government over to the mob, regarded the same changes as radical transformations in the social composition of officeholders."[3] Neither group was correct.

The growth of business from local enterprises to large-scale manufacture during the latter half of the nineteenth century was accompanied by a similar growth in governmental activity in the economy. While insisting that the free market worked for all, most businessmen showed little inclination to deliver their own interests to the stern judgments of an untrammeled, competitive economy; instead they resorted to such things as protective tariffs, public

1. Edward Pessen, *Riches, Class and Power Before the Civil War* (Lexington, Mass.: D. C. Heath, 1973), p. 278.
2. *Ibid.*, p. 304.
3. Sidney H. Aronson, *Status and Kinship in the Higher Civil Service* (Cambridge, Mass.: Harvard University Press, 1964), p. 160.

subsidies, price regulations, contracts, patents, trademarks and other legal artifacts provided by civil authority.

When government intervened in the economy, it was almost invariably on the side of the strong against the weak. The unemployment and hunger that beset great numbers of miners, farmers and laborers did little to enlist the efforts of public officials, but when rebellious workers seized the railroads, as during the depression of 1873, civil authorities were moved to energetic measures on behalf of corporate property, using the militia and then federal troops to crush the railroad strikes. "The industrial barons made a habit of calling soldiers to their assistance; and armories were erected in the principal cities as measures of convenience."[4] Short of having the regular army permanently garrisoned in industrial areas, as was the desire of some owners, government officials took steps "to establish an effective antiradical National Guard."[5]

The high-ranking officials who applied force against workers often were themselves men of wealth. President Cleveland's Attorney General, Richard Olney, a millionaire owner of railroad securities, a man of "self-righteous, ruthless, and property-loving nature"[6] used antitrust laws, court injunctions, mass arrests, labor spies, deputy marshals and federal troops against workers and their unions. From the local sheriff and magistrate to the President and Supreme Court, the forces of "law and order" were utilized to suppress the "conspiracy" of labor unions and serve "the defensive needs of large capitalist enterprises."[7] The very statutes they had declared to be unworkable against the well-known monopolistic and collusive practices of business were now promptly and effectively invoked against "labor combinations."

By the late nineteenth century, the federal government accumulated through tariffs and taxes an enormous budget surplus, distributing most of it to the wealthy in high-premium bonds. From 1888 to 1890 alone, some $45 million from the public treasury, "collected from the consuming population, and above all from the . . . poor wage earners and farmers," was paid out to big investors.[8]

4. Matthew Josephson, *The Robber Barons* (New York: Harcourt, Brace, 1934), p. 365.

5. William Preston, Jr., *Aliens and Dissenters* (Cambridge, Mass.: Harvard University Press, 1963), p. 24.

6. Matthew Josephson, *The Politicos, 1865–1896* (New York: Harcourt, Brace, 1938), p. 562.

7. *Ibid.*, p. 566.

8. Allan Nevins, *Grover Cleveland: A Study in Courage* (New York: Dodd, Mead, 1932), p. 279, quoted in Josephson, *The Robber Barons*, p. 395.

Likewise, a billion acres of land in the public domain, *almost half of the present area of the United States,* was given over to private hands. Josephson describes the government's endeavors to privatize the public wealth:

This benevolent government handed over to its friends or to astute first comers, . . . all those treasures of coal and oil, of copper and gold and iron, the land grants, the terminal sites, the perpetual rights of way—an act of largesse which is still one of the wonders of history. To the new railroad enterprises in addition, great money subsidies totaling many hundreds of millions were given. The Tariff Act of 1864 was in itself a sheltering wall of subsidies; and to aid further the new heavy industries and manufactures, an Immigration Act allowing contract labor to be imported freely was quickly enacted; a national banking system was perfected. . . . Having conferred these vast rights and controls, the . . . government would preserve them, as Conklin termed it, so as to "curb the many who would do to the few as they would not have the few do to them."[9]

For all its activities on behalf of business, the federal government did exercise a kind of laissez-faire in certain other areas: little attention was given to unemployment, poverty, education, the spread of urban slums, and the spoliation of natural resources.

The "Progressive" Era

By the turn of the century, government was to play a still more active role in helping large firms extend their hold over the economy. Contrary to the view that the giant trusts controlled everything, price competition with smaller companies in 1900 was vigorous enough to cut seriously into the profits of industries like iron and steel, copper, agricultural machinery, automobile and telephone.[10] Suffering from an inability to regulate prices, expand profits, limit competitors and free themselves from the "vexatious" laws of state and local governments, big corporations began demanding greater federal regulation. As the utilities magnate Samuel Insull said, it was better to "help shape the right kind of regulation

9. Josephson, *The Robber Barons,* p. 52.
10. Gabriel Kolko marshals a great deal of evidence to support this conclusion; see his *The Triumph of Conservatism* (Chicago: Quadrangle Books, 1967), Chapters 1 and 2.

than to have the wrong kind forced upon [us]."[11] The first major regulatory effort by the federal government under the Interstate Commerce Commission was so helpful to the railroads as to make them enthusiastic advocates of regulation after 1887; their enthusiasm persists to this day.[12]

During the 1900–1916 period, known as the Progressive Era, federal regulations in meat packing, food and drugs, banking, timber and mining were initiated at the insistence of the strongest corporations within these industries. The overall effect of regulation was to raise prices and profits for the large producers, tighten their control over markets and weed out weaker cost-cutting competitors.

Of the several White House occupants during the Progressive Era, Teddy Roosevelt might be considered most representative of the period. Hailed by many as a "trust-buster," Roosevelt actually was hostile toward unionists and reformers. Toward business he manifested bluster but virtually no bite. His major legislative proposals reflected the desires of corporation interests. Like other Presidents before and since, he enjoyed close relations with big businessmen and invited them into his administration.

However much President Theodore Roosevelt might thunder against the "malefactors of great wealth" (much as his namesake, Franklin, attacked the "economic royalists" during the New Deal) these "robber barons" and industrialists knew the attacks were largely moral and ceremonial in character—and that anyway they could often control corrupt state and even national legislatures, as well as the judiciary.[13]

What was true of Roosevelt held equally for Taft and Wilson, the other two Presidents of the Progressive Era. Neither "had a distinct consciousness of any fundamental conflict between their political goals and those of business."[14] Wilson railed against the corrupt political machines and like Roosevelt, presented himself as a "trust-buster," but his campaign funds came from a few rich contributors, most notably the copper magnate Cleveland Dodge. Wilson wrote his first inaugural speech on Dodge's yacht, conferred regularly with Dodge and other associates of Morgan and Rocke-

11. See James Weinstein, *The Corporate Ideal in the Liberal State* (Boston: Beacon Press, 1968), p. 87.

12. See Samuel P. Huntington, "The Marasmus of the ICC," *Yale Law Journal*, April 1952, reprinted in Francis Rourke (ed.), *Bureaucratic Power in National Politics* (Boston: Little, Brown, 1965), pp. 73–86.

13. Patrick Renshaw, *The Wobblies* (Garden City, N.Y.: Doubleday, 1968), p. 24.

14. Kolko, *The Triumph of Conservatism*, p. 281.

feller, and brought numerous businessmen into his administration.[15] In his Latin American interventions and his implementation of the Federal Reserve Act and the Federal Trade Commission Act, Wilson, the "liberal Democrat," showed himself as responsive to business as any of the previous Republicans. "Progressivism was not the triumph of small business over the trusts, as has often been suggested, but the victory of big businesses in achieving the rationalization of the economy that only the federal government could provide."[16]

The advent of World War I further intensified relations between industry and government. During 1917 businessmen used government agencies to convert industry to war production. If large sectors of the economy were mobilized for the business of war, it was along lines proposed by those business interests enjoying privileged access to the councils of the warriors.[17] The police and military were used without hesitation against workers. Strikes were now treated as seditious interference with war production. Federal troops raided and ransacked headquarters of the Industrial Workers of the World and imprisoned large numbers of workers suspected of socialist sympathies. Nor did things improve during the postwar "Red scare"; the federal government resorted to mass arrests, deportations, political trials and congressional investigations to suppress anticapitalist ideas.[18]

During the "normalcy" of the 1920s, prosperity was supposedly within everyone's grasp; stock speculations and other get-rich-quick schemes engaged the energies of many. Not since the Gilded Age of the robber barons had the more vulgar manifestations of capitalist culture enjoyed such an uncritical reception. But there were millions of lower-income people who remained untouched by the postwar prosperity, and with the depression of 1929, their ranks were soon joined by millions more.

15. Frank Harris Blighton, *Woodrow Wilson and Co.* (New York: Fox Printing House, 1916).

16. Kolko, *The Triumph of Conservatism*, pp. 283–284. The period between 1900 and 1916 is called the Progressive Era because of the flurry of muckraking against big business abuses, the occasional trust-busting and the municipal and state electoral reforms which introduced such things as the long ballot, the referendum and recall, and the nonpartisan election. The era was "progressive" more in tone than substance.

17. Paul A. C. Koistinen, "The 'Industrial-Military Complex' in Historical Perspective: The Inter War Years," *Journal of American History*, 56, March 1970, reprinted in Irwin Unger (ed.), *Beyond Liberalism: The New Left Views American History* (Waltham, Mass.: Xerox College Publishing, 1971), pp. 228–229.

18. See Preston, *Aliens and Dissenters, passim.*

The New Deal: Reform for Whom?

The New Deal era of the 1930s is commonly believed to have been a period of great transformation on behalf of "the forgotten man," but the definitive history of who got what during the 1930s has still to be written.[19]

From what we know, the central dedication of the Franklin Roosevelt administration was to *business recovery* rather than *social reform*. The federal government sought to revivify the economy through a system of direct subsidies, credits and supports, applying price and market regulatory methods of a kind advocated by industry. Hence, when an early version of the National Recovery Act (NRA)—allowing firms to limit production and fix prices—was opposed by corporation spokesmen, the Roosevelt administration withdrew it and substituted the approved business version.[20] The effect of the NRA was to injure small business and contribute to the concentration of American industry.[21] In attempting to spur production by financing private investments, the government in effect funneled huge sums from the public treasure into the hands of the monied few: in nine years the Reconstruction Finance Corporation alone lent $15 billion to business. As long as such measures were aimed at price and production recovery, they were popular with much of the business community, though of little help to low- and middle-income people.

The local charity arrangements of the early 1930s, almost unchanged from colonial times, were hopelessly inadequate. Faced with mass unrest, the federal government instituted a relief program which prevented widespread starvation and—more importantly from the perspective of the business community—limited the

19. The standard works on the period are often quite detailed yet lacking in any analysis of the class distributions of inputs and outputs. Only a few American historians describe how the Roosevelt administration serviced the corporate class while reserving its best rhetoric for the common man: see Paul K. Conkin, *The New Deal* (New York: Crowell, 1967); also Barton J. Bernstein, "The New Deal: The Conservative Achievements of Liberal Reform," in Barton J. Bernstein (ed.), *Towards a New Past* (New York: Pantheon, 1963); and Brad Wiley, "Historians and the New Deal," a pamphlet published by the Radical Education Project, Ann Arbor, Michigan, n.d. A good critical treatment of welfare and relief policies under the New Deal can be found in Frances Fox Piven and Richard A. Cloward, *Regulating the Poor* (New York: Pantheon Books, 1971), Chapters 2 and 3.

20. Piven and Cloward, *Regulating the Poor*, p. 72. Also Basil Rauch, The *History of the New Deal, 1933–1938* (New York: Creative Age Press, 1944), pp. 70–71.

21. Bernstein, "The New Deal . . ." p. 269.

instances of violent protest and radicalization. But as the New Deal moved toward measures that threatened to compete with private enterprises and undermine low wage structures, businessmen withdrew their support and became openly hostile. While infuriating Roosevelt, who saw himself as trying to rescue the capitalist system, business opposition probably enhanced his reformist image in the public mind.

The enormous disparity between the New Deal's popular image and its actual accomplishments remains one of the unappreciated aspects of the Roosevelt era. To cite specifics: the Civilian Conservation Corps provided jobs at subsistence wages for 250,000 out of 15 million unemployed persons. At its peak, the Works Progress Administration (WPA) reached about one in four unemployed, often with work of unstable duration and wages below the already inadequate ones of private industry. The minimum wage law reached only about a half-million of the 12 million workers in interstate commerce who were earning less than forty cents an hour. The Social Security Act of 1935 made retirement benefits payable only in 1942 and thereafter, covering but half the population and providing no medical insurance and no protection against illness before retirement. Similarly, old-age and unemployment insurance applied only to those who had enjoyed sustained employment in select occupations. Implementation was left to the states, which were free to set whatever restrictive conditions they chose. Social welfare programs were regressively funded through payroll deductions and sales taxes.

The federal housing program sought to stimulate private construction with subsidies to construction firms and middle-class buyers and protection for mortgage bankers through the loan insurance program—all of little benefit to the many millions of ill-housed poor.

Like so many other of its programs, the New Deal's efforts in agriculture primarily benefited the large producers through a series of price supports and production cutbacks, while riding "roughshod over the most destitute."[22] Thus many tenant farmers and sharecroppers were evicted when federal acreage rental programs took land out of cultivation.[23] The fate of the Roosevelt administration's

22. Piven and Cloward, *Regulating the Poor,* p. 76; and Bernstein, "The New Deal . . ." pp. 269–270.

23. By February 1935, 733,000 farm families were on the relief rolls, a rise of 75 percent in sixteen months under the New Deal's agricultural program. The lot of the small farmer did not noticeably improve under Roosevelt and frequently worsened.

"land reform" efforts was a familiar one. In rural areas the government began buying up land and redistributing it to the destitute. Some ten thousand families were resettled in 152 projects, but even this limited effort was too much for conservatives in Congress who managed to stop land distribution. Indigent farmers who wanted to buy land now had to apply for government guaranteed private loans, leaving poor Whites with little chance—and poor Blacks with even less chance—of favored treatment when it came to securing loans.[24]

Piven and Cloward argue that it was not the misery of millions which brought government aid—since misery had prevailed for years before—but the continued threat of acute political unrest. That government programs were markedly inadequate for the tasks at hand seemed less important than that they achieved a high visibility and did much to dilute public discontent. Once the threat of political unrest and violence subsided, *federal relief was cut back:* in 1936–1937 WPA rolls were reduced by over half and the emergency relief program was slashed, leaving many families with neither work nor relief, reducing them to a destitution worse than any they had known since the 1929 crash. "Large numbers of people were put off the rolls and thrust into a labor market still glutted with unemployed. But with stability restored, the continued suffering of these millions had little political force."[25]

At the same time, organized labor gained a new legitimacy, but on terms highly functional to the corporate system. Labor leaders, including most of those who had earned reputations as "militants," were dedicated to maintaining the capitalist system. In 1935 John L. Lewis warned that "the dangerous state of affairs" might lead to "class consciousness" and "revolution as well"; he pledged that his own union was "doing everything in their power to make the system work and thereby avoid it."[26] Men like Lewis, William Green and Sidney Hillman cooperated closely with management in introducing speed-up methods into production, limiting strikes and maintaining a "disciplined" labor force. The CIO's dedication, as Hillman noted, was not to changing "the competitive system" but to trying "to make the system workable."[27]

24. See Ben H. Bagdikian, "A Forgotten New Deal Experiment in Land Reform," *I. F. Stone Weekly,* July 31, 1967, p. 3. See also Conkin, *The New Deal,* Chapter 3; Piven and Cloward, *Regulating the Poor,* Chapters 2 and 3.
25. Piven and Cloward, *Regulating the Poor,* p. 46.
26. Quoted in Ronald Radosh, "The Corporate Ideology of American Labor Leaders from Gompers to Hillman," *Studies on the Left,* 6, November–December 1966, reprinted in Unger, *Beyond Liberalism,* p. 226.
27. *Ibid.,* p. 224.

Many owners relied on CIO leaders to keep a "production-minded" control over the workers, utilizing the good will of the union for management's purposes. One Baltimore manufacturer once complained to Hillman that he had been "trying to get more production for weeks" without success and asked Hillman to urge the local union leader to make more frequent appearances "because I feel that with his finesse he is able to get for us what we want, better than we can ourselves and it is urgent from many angles that we get our production."[28] To the very poor and the many millions of unemployed, the unions offered no help, giving little support to relief programs or to the wider problems of economic change.

The Roosevelt administration's tax policies provide another instance of the disparity between image and performance. New Deal taxation was virtually a continuation of the Hoover administration's program. Business firms avoided many taxes during the depression by taking advantage of various loopholes.[29] The 1935 tax law "did not drain wealth from higher-income groups, and the the top one percent even increased their shares during the New Deal years."[30] When taxes were increased to pay for U.S. military spending in World War II, some of the additional load fell on the upper-income brackets, but the major burden was taken up by those of more modest means who had never before been subjected to income taxes. "Thus, the ironic fact is that the extension of the income tax to middle and low-income classes was the only original aspect of the New Deal tax policy."[31]

In sum, the New Deal introduced some new social welfare legislation, extended the opportunities for collective bargaining and created a number of worthwhile public works projects. Yet the Roosevelt era was hardly a triumph for the "forgotten man." Of the New Deal's "three Rs," relief, recovery and reform, it can be said that *relief* was markedly insufficient for meeting the suffering of the times and, in any case, was rather harshly curtailed after the 1936 electoral victory; that attempts at *recovery* focused on business and achieved little until the advent of war spending; and that *reform,* of the kind that might have ended the maldistributions and class abuses of the capitalist political economy, was rarely

28. *Ibid.*, p. 222.
29. Conkin, *The New Deal,* p. 67 and *passim.*
30. Bernstein, "The New Deal . . ." p. 275.
31. Gabriel Kolko, *Wealth and Power in America* (New York: Praeger, 1962), p. 31.

attempted. "The welfare legislation, large in hopes generated, often pitifully small in actual benefits, hardly represented a social revolution," concludes Conkin.[32]

Along with the absence of class reform there was no noticeable attempt at race reform. The New Deal's accomplishments in regard to school desegregation, open housing, fair employment practices, voting rights, antilynch laws and other such issues are nonexistent. Blacks were excluded from jobs in the Civilian Conservation Corps, received less than their proportional share of public assistance, and under the NRA were frequently paid wages below the legal minimum.[33] The Resettlement Administration (RA) headed by Rexford Tugwell was probably the only New Deal agency to support equal benefits for Blacks. According to Conkin, the RA was one of the most honest and class-conscious of New Deal agencies. Eventually antagonizing powerful economic interests, it was abolished by Congress.

By 1940, the last year of peace, the government had poured enough money into the economy to spur production to something close to predepression levels, yet the number of ill-clothed, ill-fed and ill-housed showed no substantial decrease. Unemployment was over 9 million, almost as high as in 1933, and the national income was still lower than in 1929. One historian of the period offers this conclusion:

The New Deal failed to solve the problem of depression, it failed to raise the impoverished, it failed to redistribute income, it failed to extend equality and generally countenanced racial discrimination and segregation. It failed generally to make business more responsible to the social welfare or to threaten business's pre-eminent political power. In this sense, the New Deal, despite the shifts in tone and spirit from the earlier decade, was profoundly conservative and continuous with the 1920s.[34]

Looking back at the 1930s, erstwhile New Dealer Robert M. Hutchins offers some criticisms that are strikingly at odds with the popular notion of the New Deal as a dynamic, reformist period:

It does not seem possible that there was ever another decade like the thirties, distinguished by the air of stupefication, not to say petrification, that hung over us. We were and remained prisoners of our illusions. . . .

32. Conkin, *The New Deal*, pp. 65–66.
33. Bernstein, "The New Deal . . ." pp. 278–279.
34. *Ibid.*, p. 264–265.

We entered the thirties with a free-wheeling and autonomous economy and with no suspicion that there could be anything wrong with such a system or that it could ever come to an end. . . .

Why wasn't there a revolution? . . . [Because] everyone believed in the received ideas. The 13 million men on the bread line cherished these convictions just as deeply as did those . . . who sold their own stock short. It is a great tribute to the power of the American educational system that nobody had any other ideas.

After eight years of "recovery," nobody—including the Federal Government—had anything to show for it but deficits. The emergency did not end. The Depression would not lift. . . . As the war got closer . . . we made the adjustment easily, for the idea of unbalancing the budget to kill people was more familiar to us than the idea of unbalancing it to save the lives of fellow citizens. When the war came, it was sound to do what had been unsound in the years before.[35]

Only by entering the war and remaining thereafter on a war economy was the United States able to maintain a shaky "prosperity."

35. Robert M. Hutchins, "In the Thirties, We Were Prisoners of Our Illusions, Are We Prisoners in the Sixties?" *New York Times Magazine*, September 8, 1968, pp. 44–59, *passim*.

Politics:
Who Gets What?

6

IN THE SUCCESSIVE ADMINISTRATIONS
since the New Deal, be they Democratic or
Republican, the government's use of public
resources on behalf of private gain has never
faltered. If anything, it has grown in scope. What
follows is a sampling of the ways government
has operated in recent years in the service of
powerful interests.[1]

Welfare for the Rich

In any given year the U.S. Treasury distributes
about $20 billion to $23 billion in direct subsidies or benefit-in-kind subsidies to manufacturing, shipping, aviation, communication, mining,
timber, agriculture and other enterprises to enhance their profits. Hence, $6 billion to $7 billion
is allocated yearly mostly to high-income farmers

---

1. The best source on this subject is *The Economics
of Federal Subsidy Programs* prepared by the Joint
Economic Committee (Washington, D.C.: U.S. Government Printing Office, 1972). A compendium of information demonstrating the influence of big corporations in
and out of government can be found in Morton Mintz
and Jerry S. Cohen, *America, Inc.* (New York: Dial
Press, 1971). For an excellent analysis of how government serves large producer interests see Grant McConnell, *Private Power and American Democracy* (New
York: Knopf, 1966) and the numerous studies cited
therein. A recent more popular treatment is Jack Newfield and Jeff Greenfield, *A Populist Manifesto, The
Making of a New Majority* (New York: Praeger, 1972);
also William Proxmire, *Uncle Sam: The Last of the
Bigtime Spenders* (New York: Simon and Schuster,
1972).

and large corporations to limit acreage production and buy up crop surpluses, thereby keeping prices and profits high while subsidizing an expansion of giant corporate farms at the expense of family farms. Among those who receive agricultural subsidies are oil companies, some state universities, a bowling alley in Dallas, a municipal airport in Nebraska, a radio station in Ohio, a mental hospital in Alabama and even the Queen of England (who got $68,000 for not producing anything on her plantation in Mississippi).[2]

While the government pays agribusiness to limit production in areas of high rainfall, it spends billions on water-reclamation programs so that commercial growers can open new production in areas of low rainfall. Over the years, some $6 billion has been spent on reclamation dams. Another $2 billion was expended on a single reclamation project in Fresno County, California, for the benefit of "paper farmers, absentee landowners and several big corporations," and at the expense of small farmers and small agrarian cooperatives.[3] More than $656 million has been paid out to peanut farmers to buy their ever-expanding surplus.

The federal government gives about $1 billion a year to the shipping industry and some $200 million a year to private aviation facilities used mostly by a few thousand executives and well-to-do flying enthusiasts. In order to "promote the development of air transportation" the government reimburses private air carriers for any losses they may incur: in 1971 the sum was $57.2 million. Another $83.6 million in direct gifts goes to the sugar industry to produce sugar beets and sugar cane. The costs of one quarter of all U.S. fertilizer exports are financed by the federal government (while the profits remain with the exporters). Similarly financed are exports of iron and steel, railroad equipment, rice, textiles,

---

2. *New York Times*, July 11, 1973; see also Senator John Williams' comments as reported in the *Philadelphia Inquirer*, July 11, 1967; also Edward Higbee, *Farms and Farmers in an Urban Age* (New York: Twentieth Century Fund, 1963), pp. 139 ff.; John A. Schnittker, "The Farmer in the Till," *Atlantic*, October 1969, pp. 43–45; William Robbins, "Farm Policy Helps Make the Rural Rich Richer," *New York Times*, April 5, 1970; Larry Casolino, "This Land Is Their Land," *Ramparts*, July 1972, pp. 31–36.

3. Lynn Ludlow and Will Hearst, "The $2 Billion Giveaway," *San Francisco Examiner*, January 11, 1976. Senator Proxmire reports: "Reclamation is having disastrous effects on metropolitan water tables. Such vast quantities of underground water have been sucked out of the ground to irrigate farmlands—which account for only 10 percent of the production in states like Arizona—that local community water supplies are endangered." See his *Uncle Sam: The Last of the Bigtime Spenders*, p. 25.

petroleum, chemicals, papers, automobiles and other products. In 1976 Congress voted to spend over $6 billion to subsidize railroads, thus assuring high dividends to stockholders and big bank creditors.[4]

The government provides millions of dollars to cushion the financial losses suffered by cattle ranchers from low beef prices, shoe manufacturers from cheap foreign imports, ski resorts from poor skiing seasons and banks from bad investments. When 8 million chickens in Mississippi had to be destroyed as a result of a mysterious "contamination" from a crop pesticide, the Senate Agriculture Committee rushed $8 million to "compensate" the producers (at one dollar per chicken while the average bird brought only 67 cents on the market).[5]

The most intriguing case of compensation involves corporations like DuPont, General Motors, Ford, Exxon and ITT which owned factories in enemy countries during World War II and produced everything from tanks to synthetic fuels for the Axis war effort. GM executives like Alfred P. Sloan, Jr., served on the board of directors of GM-owned firms in Nazi Germany throughout the war. ITT produced direction finders in American plants to protect Allied convoys at sea, while manufacturing in its German plants bombers that wreaked havoc with the same Allied convoys. After the war, rather than being prosecuted for trading with the enemy, ITT collected $27 million from the U.S. government for war damages inflicted on its German plants by Allied bombings. GM and Ford subsidiaries built the bulk of Nazi Germany's heavy trucks which served as "'the backbone of the German Army transportation system." GM collected more than $33 million in compensation for damages to its war plants in enemy territories. Ford and other multinational corporations collected lesser sums.[6]

4. Blessed with such bounty from the public treasure, the railroads in question stripped themselves of their own cash assets of over $9 million and distributed the money to their stockholders in what was one of the highest dividend payments in New York Stock Exchange history. See *Workers World*, March 12, 1976.

5. The head of the Senate Agriculture Committee was Senator Eastland, himself a big Mississippi farmer. No one ever investigated the poisoning of the chickens nor the similarly suspicious poisoning of great numbers of cattle, swine and chickens in Michigan which led to an increase in milk and meat prices. See *Workers World*, April 5, 1974, and May 28, 1976.

6. The information and quotation come from documents declassified in 1974. See Bradford Snell, "GM and the Nazis," *Ramparts*, June 1974, pp. 14–16; "Memo from COPE" (AFL–CIO report), August 30, 1973; Thomas De Baggio, "The Unholy Alliance," *Penthouse*, May 1976, pp. 74–91. Some of the war plants were spared from American bombing because they were owned by big corporations. Thus while Cologne was leveled by saturation bombing,

Along with its subsidies, grants, gifts and credits, the federal government has other ways of serving the business class. It maintains prices at noncompetitive, monopolistic levels in "regulated" areas of the economy at an estimated annual cost of $80 billion to American consumers. Thus, for many years the oil import quota system limited the supply of fuel to the consumer market and raised its price by over 50 percent, resulting in an estimated $5- to $7-billion annual transfer of income from consumers to petroleum companies.[7] The regulation of trucking and railroad rates by the ICC "to prevent destructive competition" and to exclude new competitors results in costs of many hundreds of millions in excess of what competitive prices would allow; and the fixed prices and restrictions imposed on new airline competitors by the Civil Aeronautics Board allows for an estimated $2 billion to $4 billion in excess airline revenues.[8]

The federal government engages in preferential enforcement—or nonenforcement—of regulatory standards, as when the FCC sets an "allowed rate of return" for the telephone company and then ignores it, enabling American Telephone and Telegraph to earn a $169-million yearly excess over already generous rates.[9] Private electric utilities offer another illustration of the advantages of government "regulation." Utilities are nonrisk enterprises whose expenses are virtually guaranteed by the government. They never go bankrupt; they pay high dividends to their shareholders and give their managers handsome salaries and stock options. Their rates are set so as to allow them a net income as high as 15 to 25 percent, which explains why private utility rates are sometimes more than twice those of municipal-owned ones. State regulatory commissions usually grant automatic raises to the private utilities, thereby giving them little incentive to operate efficiently. In 1974 utility rate increases cost the public $6.5 billion, more than in the previous twenty-five years.[10]

Municipal-owned companies not only produce lower-cost

its Ford plant, providing military trucks for the Nazi Army, was untouched—and used by German workers as an air-raid shelter. Ford collected $1 million for some broken windows and the plant was back in operation a short time after the U.S. Army entered Cologne. See eye-witness correspondence by E. F. Patterson, *Ramparts*, August 1974, p. 8.

7. According to the Federal Trade Commission; see Mark Green, "The New Wave of Anti-Trustism," *New York Times*, March 2, 1975.

8. Peter Passell and Leonard Ross, "Mr. Nixon's Economic Melodrama," *New York Review of Books*, September 23, 1971, p. 8.

9. *Wall Street Journal*, August 30, 1971.

10. CBS television news report, March 23, 1975.

electricity but also raise revenue for a city's budget. Thus, in Boston, 500 kilowatt hours purchased from the private utility (Boston Edison) cost $13.41; in Seattle the same amount bought from the municipal-owned company costs $5. In Boston, property taxes on a home assessed at $10,000 come to $1,050 a year; in Seattle, to only $513, because Seattle's city-owned electric plant, despite lower rates, pumps millions of dollars into the city treasury, whereas the revenue from Boston Edison goes mostly to rich stockholders and corporations.[11] While the cost of producing electricity has been steadily *decreasing*, the consumer's electric bill has been *increasing*. After a thorough investigation, Senator Lee Metcalf (D.–Mont.) concluded that consumers should be paying $1 billion *less* each year due to declining production costs.

The federal government gives private corporations the use, profit and sometimes ownership of new technologies developed at public expense. Nuclear energy, electronics, aeronautics, space communication, mineral exploration, computer systems—much of the basic research and developmental work in these and other fields are done for the benefit of private firms at a cost of more than $15 billion a year to the taxpayer. For instance, through its extensive political influence in the White House and Congress, AT&T managed to have the entire satellite communications system ("Comsat") put under its control in 1962—after U.S. taxpayers had put up the initial $20 billion to develop it. Then AT&T decided not to extend the benefits of Comsat to its U.S. customers, the reason being that billions of dollars worth of the company's equipment would have become obsolete overnight if satellites were put into use within the United States. The big savings for long-distance customers would have meant huge losses for AT&T owners. In order to preserve its obsolete but highly profitable investment, AT&T withheld satellite service from the very U.S. public that had financed it.[12]

As in olden days, government continues to give away, lease or sell at bargain rates the national forests, grasslands, wildlife preserves and other public lands containing priceless timber, minerals, oil and water and recreational resources—with little consideration for environmental values or for desires other than those

11. For an expose of utilities see Lee Metcalf and Vic Reinemer, *Overcharge* (New York: McKay, 1967).
12. Steve Babson and Nancy Brigham, "Why Do We Spend So Much Money?" *Liberation*, September/October 1973, p. 19.

of the favored corporations.[13] From 1965 to 1967, for instance, several major petroleum companies leased acreage in Alaska for oil exploration, paying a sum of $12 million for leases worth upwards of $2 *billion*. In a subsequent oil lease auction, the companies paid the government $900 million for lands that are expected to be worth some $50 billion within a decade.[14]

Reviewing the peculiarly private dedications of public policy Senator Russell Long (D.–La.) concluded:

The government pays out many billions of dollars in unnecessarily high interest rates; it permits private-monopoly patterns on over twelve billion dollars of government research money annually; it permits billions of dollars of government money to remain on deposit in banks without collecting interest; it permits overcharging by many concerns selling services to government; it tolerates all sorts of tax favoritism; it fails to move to protect public health from a number of obvious hazards; it permits monopolies to victimize the public in a number of inexcusable ways. . . .[15]

Government performs other services designed to maximize private gain at public cost: it awards highly favorable contracts and provides emergency funding to insure the survival and continued profits of armaments companies; it furnishes big business with risk-free capital, long-term credits and tariff protections and provides lowered tax assessments and cost write-offs amounting to many billions of dollars yearly; it makes available to defense industries some $13.3 billion worth of government-owned land, buildings, machinery and materials, thereby in part "saving them the job of financing their own investments";[16] and it applies the antitrust laws in a manner so lackadaisical as to make them inconsequential.

13. See James Ridgeway, *The Politics of Ecology* (New York: E. P. Dutton, 1970); also The Ralph Nader Study Group Report, *The Water Lords* (New York: Grossman, 1971), James M. Fallows, project director; The Ralph Nader Study Group Report, *The Vanishing Air* (New York: Grossman, 1970), John C. Esposito and Larry J. Silverman, project directors.

14. Barry Weisberg, "Ecology of Oil: Raping Alaska," in Editors of *Ramparts* (eds.), *Eco-Catastrophe* (San Francisco: Canfield Press, 1970), p. 107 and p. 109.

15. Quoted in Richard Harris, "Annals of Politics, A Fundamental Hoax," *New Yorker*, August 7, 1971, p. 53. Senator Long should know about such matters, being himself a beneficiary of the oil depletion allowance, a holder of oil interests in at least four states, and a vigorous spokesman for the industry. See "Oil Tax Write-Off Aids Senator Long," *New York Times*, October 5, 1969.

16. Sidney Lens, *The Military-Industrial Complex* (Philadelphia: United Church Press, 1970), p. 8.

One of the ways government keeps business profits high is by pouring more money into the economy than it takes out, a process known as "deficit spending." The government subsidizes business costs, compensates for business losses, purchases billions of dollars worth of corporate goods and services, yet cuts business taxes. Approximately $50 to $60 billion in tax incentives, tax credits and loopholes go to business each year as a direct federal payment. During the Kennedy-Johnson era, corporate profits grew at a rate twice as great as the economy and *by almost four times as much as a worker's weekly wages*. This same period showed no sizable decline in unemployment. Under the Nixon and Ford administrations, real wages declined for most workers but profits continued to grow. After-tax profits in 1974 were $85.4 billion, which, despite declines in production, represented a 17 percent increase over the previous year.

With deficit spending, corporate profits grow but so does the national debt. The image of conservatives holding the line against the wild spenders in Washington is a false one, for conservative leaders have been among the wildest spenders. In its first four years, the Nixon administration added $73.8 billion to a national debt that came to over $450 billion by 1973. President Ford's budget for the fiscal year of 1976 showed a $51.8-billion deficit. As economists Huberman and Sweezy remarked some years earlier: "It is hardly surprising that businessmen are so enthusiastic about *this* kind of deficit spending. Boiled down to essentials it amounts simply to using the borrowing power of the federal government to subsidize corporate profits."[17]

As government spends more than it collects, it must borrow money from those who have it by floating risk-free, high-interest bonds. Ordinary citizens can buy nonmarketable government bonds of modest denomination through various payroll savings plans, but the bulk of federal bonds is held by banks and very rich individuals. Most federal bond issues come in nothing smaller than $5,000 denominations. As the government continues to borrow money, the national debt increases. As the national debt increases, so does the interest on it that has to be paid to the very rich. This interest payment represents another huge subsidy to the wealthy and is one of the largest single items in the federal budget each year;

17. Leo Huberman and Paul Sweezy, "The Kennedy-Johnson Boom," *Monthly Review*, February 1965, reprinted in Marvin Gettleman and David Mermelstein (eds.), *The Great Society Reader* (New York: Random House, 1967), p. 103.

in 1975, it was $31 billion, *a sum more than three times the federal money spent on all welfare payments to the poor.* The bulk of this interest is drawn from the salaried and wage-earning public; it constitutes a reverse redistribution of income, a manifestation of what one writer called the "trickle up theory" of income.[18]

In recent years the Nixon and Ford administrations attempted to curb inflation by cutting back on such things as the school milk fund, food stamps, day care assistance, rural environmental programs, and aid to the mentally retarded. But no economy measures have been taken against the multibillion-dollar handouts to big industry.

It is a simple matter to preserve the profit maximization system. American capitalism must whittle away at labor (and middle class) living standards. The Ford-Nixon . . . prescription for doing it is a *managed recession.* By tightening credit, raising interest rates, etc. the economy will be "cooled," millions will lose their jobs, demands for goods will weaken, and living standards will be reduced in an *orderly fashion—*it is hoped.[19]

The overall effect of these fiscal policies has been to diminish the buying power of the wage earner, a buying power that was considered one of the causes of inflation, without stopping the inflation itself or the growing unemployment. However, the government's intent is not to achieve full employment but to insure business profits, it being presumed that high profits will eventually bring high employment, a presumption held more firmly by those who make the profits than those looking for jobs.

In any case, as noted earlier, from business' standpoint an occasional recession is not without its compensations, since it acts as a check on wages, though not on prices, and guarantees a pool of unemployed, cheap labor. Recessions allow the giant corporations to tighten their hold on the market by taking over weakened smaller firms, thereby emerging all the stronger for the next boom.[20] Such

18. Robert Fitch, "Selling the Debt," *Ramparts,* April 1972, p. 20. The debt is not only increasing in size but consists of bonds with a shorter term maturation. In 1951 the average maturity of the debt was almost seven years. By 1972 it was three years four months and shrinking. As with any big debtor, the government is like an addict who needs stronger doses to stay in the same place. The banks are the pushers.

19. Sidney Lens, " 'Big Labor', Big Trouble," *New Politics,* 11, December 1974, p. 31.

20. R. D. Corwin and Lois Gray, "Of Republicans and Recessions," *Social Policy,* 2, November–December 1971, p. 43.

phrases as "cooling off the economy" and "weeding out the over-growth" are metaphors used effortlessly by those who do not suffer the chilling effects of the cooling and who in fact do the weeding. When it is said that the goal of government and business is a sound, stable economy, it must be asked, "Sound and stable by whose definition? For whose interests and at whose expense?

The Pentagon: Billions for Big Brother

As measured by the federal budget, the greatest devotion of the government is to the military establishment. The Department of Defense (commonly known as the Pentagon) is the largest, richest, most powerful unit of government. Its budget, $113 billion in fiscal 1976, continues to grow in leaps and bounds. Since 1946 the military has consumed about *one thousand three hundred billion* of the taxpayers' dollars and plans to spend another $636 billion during the five-year period of 1976–1980.[21] The Department of Defense owns or controls about thirty-nine million acres of land. Its total worth in land, weaponry, supplies and plant equipment in 1970 was estimated to be from $300 to $400 billion.[22]

The Pentagon repeatedly conjures up the specter of Soviet military supremacy in order to maintain its hold over the public purse. In 1956 the American public was alerted to a dangerous "bomber gap"; in 1960 it was a "missile gap," and in 1967 an "antiballistic missile gap." In each instance it was subsequently discovered that no such gap existed and that U.S. capabilities were superior to the Soviet Union's. But these revelations came only after multibillion-dollar allocations for bomber, missile and ABM programs had been voted by Congress. Then in 1975 the Department of Defense announced that it was falling behind the Russians in the development of "multiple independently targeted nuclear war-

21. David Johnson, "The Pentagon's $150 Billion Shopping List," *Ramparts*, July 1975, p. 22. The Pentagon's budgetary increases far exceed the rate of inflation, and the increases continue no matter whether there is war or peace. At the height of World War II, with 12 million in the armed services, there were 139 three- and four-star generals and admirals. Today with only 2.5 million under arms, there are 190. This lopsided growth of brass over enlisted personnel holds for all grades of officers. The Pentagon's civilian bureaucracy also grows. Between 1969 and 1972 the proportion of civilian to military personnel in the Department of Defense increased by 20 percent. See Proxmire, *Uncle Sam: Last of the Bigtime Spenders*, pp. 66–67.

22. Lens, *The Military-Industrial Complex.* Congress operates on a yearly budget amounting to less than three days' expenditure by the Pentagon.

heads" (MIRVs). In fact, as one military analyst notes, "The U.S. has had MIRVs for years. It has hundreds of them ready to use while the Soviets are just getting them."[23]

The leading beneficiaries of defense contracts, the large corporations, have helped propagate the military's cause with skillful lobbying and mass advertising that stresses the importance of keeping America "strong." And as private industry became the supporter of defense preparedness, military men spoke more openly about the blessings of free enterprise and the "American Way of Life." With 90 percent of the contracts awarded with no competitive bidding on the open market, relations between corporate and military personnel became an all-important determinant of who gets what. Military officers increasingly looked forward to early retirement and to the financial and social rewards that came with entrance into high-paying corporate jobs—usually as recompense for services rendered while in the Pentagon. One congressional committee discovered that in 1960 more than 1,400 retired officers, from the rank of major upward, were employed by the top hundred weapon concerns.[24]

As a result of this military-industrial partnership, enormous portions of American purchasing power have been siphoned off by the government through taxation and channeled into the major corporations, with the twenty-five largest contractors receiving over half the prime contracts for weapons production, thereby further centralizing corporate wealth in America.

The defense budget pays for "cost overruns" many times greater than the original bids. Many firms do not explain their cost overruns, even when requested by government to do so. The C5A transport plane eventually cost $2 *billion* more than originally contracted.[25] A study by the Brookings Institution concluded that "during the

23. James McCartney writing in the *Philadelphia Inquirer*, quoted in Richard E. Ward, "War Budget $100 Billion: What Detente?" *Guardian*, March 5, 1975, p. 3.
24. In recent years a total of eighty high-ranking Pentagon officials, including generals and admirals, have been implicated in various bribe scandals involving favored treatment for military contractors. Not one of the officers has been discharged from the service, and none of the companies, such as Rockwell, Raytheon or Northrop, has been prosecuted or penalized. See *Workers World*, April 23, 1976; also Jack Anderson's column, *Ithaca* (N.Y.) *Journal*, December 20, 1975.
25. For all its expense, the C5A has a poor performance record. Each C5A costs almost $60 million. Boeing's commercial 747, which has esentially the same size and speed requirements, costs only $23 million each. See Proxmire, *Uncle Sam . . .* , p. 83.

1950's virtually all large military contracts . . . ultimately involved costs in excess of original contractual estimates of from 300 to 700 percent."[26] A report on thirteen major aircraft and missile programs since 1955 shows that while the total cost of the programs was $40 billion, less than 40 percent of them offered "acceptable electronic performance." During these years at least sixty-eight weapons systems were abandoned as unworkable. But the rewards for inefficiency have been high: the aerospace industry earned "a 12% greater return on equity than the average of all U.S. industrial firms," despite the fact that many of its programs either failed to measure up to expectations or broke down completely.[27]

Waste and duplication are a standard part of the Pentagon's operations. Both the Navy and the Air Force spent huge amounts to build nearly identical fighter planes. In 1969 the Army allocated the grand sum of $1.5 billion to develop a heavy-lift helicopter—presumably superior to the heavy-lift helicopter it already possessed. At the same time, the Navy was building an almost identical helicopter. At a cost of many hundreds of millions, both the Air Force and Navy simultaneously developed sophisticated airborne warning systems.[28] In 1969 the Air Force admitted it had misplaced $21 million worth of oil and gasoline due to "an accounting error." In 1974 the Pentagon received $135 million from Congress for completion of a missile defense site which it planned to close down in six months.[29] The General Accounting Office published a detailed report showing that the armed forces wasted billions of dollars through poor planning and a chronic inability to decide what weapons they wanted and when they wanted them.[30] Meanwhile the Pentagon handed out $86 million in grants to defense companies to compensate for losses and mismanagement and to keep them from bankruptcy. Lockheed Corporation alone received $1 billion to keep it solvent.[31]

26. Cited in Lens, *The Military-Industrial Complex*, Chapter One.
27. See Bernard Nossiter's report in the *Washington Post*, January 26, 1969; also Lens, *The Military-Industrial Complex*.
28. *New York Times*, July 4, 1969.
29. *Rutland* (Vt.) *Daily Herald*, August 8, 1974. Original release from *New York Times* news service.
30. *New York Times*, February 8, 1971. In 1976 it was disclosed that the defense budget was deliberately padded by an estimated $3 billion to $5.7 billion to insure against congressional cuts. *New York Times*, February 4, 1976.
31. The grant is known in the Pentagon as an "amendment without consideration," meaning money given without assurance of getting anything in return. See A. Ernest Fitzgerald, *The High Priests of Waste* (New York: Norton, 1972); also *New York Times*, April 30, 1973. For a good overall critique of Pentagon spending see Richard F. Kaufman, *The War Profiteers* (New York: Bobbs-Merrill, 1971).

The huge $113-billion defense budget does not encompass all military-related spending. The government distributed more than $13 billion in veterans benefits and services in 1976. The $31-billion interest paid in 1976 on the national debt was mostly for deficits incurred because of the huge wartime and peacetime military budgets. In addition, $4 billion yearly for space satellites and moon landings of widely proclaimed but unspecified scientific benefit, and expensive underground atomic tests allegedly essential to our defense but "harmless" to our environment, also must be considered in any calculation of what military spending costs the American people, as must the billions in military aid sent to foreign dictators.

It is not enough to condemn the waste and profligacy of the Pentagon, however; we must also try to understand its function in the existing capitalist society. For the millions of taxpayers who are deprived of essential domestic services because the military budget devours such a large chunk of the public treasure, defense spending is wasteful. But for the industrial empire that has grown rich and immense by servicing the U.S. military, defense spending is wonderful. First, the taxpayers' money underwrites all the risks and most of the costs of weapons development and sales. Unlike automobile manufacturers who must worry about selling the cars they produce, the weapons manufacturer has a precontracted market complete with cost-overrun guarantees. Second, the defense industry is the most lucrative business there is. With a customer as spendthrift as the Pentagon, profits are far higher than those in the private consumer market. Third, the armaments market does not compete with the consumer market, rather it creates a whole new area of demand, investment and profit. Multibillion-dollar weapon systems, technologically obsolete almost by the time they come off the production line, are replaced by new generations of weapon systems. The defense industry has its own built-in obsolescence which creates its own endless demand. And as weapon systems become increasingly sophisticated, they become ever more expensive and profitable. Thus, despite the end of a costly Indochina war and despite arms control agreements and detente with the Soviet Union, the military budget continues to expand. Its growth is a perfectly functional, rational, desirable arrangement for corporate capitalism.

Taking into account the multiplier effect of a dollar spent and the network of subsidiary services that feed on the defense dollar, possibly a fifth of all economic activity in the United States is dependent on military expenditures.[32] Without the enormous increase in defense appropriations since the 1930s, the United States would slide back into a deep depression. After World War II, business and government leaders, in effect, decided that if private business could not create enough new investment opportunities and jobs, then the Pentagon would. By 1970, 14 million Americans relied on military spending for their jobs.[33] In 1974 then–Defense Secretary Schlesinger defended a last minute $1-billion increase in the military budget on the grounds that it would provide a stimulus to a lagging domestic economy. He thereby acknowledged that Pentagon spending was dictated, as the *Times* noted, "in part by domestic fiscal considerations and not strictly by military requirements."[34]

Many people have defended military spending because it provides jobs. So do the heroin, prostitution, pornography and advertising industries. The millions of highway accidents each year provide employment for wreckers, repairmen and hospital workers. The cigarette industry provides jobs but that is no reason to encourage cigarette consumption. There are many useful and needed things that our labor and resources might be expended on, but these do not include the capacity to blow up the world a hundred times over or produce mountains of obsolete, death-dealing weapons. The growing enrichment of the military sector leads to the increasing impoverishment of the civilian sector. The people of New York City, for instance, pay more money in taxes to the Pentagon than to New York City. Thus we have the spectacle of the military feasting on billions while day care centers, schools, hospitals and nursing homes are closed down for want of funds.

Measured by the number of jobs created, military spending is not the most efficient job provider. The Public Interest Research Group in Michigan, in a depth study, found that (1) the nation as a whole suffered a loss of 840,000 jobs by the diversion of such huge sums from the civilian to the military sector; (2) military spending creates fewer jobs per billion dollars spent than any other government spending except the space program; (3) if armed forces personnel and spending were cut and the number of firemen,

32. Bert Cochran, *The War System* (New York: Macmillan, 1965), pp. 142–144.
33. Three million in the armed forces, 1 million in civilian Pentagon jobs, 3 million working in defense industries, and 7 million employed by the "ripple effect" of military spending on the rest of the economy. See *Monthly Review*, April 1971.
34. *New York Times*, February 27, 1974.

teachers and other government employees increased, the economy would gain 21,000 jobs per billion dollars transferred to state and local governments.[35]

In addition, military spending is one of the major causes of inflation. While creating many jobs and many billions in income, and consuming vast amounts of labor and material resources, it does not create the things people need in the way of housing, food, fuel and other human and social services. Shortages, soaring prices and a growing national debt are the result.[36]

In his farewell address, President Eisenhower warned that there had grown in our midst a vast "military-industrial complex" whose influence "is felt in every city, every state house, every office of the Federal Government." Indeed, the corporate-military elites influence the development of whole communities. Of the many agencies engaged in propagandizing the public, none is more active than the Pentagon.[37] The armed services currently compose the strongest lobby in Washington, exerting more influence over Congress than that body exerts over the Defense Department.

That it happens to be a federal offense to use the taxpayers' money to propagandize the taxpayers seems not to have deterred the military. The Pentagon spends more than $30 million a year on propaganda, including exhibitions, films, books, armed services magazines and brochures, recruitment tours to colleges and high schools and a flood of press releases which, publicized as "news reports" and "news events" in thousands of newspapers and magazines and on radio and television shows, propagate the military's view of the world without identifying the military as their source.[38]

The influence of our military state is nowhere more heavily felt than in the academic community. Many institutions of higher

35. The report is summarized in the *Progressive*, April 1976, p. 11. See also Adam Yarmolinsky, *The Military Establishment* (New York: Harper and Row, 1973) for a discussion of the military's impact on the domestic economy; also Seymour Melman, *Pentagon Capitalism: The Management of the New Imperialism* (New York: McGraw-Hill, 1970).

36. See the lively and well-illustrated book *Q. What's Happening to Our Jobs?* (Somerville, Mass.: Popular Economics Press, 1976).

37. See J. William Fulbright, *The Pentagon Propaganda Machine* (New York: Vintage, 1971); Lens gives a description of the public relations efforts of the Pentagon in his *The Military-Industrial Complex*. An interesting account of the propaganda techniques used by NASA to sell the $30-billion space shuttle and space station programs can be found in Les Aspin, "The Space Shuttle: Who Needs It?" *Washington Monthly*, September 1972, pp. 18–22.

38. Fred C. Cook, "The Juggernaut," *Nation*, October 28, 1961, p. 286; also Lens, *The Military-Industrial Complex*, Chapter Five.

education donate space, building funds and maintenance service to programs financed by the Pentagon and draw anywhere from 10 to 80 percent of their budgets from government sources. "These schools must maintain their governmental research projects or face bankruptcy," Edward Greer concludes.[39] By 1971, at least ninety universities and colleges were researching problems of counter-insurgency, command-control systems, defoliation techniques, internal security and antiriot strategies, population relocation methods and seismic and magnetic detection systems. At least fifty-six universities and colleges have been engaged in research on chemical and biological warfare.[40] Dr. A. J. Hill, a weapons research man at MIT, noted: "Our job is not to advance knowledge but to advance the military."[41]

Many social scientists have joined programs financed by the military, including psychological, sociological, economic and political studies devoted to counterrevolutionary techniques and the manipulation of opinion at home and abroad. In hundreds of conferences and in thousands of brochures, articles and books written by members of the intellectual community who are in the pay of the government, military propaganda is lent an aura of academic objectivity, complete with statistical and sociological embellishments. Casting a shadow on their own integrity as scholars and teachers, such intellectuals transmit to an unsuspecting public the military view of reality and the Pentagon's sense of its own indispensability.

The proliferation of Pentagon-financed "independent" corporations such as RAND and the Hudson Institute—the "think-tanks" that solve technical military problems for a fee—testifies to the growing role played by the nonmilitary man. The armed services, progressively less able to provide the brainpower for all their needs, simply buy up such human resources from the universities, corporations and planning institutions. The staggering fact is that over two-thirds of all the technical research in America is being consumed by the military.

If we define "military state" as any polity that devotes a major portion of its public resources to purposes of war, then the United

39. Greer, "The Public Interest University"; also Clark Kerr, *The Uses of the University* (New York: Harper and Row, 1966), p. 55.

40. See the wealth of data—most of it from published government and university sources—gathered by Greer, C. Brightman, C. McAffee, M. Klare, D. Ransom, B. Leman, R. Rapoport, and M. Locker in *Viet Report*, January 1968.

41. Quoted in Cochran, *The War System*, p. 307.

States is a military state, the strongest in history. Our leaders proudly proclaim that fact. Contrary to the conventional view, a civilian constitutional government is as capable of becoming a militarist power as is a dictatorship. The political system of a nation is of less importance in determining its military capacity than is the level of its industry and wealth, the intensity of its anxiety about domestic and foreign enemies and the scope of its overseas investments and ambitions.

The Sword and the Dollar: Travels Abroad

Large corporate profits, including those from defense expenditures, help feed overseas investments, and as these investments grow, so does the need for military intervention and big military budgets. Let us explore this point. The postwar growth of American corporations has been nothing less than stupendous, but problems come with such success; enormous surplus profits remain after operational expenses are paid and even after the more than $25 billion in yearly dividends are distributed—chiefly to the wealthiest 1 or 2 percent of America's families. The remaining undistributed profits must be invested somewhere. As noted earlier, the growth in profits intensifies the search for new profit yielding opportunities which, in turn, create more profit surplus and a still more strenuous pursuit of investment (i.e., profit) opportunities. In a word, profit abundance and profit hunger are but two sides of the same coin. Overseas investments—especially in underdeveloped countries—become increasingly attractive because of the cheap native labor, the high profit return, the absence of corporate taxes, the marketing of products at monopoly prices and the opportunity to invest a surplus capital that would only depress the profit rate at home or bring a lower return in other industrialized nations.[42] As of 1975 U.S. corporate investments in foreign countries amounted to $300 billion.

A central function of capitalist governments is, as Adam Smith said, to facilitate commerce "carried on with barbarous and uncivilized nations."[43] To this day, the U.S. government performs that function—first, by subsidizing and financing corporate overseas investments with sums amounting to billions yearly and, second, by

42. See Harry Magdoff, *The Age of Imperialism* (New York: Monthly Review Press, 1969).

43. Adam Smith, *An Inquiry into the Nature and Cause of the Wealth of Nations* (Chicago: Encyclopaedia Britannica, Inc., 1952), p. 309.

providing a global military force which protects private investments and capitalist social orders from revolutionary change. Let us consider each of these in turn.

The U.S. government provides a multibillion-dollar foreign aid program that ostensibly is designed to help poorer nations help themselves but which actually helps "the United States maintain a position of influence and control around the world," as President John Kennedy once proudly noted.[44] American aid is allocated to Third World countries usually on the condition that it be used to buy American goods at American prices, to be transported in American ships. The highways, roads, ports, dams and utilities constructed in foreign lands with U.S. government funds frequently are planned around the needs of American-owned factories, mines, oil fields, refineries and plantations. Abroad, as at home, the U.S. taxpayer pays for the "social overhead capital" needed to service the multinational corporations.

The U.S. government finances overseas loans and investments and subsidizes business exports. The government compensates corporate investors for losses due to war, revolution, insurrection or confiscation by a foreign government, and the government refuses aid to any country which nationalizes without compensation assets owned by U.S. firms.

In Latin America, Alliance for Progress funds were given to native governments for the purpose of having them expropriate *unprofitable* U.S. firms at *above market prices*. "In turn," James Petras notes, "U.S. corporations used the funds procured to invest in more profitable activities . . ."[45] The poor are almost always left out of such arrangements. Of the 25,000 tons of meat shipped to Brazil under the Alliance for Progress, for instance, 85 percent ended up in the hands of wealthy ranch owners. The much publicized "Green Revolution" has been of great benefit to the large landowners of India, Asia and Latin America and a disaster to small farmers.

The net effect of overseas aid and capital investments is to retard rather than advance the economic development of Third World countries. Many liberals have wondered why the gap between rich and poor nations grows wider despite the increase in Third

44. Quoted in Teresa Hayter, *Aid as Imperialism* (Baltimore: Penguin Books, 1971).
45. James Petras, "U.S. Business and Foreign Policy," *New Politics*, 6, Fall 1967, reprinted in Michael Parenti (ed.) *Trends and Tragedies in American Foreign Policy* (Boston: Little, Brown, 1971), p. 98.

World investments. The answer is that the gap widens *because* of such investments. Unless we assume that corporations are in the business of social philanthrophy, it is clear that investments have the ultimate purpose of *extracting* wealth from poorer nations rather than donating wealth. Between 1950 and 1972, U.S. corporations showed *a $50-billion overseas investment outflow and a $99-billion profit influx.*[46] Foreign aid and investments help U.S. capital exploit the recipient country's labor, monopolize its resources, control its politics and influence its tastes, markets and technical needs so that dependency on American products continues well after the aid program has ceased.[47] The effect of foreign aid and private U.S. investment is to dislocate the economy of the poorer country, retarding its productive capacity by limiting it to a few specialized extractive industries like oil, timber, tin, copper and rubber or cash crops like sugar, coffee, cocoa, cotton or tobacco. The labor and resources of the land are mobilized to fit the interests of U.S. corporations rather than the needs of the populace. The result is widespread unemployment for the indigenous population, low wages, high illiteracy and chronic poverty. In a country like Guatemala, while U.S. corporations own three-fourths of the arable land and extract enormous profits, the rural population has a smaller per capita food supply today than during the Mayan civilization.[48]

U.S. aid and investment programs leave Third World countries deeply indebted to U.S. banks. Like addicts, debtor nations become hooked on U.S. credit to remain solvent, borrowing increasingly larger sums at high interest rates to pay off an ever-growing debt, the temporary relief of each new loan only creating a heavier debt obligation for the future. Some Third World nations devote the major part of their export earnings to paying off their debts to American banks and the U.S. government.

The growth of American capitalism from a weak domestic position to a dominant international one has been accompanied by a similar growth in American military interventionism. Sometimes the sword has rushed in to protect the dollar, and sometimes the dollar has rushed in to enjoy the advantages won by the sword. To

46. Paul Sweezy, "Growing Wealth, Declining Power," *Monthly Review*, March 1974, pp. 6–7.

47. Magdoff, *Age of Imperialism*, pp. 129 ff.

48. For a closer look at the effects and purposes of overseas corporate investments and government aid, see Felix Greene, *The Enemy: What Every American Should Know About Imperialism* (New York: Vintage, 1970); Paul Baran and Paul Sweezy, *Monopoly Capital* (New York: Monthly Review Press, 1968), pp. 186–207; Petras, "U.S. Business and Foreign Policy."

safeguard the ever-expanding U.S. corporate empire, the United States government has had to embark on a global counterrevolutionary strategy, surpressing insurgent peasant and worker movements throughout Asia, Africa and Latin America. But the interests of the corporate elites never stand naked, rather they are wrapped in the flag and coated with patriotic appearances. Knowing that the American people would never agree to sending their sons to fight wars in far-off lands in order to protect the profits of Gulf Oil, ITT and General Motors,[49] the corporate elites and their political spokesmen play upon popular fears, telling us that our "national security" necessitates our intervention in Vietnam or Cambodia or Angola or wherever a capitalist, colonial order is threatened by a popular uprising seeking to establish a socialist economic system.

Frequently our policymakers claim they are defending democracy against the impending tyranny of communist insurgents in Asia, Africa and Latin America. But closer examination shows they are defending the capitalist world from social change—even if the change be peaceful, orderly and democratic. Guatemala in 1954 and Chile in 1973 are two cases in point. In both countries popularly elected governments began instituting progressive changes for the benefit of the more destitute classes and began to nationalize or threatened to nationalize multimillion-dollar U.S. corporate holdings. And in both countries the United States was instrumental in overthrowing these governments and instituting right-wing fascist regimes that accommodated U.S. investors and ruthlessly repressed the peasants and workers. Similarly, in countries like Iran, Greece, the Philippines, Indonesia, East Timor and in at least ten Latin American nations over the past fifteen years, popular governments have been overthrown by military oligarchs, largely trained and financed by the Pentagon and the CIA, who prove themselves friendly to the investment interests of American capitalism. Far from defending freedom, the United States government has been propagating fascist regimes throughout the world, using assassination squads, torture and terror when necessary, finding such regimes to be "stable" allies of the corporate world order.

This policy of containing social change in order to make the

49. A Harris poll in 1975 found that the American people opposed sending U.S. troops to aid countries under attack. If North Korea invaded South Korea, 65 percent of the respondents opposed and 14 percent favored sending troops. If China invaded Taiwan, 59 percent opposed and 17 percent supported sending troops. The only country Americans supported (by a 77 to 12 percent margin) sending troops in case of invasion was Canada. See *Burlington* (Vt.) *Free Press*, March 25, 1975.

world safe for capitalism has had its serious setbacks. In recent years successful national liberation movements in Vietnam, Cambodia, Laos, Guinea-Bissau, Mozambique and Angola vanquished U.S. or U.S.–backed forces and have instituted popular socialist governments in their respective nations. But if military-corporate America lost the war in Indochina, it was not from want of trying. The United States government, under the leadership of Democratic and Republican administrations, spent $150 billion and more than ten years prosecuting the Indochina war, dropping almost 8 million tons of bombs, 18 million gallons of chemical defoliants and nearly 400,000 tons of napalm. The Vietnamese, Laotian and Cambodian countrysides were desolated by saturation bombings; 3 million Vietnamese and 1 million Cambodians and Laotians were killed, maimed or wounded and almost 10 million Indochinese were

left homeless; 55,000 Americans lost their lives and hundreds of thousands more were wounded. The only ones to profit from the war were corporate defense contractors like DuPont and ITT.

If we define "imperialism" as that relationship in which one country dominates, through use of economic and military power, the land, labor, resources, finances and politics of another country, then the United States is the greatest imperialist power in history. The American empire is of a magnitude never before equaled. More than 1.5 million American military personnel are stationed in 119 countries. The United States maintains 429 major military bases and 2,972 lesser bases in thirty countries, covering some 4,000 square miles and costing almost $5 billion a year. The military has some 8,500 strategic nuclear weapons and 22,000 tactical ones deployed throughout the world. The U.S. Navy deploys a fleet larger in total tonnage than all the other navies of the world combined, consisting of missile cruisers, nuclear submarines, aircraft carriers, destroyers and spy ships which sail every ocean and make port on every continent. Two million native troops and large contingents of native police, under the command of various military juntas, have been trained, equipped and financed by the United States and assisted by U.S. counterinsurgency forces, their purpose being not to defend these countries from outside invasion but to protect capital investments and the ruling oligarchs from the dangers of domestic insurgency.

Since World War II more than $60 billion in military aid has been given away by the United States to some eighty nations. In 1975 the United States sold $8.6 billion in arms to 136 nations and provided military aid to fifty-one countries.[50] No one knows precisely how much is being given away in military aid; estimates range from $4.8 billion to $7 billion a year. Congress exercises no effective oversight on military aid, and details of the program are withheld from the public and from Congress in "the interests of national security."[51]

This American global expansionism demands government expenditures that are terribly costly. But, as Veblen pointed out in 1904, "the costs are not paid out of business gains, but out of the industry of the rest of the people."[52] The *profits* of empire flow into private hands, while the growing military and overhead *costs* are socialized and carried by the taxpayer.

This is not to say that U.S. expansionism has been impelled by purely material motives but that various other considerations, such as national security and patriotism, are defined in a way that serves the material interests of a particular class. Indeed, much of what passes for "the national interest" in capitalist America, not surprisingly, has been defined from the perspective of a capitalist social order. "A serious and explicit purpose of our foreign policy," President Eisenhower observed in 1953, "[is] the encouragement of a hospitable climate for investment in foreign nations."[53] Since American "security" is supposedly dependent on American power, and such power depends in part on American wealth (i.e., a "sound economy," "secure markets," "essential raw materials," etc.), then

51. See "Curbing Arms Aid," *Progressive*, April 1971, p. 7.
52. Thorstein Veblen, *Theory of Business Enterprise* (New York: New American Library Edition, n.d.), p. 217.
53. *New York Times*, February 3, 1953, quoted in Magdoff, *The Age of Imperialism*, p. 126.

policies which are fashioned to expand U.S. corporate wealth abroad are presumed to be in the national interest. Thus we avoid any question as to whose interests are benefited by military-industrial global expansionism, at whose cost, and in pursuance of whose particular definition of "security" and "national interest."[54]

Taxes: The Unequal Burden

Our nominally "progressive" tax structure is thought to burden the rich more than the poor and therefore lessen class inequalities. In truth the tax load tends to fall most heavily on those least able to pay. Most state and local taxes are regressive, that is, they take larger percentages from the earnings of low-income persons than from high-income persons. A study in 1965 showed that sales and excise taxes claimed 6.1 percent of the annual income from families under the $2,000 level but only 2.6 percent from families earning above $15,000.[55] The percentage of income taken by all taxes, including state and federal *income* taxes, was 33 percent for families in the $5,000 to $7,000 bracket and 28 percent for families earning above $15,000.[56] Kolko has shown that families earning less than $4,000 together contribute substantially more in federal taxes than the government spends "on what by the most generous definition may be called 'welfare.'"[57]

The steeply progressive federal tax rates on income give the misleading appearance that the rich are taxed more heavily than the poor. In reality, the wealthier the person, the greater are his

54. For further discussion of this and related points see Michael Parenti, "The Basis of American Interventionism," in Parenti, *Trends and Tragedies in American Foreign Policy*, pp. 215–228; David Horowitz (ed.), *Corporations and the Cold War* (New York: Monthly Review Press, 1969); Magdoff, *The Age of Imperialism*; Greene, *The Enemy*.

55. *Allocating Tax Burdens and Government Benefits by Income Class* (New York: Tax Foundation, Inc., 1967), p. 7, cited in Robert Lineberry and Ira Sharkansky, *Urban Politics and Public Policy*, 2nd ed., (New York: Harper and Row, 1974), p. 37.

56. See Brendan and Patricia Sexton, *Blue Collars and Hard Hats* (New York: Random House, 1971), p. 155.

57. Gabriel Kolko, *Wealth and Power in America* (New York: Praeger, 1962), p. 39. The documentation on the regressive quality of our tax structure is ample. See Joseph Pechman, *Federal Tax Policy* (Washington, D.C.: Brookings Institution, 1966); Ferdinand Lundberg, *The Rich and the Super Rich* (Garden City, N.Y.: Doubleday, 1968); Herman P. Miller, *Rich Man, Poor Man* (New York: Crowell, 1971); Philip Stern, *The Rape of the Taxpayer* (New York: Random House, 1973).

opportunities to enjoy nontaxable income from capital gains, expense accounts, tax-free municipal and state bonds, stock options and various other kinds of business and professional deductions.[58] Philip Stern calculated that families with yearly incomes of $100,000 and above—about .3 ₋percent of the population—receive tax preferences of more than $11 billion annually.[59] In 1964 thirty-five persons making over $1 million paid no income taxes at all. In 1970 112 millionaires paid not a penny to the federal treasury.[60]

The income of right-wing Texas oil billionaire, the late H. L. Hunt, was estimated back in 1957 to be $1 million each *week*, and the late J. Paul Getty's income was estimated at $300,000 each *day*. Yet both Hunt and Getty paid only a few thousand dollars a year in taxes. Several thousand other persons who earn over $200,000, including millionaire politicians like Nelson Rockefeller and Ronald Reagan, have paid little or nothing. In contrast, the low-wage earner has few opportunities for deductions and pays close to the full amount demanded by law. Loopholes to avoid inheritance taxes allow rich families to hold onto and increase their fortunes from generation to generation.[61]

Perhaps most unjust of all are property taxes, the bulk of which are paid by small homeowners and tenants (in the form of higher rents). One California study showed that the richer the family, the lower the percentage of property taxes paid.[62] Property taxes on business establishments are generally assessed on amounts far lower than the real value of the property and are shifted to the consumer.

58. If you're very rich, almost any investment can be turned into a tax shelter. Herds of cattle, railroad cars, baseball teams, orange groves, amusement parks or whatever can provide depreciation and maintenance allowances and write-offs during the time they are not producing income. Imaginary income that did not come in can be claimed as a loss so that one can make a substantial real earning yet show a loss and enjoy a hefty tax deduction.

59. Stern's estimates are reported in Erwin Knoll, "It's Only Money," *Progressive,* March 1972, p. 25.

60. Congress attempted to strengthen the minimum tax in 1975 to eliminate the possibility of complete avoidance of tax payments. But the required minimum amount was only 14 percent, which is what persons in the lowest income bracket pay. *New York Times,* September 19, 1975.

61. See the study done by the Cambridge Institute, cited in *Society,* 9, September–October 1972, p. 16.

62. G. Rostvold, *Financing California Government* (Dickenson, 1967), cited in Thomas Bodenheimer, "The Poverty of the State," *Monthly Review,* November 1972, pp. 13–14. Rostvold's study found that families earning $1,000 a year pay 13 percent of their income in property taxes; those making $4,000 to $5,000 pay 5 percent; and families earning over $15,000 pay only 2 percent in property taxes.

States and local communities, competing to attract industry into their areas, often grant tax dispensations to businesses for periods of many years.

The Internal Revenue Service (IRS) makes a great claim to being nonpolitical, yet its rulings seem to manifest a political bias. Hence, conservative and right-wing veterans' organizations like the American Legion and Veterans of Foreign Wars receive tax-exempt status even though they lobby and take public stands on various political issues. The left-oriented Vietnam Veterans Against the War also takes stands on public issues and has been consistently denied tax-exempt status for doing so. The purpose of the IRS is to enforce tax laws not to enforce political orthodoxy, yet a Senate subcommittee revealed in 1975 that the IRS engaged in political surveillance "unauthorized by law," compiling files on 11,458 politically active organizations and individuals.[63] Documents collected by Senate investigators during the Watergate hearings reveal that the tax records of "ideological, militant, subversive, radical or other" organizations were made available by the IRS to a White House team whose function was to hamstring and damage dissident groups.[64] IRS files also were used to compile dossiers on political opponents in Congress, the news media and the entertainment world.

Rich corporations, like rich individuals, pay very little in taxes. In 1974 Chase Manhattan Bank, Ford Motor Company and six other corporations paid no income taxes despite hundreds of millions in profits. Ford not only escaped paying taxes but received $57 million in tax credits which it could deduct from taxes in future years. Millions in tax credits were given to other major firms. The twelve largest oil companies with a combined profit of $8.2 billion in 1973 paid only 9.6 percent taxes that year, less than the rate paid by most persons living below the poverty line. "Corporations have managed to get tax breaks for doing much of what they have to do anyway to stay in business. Perhaps it won't be long before we're told that

63. *Washington Post*, March 24, 1975; also *Durham* (N.C.) *Morning Herald*, November 18, 1974. It should also be noted that low-income taxpayers get rougher treatment from the IRS than higher-income people, according to a federal study: in 1974 it was found that 3.6 percent of the itemized returns submitted by low-income people were subject to IRS audits as compared to only 2.4 percent of the itemized returns of persons in the $10,000 to $50,000 bracket. The agency was also far more successful in collecting on claims assessed against low-income people than upper-income persons. See *New York Times*, November 17, 1975.

64. See editorial in the *Washington Star*, April 16, 1974; also *New York Times*, October 3, 1975.

the higher a company's profits are, the less taxes they should pay as a reward!"[65] Corporate tax evasion represents a continual trend. While the share of federal revenues coming from individual tax-payers has been rising steadily, the portion paid by corporations has dropped from 23 percent in 1950 to 14 percent in 1974.[66]

Private utilities not only fail to pay their fair share, they also pocket millions of dollars in taxes charged to their customers. Thus an electric utility in upstate New York collected $45 million in taxes on its monthly billings to customers, but by taking advantage of loopholes and write-offs, paid only $5.8 million to the government. Even more impressive: Con Edison charged its customers almost $100 million in federal taxes for 1974 and the first half of 1975 and actually paid only $100,000 to the government.[67] In addition, an estimated 350,000 companies are illegally withholding Social Security and income taxes from their employees' paychecks and then keeping the money for themselves. During the first half of 1975, business firms pocketed over $1 billion. Few of these delinquent firms have been prosecuted by the IRS.[68]

To summarize the major points in this chapter: the outputs of the political system, as manifested by the services, subsidies, prices, protections, taxes, leases, credits and market quotas established by public authority, affect the various areas of business enterprise and socioeconomic life mostly to benefit those who own the wealth of the nation and at the expense of the working populace. In almost every area of enterprise, government has provided business with un-surpassed opportunities for nonrisk investments, gainful inefficiency, monopolistic pricing, lucrative contracts and huge profits. Government feeds capital surplus through a process of deficit spending, offers an endless market in the defense, space and nuclear industries, and provides for the financial aid, global expansion and military protection of modern multinational corporations. From ranchers to resort owners, from doctors to bankers, from auto makers to missile makers, there prevails a welfarism for the rich of such stupendous

65. "Corporate Taxes Wither," *Dollars and Sense*, April 1976, p. 3.
66. *Ibid.* It was estimated in 1975 that $91 billion would be lost to the federal government in the form of tax preferences and write-offs—the largest share going to the business community. The sum included over $4 billion uncollected because of the special low rate of capital gains taxes and the $500 million that U.S. corporations would not pay on their overseas operations. See *New York Times*, March 2, 1975. The oil depletion allowance for large oil companies was repealed in 1975 but retained for "small" companies. These latter enjoyed a tax write-off of $3 billion in 1975.
67. *New York Times*, September 28, 1975.
68. *Moneysworth*, October 13, 1975; *National Enquirer*, May 6, 1975, p. 4.

magnitude as to make us marvel at the big businessmen's audacity in preaching the virtues of self-reliance and private initiative whenever lesser forms of public assistance threaten to reach hands other than their own.

Health, Education and Welfare: The Leaky Pump

7

GOVERNMENT EFFORTS ON BEHALF OF health, education and welfare, while composing a substantial portion of the federal budget, represents an increasingly smaller percentage of the Gross National Product. And of the monies spent on human services, only a pittance reaches those most in need.

The Poor Get Less

The much publicized "war on poverty" of the 1960s brought no noticeable betterment to the millions living in destitution, nor to the millions of others who, technically above the poverty level, are still burdened by debts, low wages, high taxes, inflation and lack of job security.[1]

After studying antipoverty programs in a dozen cities, Kenneth B. Clark concluded: "The poor serve as pawns in a struggle in which their interests are not the primary concern. The leaders talk in the name of the poor and extensive funds are appropriated and spent in their name without direct concern for, or serious attempts at, involvement of the poor."[2] What is true of urban America seems equally true of rural America. During the 1960s, $7 billion was invested by federal, state and local governments

1. See Richard Parker, *The Myth of the Middle Class: Notes on Affluence and Equality* (New York: Liveright, 1972).
2. Quoted in the *New York Times*, November 9, 1969.

in the Appalachia region, yet, according to a *New York Times* report, the bulk of the poor "remain largely untouched" by the expenditures.[3] Some Office of Economic Opportunity (OEO) officials complained that the poverty program was "chiefly a boon for the rich and for the entrenched political interests," specifically Appalachia's suburban and town "Main Streeters"—merchants, bankers, coal industry leaders, civic boosters and road contractors.[4]

Low-income families are shortchanged by government programs supposedly designed to serve them. One study shows that federal transfer payments, such as Social Security, workman's compensation, unemployment benefits and veteran's disability compensation, distribute $7 billion more to people earning above $10,000 than to those below, with a person under the $5,000 income level receiving only a third the share available to someone in the $25–50,000 bracket.[5] Social Security, better described as "social insecurity," condemns most elderly to a life of poverty. Old persons living alone received benefits averaging $2,256 in 1976, while aged couples were paid about $3,700 to meet all their living needs.[6]

The growing poverty of the late 1960s and the 1970s has led to a doubling of the welfare rolls. While some people complain about "welfare chiselers," the truth is that 50 percent of those on welfare are children, 13 percent are mothers without means of support, 37 percent are aged, disabled or blind, less than 1 percent are able-bodied men, and about 55 percent are White. Large numbers of welfare recipients suffer from poor diet, insufficient clothing, overcrowded housing, chronic illnesses and inadequate or nonexistent medical care. Approximately one-fourth of all welfare children, ages five to fourteen, have never seen a dentist; at least half suffer from malnutrition.[7] An estimated 112,000 to 225,000 children of poverty, living in dilapidated housing, fall victim every year to lead poisoning; the toddlers eat chips of peeled paint containing

3. *New York Times,* November 29, 1970.
4. *Ibid.*
5. Taylor Branch, "The Screwing of the Average Man. Government Subsidies: Who Gets the $63 Billion?" *Washington Monthly,* March 1972, p. 22. Branch was referring to a study done by Joseph Pechman and Benjamin Okner for the Brookings Institution.
6. The regressive quality of Social Security funding should be noted. A corporate executive with a $200,000 salary pays no more Social Security tax than one of his accountants who earns $15,000 and only a little more than the janitor who cleans his office and makes $6,500. Those in the lowest paying jobs who are too poor to pay income taxes must still pay Social Security.
7. See data published by Children's March for Survival in the *New York Times,* March 19, 1972.

lead, which, when ingested in sufficient amounts, causes brain damage and other serious disabilities.[8] Almost nothing has been done about this situation by federal or local authorities.

The welfare program in the United States does little to advance the life chances of persons in dire need; its funding is grossly inadequate and its administration is usually punitive in spirit and abusive of the rights of recipients.[9] One welfare expert estimates that, under the present program, for every two people receiving support, there are between two and three entitled to assistance who do not get it, not including those who receive payments smaller than they legally deserve.[10]

Millions of poor Americans receive no assistance at all. They find themselves too young for Social Security or not covered by it, too old for Aid for Dependent Children, not disabled enough for Aid to the Totally Disabled, not covered by unemployment benefits, eligible for food stamps but without money to buy them, often eligible for welfare but unable to collect it. In many states the number of welfare recipients has been reduced by administrative fiat even as needs have increased. Other services to low-income people, however paltry, were cut by the Ford administration in 1976, including slashes in aid to the handicapped and in day care and child nutrition programs.[11]

Most federal assistance programs do little for the have-nots. The following are only a few examples:

(1) Under the federal school-lunch program, most lunches are distributed to middle-class children rather than to the poor. Food programs reach only about 18 percent of the poor. The very poor are least likely to benefit from the food programs because they have

8. *New York Times*, March 26, 1969.
9. For detailed accounts of the inhumane effects of welfare programs, see Paul Jacobs, *Prelude to Riot* (New York: Random House, 1966); James J. Graham, *The Enemies of the Poor* (New York: Random House, 1970) Chapters 1–4; Gilbert Y. Steiner, *Social Insecurity* (Chicago: Rand McNally, 1966); Dorothy James, *Poverty, Politics and Change* (Englewood Cliffs, N.J.: Prentice-Hall, 1972).
10. David Steinberg, "Life Under the Plague," *Activist*, 7, Fall 1966, p. 20. See also Francis X. Clines, "Relief Clients Feel the Loss of Quarterly $25," *New York Times*, July 26, 1969; Homar Bigart, "Hunger in America: Stark Deprivation Haunts a Land of Plenty," *New York Times*, February 16, 1969.
11. On the same day (UPI release, May 4, 1976) that the Ford administration announced the $1.2-billion cut in food stamps, thus eliminating over 5 million people from the program and raising the cost of stamps by 30 percent for another 5 million, it asked Congress to add $1.2 billion to the military budget so that the Navy might build five more ships.

insufficient funds to pay for them.[12] Furthermore, since the food programs are under the jurisdiction of a Department of Agriculture primarily dedicated to serving large agricultural producers, poor children often are fed whatever tends to accumulate in farm surplus programs, mostly white flour, white sugar and other low-nutrient products, their diets being more "a result of economic policies rather than the types of food they really need," according to two nutrition experts.[13]

(2) The federal manpower programs, expending billions, have been described as a "windfall" and a "business bonanza" for the private firms that run the training programs at considerable profit to themselves, but few jobs have been generated for the mass of unemployed and unskilled.[14] Federal job aid intended for the disadvantaged has been channeled by local governments to rehire laid-off workers and ease budget crises. There has been a major shift from aid to the poor "to aid for more middle-class Americans in the suburbs and smaller towns."[15] "Community" programs like VISTA have mostly benefited corporations like General Electric which pick up the multimillion-dollar yearly training fees for program volunteers. Such programs seem primarily intended to foster quiescence among the have-nots by performing minor services on their behalf.[16]

(3) The use of funds on behalf of the privileged and powerful sometimes takes cruder forms. Thus the Farmers Home Administration, a federal agency supposedly concerned with the problems of rural America, provided multimillion-dollar no-risk loans for the construction of over five hundred private golf courses. The government allocated $4 million from funds earmarked for "economically depressed areas" to construct a convention center for businessmen in an affluent Missouri resort area, and another $2.5 million to finance airports for the convenience of the resorts' prosperous clien-

12. *Hunger, U.S.A.*, a report by the Citizens' Board of Inquiry into Hunger and Malnutrition in the United States (Boston: Beacon Press, 1968).

13. Dr. Michael Latham and Dr. Jean Mayer testifying before a Senate subcommittee, *New York Times*, December 18, 1968.

14. The training of people for jobs presumes the existence of the jobs. The training programs do nothing to answer the unemployed's first need, which is the creation of a faster expanding job market. On the shortcomings of one program, see Ivar Berg and Marcia Freedman, "The Job Corps: A Business Bonanza," *Christianity and Crisis*, May 31, 1965, pp. 115–119.

15. *New York Times*, September 26, 1975.

16. VISTA workers I interviewed in Vermont and others from Boston and eastern Kentucky all seem to agree that their efforts were essentially useless in helping the poor overcome the economic forces that perpetuate their poverty.

tele.[17] (The resorts happened to be located in a county classified as "depressed.") The U.S. Public Health Service—an agency supposedly dedicated to safeguarding our health—was, according to a Senate investigation, "deeply involved" in the production of a deadly shellfish poison that the Central Intelligence Agency was storing despite a presidential order that biochemical weapons be destroyed. Personnel in the "milk and food research group" carried out most of the research for the CIA.[18]

(4) Federal funds for day care centers provide needed services to some working families but at an exorbitant cost. In most cities the centers are leased from private landlords at high rents. The city pays the rent money directly to the landlord along with all utility bills and real estate taxes. These centers cost New York City $14 a week more per child than the ones operated by community groups and $10 million a year in municipal and federal funds. Landlords in the "day care business" have grown rich. When austerity hit New York, the centers were closed but the city continued to honor the leases, some of which ran for fifteen- and twenty-year durations.

(5) Most of the billions intended for underprivileged school children have been used to replace rather than supplement state and local funds, often perpetuating racially segregated facilities in both North and South, with little of the monies going to instructional programs. The main beneficiaries have been the "textbook publishers and professional producers of education hardware," who lobbied hard for the federal act and who since have sold millions of dollars worth of their products to the schools under the act's program.[19] Millions of dollars intended for the education of impoverished Native American children were used to buy expensive equipment for White students and to cover general operating expenses in order to reduce taxes for non-Indian property owners. Parents of Native American students were seldom informed about the money available to them.[20]

(6) Publicly funded "educational research" is frequently little more than publicly supported commercial research in disguise. Federal and state monies help finance the schools of business, law,

17. *National Enquirer,* February 21, 1971.
18. *New York Times,* September 18, 1975.
19. The report was prepared by the NAACP and the Washington Research Project; see the *Chicago Sun-Times,* November 9, 1969.
20. *Champaign-Urbana Courier,* January 12, 1971. By "Native American" I mean those indigenous peoples usually described as "Indians."

agriculture and technology that provide expensively trained personnel, specialized consultations, research skills and various other services to the large firms in these respective fields.

(7) Almost without exception the beneficiaries of public aid to higher education have been in the upper-income quartile. Thus the students who attended the University of California in the mid-1960s and received an average subsidy of about $5,000 were mostly upper and upper-middle class, while lower-middle or working-class students were concentrated in the California junior colleges where the per capita subsidy was only about $1,000.[21] A similar situation exists in public support for elementary schools. State aid is supposed to counter-balance the great inequities between rich and poor school districts, but most states dispense money through matching funds, giving larger sums to upper-income districts and smaller sums to lower-income districts and thereby doing little to lessen inequities and much to intensify them.[22] Educational opportunities are limited according to one's ability to pay rather than one's ability to learn. The children of the sharecropper, the underemployed, the migrant worker and the ghetto poor have little chance of getting an advanced education.

"Urban Removal" and the Death of Cities

American cities are among the prime victims of the profit system. Consider the housing crisis and the problem of urban decay. About one out of every five renters lives in a substandard domicile lacking adequate plumbing, heat, electricity, insulation and space. Millions more pay excessive portions of their incomes for standard housing. The scarcity of decent homes allows landlords to charge exorbitant rates. New housing is beyond the means of 85 percent of the nation's families.[23] But lavish assistance has been provided for upper-income home owners in the form of low-cost federal guaranteed credit, income tax deductions and other subsidies amounting to as much as $5 billion a year by 1976.[24] (These subsidies are also a

21. See W. Lee Hansen and Burton A. Weisbord, *Benefits, Costs and Finance of Public Education* (Chicago: Markham, 1969).

22. John E. Coons, William H. Clune and Stephen Sugarman, *Private Wealth and Public Education* (Cambridge, Mass.: Harvard University Press, 1970).

23. According to a study by the Department of Housing and Urban Development, reported in the *Progressive*, May 1976.

24. One housing expert, formerly of HEW, calculated that the wealthiest fifth of the population received $1.7 billion a year in housing subsidies, or

benefit to banks, construction firms, realty interests and others in the housing industry.) "Today," the New York Times reports, "the bulk of urban aid from Washington is targeted not at the still festering poverty sections but at . . . well-to-do neighborhoods . . . and suburbs."[25]

Government does little to protect the poor from their landlords. In places like New York City landlords take ownership of a building and milk it ruthlessly, paying neither the real estate taxes, mortgage payments nor fuel bills, permitting violations to pile up without making repairs, but at the same time collecting rents from the tenants. The landlord eventually abandons the building in a ruined condition and disappears with thousands of dollars in excess of his or her initial investment. Yet there exists no federal or state law which makes such conduct criminal.[26] "The economics of ghetto housing insures that bad housing is profitable and that good housing cannot be maintained."[27]

The billions spent by the Federal Housing Administration (FHA) supposedly to provide homes for the poor have failed to do so because the real function of FHA spending has been to guarantee profits for big developers, banks and speculators. By assuring bankers and real estate interests payment on their investments no matter what the performance, the government opened the door to manipulation of low-income housing for massive profit. Speculators buy up large numbers of old houses, apply cosmetic improvements, then get an inflated appraisal of the property's worth, often at three or four times its actual market value. Incredibly enough, FHA has no practice of actual inspection of these properties, and decrepit structures are routinely certified as "up to standard." The houses are then sold to low-income families with a federal guarantee covering the mortgage. Once they take possession, the families find their homes to be in unlivable condition. Unable to afford the major repairs, they eventually abandon the houses. At this point FHA is obliged to pay off the mortgage holders at the inflated value and take possession of the home.[28]

twice as much as the poorest fifth. See William Proxmire, Uncle Sam: The Last of the Bigtime Spenders (New York: Simon and Schuster, 1972), pp. 196–197.

25. New York Times, April 19, 1976.

26. See the correspondence in the New York Times, June 25, 1976, from Franklin Nieves and Julia Paz.

27. William K. Tabb, The Political Economy of the Black Ghetto (New York: Norton, 1970), pp. 13–14.

28. G. C. Thelen, Jr., "Homes for the Poor: The Well-Insured Swindle," Nation, June 26, 1972, pp. 814–816.

Speculators have made an average profit of over 100 percent on FHA guaranteed houses, according to Justice Department investigators.[29] Defaults on FHA mortgages have created hundreds of thousands of abandoned domiciles in our cities, making the Department of Housing and Urban Development the leading slumlord in the United States.

Urban renewal, better described as "urban removal," provides another instance of how the resources of government are used to benefit the haves at the expense of the have-nots. The billions expended by government in urban renewal programs have forced low-income people to double up in the remaining low-rent areas so that their neighborhoods can be demolished and replaced by luxury apartments, office buildings, banks, department stores, shopping centers, throughways and parking lots, as has happened in just about every city with a housing program.

Urban renewal projects might best be characterized as "land grabs." By the power of eminent domain, the municipal or state government is able to do for realty investors and corporations what they could not do for themselves—namely, forcibly buy large tracts of residential areas from reluctant small owners and small businessmen, or from "far-sighted" speculators who, armed with inside information, buy up land in the "condemned" area for quick resale to the city at substantial profit. Then the city sells this land, often at less than the market value, to big developers, underwriting all investment risks on their behalf. The losses suffered by the municipality in such transactions are usually made up by federal funds and constitute another public subsidy to private capital.[30]

The chairman of the President's National Commission on Urban Problems, former Senator Paul Douglas, concluded that "Government action through urban renewal, highway programs, demolition on public housing sites, code enforcement and other programs has destroyed more housing for the poor than government at all levels has built for them."[31] Blacks, Chicanos, Native Americans, Chinese and other racial minorities occupy a disproportionate share of the nation's bad housing. According to a 1971 report by the McGovern Senate Committee on Nutrition and Hu-

29. *Guardian,* June 16, 1976.
30. See Paul Baran and Paul Sweezy, *Monopoly Capital* (New York: Monthly Review Press, 1968), pp. 289–300; also Edward C. Higbee, *The Squeeze: Cities Without Space* (New York: Morrow, 1960).
31. Quoted in Michael Harrington, "The Betrayal of the Poor," *Atlantic,* January 1970, p. 72. See also *New York Times,* July 17, 1968.

man Needs, "from 1960 to 1968, the percentage of non-whites occupying substandard housing actually increased from 22 to 33 percent."[32] Nor has that trend been reversed in the 1970s.

The transportation system in America is a prime example of how the well-to-do get the most and the needy the least. Twenty percent of all federal transportation outlays goes to the airlines. Another 63 percent is spent on highways—of little use to the millions of very poor, elderly and others who cannot afford automobiles. Only 2.8 percent is given to mass transit systems.[33] Thus relatively high-income air travelers are sumptuously subsidized while urban low-income subway or bus riders are expected to pay nearly the full cost of their transportation. The urban areas "where the greatest number of persons suffer from the most severe problems deriving from transportation," including "pollution and congestion," receive the least support.[34]

As public transportation declines because of the austerity imposed on it by federal and state budgets, a growing reliance is placed on the automobile—leading to a further decline in public transportation. The social costs of the automobile are staggering. About 50,000 people are killed on the highways each year and hundreds of thousands more are injured and maimed. More than 60 percent of the land of most U.S. cities is taken up by the movement, storage and servicing of automobiles.[35] Homes, schools, churches, recreational areas and whole neighborhoods, particularly in working-class communities, are razed to make way for highways. The single greatest cause of air pollution in urban areas is the automobile: its carbon monoxide exhaust now claims about a thousand lives a year, and deaths from emphysema, a related lung disease, have been increasing by about 12 percent each year for the past twenty years.[36] As the number of cars grows (from 31 million in 1945 to 114 million in 1972), so do the revenues from the gasoline tax that are put into the Highway Trust Fund. As more superhighways are built with these accumulated billions, the carnage, environmental devastation and—just as significantly—the profits of

32. Quoted in "Rural Housing Famine," *Progressive*, April 1971, p. 8.
33. Robert S. Benson and Harold Wolman (eds.), *Counterbudget, A Blueprint for Changing National Priorities 1971–1976* (New York: Praeger, 1971), p. 157.
34. *Ibid.*
35. According to the Highway Action Coalition, a public interest group in Washington, D.C., as reported in Renee Blakkan, "Profits Clog the Highways," *Guardian*, November 29, 1972.
36. *Ibid.*

the oil, auto, trucking, tire, cement, construction, motel and other businesses increase. At the same time the mass transit systems—the most efficient, cleanest and safest form of transporting large numbers of people—fall into further decay.

Most of the municipal transit systems are funded by deficit spending, with bond issues that are sold to wealthy individuals, banks and business firms. In any one year these transit systems pay out millions of dollars for the enrichment of privileged bondholders, while themselves coming close to bankruptcy and being forced to cut services for the ordinary citizens who pay the bill. In 1973, for example, the Chicago Transit Authority proposed an additional fare rise and threatened to cut services and lay off workers because it was $42 million in debt. Yet CTA bondholders, led by First National Bank of Chicago and Continental Illinois, collected some $7 million in interest on their holdings that same year.[37] Much of what is called "public ownership" in transportation, roads, airports, bridges and other facilities and services is really privately bonded, with tax-free, risk-free dividends going to the rich and the costs being paid by taxpayers.

What is true of municipal transit systems is true of cities in general. Like the Third World debtor nations discussed in the previous chapter, cities are the victims of private "aid" and investment. Unable to meet the expenses of servicing the business community and satisfying minimal public needs, the cities borrow huge sums from banks and rich individuals at high dividend rates. With each bond issue a city goes deeper into debt. Speaking of New York City, Jack Newfield observes, "The banks acted like a drug dealer, and the city became a junkie. The banks made a pusher's profits, and the city got addicted."[38] New York City pays out more than $1.5 billion a year to the banks and "investment community" in the form of debt and interest payments. In 1975 New York faced bankruptcy when it could not sell a half-billion dollar bond issue needed to pay off earlier debts that had fallen due. The city was put in receivership by large creditors, led by David Rockefeller,

37. The CTA purchased highly inflated bonds to buy up bankrupt private transit companies, after the companies had been milked by their investors. (The New York City subway system came under municipal ownership in the same way.) About $300 million will eventually be returned to bondholders who originally paid $138 million, that is a 220 percent profit from a "public, nonprofit" transit authority. See *Workers World*, April 5, 1974, and September 26, 1975.

38. Jack Newfield, "Who Killed New York City?" *New Politics*, 11, Winter 1976, pp. 34–38.

who formed the Municipal Assistance Corporation (Big MAC.) This group then issued $3 billion worth of bonds for the city budget. The bonds paid a staggering 11 percent interest, and were virtually default-proof because they were backed by city taxes. City revenues normally spent on services would have to be used first to pay off Big MAC, which stood to make roughly $400 million from the crisis, all of it tax free.

In addition, New York City residents paid a total of $16 billion in federal taxes in 1974 and only got back $8 billion in federal funds. Most large municipalities are similarly shortchanged, and the annual drain of tax dollars has a devastating impact on their economies. To "rescue" the cities from their plight, the federal government and the banks had a plan, first applied to New York City and later to be used against other major urban centers: drastically cut services to the people. In 1975–1976 New York closed down day care and drug rehabilitation centers, neighborhood health clinics, every VD clinic, senior citizen centers and summer park services for children; 30,000 city employees, including hospital workers, sanitation workers, firemen and teachers, were laid off; $300 million in new taxes were introduced; free tuition at City University was abolished and the subway fare was raised. Yet in the midst of all this austerity, the city granted $276 million in tax deductions to rich landlords, including some big contributors to Mayor Beame's election campaign, and spent $100 million to renovate Yankee Stadium for the benefit of its rich owners. Meanwhile the state government was considering giving big tax breaks to corporations and Wall Street firms.[39]

At present, every indicator suggests that the urban crisis will deepen. The cities are caught in the squeeze of a capitalist system working its inexorable effect. The juxtaposition of private wealth and public poverty so frequently found in the United States is no mere curiosity. The two go together and reenforce each other.

Health and Safety for Nobody

Consumer protection is another area in which government efforts seem designed to advance the interests of private producers at the expense of the public. Adulterated products, contaminated meats

39. *New York Times*, May 26, 1976; also Newfield, "Who Killed New York City?"; and Andy Stapp, "NYC in Crisis: Bonanza for the Rich, Hardship for the Poor," *Workers World*, October 10, 1975, p. 11.

and fish, unsafe additives and preservatives, deceptive labeling, false advertising, overpricing, planned obsolescence, shoddy and dangerous commodities—such evils of the consumer market not only go uncorrected but are sometimes even encouraged by public authorities.[40] The Food and Drug Administration (FDA) does little policing of the drugs and foods that are marketed; it samples but 1 percent of the millions of yearly shipments of products, yet issues reassuring pronouncements on the safety of numerous drugs, additives and preservatives whose long-range, or even immediate, effects are highly suspect.

Certain additives and artificial hormones like diethystilbestrol (DES) are known to be carcinogenic (cancer causing), yet FDA still approves their use in foods.[41] Hundreds of hair dyes, cosmetics and drugs marketed for years without benefit of FDA testing have recently been linked to cancer and birth defects.[42]

With annual sales of over $15 billion, the drug industry is one of the most profitable of U.S. enterprises. Drug companies spend $1 billion a year for medical journal advertising and for samples and gifts to physicians in order to promote sales—three times more than they spend on research and development. Physicians admit that drug salesmen, who know almost nothing about medicine, are their first source on the uses of new drugs.[43] Drugs sold under their commercial label in the United States cost as much as eighteen times more than the exact same drug sold on a regulated market in Canada or Europe under its generic name.[44]

As with drugs, medical devices such as heart pacemakers, incubators, emergency oxygen units, marketed virtually without

40. A collection of articles documenting the ways consumers are cheated and endangered by business, often with the complicity of government, is David Sanford (ed.), *Hot War on the Consumer* (New York: Putnam, 1969). See also David Caplovitz, *The Poor Pay More* (New York: Free Press, 1967).

41. Proxmire, *Uncle Sam . . .* p. 222.

42. *New York Times,* July 22, 1973, and March 18, 1975. About 60,000 Americans are badly injured by cosmetics every year. See *Liberation,* December 1973, p. 5.

43. Amanda Spake, "The Pushers," *Progressive,* April 1976, p. 18. Testifying before a Senate subcommittee, one doctor estimated that one out of every twenty patients in hospitals is there because the drugs prescribed made her or him worse. See Saul Heller, "Crime and the Bedside Manner," *The Realist,* November 1968, p. 24. The medical profession has never been called to account for its excessive and often ignorant reliance on drugs, to the exclusion of other forms of therapy and medical care, including herbal medicine, nutritional treatments and acupuncture.

44. See Senator Gaylord Nelson's comments in the *National Enquirer,* January 6, 1976; also *New York Times,* January 6, 1975, for pricefixing among drug companies.

regulation by any public agency, have frequently proven faulty and dangerous. "The number of recalls after people have been injured or even killed by them has become alarming. Yet neither physicians nor manufacturers are legally required to report such mishaps."[45]

FDA's claim that it has not enough staff to police the food, drug and cosmetics industries has not prevented its agents from spending much time investigating, harassing, prosecuting and stigmatizing as "faddists" those health food innovators whose ideas about nutrition and medicine are critical of established drug and food enterprises.[46]

Given the way health care is organized in the United States, money often makes the difference between life and death. Many sick people die simply because they are poor and cannot afford medical assistance.[47] They are covered by no insurance and live in areas where advanced treatment is unavailable except for substantial fees. Almost all Americans, including those who can afford to pay their doctor's bills, have fallen prey to a rapacious medical industry. Every year it costs the government some $7.4 billion in Medicaid (with matching funds from state and local governments). Yet it is almost universally agreed that people are not receiving better care, only more expensive care.[48] To offer one small instance: a Maryland man incurred $445 in hospital bills during the fifty minutes that elapsed between the time his auto crashed and his death in an emergency room.[49]

Doctors' fees have doubled in recent years and hospital bills have been rising five times faster than the overall cost of living,

45. Sylvia Porter in the *Rutland* (Vt.) *Daily Herald*, June 25, 1974.
46. Omar V. Garrison, *The Dictocrats' Attack on Health Foods and Vitamins* (New York: Arco Publishing, 1971); also Alex A. Rozental, "The Strange Ethics of the Ethical Drug Industry," *Harper's*, May 1960, pp. 73–84; Estes Kefauver, *In a Few Hands* (New York: Pantheon Books, 1965); and Richard Harris, *The Real Voice* (New York: Macmillan, 1964). One spokesman for FDA, Dr. Ogden Johnson, revealed his real concern by noting: "We have been quite frankly appalled at the degree to which the consumer does not trust the manufacturer," quoted in the *Militant*, December 24, 1971, p. 7.
47. According to some of the nation's leading medical people interviewed in the *National Enquirer*, June 16, 1968.
48. See Richard Lewisohn, "Medicaid Mess—Let's Clean It Up," *Village Voice*, November 24, 1975, p. 10. The second largest item in the Medicaid administration budget has been for data processing services, contracted at nearly *40 percent profit* to a company owned by a right-wing businessman who became a billionaire by servicing various state and federal welfare and medical programs. See Robert Fitch, "H. Ross Perot: America's First Welfare Billionaire," *Ramparts*, November 1971, pp. 43–51.
49. *Progressive*, September 1975, p. 11.

while the quality of health care has shown little improvement and in some areas has deteriorated. The additional billions spent on health care have not gone into services for the people but to doctors, hospital administrators, the drug industry, health insurance companies and other businesses. This health care empire netted $9 billion in profits in 1975. Most hospitals are "nonprofit" in name only. While they have no stockholders who collect dividends, they do have boards of directors composed of staff doctors and administrators who vote themselves sumptuous salaries, and businessmen whose firms supply the hospitals with everything from pharmaceuticals and medical equipment to loans and legal counsel—at exorbitant cost.[50] Many hospitals are caught in the same cycle of profiteering prices, deficit spending and deeper indebtedness that is strangling our cities. For this reason county and municipal hospitals are closing down at an alarming rate.[51]

Another profitable enterprise feeding off Medicare and Medicaid, to the special detriment of the elderly, are nursing homes. Within a decade nursing homes have become a major profit-growth industry, run not by geriatric specialists but by builders, contractors and fast-buck operators like the notorious Dr. Bernard Bergman. The homes have netted huge profits by fraudulent billing and by maintaining services at hardship levels. The picture revealed by investigations is of elderly patients beaten, drugged and tied up all day; patients left unattended for days; patients in shock from cold, dehydration or lack of medical attention; and starved patients who fight each other for food.[52]

Doctors organize their practices as would any private entrepreneur, incorporating themselves to avoid taxes, selling a service to customers who are charged what the market will bear. Doctors have cheated Medicaid and Medicare of hundreds of millions of dollars by consistently overcharging, by fraudulent billing for nonexistent patients,[53] by charging for unneeded treatments and

50. Government regulations in some cities forbid this kind of conflict of interest, but the regulations are seldom enforced. At a New York hospital, one director was awarded a construction contract that eventually cost the hospital $673,000, another collected $38,472 on insurance premiums, and others made money from the hospital for legal services and electrical supplies. See the *New York Times*, December 26, 1975.

51. Elinor Blake and Thomas Bodenheimer, "Hospitals for Sale," *Ramparts*, February 1974, pp. 27–33.

52. Renee Blakkan, "Nursing Homes a Profit 'Industry'," *Guardian* February 5, 1975. The best book on this subject is Mary Adelaide Mendelson, *Tender Loving Greed* (New York: Knopf, 1974).

53. *New York Times*, June 25, 1976.

hospital admissions, by getting kickbacks for unnecessary but expensive laboratory tests[54] and—most unforgivably of all—by performing unnecessary surgery. An estimated 2.4 million of the 18 million operations performed yearly are totally without medical justification and lead to the death of some 11,900 patients as the result of complications.[55] Doctors and businessmen have become rich by running methadone clinics for drug addicts. Methadone neither cures nor rehabilitates addicts but it "has created a new class of millionaires."[56]

The health insurance companies, doing a $29-billion business in 1973, are controlled by giant insurance firms and other multinational corporations. Originally designed to protect families from financial hardship, Blue Cross and Blue Shield premiums are now themselves something of a hardship, offering less protection for more money with each passing year.[57]

The conditions Senator Edward Kennedy found during his Senate investigation of health care were the same throughout the nation: people denied emergency treatment because they could not show proof of ability to pay, others ejected from hospitals in the midst of an illness because they were out of funds, still others bankrupted by medical bills despite supposedly "comprehensive" insurance coverage, many who were victims of surgery done for the sole purpose of profiting the physicians, many who suffered injury and death in hospitals that were below minimal federal standards of cleanliness, safety and staff.[58]

Health care will continue to worsen no matter how many more billions are spent on it. As with agriculture, housing and transportation, medical care is organized as a private enterprise

54. *New York Times,* January 11, 1973.
55. *New York Times,* January 26, 1976.
56. Doug Garr, "How M.D.s Gross Methadone Millions," *Village Voice,* November 24, 1975, pp. 9–10. See also the booklet "Uncle Sam the Pusherman: The Story of How the U.S. People Got Hooked on Morphine, Heroin and Methadone," (Palo Alto Community Drug Abuse Project, Palo Alto, California, circa 1974).
57. Vicente Navarro, "Health and the Corporate Society," *Social Policy,* January/February 1975, pp. 41–49.
58. Edward Kennedy, *In Critical Condition: The Crisis in America's Health Care* (New York: Simon and Schuster, 1972); also *New York Times,* May 26, 1976. One of the best critiques of the economics of medical care in the United States is Barbara and John Ehrenreich, *The American Health Empire: Power, Profits and Politics* (New York: Vintage, 1970); also Ed Cray, *In Failing Health: The Medical Crisis and the AMA* (New York: Bobbs-Merrill, 1971); Richard Kunnes, M.D., *Your Money or Your Life* (New York: Dodd, Mead, 1975).

for the purpose of making a profit for those who control it. Unless the service itself is reorganized on a nonprofit basis, additional monies will only lead to more profits for the few not better services for the many.

One cannot talk about the health of America without mentioning the awesome problem of occupational safety. Every year 16,000 workers are killed on the job. Another 100,000 die prematurely from work-related diseases, such as black lung, brown lung and cancer. More than 8 million workers annually require medical attention for job injuries and illnesses. At least one out of every four workers in factories, small businesses, and on farms suffers from occupationally connected diseases.[59] One out of every six coal miners sustains a serious injury within any given year. Up to 50 percent of asbestos workers eventually die of cancer.[60] In one Georgetown, Pa., steel mill, *one-third* of the labor force suffered injuries within a year.[61] Pesticide poisoning seriously affects over 75,000 farm workers each year.[62] Rubber industry workers get bladder cancer from benzidine and other chemicals; coke oven workers get lung cancer; workers in paint, dye and chemical industries suffer brain damage and disorders of the central nervous system; and workers dealing with polyvinyl chloride plastics get liver cancers.[63] The casualties that working people suffer daily are many times higher than what Americans sustained during the Vietnam war, yet no one is organizing mass protests against this industrial slaughter.

It may well be that industrial production will always carry some kind of risk, but the present high rate of death, injury and illness can be ascribed to the lack of adequate safety standards and lax enforcement of safety codes. Thus mine owners argue that coal mining is the most dangerous occupation because of natural and unavoidable hazards like underground gas explosions. But almost all coal mine accidents could be avoided if proper safety measures were taken. Safety conditions in U.S. mines are among

59. *New York Times,* April 28, 1975 and May 12, 1976.

60. According to Dr. Samuel Epstein of Case Western Reserve; see "Death on the Job," *Progressive,* May 1976, p. 7.

61. Rita Millins, "Georgetown Steel Company Strike," *Workers World,* December 25, 1970.

62. I. C. Van Buskirk, "Pesticides Kill Farm Workers," *Guardian,* April 21, 1976. Much of the information herein is drawn from Jeanne M. Stellman and Susan M. Daum, *Work Is Dangerous to Your Health* (New York: Pantheon, 1973); Rachel Scott, *Muscle and Blood* (New York: E. P. Dutton, 1974).

63. *Ithaca* (N.Y.) *Journal,* June 24, 1976; also *Philadelphia Inquirer,* March 14, 1976.

the worst in the world. In Poland, the world's second largest exporter of coal, accidents are "rare," according to the *New York Times,* because of elaborate safety measures.[64] This same emphasis on worker safety is found in other noncapitalist countries.[65]

In the United States, however, government and business have been criminally negligent in the matter of safety. In Kentucky miners breathe sixty-seven times the maximum amount of coal dust declared to be safe by federal law. Federal standards in asbestos plants permit workers to inhale 20 to 30 million asbestos fibers in a single working day. Government safety standards currently exist for only 450 of the tens of thousands of chemical and physical agents in industry. Corporations introduce new chemicals into the work place every day—without testing their effects on workers and without government supervision. Of 1,339 companies doing business with the government, 95 percent violate minimum safety and health standards.[66]

When officials do get around to acting on violations, the average fine against employers in a year like 1974 was $15. And over 80 percent of the violations filed lead to no penalties at all.[67] In a routine call on a Florida agribusiness farm in 1976, Labor Department inspectors found sixteen separate health and safety violations and fined the farm a grand sum of $230.[68] Federal health officials found an oil company responsible for the death of three workers and fined it $500. When six workers at a Gulf refinery were killed due to company negligence, the fine was $600. A factory guilty of producing a highly toxic chemical was fined $6 for each of its violations.[69] In 1975 eight people were killed by gas

64. *New York Times,* October 26, 1974.
65. See the eye-witness report of a West Virginia miner who visited the Soviet Union, *United Mine Workers Journal,* November 1, 1974.
66. Sylvia Porter, "Accident Toll of Workers," *San Francisco Chronicle,* July 30, 1968, cited in G. William Domhoff, *The Higher Circles* (New York: Vintage, 1971), p. 201. See also Morton Mintz, "Danger and Death in the Trucker's Cargo," *New York Post,* September 3, 1969; Millins, "Georgetown Steel Company Strike." For a report on the plight of farm workers see Fay Bennett, "The Condition of Farm Workers and Small Farmers in 1969," *Report to the Board of Directors of National Sharecroppers Fund* (New York: 1969); Tom Foltz, "Florida Farmworkers Face Disaster," *Guardian,* April 3, 1971, p. 4; Rod Such, "New Growth in Use of Child Labor," *Guardian,* June 2, 1971, p. 5; and the *New York Times* report on migrant workers, September 16, 1971.
67. "Your Job May Be Hazardous to Your Health," *Dollars and Sense,* February 1976, p. 11.
68. Jack Anderson's column, March 13, 1976.
69. Bob Kuttner, "When the Job Disables the Worker," *Village Voice,* May 18, 1972. See also Joseph A. Page and Mary-Win O'Brien, *Bitter Wages* (New York: Grossman, 1973).

seepage from a faulty Atlantic Richfield well. Federal investigators fined the company $550.[70]

The absence of worker safety is the result of something more than just "negligence" on the part of business and government. The overbearing imperative of the capitalist economy is to maximize profits. One way of doing this is by cutting costs, including the substantial costs of maintaining safe conditions.[71] Money spent not on production for profit but on safety for the worker is money spent primarily in the worker's interest rather than the owner's. Indeed, a major determinant of how much industry expends on safety measures is how much it will save when it reduces injury. Low-wage workers are less expensive to "damage"—that is, the amount of production lost is less than when a highly skilled, better-paid worker is disabled. Hence, in those industries where it is cheaper to replace the injured worker than make safety changes, injury rates tend to be higher.[72] Consider the testimony of a farm worker (among the lowest paid of unskilled laborers) about conditions on a big commercial farm in California:

I began to see how everything was so wrong. When growers can have an intricate watering system to irrigate their crops but they can't have running water inside the houses of workers. Veterinarians tend to the needs of domestic animals but they can't have medical care for the workers. They can have land subsidies for the growers but they can't have adequate unemployment compensation for the workers. They treat him like a farm implement. In fact, they treat their implements better and their domestic animals better. They have heat and insulated barns for the animals but the workers live in beat-up shacks with no heat at all.

. . . Stoop labor is very hard on a person. Tuberculosis is high. And now because of the pesticides, we have many respiratory diseases. The University of California at Davis has government experiments with pesticides and chemicals, to get a bigger crop each year. They haven't any regard as to what safety precautions are needed.[73]

To ask why government has been unable to force business to change its ways is to presume that government acts according to the dictates of justice rather than the realities of power and in-

70. *Guardian*, January 14, 1976.
71. See the discussion in Chapter Two concerning the imperatives of the profit system.
72. See the study by labor economist Robert S. Smith, reported in the *New Haven Register*, December 22, 1972.
73. Farmworker quoted in Studs Terkel, *Working* (New York: Pantheon Books, 1972), p. 12.

terest. By now it should be clear that government is hardly an entity independent of the corporate system in which it operates. The ways that business keeps government subservient to its interests have already been touched upon and will be explored further in the pages ahead.

On Behalf of Pollution

The federal government's widely publicized "war on pollution" of the 1970s, like its "war on poverty" of the decade before, has brought few results. Like sin itself, pollution is regularly denounced but vigorously practiced. In 1970 corporations spent $1 billion to advertise what they were supposedly doing to "save the environment," an amount that was ten times more than all U.S. firms spent for pollution control devices that same year. Strip mining, deforestation and offshore oil drilling continue to bring ruination to millions of acres.[74] Industry pours tons of poisonous chemicals into our rivers, lakes and water supplies each year, much of it working its way into the food chain.[75] At least 25,000 synthetic chemicals are now in the atmosphere, with over 500 added yearly.

Consider the Allied Chemical plant in Hopewell, Virginia, which produced kepone, a poisonous insecticide more potent than DDT. Kepone is, in effect, nonbiogradable. It merges with blood cells and one's body cannot get rid of it. Because of the uncontrolled dumping of waste products from the plant, the multi-billion-dollar fishing and shell fish industries in the James River and Chesapeake Bay had to be closed, putting 3,000 people out of work. As many as 149 of the plant's workers suffered total dis-

74. Having stripped their own lands of every major stand of virgin timber, the timber companies are now scourging public lands. See Bartle Bull, "'Harvesting' the National Forests," *Village Voice*, August 17, 1972, pp. 6 ff. For an account of the Santa Barbara oil spillage, see Ross Macdonald, "Life with the Blob," in Walt Anderson (ed.), *Politics and Environment* (Pacific Palisades, Calif.: Goodyear, 1970), pp. 123–132. For a general critique of what is happening to our environment, see James Ridgeway, *The Politics of Ecology* (New York: E. P. Dutton, 1970).

75. For information on pesticides see the *New York Times*, July 31, 1975. Evidence is accumulating that the carcinogens introduced by humans into the environment could be the cause of almost all cancer. See the *Ithaca* (N.Y.) *Journal*, January 24, 1976. Certainly the instances of cancer are highest in areas most heavily affected by industrial pollution. See "Cancer: The Pollution Link," *Public Occurance, A Vermont Magazine*, June 1975, p. 35.

ability and were expected to die within a few years because of their exposure to kepone. Their families have also been poisoned. The drinking water in the area contained dangerous amounts of the poison. During plant production hours, at least 50 percent of Hopewell's air dust was kepone, according to a monitoring done by a federal agency.[76] But when the chief of the State Water Control Board, a former employee of Allied Chemical for seventeen years, was warned about the kepone situation by a member of his staff, he refused to do anything. After much publicity Allied Chemical was prosecuted and fined over $2 million, but a federal judge may waive the fine if the company ceases polluting and pays minimal damages. Allied's directors were acquitted of all charges.

Pollution continues unabated because it is profitable for the polluters. Production costs are cheaper when industrial wastes can be dumped into waterways or the atmosphere. Rather than instituting costly pollution controls, industry passes the social and human costs to the public in the form of ecological devastation, illness and death. Pollution costs billions a year in depressed property values, contaminated municipal water supplies and other forms of destruction. The pollution of some businesses destroys the production of others, notably recreational and fishing industries. Thus the water pollution caused by the paper companies in Maine has driven that state's rivers into ecological bankruptcy, destroying a $9.4-million salmon fishery on the Penobscot River and a $13.8-million fishery on the St. Croix River.[77]

Enforcement of pollution laws is so rare as to be newsworthy, and the penalties so minor as to be farcical. After the first oil spillage at Santa Barbara, the petroleum companies were charged with 343 violations of the Fish and Game code; upon conviction, each company was fined the grand sum of $500. The multibillion-dollar U.S. Steel Corporation was indicted on five counts of dumping poisonous industrial wastes into Lake Michigan—if convicted it could receive a maximum fine of $2,500 on each count. A little publicized provision of the Pesticide Control Act even makes pollution a money-making venture for some industries, allowing the government to compensate—at retail prices—the producers of pesticides for financial losses suffered if their products are ordered off the market as unsafe. One Congressman observed: "This measure

76. *Workers World,* January 2 and 9, 1976.
77. *New York Times,* May 18, 1973.

may set a precedent for the Government to pay compensation to private enterprise every time a legitimate Government action taken in the public interest results in a loss of profit for the business community."[78]

The approach taken by state, local and federal government in regard to pollution, like the approach taken in most other problem areas, hews closely to three principles: (1) the forms of public control must never compete or interfere with the basic profit interests of private investment—that is to say, the solutions to pollution must be accommodated to the capialist production system; (2) in keeping with the above requirement, the costs of pollution control are to be borne by the public rather than by the producers; and (3) the companies that pollute the most will get the most. Thus the larger the company's profits, the greater is its pollution subsidy under the 1969 Tax Reform Act. This measure is in pursuance of a certain perverse logic: big profits are made by big producers, and big production generally means big pollution, which, in turn, demands big clean-up subsidies and big tax credits. In sum, the polluter is rewarded rather than punished.[79]

Not yet mentioned is probably the greatest environmental menace of all: nuclear power. A major accident at a nuclear reactor site could kill as many as half a million people and contaminate an area the size of California—and there have been some frightfully close calls.[80] Nuclear plants are so hazardous that insurance companies refuse to handle them. Breakdowns in safety systems, causing contaminating leakages are fairly common occurrences.[81] Perhaps more dangerous than a catastrophic accident is the daily radioactivity emitted by the nuclear plants often in excess of "permissible" levels established by the Atomic Energy Commission. (AEC). No one has ever demonstrated that there *is* such a thing as a "permissible" level of radioactive leakage. The best scientific evidence indicates that *any* amount of emission can have

78. Richards D. Lyons, "Pesticide Compensation Bill Seen Costing Billions," *New York Times*, October 15, 1972.

79. See Branch, "The Screwing of the Average Man: Government Subsidies . . . ," p. 15; also "Eco-profits," *Hard Times*, May 11–18, 1970, p. 1; and Martin Gellen, "The Making of a Pollution-Industrial Complex," *Ramparts*, May 1970, pp. 22–27. For an excellent analysis of the effects of capitalism on the natural environment, see Barry Weisberg, *Beyond Repair—the Ecology of Capitalism* (Boston: Beacon Press, 1972).

80. John G. Fuller, *We Almost Lost Detroit* (New York: T. Y. Crowell, 1976).

81. John W. Gofman and Arthur R. Tamplin, *Poisoned Power* (New York: Signet, 1971).

a damaging effect on health and genetic structure.[82] Within a decade, the instances of leukemia among children who resided within a twenty-mile radius of the first nuclear plant built in Pennsylvania increased by 300 percent. About 100 million Americans live within a fifty-mile radius of one of the fifty-six reactor sites and are subjected to some amount of radioactive emissions. Sixty-three more nuclear reactors are being built and the Ford administration wanted 200 plants operating by 1985. At this rate most Americans would have a nuclear plant in their locale.

The reactors produce wastes that remain radioactive for upwards of 250,000 years and which cannot be safely stored. At Hanford, Washington, the world's largest nuclear dump, it was discovered in 1975 that more than half a million gallons of radioactive liquids had leaked from the steel and concrete storage tanks and ended up in groundwater and in the Columbia River. Anyone eating a pound of duck from the nearby Hanford Reservation suffers an exposure to radioactivity three times the AEC's maximum "safe" and "permissible" level.[83] As of now the nuclear industry has no long-term technology for safe waste disposal. Corrosive nuclear wastes are stored in tanks that have a life expectancy of fifteen years.[84]

The performance of nuclear plants indicates that nuclear energy is the most expensive and least efficient large scale method of producing electricity.[85] The costs of building a plant are now five times higher than the original estimates given to Congress by the AEC.[86] But the costs are part of the attraction. Dominated by a few giant manufacturers who work in conjunction with the AEC and the Energy and Research Development Agency, the nuclear industry draws billions each year from the federal treasury for construction, research and uranium price supports. In its first twenty-four years, the AEC spent $49 billion and bought more than $3 billion worth of uranium ore from domestic producers at high, fixed prices. The nuclear industry, like the defense industry, is a government-contracted market for the benefit and profit of giant private suppliers. The more expensive things get, the more the contractors rake in.

82. *Ibid.*
83. John Ghrist, "Nuclear Power: Breaking Up Is Hard to Do," *Vermont Cynic,* April 3, 1975.
84. Liberation News Service, "Nuclear Leaks Abound," *Guardian,* June 9, 1976, p. 7.
85. Gofman and Tamplin, *Poisoned Power;* also "Nuclear Power Costs More and More," *Dollars and Sense,* April 1976, pp. 4–5.
86. Ghrist, "Nuclear Power . . ."

The AEC has served as a tool of the nuclear industrialists, spending millions to publicize the false notions that nuclear energy is safe and cheap, and repeatedly suppressing findings by its own scientists that demonstrate the contrary.[87] The devotion to nuclear power and profits is such that the government spends almost nothing on alternate fuel sources such as solar, geothermal and tidal energies. Much of the federal money for solar energy development has gone to Westinghouse and General Electric, the two major nuclear reactor builders, who, not surprisingly, announced that solar energy technology is not yet commercially viable—although tens of thousands of people around the world are already relying on solar heating devices.[88]

In the energy field as elsewhere we discover the basic contradictions between our human values and our economic system: the social and ecological need to conserve energy as opposed to the corporate need to get people to consume still more energy in order to maximize profits; the human need for safe, clean energy sources versus the corporate need for profitable energy markets, no matter how destructive and lethal they may be.

To conclude this chapter: a large part of the domestic budget appears to be spent on worthwhile things, and indeed *some* of these monies get to the have-nots; *some* school lunches, child care centers and rehabilitation programs help the needy. But the methods of spending—through private producers in a capitalist economy—most often brings great costs to the taxpayer, fat profits to the corporate few and little benefit to the people. The government's programs in housing, health, transportation, urban development, energy and ecology do not achieve the goals we would want because they are not designed to. Their purpose is not to pursue the public interest and fulfill human needs but to satisfy the profit needs of a few giant producers usually at the expense and suffering of the many, thereby fulfilling the capitalist dictum: "To them that have shall be given. From them that have not shall be taken even what little they have."

87. *New York Times,* November 10, 1974; also Gofman and Tamplin, *Poisoned Power,* pp. 103 ff.

88. See the excellent article by Tom Zeman, "Solar Power Now," *Ramparts,* April 1975, pp. 22–25, 55–58. In the same 1976 election which saw former AEC director Dixey Lee Ray elected governor of Washington (she had said "The hazards of nuclear energy are trivial"), a nuclear safeguards initiative was defeated. The opponents spent seven times as much as the proponents and most of this money came from out-of-state nuclear-related corporations.

Law and Order: The Double Standard

8

SINCE WE ARE TAUGHT TO THINK OF the law as an institution serving the entire community and to view its representatives—from the traffic cop to the Supreme Court Justice—as guardians of our rights, it is always discomforting to discover that the law is often written and enforced in the most tawdry racist, class and sexist ways.

The Protection of Property

Far from being a neutral instrument, the law belongs to those who write it and use it—primarily those who control the resources of society. It is no accident that in most conflicts between the propertied and the propertyless, the law intervenes on the side of the former. The protection of property is deemed tantamount to the protection of society itself and of benefit to all citizens, presumably even the propertyless. Those who equate the interests of property with the "common interest" seldom distinguish between (a) large corporate property used for the production of profit and (b) consumer-use possessions like homes and personal articles. Most political conflicts are concerned with the distribution and use of (a), not (b); yet segments of the public, believing that their modest and highly mortgaged personal-use possessions (b) are being threatened in controversies arising over (a), will give sympathetic support to the corporate property system.

The law's intimate relationship to property can be seen in the curriculum of the average law school: one learns corporate law, tax law, insurance law, torts and damages and realty law chiefly from the perspective of those who own the property. Owners, trustees and landlords have "rights," but workers, students, consumers and tenants have troublesome "demands." In most instances crime is defined by law as something which the have-nots commit against the haves. Under the property law, management may call in the police to lock out workers, but workers cannot call in the police to drive out management. University trustees may bring in the police to suppress striking students, but students cannot call on the police to control trustees. Landlords can have the police evict rent-striking tenants, but tenants cannot demand that police evict rent-gouging landlords. The landlord's rights are usually automatically upheld by the courts, the burden being on the tenant to prove violations. Low-income residents soon learn that laws dealing with the collection of rents, eviction of tenants and protection of property are swiftly enforceable, while those dealing with flagrant violations of building and safety codes, rent overcharging and the protection of people go unenforced.

The biases written into the law, which reflect the one-sided and often unjust property relations of the society, are compounded by the way the law is enforced. Even when the letter of the law is on their side, the poor have little else working for them. Although they are in greatest need of legal protection, they are least likely to seek redress of grievances through the courts, having neither the time nor money. And when they find themselves embroiled in court cases, it is almost always at the initiative of the bill collector, merchant, or landlord who regularly use the courts as a means of asserting their property interests. In the absence of strong tenant and consumer organizations, the individual has little to fall back on. It is futile for "individual consumers one by one to bring their grievances to the courts where the laws are so rigged against consumers that not even the most sympathetic judge can grant much redress."[1]

Business crime is socially more damaging than most working-class crime, since it involves the health, safety and earnings of millions of workers and consumers. Ralph Nader estimated that each year orange-juice companies steal more money from the

1. Jean Carper, "Defense Against Gouging," *Nation*, November 3, 1969, p. 473.

American public by watering down their product than bank robbers steal from banks. A Nader task force estimated that monopolies are costing American consumers $48 to $60 billion a year because of fixed prices, lost production and lack of innovation.[2] The President's Commission on Law Enforcement reported that the property losses from crimes like robbery, burglary, auto theft and larceny account for only 15 percent of the money costs against property, while business crimes like embezzlement, fraud, forgery and commercial theft account for 78 percent.[3]

Lawlessness is endemic to the business community. A routine inspection of lumber establishments found that approximately three-fourths of them were violating major provisions of the Fair Labor Standards Act.[4] And three-fourths of all banks were violating the banking laws. The criminality of corporations, Sutherland concludes, is persistent, "like that of professional thieves."[5] Looking at seventy of the largest corporations in the United States, he found that in several decades they had been convicted of an average of ten criminal violations each (a figure that greatly underestimates the actual amount of crime, since most violations go unchallenged or never reach court). Any ordinary citizen with such a conviction record would be judged an "habitual offender" deserving of heavy punishment. Yet the guilty companies were provided with special stipulations, desist orders, injunctions and negotiated settlements or were let off with light penalties. The fines they are required to pay "are generally so small that many corporations have found it far cheaper to operate on the shadowy side of the law than take the necessary steps toward compliance."[6]

Often companies are not even obliged to appear in court. They also are allowed to file "consent decrees" which, in effect, say that the firm has done nothing wrong and it promises never to do it again. Then the government's files are made confidential and all the evidence against the company is locked away. Persons seeking damages in civil suits must try to uncover the evidence on their own. Wealthy corporate criminals are separated administratively

2. "Nader Report: Consumers Lose Billions to Invisible Bilk," *Crime and the Law* (Washington, D.C.: Congressional Quarterly, 1971), p. 21.

3. President's Commission on Law Enforcement and Administration of Justice, 1967, reported in *Crime and the Law*, p. 20.

4. Edwin Sutherland, *White Collar Crime* (New York: Holt, Rinehart and Winston, 1949), p. 150.

5. *Ibid.*, pp. 210–222.

6. Sarah Carey, "America's Respectable Crime Problem," *Washington Monthly*, April 1971, p. 3.

from low-income offenders, facing "a far gentler disciplinary system composed of inspectors, hearing examiners, boards and commissions. . . . For the affluent, the loopholes are so abundant that it takes determination to avoid them."[7]

Nonenforcement of the law is common in such areas as price fixing, restraint of trade, tax evasion, environmental and consumer protection, child labor and minimum wages. The antitrust laws, supposedly intended to restrict the unfair practices of large firms and protect the consumer and smaller producers, have snared almost no businessmen in the eighty years of their existence: from 1890 to 1946 only seven were sentenced to prison, and all seven had their sentences suspended. In the early 1960s, thirty-two electrical firm executives were found guilty of conspiracies to fix prices in contracts valued at over $27 million. Thirty were given jail sentences; twenty-three of these were suspended and the other seven served thirty days. The treble damage payments which the electrical firms had to pay their customers, however, were ruled to be tax deductible business expenses by the IRS. In effect, the government picked up the costs—another case of the taxpayers being punished for the crimes of the corporations.

The law leans consistently in the direction of business. To break strikes, and unions, the courts can impose injunctions and massive fines. Thus in 1975 a federal district judge imposed a $5-million fine on the United Mine Workers for failing to contain a wildcat strike by its rank and file, and an additional $100,000 every day the strike continued.[8] In contrast, the maximum fine for a violation of the Sherman Anti-Trust Act is $50,000, a figure not likely to terrorize Wall Street.

A study of the New York State court system found that persons who committed crimes like burglary, theft and small-time drug dealing received harsher sentences than persons convicted of securities fraud, kickbacks, bribery and embezzlement.[9] One judge imposed a small fine on a stockbroker who had made $20 million through illegal stock manipulations and, on the same day, sen-

7. Senator Philip Hart, "Swindling and Knavery, Inc.," *Playboy*, August 1972, p. 156.
8. *New York Times*, September 2, 1975.
9. *Guardian*, October 18, 1972. In federal courts in 1971, 71 percent of the persons convicted of auto theft went to jail for an average of three years. Only 16 percent of those convicted of securities fraud—involving sums many times greater than the worth of any automobile—were jailed, for an average term of 1.7 years. Whitney North Seymour, Jr., *Why Justice Fails* (New York: William Morrow, 1973).

tenced an unemployed Black man to one year in jail for stealing a $100 television set from a truck shipment.[10] When a low-income Black man was convicted of robbing a crap game, he was sentenced to fifteen years. But a rich doctor caught having forged a check for over $36,000 received a conditional discharge and paid a restitution of $18,000 (thus profiting $18,000 for his crime).[11] A Dallas court gave a five-time petty offender 1,000 years in prison for stealing $73.[12] And a New Orleans court gave a four-time offender life imprisonment for possession of a stolen television set and sentenced another man to fifty years for an armed robbery that netted him $3.[13] In contrast, Dr. Bernard Bergman, convicted of swindling millions of dollars in the nursing home business was sentenced to four months.

Relations between the judiciary and the business community may be described as close and loyal. In 1958 twenty-nine oil companies were indicted for fixing prices and creating artificial scarcity. The evidence compiled by the Justice Department was detailed and devastating, including letters and testimony from various company executives. But Federal Judge Royce Savage dismissed the case as based on "hearsay," without bothering to hear the defense. A year later Savage become a top executive at Gulf Oil, one of the twenty-nine companies.[14] In 1976 when Federal Judge Miles Lord ordered a Minnesota company to pay $100,000 to the city of Duluth for water filtration (after the company had been contaminating the city's water for several years), the U.S. Court of Appeals reversed the decision and ordered Lord removed from the case for showing "bias" against the polluters. It was the first time in more than twenty years that an appellate court had removed a district judge without a complaint being officially brought against him.[15]

Persons in public office usually are drawn from the same social strata as businessmen, and many return to business when they leave office. "Almost every important person in government has many close personal friends in business, and almost every impor-

10. Leonard Downie, Jr., *Justice Denied* (New York: Praeger, 1971).

11. Sharon Krebs, "Attica Profile: Big Black Speaks," *University Review*, November 1974, p. 15; and Deborah Larned, "Monitoring Abortion Clinics," *ibid.*, p. 13.

12. Gary Cartwright, "The Tin-Star State," *Esquire*, February 1971, p. 100.

13. Bob Pratt, "How One U.S. City Has Slashed Its Crime Rate," *National Enquirer*, June 8, 1976.

14. Burton H. Wolfe, "The Judge Who Saved the Oil Companies," *San Francisco Bay Guardian*, January 9–16, 1975. Fifteen years later Savage appeared as a key figure involved in Gulf's illegal political contributions.

15. *Workers World*, February 27, 1976.

tant person in business has many close personal friends in government."[16] Sutherland writes: "Legislators admire and respect businessmen and cannot conceive of them as criminals. . . . The legislators are confident that these respectable gentlemen will conform to the law as the result of very mild pressure."[17]

Criminal Enforcement:
Unequal Before the Law

Looking at the criminal law enforcement process, we find that various racial, sexual, political and class factors—external to any actual criminal behavior—bear a clear relationship to the treatment accorded an individual from the time of arrest to the time of imprisonment.

ARREST

An arrest is not only the first step in the enforcement process; it is often a punishment in itself, leading to incarceration, legal expenses, psychological intimidation, sometimes severe physical abuse and loss of job. Of the 7.5 million people arrested in 1969 for all crimes, excluding traffic offenses, more than 1.3 million were never prosecuted or charged, and 2.2 million were acquitted or had the charges against them dismissed, according to the FBI Uniform Crime Report. The large number of arrests without charges or conviction, especially of ghetto residents and antiwar demonstrators, suggests that frequently the purpose of arrest is not to convict but to harass, intimidate and immobilize. In some cities, as many as 90 percent of arrests are made without warrants. Police have the power to jail anyone for up to two or sometimes three days without pressing charges and once charged, a suspect can have a "hold" placed on him by the District Attorney or some law enforcement official and be kept in prison until trial time.

In many instances the class and racial prejudices of the police are a crucial determinant of who gets arrested and who does not. "If you are stopped by the cops for weaving boozily through late-night traffic," Russell Baker writes, "you will be far wiser to be a

16. Sutherland, *White Collar Crime*, p. 248.
17. *Ibid.*, p. 47.

Congressman in a large new car than an unemployed hod carrier in a 1950 Chevrolet with one fender missing."[18]

CHARGES

The kind of charges brought against an arrested person may depend on the kind of person he is. Members of rich and influential families and persons who occupy high public positions are often able to hush up an embarrassing arrest and not be charged with anything.[19] Every arrest situation has enough ambiguity to allow authorities some discretion in determining charges. Whether a situation is treated as "disorderly conduct" or "mob action," whether it is to be "aggravated battery" or attempted murder," depends somewhat on the judgment of the law enforcers, both police and prosecutors, and their feelings about the suspect.

A factor sometimes determining the seriousness of the charges is the degree of injury *sustained*, not inflicted, by the individual during the course of his arrest. Police are inclined to bring heavier charges against someone whom they have badly beaten—if only to justify the beating and further punish the "offender." The beating itself is likely to be taken as evidence of guilt. "I cannot believe a state trooper would hit anyone for no reason," announced one judge in a trial involving a college professor who had been repeatedly clubbed by troopers while participating in an antiwar demonstration.[20] "In the eyes of the police," Paul Chevigny argues, "arrest is practically tantamount to guilt, and the police will supply the allegations necessary for conviction; the courts are treated as a mere adjunct to their purpose."[21]

BAIL AND LEGAL DEFENSE

After being charged and booked, the suspect is held in jail to await arraignment.[22] At arraignment the judge has the option of doing

18. Russell Baker's column, *New York Times*, September 14, 1974.
19. The former lobbyist Robert Winter-Berger gives an interesting account of his successful efforts to cover up the arrest of a U.S. Senator in a gay bar in New York; see his *The Washington Pay-Off* (New York: Dell, 1972), pp. 82–84.
20. Michael Parenti, "Repression in Academia: A Report from the Field," *Politics and Society*, 1, August 1971, pp. 527–537.
21. Paul Chevigny, *Police Power* (New York: Pantheon, 1969), pp. 276–277.
22. Procedures vary somewhat from state to state and according to the

anything from releasing the defendant on his own recognizance to imposing a bail high enough to keep him in jail until his trial date—which might come a couple of years later—as was the fate of numerous Black Panthers arrested in police raids in various cities and held on bonds of $100,000 and $200,000. Even if found innocent, as was the case of the New York and New Haven Panthers, the defendant will have suffered the immense costs and anxieties of a trial and an extended imprisonment. This "preventive detention," commonly employed against large numbers of persons rounded up during urban disturbances, allows the state to incarcerate and punish people without having to convict anyone of any crime.[23]

"Recognizance" would be most helpful to those unable to afford bail but it is usually granted to "respectable" middle-class persons and seldom to indigents. Stuart Nagel shows that in state cases 73 percent of all indigents were denied pre-trial release as opposed to 21 percent of nonindigents.[24] The 1970 census discovered that more than half the people held in all county and municipal jails had been convicted of no crime but were awaiting either a trial or hearing.[25] Pre-trial detention makes it almost impossible for the poor to assist their attorney in the preparation of an adequate defense. Brought into court directly from jail, a defendant is more likely to be convicted and likely to be sentenced to a longer term than someone who has been free on bail and whose lawyer can point to his "rehabilitation" and law-abiding life since the original arrest.[26] Poor people also are more likely to be persuaded to plead guilty to reduced charges ("plea bargaining"). Ninety percent of all defendants plead guilty without a trial; of the other 10 percent, more than half are convicted of something. This statistic hardly fits with the image of "coddled" criminals and "soft-hearted" courts propagated by the get-tough advocates.

nature of the crime. For a standard textbook account of law enforcement procedures, see Delmar Karlen, *The Citizen in Court* (New York: Holt, Rinehart and Winston, 1964).

23. See Jerome Skolnik, "Judicial Response in Crisis," an excerpt from Skolnik's book, *The Politics of Protest* (New York: Simon and Schuster, 1969), reprinted in Theodore Becker and Vernon Murray (eds.), *Government Lawlessness in America*, (New York: Oxford University Press, 1971), p. 162, especially the comments by Judge Crockett of Detroit.

24. Stuart Nagel, "Disparities in Criminal Procedure," *UCLA Law Review*, 14, August 1967, pp. 1272–1305.

25. 1970 National Census, statistics reproduced in *Crime and the Law*, p. 12.

26. Ralph Blumenfeld, "The Courts: Endless Crisis," *New York Post*, May 15, 1973. See also Stuart Nagel, "The Tipped Scales of American Justice," *Transaction*, 3, May–June 1966, pp. 3–9; and Nagel's "Disparities in Criminal Procedure."

LAWYERS, JURIES AND JUDGES

Like medical service, legal service in our society is commercial; it best serves those who can pay for it. The man who has the $100,000 for top legal assistance experiences a different treatment from the law than the poor person with a court-appointed lawyer. Public Defender or Legal Aid lawyers are overloaded with cases and have little time for the defendant, sometimes seeing him for the first time on the day of his trial. Being mostly of White middle-class background, they often share the same prejudices about their non-White, poor clients as do police, prosecutors, judges, juries and probation officers, a factor that can further influence their efforts.[27]

In most states prospective jurors are chosen from voter registration rolls or county tax lists which underrepresent racial minorities, the young, the propertyless, the poor and the transient. Sometimes whole precincts are excluded from jury selection if they are unusually poor or have a high percentage of Blacks. A study of Erie County, N.Y., found that Blacks were underrepresented by 34 percent in the jury selection pool, women by 68 percent and persons between the ages of twenty-one and twenty-nine by 84 percent. Women were granted exemptions without even requesting them and college students seem to have been "automatically disqualified."[28]

The few cultural or political "deviants" who might get called for jury duty are usually weeded out at selection time by the peremptory challenges of the prosecutor. Juries in most areas of the country will contain a disproportinately high percentage of White, middle-aged or elderly middle-class Americans of conventional and often conservative stripe. The same is true of grand juries, which commonly function as extensions of the prosecution rather than as impartial citizens' panels. The grand jury bringing indictments against prisoners who allegedly had taken part in the 1971 Attica uprising contained twelve persons who stated in open court that they had friends or relatives working as guards in Attica prison.

27. According to a study conducted through Boston University Law School, reported in the *Guardian, November* 26, 1975, most indigents go to court without benefit of even this token legal representation. Judges, especially in the lower courts, openly encourage defendants to waive their right to counsel.

28. *Buffalo Courier Express,* March 29, 1974, and *Spectrum* (Buffalo, N.Y.), April 1, 1974. In 1976 it was disclosed that thousands of persons called for federal jury duty have been subjected to background checks by the IRS without their knowledge, as U.S. prosecutors have sought to pinpoint and exclude those with "antigovernment biases." *New York Times,* April 19, 1976.

Five jurors had friends who had been held hostage by the rebelling prisoners. The judge did not believe these connections were evidence of bias or prejudice.[29]

As portrayed in the media, judges are distinguished looking persons possessed of a wise and commanding air, making fair-minded decisions, calming courtroom passions with measured admonitions, showing fear and favor toward none yet capable of a certain compassion for the accused. Turning from Hollywood to reality, we discover that judges are often arrogant, corrupt, self-inflated persons. After observing courtroom procedures for two years, the investigative journalist Jack Newfield concluded that along with "personal venality" many judges were marked "by cruelty, stupidity, bias against the poor, short tempers or total insensitivity to civil liberties."[30] Investigations by a special prosecutor in 1975–1976 in New York found widespread sale of judgeships to monied persons. Once on the bench, these individuals commonly sold "not guilty" verdicts to rich businessmen, crime syndicate bosses and corrupt politicians brought before them.[31]

A study of state courts found that judges were considerably more inclined to send poorly educated persons to prison and less likely to give them suspended sentences or probation than better educated and better-income persons convicted of the same crimes.[32] A study of courts in Seattle, Washington, found that persons who convey the appearance of a middle-class status are treated as more worthy of leniency by judges than those who by dress or attitude do not seem to value "the same things which the court values."[33] One federal judge observes that his colleagues are "likely to read thick briefs, hear oral arguments, and then take days or weeks to decide who breached a contract for the delivery of onions"—such are the efforts devoted to business cases—but when dealing with

29. See Nick Coles, "Massive Crackdown Hits Attica," *Guardian*, January 3, 1973; also John Conyers, Jr., "Grand Juries: The American Inquisition," *Ramparts*, August/Septemver 1975, pp. 14–16.

30. Jack Newfield, "The Next 10 Worst Judges," *Village Voice*, September 26, 1974, p. 5; also Charles Ashman, *The Finest Judges Money Can Buy* (Los Angeles: Nash, 1973) for an expose of venality on the bench.

31. The Special Prosecutor, Maurice Nadjari, launched 500 investigations, got 79 convictions and 296 indictments against judges and other officials. His efforts proved so troublesome to the powers that be that he was eventually fired by Governor Carey.

32. Nagel, "Disparities in Criminal Procedure."

33. For a report on the study see Ray Bloomberg, "Court Justice Tied to Middle-Class Values," *Quaker Service Bulletin*, 54, Spring 1973, p. 8. This study found poverty to be a bigger factor in court bias than race. Nagel finds the same, although he allows that there is much overlap.

criminal charges against a common defendant, "the same judge will read a pre-sentence report, perhaps talk to a probation officer, hear a few minutes of pleas for mercy—invest, in sum, less than an hour in all—before imposing a sentence of 10 years in prison."[34]

Like police, many judges are inclined to see any defendant who enters their court as guilty of something. One observer of New York City courts concluded: "Favoritism to the prosecution is the rule among most judges here. . . ."[35] Judges not only identify with the prosecutor, they frequently *are* former prosecutors, having made their way to the bench via the office of district attorney or state attorney or the Justice Department. Thus a Justice Department lawyer, Myles Lane, one of the prosecutors in the Rosenberg "atom spies" trial, became, twenty years later, the judge who sentenced the Black revolutionary H. Rap Brown to five to fifteen years for armed robbery. The image we have in our heads of an orderly, even-handed, dignified system of justice does not coincide with the picture drawn by Newfield:

Routinely, lives are ruined and families broken by 30-second decisions. Some judges quit work at 2:00 P.M. to play golf, while some 8,000 men and women presumed innocent under the Constitution wait months for trials in the city's overcrowded detention jails. Other judges have tantrums on the bench and call defendants "animals" and "scum." Cops pay court attendants ("bridgemen") $5 to call their cases first. Legal Aid lawyers defend 50 poor clients a day with not a second for preparation. The bail system lets bondsmen buy freedom for the rich and well-connected. Clerks sell advance word on court assignments and decisions. Civil cases almost always get decided in favor of the landlord or business-man, or city agency.[36]

PENALTIES AND PRISONS

Echoing a favorite conservative theme, President Nixon complained of "softheaded judges" who showed more concern for "the rights of convicted criminals" than for "innocent victims."[37] But an Amer-

34. Marvin E. Frankel, *Criminal Sentences: Law Without Order* (New York: Hill and Wang, 1973).
35. Ralph Blumenfeld, "The Courts: Endless Crisis," *New York Post,* May 15, 1973.
36. Jack Newfield, "New York's Ten Worst Judges," *New York,* October 1972, p. 32.
37. See the response by Marvin E. Frankel, "An Opinion by One of Those Softheaded Judges," *New York Times Magazine,* May 13, 1973, p. 41. In his

ican Bar Association study found that, far from coddling criminals, American jurists imposed much severer sentences than their opposite numbers in Western European countries. Sentences of over five years for felony convictions are rare in Europe but common in the United States,[38] where jail terms sometimes have an eighteenth-century quality about them. In Norfolk, Virginia, a man received ten years for stealing eighty-seven cents; in Detroit, a Black youth was found guilty of stealing seven dollars and given three to ten years; in Georgia, a White youth and a Black youth were each sentenced to thirty years for possession of marijuana; in Los Angeles a twenty-year-old Mexican-American drug addict was sentenced to life in prison for selling some narcotics to a police informer; a youth in Louisiana got fifty years for selling a few ounces of marijuana.

In contrast, Robert F. Kennedy, Jr., received a suspended sentence for possession of marijuana. The son of a well-established New York politician, arrested for possession of heroin, was paroled and placed in a narcotics treatment program. A major heroin dealer, with previous arrests and important mob connections, was given a conditional discharge. A big-time racketeer had felony charges against him dismissed by a compassionate judge known for his stern rulings against hippies and Blacks. A detective with gangland connections, caught dealing in heroin, was convicted of a misdemeanor and given a suspended sentence. "What criminal cases reveal," Mitgang writes, ". . . is that there is one law for the poor, another for the organized criminal with the expensive name lawyers."[39]

Consider how the law was applied in these cases: (1) A White, unemployed migrant farm worker, Thomas Boronson, and his family were eating one meager meal each day from money earned by selling their blood. Boronson and a friend, Lonnie Davis, took over a welfare office in a desperate attempt to get the several hundred dollars owed to the Boronson family. The youngest of Boronson's six children was a sick infant who had been denied medical care by local doctors because the family could not afford to pay. Boronson and Davis were arrested and convicted of kidnapping, assault and robbery, even though the welfare worker refused to

book *Criminal Sentences*, Judge Frankel describes judges as "arbitrary, cruel and lawless" in the ways they determine sentences.
38. Frankel, "An Opinion by One of Those Softheaded Judges."
39. Herbert Mitgang, "The Storefront Lawyer Helps the Poor," *New York Times Magazine*, November 10, 1968.

press charges. They were sentenced to nine and seven years respectively.[40]

(2) In 1975 a Black student, Philip Allen, joined a small crowd watching a drunk smash a store window. When the police arrived they jumped Allen with drawn pistols, according to witnesses. The police claim that Allen, who is 5′ 3″ and weighs 135 pounds, over-powered several of them, seized one of their guns, shot three of them—killing one—without leaving any fingerprints on the gun and then was captured by the other two. No witnesses saw Allen hold-ing a gun at any time. The police most likely shot each other in the scufflle. Allen was convicted and given a life sentence.[41]

(3) William Wesler, a husky 6′ 1″ White man, repeatedly terrorized and molested the children of a young Indian woman, Yvonne Wanrow, and the children of a woman who lived next door to Wanrow. Wesler had a record of sexually abusing children and had recently raped a neighbor's seven-year-old daughter. Despite frantic and repeated calls to the police, he was never arrested. Then one night, Yvonne Wanrow killed Wesler when he broke into the house and made sexual advances upon her and her three-year-old nephew. She was convicted and sentenced to twenty-five years in prison.[42]

(4) In 1974 in Louisiana, a bus carrying Black children was attacked by a mob of Whites, some of whom were armed. Accord-ing to the bus driver, a gun was fired from the crowd; it missed the bus but killed a White youth. When the Black students were forced out of the bus and to their knees by police, one of them, Gary Tyler (age fifteen at the time), was arrested for "interfering with an officer" when he objected to the deputy sheriff's putting a gun to the heads of Black students. The police "found" a gun in the bus, but it curiously turned out to be a police revolver with no fingerprints. Tyler was charged with murder, convicted by an all-White jury, and sentenced to die in the electric chair. The prosecution's case rested entirely on two witnesses; however, both recanted their testimony, charging that police had coerced them into fingering Tyler. The police had threatened to take one witness'

40. *Guardian*, May 26, 1976.
41. *Guardian*, October 29, 1975.
42. *Workers World*, October 24, 1975.
43. *Guardian*, May 12, 1976; *Workers World*, May 21, 1976. For a general critique of the problem of justice for Blacks, see Haywood Burns, "Can a Black Man Get a Fair Trial in This Country?" *New York Times Magazine*, July 12, 1970, pp. 5, 38–46.

child away from her and charge her as an accessory to the murder. The judge refused to grant a new trial.[43]

Those who are convicted of crimes must then face our "correctional institutions." American prisons are overcrowded, filthy, unhealthy places, breeding crime, violence, homosexual rape, murderous and sadistic guards, mental degradation and physical deterioration. Joan Bird, a founder of the Women's Bail Fund, describes the conditions faced by women inmates throughout the country: "The basic right to bathe, the right to decent food and clothing, adequate medical care, exercise and fresh air, the right to internal cleanliness—the right to exist as human beings are denied to them."[44] Eighty percent of all prison inmates are Black, Chicano, Puerto Rican, Native American and Asian. Blacks tend to get substantially longer prison terms than Whites who commit the same crimes (even when the Black is a first-time offender and the White is a second- or third-time offender).[45]

Prisoners who attempt to protest the inhumane conditions they suffer are likely to be subjected to the most extreme retribution. One of the better-known, George Jackson, was murdered by guards at Soledad State Prison. At Atmore and Holman prisons in Alabama, forty-five of the inmates who organized for better prison conditions were indicted on charges. In a year and a half, five of the leaders had been either shot, hanged or beaten to death while handcuffed—by prison guards.[46]

Prisons may be places of sadism, racism and moral horror, but they are also one of the big profit-making industries in the country. In fiscal 1974 federal prison labor grossed $67 million in sales. State prisoners are forced to work twelve-to fourteen- hour days on corporate farms producing multimillion-dollar sugar cane, cucumber,

44. Quoted in the *New York Post*, December 19, 1970. For a critique of the American penal system, see Jessica Mitford, *Kind and Usual Punishment* (New York: Vintage, 1971); also Frankel, *Criminal Sentences;* and Alan Dershowitz, "Let the Punishment Fit the Crime," *New York Times Magazine,* December 28, 1975.

45. Frank L. Morris, "Black Political Consciousness in Northern State Prisons," paper presented at the National Conference of Black Political Scientists, New Orleans, May 1973. Statistics show that in cases of Black-against-White rape, a Black man is eighteen times more likely to be executed than someone convicted of a Black-against-Black, White-against-White or White-against-Black rape. In the South no White man has ever been executed for raping a Black woman, although such rapes have been common occurrences. See the study by the Southern Poverty Law Center reported in the *Guardian,* March 10, 1976.

46. Walt Shepperd, "Alabama's State Prison System: Unfit for the Shelter of Animals," *Ithaca* (N.Y.) *New Times,* February 1, 1976.

tobacco and cotton crops. For this inmates are paid as little as 25 cents a week or often nothing at all.[47]

To sum up what might be said about criminal enforcement: poor and working-class persons, the uneducated and the racial minorities are more likely to be arrested, less likely to be released on bail, more likely to be induced to plead guilty, more likely to go without a pre-trial hearing even though entitled to one, less likely to have a jury trial if tried, more likely to be convicted and receive a harsh sentence and less likely to receive probation or a suspended sentence than are mobsters, businessmen and other upper- and middle-class Whites. "The rich have little reason to fear the system and the poor have little reason to respect it."[48] Many poor understand that the person who steals $5 is called a thief while the person who steals $5 million is called a financier. And they see that the law rather consistently works against people like themselves.

Women of upper-class social background are more likely to receive favored treatment at the hands of the law than low-income or impoverished people of either sex, and in most kinds of cases White women receive better consideration than Black men. But race and class aside, women suffer legal injustices of their own.[49] Most laws against prostitution, for example, are either written or enforced so as to place all the guilt on the prostitute and none on her male clients. In some states, wives still have not achieved equality with their husbands in regard to consent in contracts and handling of property. In most states a woman under eighteen still does not have the right to consent to sexual love without running the risk of having the act declared unlawful and her lover prosecuted for "statutory rape." But men under eighteen are under no similar consent restriction with women of "legal age." As victims of rape, women often receive little justice in the courts, it frequently being assumed by police, attorneys, judges and jurors that the rape victim "was asking for it" (an assumption that is far less likely to be made if the alleged rapist is Black). Women in prison are subjected to repeated sexual abuse from male guards, sheriffs and jail trustees. In one women's prison in Alabama there were eight births a year, mostly the result of sexual assaults by male guards.[50]

47. "Profits from Prison Labor," *Workers World*, December 12, 1975.
48. Hart, "Swindling and Knavery, Inc., . . ." p. 162.
49. Karen De Crow, *Sexual Justice* (New York: Random House, 1974).
50. *Workers World*, March 5, 1976. One such case is that of Jo-Ann Little, the Black woman who killed a guard who sexually abused her. Because of its sensational aspects, the Little case won national publicity. Many other cases of prison rape receive no attention.

In many states there still exists a host of female "juvenile crimes," such as going into a bar, getting pregnant, fighting with parents, running away from home and staying out late at night, that are not crimes and should be taken off the books but which are used to incarcerate many young and spirited women.

Every year thousands of women are hospitalized because of prolonged and repeated beatings from their spouses. It is a crime to assault anyone, yet the law is seldom enforced against husbands who batter their wives. The law also has yet to prove effective in breaking down discriminatory employment and wage practices. If anything, the women's liberation groups fighting such discrimination have been the object of FBI, CIA and Military Intelligence surveillance over the years. The feminist struggle against all forms of sexism, which is part of the struggle for democracy and equality, is treated by government agencies as subversive of the existing system—as indeed it may be. "If you have ever been even moderately active in any phase of the Women's Movement, you are likely to have your very own dossier in the gracious J. Edgar Hoover Building in Washington," Nat Hentoff reports.[51]

As with Blacks, the poor and women, so with homosexuals: the oppression practiced in the wider society is reflected and re-enforced in the law and the courts. Thus when gay people go to court to contest the discrimination they suffer in housing and employment, they are most likely to find that the rights of property take precedence over the rights of people, and the doctrine of equal protection under the law does not apply to them. Within the last several years more than a dozen states have removed penalties against consenting adults who engage in homosexual acts. But in thirty-six states gay love is still punished under "sodomy" or "unnatural acts" laws, and two people who love each other but are of the same sex find themselves treated as criminals or "perverts" to be hustled off to jail or a mental institution for "treatment" and "cure." In 1976 the Supreme Court ruled, 6 to 3, that states may prosecute and imprison people committing homosexual acts even when both parties are consenting adults and the act occurs in private.[52]

Gays have been barred from sensitive government jobs on the highly dubious assumption that their homosexuality is indicative of personal instability and leaves them open to corruption or black-

51. Nat Hentoff, "How the Government Protects You from Dangerous Women," *Village Voice*, May 31, 1976.
52. *New York Times*, March 30, 1976.

mail, making them poor security risks. Both female and male gays have been discharged from the armed services for no other reason than that they were homosexuals. Lesbian mothers have been denied custody of their children on the grounds that their sexual preferences made them unfit parents. Gay bars are frequently raided by police or closed down by municipal authorities and gay individuals often are "cruised" by undercover police, posing as fellow gays, whose intent is to entice and entrap them, an undertaking that some law officers perform with an enthusiasm that seems to involve something more than the call of duty.

Police Terror: Who Guards the Guardians?

No discussion of law and order would be complete without some mention of that violent and often criminal element, America's only armed minority: the police. Despite cutbacks in city budgets, the police remain the fastest growing public occupation in the United States. In 1975 the various metropolitan police forces received the largest outlay ($4.7 billion) from municipal budgets, and U.S. cities were spending almost 200 percent more on police than ten years before.[53] The budgets of some cities resemble the federal budget in their lopsided dedication to "defense spending." The largest single item in the 1974 municipal appropriations of Philadelphia was the $110 million given to the police. Yet despite these growing expenditures, the urban crime rate continues to rise.[54]

If the police have been unsuccessful in the "war against crime," they have not been idle in their war against workers, poor people, youth, racial minorities and other elements that might prove troublesome to the interests of property and propriety. The police are like an occupying army patrolling the exploited and hostile low-income areas, keeping the sullen population in line with large does of terror. In the two years before the Watts riot, sixty Black people were killed by Los Angeles police: twenty-seven were shot in the back or the side; twenty-five had been completely unarmed; and there was some question whether many of those listed as armed were in fact so. In many instances there was no evidence of any crime having been committed by the victims. Scores of other Blacks and Chicanos were shot and survived, and many more were

53. *Workers World,* December 12, 1975.
54. *New York Times,* May 24, 1973.

badgered, threatened, arrested and beaten by the police.[55] If the Watts riot was eventually suppressed by the police, it also was in large part ignited by police murder and brutality—one of the major grievances of the ghetto.

Studies show that Blacks, Chicanos, Puerto Ricans and low-income Whites have many more personal encounters with police brutality than middle-class White "respectables."[56] In recent years there have been hundreds of killings of members of low-income groups and non-Whites by police in situations having every appearance of murder: a Black man is forced to lie face down in a Detroit motel and a policeman cold-bloodedly pumps a bullet into his head. A Black man, father of five children, is killed by an angry off-duty San Fransico policeman whose car has been accidentally scraped by someone else. In Newark a grinning state trooper, holding a Black youth captive in an alley, repeatedly shoots him in the head and body, pausing only to place a knife in the victim's hand. A White working-class youth is beaten to death by police in a paddy wagon in Cambridge, Mass. A patrolman in Eureka, Calif., accosts a thirty-eight-year-old Native American father of five and shoots him through the forehead for no reason. A twelve-year-old Chicano boy, arrested in Dallas as a "burglary suspect," is shot through the head and killed while sitting handcuffed in a patrol car. A Black man, father of three, driving without a license, becomes frightened when finding himself followed by police and flees from his car in Urbana, Ill., only to be shot dead by a policeman who utters no warning. A White hippie, finding his house surrounded by armed, unidentified men in Humboldt County, Calif. (they turn out to be county police and narcotics agents raiding the wrong place), flees in terror out the back door and is shot dead. A Puerto Rican teenager is killed by a patrolman while climbing a park fence one night in New York. A ten-year-old Black boy walking with his foster father in Queens, New York, is killed by a plainclothes policeman who leaps from his unmarked car without identifying himself, shouts "Hey niggers!" and opens fire. A Black shell-shocked Vietnam veteran, walking down the street, is shot to death in Houston by two White officers as he reaches into his pocket to take out a Bible.[57]

55. Paul Jacobs, *Prelude to Riot* (New York: Random House 1968), pp. 29–30.

56. David H. Bayley and Harold Mendelsohn, *Minorities and the Police* (New York: Free Press, 1971), p. 122.

57. For accounts of these and similar incidents the reader is referred to Tom Hayden, *Rebellion in Newark* (New York: Vintage Books, 1967); John

A study of police forces in three major cities found that all the victims of brutality had one thing in common: they were from low-income groups.[58] Sometimes it is enough just to be Black—even if middle class. The case of Carl Newland is not a rarity. Newland, a Black forty-eight-year-old accountant, happened to be walking by a newsstand that had just been robbed. He was roughed up and handcuffed by the police and then brought before the newsstand clerk, who emphatically denied that he was the stickup man. Nevertheless, because of his "belligerent attitude" he was taken to city jail, charged with armed robbery and, according to statements by several prisoners, repeatedly and severely beaten by the police. He died in his cell that night.[59]

To note a few more of the many instances of police murder: Martin Perez, a community organizer and advocate of Puerto Rican independence, was arrested in 1974 for "disorderly conduct" while waiting for a subway train in New York, then found two hours later hanged in a cell by a belt—with his hands still handcuffed. He was declared a "suicide" by police. The precinct station to which he had been taken had a long history of beatings and harassment of Blacks and Puerto Ricans.[60] A Black community leader in Texas, Clifford Coleman, was arrested in 1975 while sitting quietly in his car outside a drive-in grocery. Coleman had been repeatedly harassed by police. This time he was beaten at the police station, then shot in the back and again beaten, according to an eye-witness account by a clergyman who had come to bail him out. Coleman died shortly afterward.[61] In 1975 a Puerto Rican,

Hersey, *The Algiers Motel Incident* (New York: Knopf, 1968); Art Goldberg and Gene Marine, "Officer O'Brien: 'I Want to Kill a Nigger So Goddamned Bad I Can Taste It!' He Killed George Baskett," *Ramparts*, July 1969, pp. 9–16; Murray Kempton, "The Harlem Policeman," in Becker and Murray (eds.), *Government Lawlessness in America*, pp. 47–49; Joe Eszterhas, "Death in the Wilderness: The Justice Department's Killer Nark Strike Force," *Rolling Stone*, May 24, 1973, pp. 28–34, 44–54. See also various back issues of the *Guardian*, the *Militant*, *Workers World* and the *Daily World* for accounts of criminal and murderous actions against radicals and racial minorities. *Akwesasne Notes*, official publication of the Mohawk nation, has carried numerous accounts of atrocities committed against Native Americans in recent years by law officers and other Whites. The *Black Panther Intercommunal News Service* has carried similar accounts involving Black victims.

58. Albert J. Reiss, "How Much 'Police Brutality' Is There?" *Trans-action*, July/August 1967, reprinted in Stephen M. David and Paul E. Peterson, *Urban Politics and Public Policy* (New York: Praeger, 1973), p. 282.

59. *Workers World*, June 4, 1976.

60. *Guardian*, December 18, 1974. Atrocities like these are reported weekly in publications like the *Guardian* and *Workers World* but seldom in the established business-owned press.

61. *Guardian*, January 29, 1975.

Israel Rodriguez, was in his Bronx home with his pregnant wife when the police, allegedly investigating a robbery, broke in and started beating him. "They beat him and beat him and then took him away," his wife said. At the station he was beaten again and soon died from internal injuries.[62] A Blackfoot Indian in Montana, Clayton Hirst, suffered repeated harassment by county officials ever since winning a suit against them in 1973. He was arrested in 1975 on a drinking charge and was later found hanged in his cell and declared a suicide. But an autopsy done by criminal pathologists at the request of Hirst's family found that he had been electrocuted to death and then strung up to give the appearance of suicide.[63]

Few of the law officers involved in these kinds of cases have ever been indicted for murder. Most have been exonerated by review boards despite the highly incriminating testimony of eyewitnesses. A few have been suspended from the force, and a few have been tried for "justifiiable homicide" or "manslaughter" and acquitted.[64] One White officer, who had held a young Black boy with one hand and shot him with the other, was awarded tax-free disability pay of $1,000 a month for the rest of his life because of the "trauma" he supposedly suffered after murdering the boy.[65] In Mobile, Alabama, a grand jury investigation of police terror concluded that "police department command personnel not only accepted but encouraged such behavior," a finding that could be applied to any number of departments in the nation.[66] Grand jury investigations in places like Newark show that the police, from superior officers to patrolmen, offer no cooperation in identifying those in their ranks who might have committed brutal and unlawful acts.[67]

Police frequently ally themselves with unlawful elements whose prejudices they share. In places like Boston, East Boston, Queens (N.Y.), Buffalo and Detroit, Black homeowners have been repeatedly terrorized by White mobs and arsonists but have been unable to secure protection from law agents or, worse still, have themselves been subjected to police attack. To describe only one

62. *Workers World,* June 27 and October 17, 1975.
63. *Guardian,* November 19, 1975.
64. See Sara Blackburn (ed.), *White Justice: Black Experience Today in America's Courtrooms* (New York: Harper, 1972).
65. *Workers World,* February 7, 1975.
66. *Guardian,* May 19, 1976.
67. *New York Times,* March 2, 1975; see also Peter Maas, *Serpico* (New York: Bantam, 1974) for an account of widespread corruption and cover-up in the New York City police department.

of many such incidents: when a Black home was attacked by a racist mob in East Boston in 1976, the police did nothing to stop the attack and instead broke into the home and arrested the resident and seven visitors for "loud and abusive language." Witnesses for the defense, including a priest, a lawyer and a local resident, testified that no loud or abusive language had been uttered and that the defendants had acted peacefully at all times. Nevertheless, the eight were convicted and received jail sentences of six to eight months.[68]

The history of the labor movement in the United States reveals a similar pattern of police harassment, violence and terror. From the earliest industrial conflicts to the most recent struggles of the United Farm Workers, agents of the law have consistently sided with the propertied and powerful, either looking the other way or actively cooperating when company goons and vigilantes attack workers, organizers, union headquarters and pickets.[69]

The law and its enforcement agents, the police, do many worthwhile things. Many laws are intended to enhance public safety and individual security. The police sometimes protect life and limb, direct traffic, administer first aid, assist in times of community emergency and perform other vital social services with commendable dedication and courage. But aside from this desirable *social service* function, the police and the law serve a *class control* function—that is, they protect those who rule from the protests and confrontations of those who are ruled. And they protect the interests of property from those who would challenge the inequities of the system. The profiteering corporate managers, plundering slumlords, swindling merchants, racist school boards, self-enriching doctors, special-interest legislators and others who contribute so much to the scarcity, misery and anger that lead to individual crimes or mass riots leave the dirty work of subduing these outbursts to the police. When the police charge picket lines—beating, gassing and occasionally shooting workers—they usually are operating with a court injunction which allows them to exert force in order to protect the interests of the corporate owners. When police harass and terrorize racial minorities and slum dwellers, they usually have the support of the White middle-class community and government officials, who want problems like protest and poverty

68. *Workers World*, October 17 and November 14, 1975; March 5, 1976. For other instances of this kind of treatment, see the *Guardian*, April 14, 1976; *Workers World*, April 18 and June 20, 1975.
69. Jeremy Brecher, *Strike!* (Greenwich, Conn.: Fawcett, 1974).

swept under the rug—even if it takes a club or gun. Repressive acts by police are not the aberrant behavior of a few psychotics in uniform but the outgrowth of the kind of class control function law officers perform and rulers insist upon—which explains why the police are able to get away with murder.

Law and Order: The Repression of Dissent

9

AMONG THOSE WHOM THE LAW TREATS repressively are persons who oppose capitalism and advocate alternative social orders. Since capitalism is considered an essential component of Americanism and democracy, anticapitalists are treated as antidemocratic, un-American and a subversive threat to the "national security," and thus fair game for repression. As repression gathers momentum, it is directed not only against socialists but against anyone who shows an active interest in progressive causes. Under the guise of defending democracy, security agencies are able to deny dissenters their democratic rights and move the nation closer to a police state.

The Methods and Victims of Repression

When directed toward social reform, the law usually proves too weak for effective change. But when mobilized against political dissenters, the resources of the law appear boundless, and enforcement is pursued with a punitive vigor that itself becomes lawless. Dissident groups have had their telephones tapped, their offices raided, their records and funds stolen by law officers, their members threatened, maligned, intimidated, beaten, murdered, or arrested on trumped-up charges, held on exorbitant bail, subjected to costly, time-consuming trials which, whether won or lost, paralyzed their leadership, exhausted their funds and consumed their energies.[1] With these kinds of attacks, the government's message comes across loud and clear: people are not as free as they think. They may organize and propagandize against government policies, but their public utterances and private behavior will be watched by one or more of the many security agencies. And if they persist, they run the risk of being struck down by police violence or devoured by the repressive legal mechanism of the state. The law is a weapon used against people who want to change the class and racial relations of the society.

Consider some specific cases: the Black socialist Martin Sostre, long an opponent of heroin traffic in the ghetto, was convicted of dealing in heroin—on the sole testimony of a convict who was released from prison after appearing against Sostre and who subsequently admitted in a sworn statement that his testimony had been fabricated. The trial judge refused to believe his recantation and Sostre remained in prison, sentenced to thirty years. He served nine years, mostly in solitary confinement and was subjected to sadistic treatment at the hands of prison authorities. In 1975 after much protest from progressive and humanitarian groups, the governor of New York granted Sostre amnesty.[2]

Then there was George Jackson. Sentenced as a youth to a long, indeterminant prison term for a relatively minor crime, Jackson became radicalized while in the penitentiary. He began organizing inmates and writing books about his revolutionary creed which won public attention.[3] For this he was placed in solitary for long periods, repeatedly beaten and eventually shot dead by guards. In 1976 at the trial of the surviving Soledad brothers, the defense produced a Black undercover agent who described the elaborate and successful plans of the police to kill Jackson during what was to appear as an "escape attempt."[4]

1. Note how the leadership of the antiwar movement was harassed on trumped-up "conspiracy" charges. See Jessica Mitford, *The Trial of Doctor Spock* (New York: Knopf, 1969); and Jason Epstein, *The Great Conspiracy Trial* (New York: Vintage, 1971).

2. *New York Times*, December 25, 1975.

3. See George Jackson, *Soledad Brother: The Prison Letters of George Jackson* (New York: Bantam, 1970); also Eric Mann, *Comrade George: An Investigation into the Life, Political Thought and Assassination of George Jackson* (New York: Harper and Row, 1974).

4. *Guardian*, April 21, 1976. The agent, Louis Tackwood, told of his experiences as an undercover provocateur in a book: see Citizens Research and Investigation Committee and Louis Tackwood, *Glass House Tapes* (New York: Avon, 1973); also Mann's examination of Jackson's murder in *Comrade George*.

Frank Shuford, a Black community organizer and a socialist in Santa Ana, California, campaigned against police brutality, drug pushers and police complicity with the drug traffic. In 1975 he was arrested for the shooting of two store clerks, although at the time of the crime Shuford was home with his family. The clerks could not identify him as the gunman. The first trial ended in a hung jury. In the second trial Shuford's former lawyer, who was himself now facing charges of having received stolen goods, testified that prior to the shooting Shuford had come to him in an "irate and dangerous mood." The prosecution told the all-White jury that Shuford was a "revolutionary troublemaker." Shuford was found guilty and sentenced to thirty years. Once in Vacaville prison, he met the kind of cruelty reserved for political prisoners. He was drugged, beaten, provoked, denied medical care and forced to live in a filthy cell. When his spirit would not break, Shuford was scheduled for a lobotomy. Only community support for him prevented the operation from taking place.[5]

When a White mob invaded the Black community in Wilmington, N.C., in 1971, setting fire to several buildings, police did nothing to stop them. But a year later, in connection with those same fires, the Reverend Ben Chavis and nine other Black leaders were arrested on charges of arson and "conspiracy to attack police and firefighters." On the first day of the trial, faced with a jury of ten Blacks and two Whites, the prosecutor developed a sudden stomach pain. Instead of calling a recess for a few days, the judge declared a mistrial. At the second trial a jury of ten Whites and two Blacks was seated. The "Wilmington ten were found guilty on the testimony of two young men who were themselves facing long jail terms for an unrelated crime. Chavis was sentenced to thirty-four years while the others received sentences of twenty-nine to thirty-four years. Chavis had been previously arrested on seventy-eight separate charges over a three-year period and acquitted on all.[6]

The repression of dissent usually reveals the criminal nature of those who say they are dedicated to fighting crime. This account

5. *Guardian*, September 24, 1975.
6. See Buffy Spencer, "North Carolina: Laboratory for Racism and Repression," *Outfront* (Amherst, Mass.), August 1976, p. 9. The key prosecution witness against the Wilmington 10 has repudiated his testimony, but Chavis and the others remain in prison. Cases like the above are only a few of the more prominent. Almost any political activist who occupies a leadership position (and many who don't) runs into confrontations with the law. As the above might indicate, the treatment of Black and other minority group dissenters has been especially severe.

of a police attack against a peace demonstration in New York in 1969 is typical of many such incidents that occur throughout the United States during political protests and labor conflicts:

A number of policemen came charging into the crowd, many, but not all, with their clubs in hand raised to the levels of their heads. . . . I saw other people being beaten. Some were arrested and others were not. It appeared to me that the police were just beating people at random with no clear indication that the people they were attacking had committed an illegal act. I saw none of the people being attacked fight back or attempt to hit the police. Most attempted to protect themselves by covering their heads or tried to run.[7]

Witness this assault on an antiwar protestor in front of the Pentagon in 1967:

At least four times that soldier hit her with all his force, then as she lay covering her head with her arms, thrust his club swordlike between her hands onto her face. Two more troops came up and began dragging the girl toward the Pentagon. . . . She twisted her body so we could see her face. But there was no face there: all we saw were some raw skin and blood. We couldn't even see if she was crying—her eyes had filled with the blood pouring down her head. She vomited, and that too was blood. Then they rushed her away.[8]

The police have killed many unarmed people participating in collective protest actions. Of the one hundred or so murders of persons associated with the civil rights movement during the 1960s, almost all were committed by police and White vigilantes. Few of the murderers were caught; none was convicted of murder. From 1968 to 1971 local police stormed into and wrecked Black Panther headquarters in more than ten cities, stealing thousands of dollars in funds and arresting, beating and shooting the occupants in well-planned, unprovoked attacks. More than forty Panthers were killed by police in that period, including Chicago leader Fred Hampton, who was shot while asleep in his bed. More than 300 were arrested and many were imprisoned for long periods without bail.

7. Quoted in Peggy Kerry, "The Scene in the Streets," in Theodore Becker and Vernon Murray (eds.), *Government Lawlessness in America* (New York: Oxford University Press, 1971), p. 61.
8. Eyewitness testimony by Harvey Mayes, *New York Times*, December 3, 1967. Descriptions of brutality at the Pentagon were not carried in the *Times* or other newspapers. Mayes' account along with numerous others appeared in a full-page paid advertisement.

In Orangeburg, S.C., three Black students were killed and twenty-seven wounded when police fired into a peaceful campus demonstration. No guns were seen or found among the students, and some of the victims had been shot in the back while fleeing.[9] During a nonviolent demonstration at Southern University in Louisiana, two unarmed Black students were killed by police. In antidraft and anti-ROTC demonstrations in 1970, unarmed Black students at Jackson State were murdered by police. At Kent State, White students were murdered by National Guardsmen. In the latter two instances, the evidence gathered by government agencies clearly indicated that the lives of the law enforcement officers and Guardsmen were never in danger and that the men who did the shooting got together after the event and agreed to tell investigators the false story that their lives had been in danger. In both cases, state grand juries refused to indict the murderers but did indict demonstrators, including several who had been wounded.[10]

The list of killings could go on, but the pattern remains the same: law enforcement agents have used lethal weapons against antiwar activists, ghetto protestors, rebellious prisoners and political radicals, none of whom were armed, a few of whom were reported to be hurling rocks or making "obscene gestures." In almost every instance, an "impartial investigation" by the very authorities responsible for the killings exonerated the uniformed murderers and their administrative chiefs. The few killers who are indicted are not usually convicted.

Political dissenters in the military are often meted out harsh treatment; they have been denied access to socialist publications, confined to quarters, subjected to racial insults, physically threatened, given the least desirable assignments, framed on trumped-up charges, courtmartialed and incarcerated in the stock-

9. *New York Times*, December 12, 1968; also Jack Nelson and Jack Bass, *The Orangeburg Massacre* (New York: World, 1969). A federal grand jury refused to indict any of the highway patrolmen involved in the action.

10. I. F. Stone, "Fabricated Evidence in the Kent State Killings," *New York Review of Books*, December 3, 1970, p. 28. After much public pressure the Justice Department indicted the Guardsmen involved in the Kent State killings. However, the judge threw the case out without even hearing the defense, arguing that the prosecution had proven excessive and unjustified force had been used against the students but had not shown that the Guardsmen had acted with premeditation to punish or deprive students of their constitutional rights. *New York Times*, November 9, 1974. Guardsmen who admitted to having lied under oath in an earlier state grand jury investigation were never tried for perjury. See Peter Davies, "Kent State Questions," *New York Times*, May 4, 1976.

ade.[11] Similarly, persons who organize and develop a political consciousness in prison do so at the risk of their lives. The rebellion at New York's Attica State Penitentiary in 1971 against inhumane conditions revealed the murderous force of the state. Asserting that the uprising was the work of "revolutionaries," Governor Nelson Rockefeller ordered an armed assault by troopers. The attack was not planned to minimize the loss of life; no safeguards were taken to avoid excessive use of force; and no check against violent reprisals by guards was imposed. Blasting their way into the prison yard, the troopers killed thirty-three inmates and ten prison guards who were being held as hostages and wounded more than a hundred other inmates. Not a single gun was found among the prisoners. A Special Commission on Attica declared the assault to be "the bloodiest attack by Americans on Americans" since the 1890 U.S. Army massacre of Indians at Wounded Knee.[12]

Among those singled out for special oppression have been members of the American Indian Movement (AIM), a group that has persistently challenged the injustices accorded Native Americans.[13]

The case of Russel Means, AIM leader, is instructive. Within a five-year period, Means was pistol whipped by a sheriff while getting out of a car; assaulted and arrested by tactical squad police because, as a spectator in court, he refused to stand when the judge entered, then convicted of "rioting" and sentenced to four years because of the courtroom incident; faced with four other trials with sentences threatened of more than 111 years; shot in the back by a police agent while a candidate for election on an Indian reservation; shot again as he rode in a car, the sniper's bullet grazing his forehead; arrested and charged with murder after visiting a bar to buy a six-pack of beer—even though the dying victim told police

11. See Robert Sherrill, *Military Justice Is to Justice as Military Music Is to Music* (New York: Harper and Row, 1970).

12. Annette T. Rubinstein, "Attica Now," *Monthly Review*, January 1976, pp. 12–20. In the next four years the state spent $10 million to prosecute sixty-two of the surviving inmates on charges as serious as kidnapping and murder. Two convictions were won; several were lost by the prosecution and fifteen indictments had to be dropped for lack of evidence. No guards or troopers were indicted for the murders committed against inmates after the take-over of the prison yard.

13. *Workers World*, July 4, 1975. In one 48-hour period, twenty AIM activists, over a three-state coordinated raid, were imprisoned and charged with such felonies as "assault with intent to kill" and "criminal syndicalism" and held under cash bonds of as high as $50,000. See *Workers World*, March 14, 1975.

that Means had not been in the bar when the shooting occurred; and forced out of a house he was visiting by unidentified armed men who shot and wounded him and another AIM activist "at close range in an execution attempt," as one witness put it.[14]

Along with the club and the gun, the state has more subtle instruments of oppression. One of these is the grand jury. Supposedly, grand juries are groups of citizens who weigh prosecution evidence to see whether there are sufficient grounds for a trial. Intended to protect the innocent from unjustifiable prosecution, the grand jury has been turned into its very opposite, usually doing what the prosecutor wants.[15] A common device is to grant a witness immunity from prosecution. The Fifth Amendment right against self-incrimination ceases to apply, and if one refuses to testify, one can be imprisoned for contempt. The upshot is to turn anyone into an involuntary informer regarding any conversation or activity to which she or he has been privy. Persons who refuse to answer questions when visited by FBI agents (and no one is obliged to talk to any law officer) are often summoned before a grand jury. The purpose is not to begin prosecution for a specific crime, but to carry out "fishing expeditions" against dissenters in the hope of turning up unexpected violations of law and to intimidate persons engaged in political activities and jail those who refuse to cooperate. Within three years the Justice Department ran more than one hundred grand juries in over eighty cities, subpoenaing some two thousand witnesses. People have been required to appear with little or no notice, without benefit of counsel and without being told the nature of the investigation. They can be forced to answer any question about political ideas and associations with friends, neighbors or relatives—or face up to eighteen months in prison without trial.

14. *Workers World*, July 4, 1975; *News and Observer* (Raleigh, N.C.), July 17, 1975; *Guardian*, April 14, 1976; *Workers World*, May 14, 1976. Dennis Banks, another AIM leader, has faced a succession of false charges and assassination attempts. Among the many Indian dissidents who face jail sentences or have been incarcerated are Leonard Crow Dog, Darlene Nichols Banks, Darelle Butler, Robert Robideau, Anna Mae Aquash, Russell Redner, Ken Loudhawk and Leonard Peltier. See Rusty Conroy, "Indian Activists Framed," *Guardian*, March 3, 1976. Another AIM member, Dick Marshall, was convicted in the same barroom shooting involving Means by an all-White jury on the basis of testimony by an FBI informer and several witnesses who have since changed their testimony. Marshall had accompanied Means into the bar; the shooting victim had not identified him as the attacker. He is now serving a life sentence at hard labor.

15. John Conyers, Jr., "Grand Juries: The American Inquisition," *Ramparts*, August/September 1975, p. 15.

Socialists and other dissenters also encounter oppression within the "private sector" of society. Employment oportunities, job tenure, and professional certification may often depend on how well one conforms to the sociopolitical attitudes of those who control the jobs. Employees who agitate for better working conditions or enunciate unpopular political opinions risk loss of job. Professionals who take unpopular stands, such as doctors who show themselves sympathetic to socialized medicine or lawyers who sympathetically defend socialists, may become the objects of professional sanction and harrassment. At numerous universities, students and faculty who espouse Marxist or other unorthodox political ideas have been hounded by campus police and university authorities. Students seldom get the opportunity to investigate the world from an anticapitalist perspective, since the bulk of their readings and almost all their instructors are either ignorant of, or hostile to, socialist perspectives. Socialist faculty members usually find their contracts not renewed. At Dartmouth College in 1969, a dozen radical faculty members regularly met together for lunch, but within three years all but one had been terminated—a dramatic but not unique example of the quiet purge conducted on campuses throughout the nation.[16]

Our government also protects us from ideas imported from abroad. In recent years a score of Marxist scholars, novelists, artists and union leaders, including people like Ernest Mandel and Carlos Fuentas, have been denied visas and prevented from entering the United States to participate in cultural events and conferences to which they had been invited by private groups.

Agents of National Insecurity

At least twenty well-financed federal agencies (of which the FBI and the CIA are only the best publicized) and hundreds of state and local police units actively engage in the surveillance, infiltration, entrapment and suppression of dissenting groups.[17] The Army

16. For summaries of repressive actions on campus, see Michael Miles, "The Triumph of Reaction," Change, The Magazine of Higher Learning, 4, Winter 1972–1973, p. 34; and J. David Colfax, "Repression and Academic Radicalism," New Politics, 10, Spring 1973, pp. 14–27.

17. See Frank Donner, "The Theory and Practice of American Political Intelligence," New York Review of Books, April 22, 1971, p. 27. A good collection of studies of government repression is Theodore Becker and Vernon Murray (eds.), Government Lawlessness in America (New York: Oxford University Press, 1971). See also Michael Parenti, "Creeping Fascism," Society, 9, June 1972, pp. 4–8; and Murray Levin, Political Hysteria in America (New York: Basic Books, 1971).

employs an estimated 1,200 agents for *domestic* spying. Counterinsurgency methods developed by the government for use in other lands are applied at home to combat civil disturbances caused by racial minorities, student radicals and striking workers. The Army has contingency plans enabling it "to strike concurrently at rioters in as many as 25 major cities."[18] The Justice Department's Law Enforcement Assistance Administration provides electronic sensors, wall-penetration surveillance radar, voice-print equipment, night-vision devices, command and control systems, television street surveillance systems and other electronic materials, at an estimated yearly cost of more than $400 million, to police departments throughout the nation. One of the fastest growing commodity markets involves the sale of counterinsurgency equipment to U.S. police. The unrestricted adoption of surveillance technolgy by police moved one Rand Corporation engineer to speculate that "we could easily end up with the most effective, oppressive police state ever created."[19]

In cities like Philadelphia and Chicago and even in smaller urban areas where organized crime and corruption are rife, the new police units have devoted more time to radicals, hippies and politically conscious Blacks than to mobsters or violent criminals. The Berkeley police budget was doubled between 1967 and 1970, yet over that same period there was a 65 percent rise in major criminal offenses, including burglary, rape and murder, and a 5 percent decrease in arrests for these offenses from the previous year. The Berkeley police were simply too interested in pursuing drug users, hippies, "street people" and radicals to worry about ordinary crime. (Drug arrests of youth increased by 231 percent.)[20] In most urban areas, according to Illinois Police Superintendent James McGuire, there are more police "on political intelligence assignments than are engaged in fighting organized crime."[21] The same seems true of federal law officers, which might explain why agencies like the FBI have such lackluster records in battling the organized rackets. Files stolen from a Media, Pennsylvania, FBI office in 1971 and subsequently published revealed that a great portion of FBI

18. *New York Times*, March 5, 1972.
19. Quoted in Robert Barkan, "New Police Technology," *Guardian*, February 2, 1972. See also Les L. Gapay, "Pork Barrel for Police," *Progressive*, March 1972, pp. 33–36, for data on law enforcement technology.
20. Frank Browning, "They Shoot Hippies, Don't They?" *Ramparts*, November 1970, p. 14.
21. Quoted in Donner, "The Theory and Practice of American Political Intelligence," p. 28 *fn*.

work in the mid-Atlantic region was directed against Black militants, White radicals and antiwar organizers. Relatively little attention was being given to organized crime.

As long as street gangs confined their activities to rape, robbery and burglary within the inner-city communities, they had relatively little trouble from the police. But when these gangs began to become radicalized, as did the Devils Disciples and the Young Lords in Chicago and New York, they became the objects of intensive police intimidation and attack. Here we might understand one reason why law officers cannot win the "war against crime"—they are not engaged in it, being too busy protecting us from the "Red Menace."

The intelligence business is a massive enterprise. By 1976 government agencies were expending approximately $10 billion a year on intelligence at home and abroad. This is, at best, a rough estimate, since Congress has no exact idea how much money organizations like the CIA are spending or for what purposes.[22] Millions of dossiers are kept on individuals suspected of harboring unorthodox political views. Data on political dissenters are shared by federal, state and local intelligence units and are sometimes fed to the press and to employers, landlords and others who might have opportunity to harass the persons under surveillance.[23]

"Justice," as the late FBI chief J. Edgar Hoover said in a 1970 television interview, "is merely incidental to law and order. It's a part of law and order but not the whole of it." Indeed, the whole of it, the indispensable goal of law and order, Mr. Hoover made clear on many occasions, is the preservation of the American socioeconomic status quo. In pursuance of that goal, the FBI has conducted hundreds of illegal burglaries against dissident individuals and organizations, stealing private files, letters and documents, while

22. See the excerpts from the report of the House Select Committee investigating the CIA, published in the *Village Voice*, February, 16, 1976. The CIA officials questioned by the Committee refused to state the size of their budget.

23. *New York Times*, October 3, 1975. In 1974 the Senate Judiciary Committee discovered that at least fifty-four federal agencies had data banks (few of which were authorized by law) containing over a billion pieces of personal information about Americans, primarily of a political nature. In addition, more than 2,500 private dossier companies maintain secret files on over 100 million Americans. These "credit" companies are protected by law from one's efforts to see one's own file and challenge its accuracy. Yet some of them will give information to anyone claiming to be a potential employer or creditor. See James B. Rule, *Private Lives and Public Surveillance* (New York: Schocken, 1974).

repeatedly denying any knowledge of such crimes.[24] As the *New York Times* noted: "Radical groups in the United States have complained for years that they were being harrassed illegally by the Federal Bureau of Investigation and it now turns out that they were right."[25] FBI agents have infiltrated leftist organizations and liberal ones including the Southern Christian Leadership Conference and Americans for Democratic Action with the intent of sabotaging their operations. Undercover agents have fomented ideological divisiveness among political groups, instigated violent conflict between rival Black militant groups and planted false information identifying prominent members of political organizations as federal agents.[26]

At the behest of every President from Franklin Roosevelt to Richard Nixon, the FBI supplied secret dossiers, conducted wiretaps and carried out physical surveillance of White House political opponents, journalists, Congressmen and members of congressional staffs.[27] The Bureau infiltrated and spied on several labor unions in an attempt to brand them as "communist controlled."[28] At a time when organized crime was expanding its operations in New Jersey, FBI officers in that state were working at fever pitch, planting false information and in other ways attempting to drive a scoutmaster in Orange, N.J., from his job, their reason being that he might contaminate young minds because his wife was a socialist.[29] The FBI keeps a "security index," a list of 15,000 persons, mostly members of leftist groups, who are slated for arrest and detention in case of a "national emergency." Although the law authorizing this practice was declared unconstitutional, the Bureau still maintains the detention list—despite statements to the contrary by its director.[30]

In contrast to the way they treat the left, the FBI and the

24. *New York Times*, September 26, 1975, March 29 and June 24, 1976. FBI agents continued to conduct illegal break-ins even after being ordered to stop by FBI Director Clarence Kelley, *New York Times*, August 11, 1976.
25. *New York Times*, November 24, 1974.
26. *New York Times*, November 24, 1974, and January 29, 1975; *Guardian*, April 2, 1975; *Chicago Tribune*, January 5, 1975. Among the persons whom the FBI tried to hound and defame was the late civil rights leader Martin Luther King. See the *New York Times*, November 19, 1975. An FBI undercover agent in the Black Panther party in Chicago provided the information needed for the police attack which killed Panther leaders Mark Clark and Fred Hampton. *Guardian*, May 22, 1974, and April 14, 1976.
27. *New York Times*, December 4, 1975.
28. *New York Times*, February 24, 1975.
29. *New York Times*, March 23, 1975.
30. *New York Times*, August 3 and October 25, 1975.

police have given a free hand to, or actually assisted right-wing extremists. Thus the Bureau provided information and encouragement to organizations like the Minutemen and the John Birch Society in their harassment campaigns against progressive groups. In San Diego, the FBI created and financed a crypto-fascist outfit called the Secret Army Organization (SAO) whose members were heavily armed with automatic weapons and explosives. All SAO activities, ranging from burglary and mail theft to bombings, kidnapping, assassination plots and attempted murder, were conducted under the supervision of the FBI.[31] Bureau agents infiltrated the Ku Klux Klan and took part in numerous acts of racist terrorism and violence, including the killing of a civil rights activist. According to the sworn testimony of one undercover informer, the FBI rarely acted to head off violent Klan attacks against Blacks and civil rights workers despite advance notice.[32]

Supposedly it is the left's propensity for violence that brings it into confrontations with the law: more truthfully, it is the left's propensity for challenging the established interests. Violence as such has never bothered the FBI or the police; it depends on who is using it against whom. To note a few of many such instances: in 1973 the Center for Cuban Studies in New York City was shattered by a bomb. Right-wing Cuban exile groups had repeatedly threatened to blow up the center, but the FBI made no arrests and instead harassed members of the center with interrogations. In 1974, when two Chicano socialists were killed by bombs planted in their respective cars, the FBI made no arrests. A powerful bomb wrecked the offices of several progressive and civil-libertarian groups in New York, injuring three people; the police made only a perfunctory investigation.

The Unidos Bookstore in the East Los Angeles Chicano community was bombed twice. A group calling itself the provisional wing of the American Nazi party publicly claimed credit for the first attack, but the police failed to arrest anyone. A progressive book store in Venice, California, was the target of a fire bomb. Police arrived a half hour after being called. No arrests were made.[33]

The largest army of domestic political spies is not in the FBI

31. *San Francisco Examiner*, January 11, 1976.
32. *New York Times*, December 3, 1975; *Workers World*, December 12, 1975.
33. For accounts of some of these incidents see the *Guardian*, December 12, 1973, March 12 and May 21, 1975.

but in the local police "red squads" operating throughout the country. Two hundred of these political intelligence units in almost every major American city belong to the federally funded Law Enforcement Intelligence Unit, through which they exchange files and other information. Investigations of red squads in cities like Detroit, Chicago, New York, Washington, D.C., Indianapolis and Baltimore reveal the same dismal record of unlawful burglaries and wiretapping, infiltration of groups engaged in no illegal activity, aid to right-wing terrorist organizations and attacks against the left.[34]

The Central Intelligence Agency matches the FBI and the red squads in its readiness to violate the rights of Americans. The CIA's legal mandate is to act as an overseas intelligence-gathering agency. It is prohibited from engaging in domestic spying. But it was revealed in 1974 that the Agency was heavily involved in extensive domestic intelligence work, including wiretapping and break-ins, and that it had collected dossiers on at least 10,000 Americans involved in antiwar and other protest activities.[35] In addition, (1) for twenty years the CIA opened the mail of private citizens. Agency officials knew it was illegal and took measures to conceal it. (When the FBI found out about the program, it became an active participant.) (2) The CIA infiltrated the campaign organizations of candidates running for Congress and admitted to maintaining active surveillance on members of Congress. (3) The CIA has given thousands of dollars to private corporations but has refused to disclose the purpose of such payments. The Agency also owns a complex of insurance companies whose profits are secretly invested in private securities. (4) The CIA has conducted electronic and physical surveillance of newspaper reporters to find out their sources of information concerning government practices. The Agency has infiltrated various news services, and at least forty overseas American correspondents are in the pay of the Agency. (5) The Agency has maintained several hundred college faculty on its payroll, even after President Johnson issued a ban on this practice in 1967, and is deeply involved in the operations of non-profit "educational centers" and foundations.[36] The CIA has infiltrated

34. *Guardian*, March 24, 1976.
35. *New York Times*, December 22, 1974.
36. See the *New York Times*, March 6, June 11 and December 29, 1975, January 26, 1976. For an early study of the CIA see David Wise and Thomas B. Ross, *The Invisible Government* (New York: Random House, 1964).

student, labor, scientific and academic groups, has secretly financed the writings of "independent" scholars and has subsidized publishing houses and periodicals (e.g., *Encounter*). CIA agents were staff members of the Michigan State University research programs for the early U.S. ventures in Vietnam. The Center for International Studies at MIT was financed in part by the CIA. And numerous local police departments around the country have received training in surveillance, detection and counterinsurgency from the CIA, all despite the congressional prohibition against domestic activity.

In 1975–1976 it was revealed that: the White House and the Treasury and Commerce departments were infiltrated by CIA agents; the CIA had been experimenting with LSD on unsuspecting subjects for nine years and was responsible for the death of at least one government employee; the Agency was involved in the southeast Asia heroin trade and had talked the Justice Department into dropping an indictment against a CIA agent charged with smuggling 100 pounds of opium into the United States; it had used notorious Mafiosi gangsters to assist in CIA assassination plots against Fidel Castro; and it retained a stockpile of poisonous gas despite a previous presidential order to destroy it.[37]

The CIA's crimes against the peoples of other nations are too numerous to record here in any detail. In places like Latin America, the CIA has used military force, terror and sabotage to bring down democratically elected governments and install right-wing dictatorships that were friendly to American corporate interests. It has infiltrated and fractured the trade union movements of other nations. It has funded secret armies, death squads and "destabilization" campaigns. It has been involved in the assassination of popular activists and heads of state. And it has meddled in the electoral processes of other nations, financing conservative parties and various reactionary movements.[38]

37. *New York Times*, June 11 and 20, 1975, July 9 and 10, 1975, April 13, 28 and 29, 1976. The two Mafia gangsters agreed to appear before a Senate committee about their involvement with the CIA, but one was gunned down in June 1975 shortly before he was slated to testify and the other, after testifying, was found murdered gangland style in July 1976.

38. For exposes of the CIA see Victor Marchetti and John D. Marks, *The CIA and the Cult of Intelligence* (New York: Knopf, 1974); and Philip Agee, *Inside the Company: CIA Diary* (London: Allen Lane, 1975).

Watergate:
"The System Works"—for Itself

In June 1972 a group consisting mostly of ex-CIA agents, some of whom were associated with President Nixon's campaign staff, were caught breaking into the Democratic party headquarters in the Watergate building in Washington. Subsequent investigations revealed that the burglary was only a small part of an extensive campaign involving political espionage, electoral sabotage, wiretapping, illegal entry, theft of private records, destruction of campaign finance records, illegal use of funds, perjury, conspiracy to obstruct justice and other such acts, planned and directed by members of Nixon's campaign staff and White House staff and directly implicating the President himself. Testimony by persons close to the President alleged that Nixon withheld for a month evidence of a break-in at the office of Daniel Ellsberg's psychiatrist and may have even ordered it, that he tampered with the judge presiding over the "Pentagon Papers" trial of Ellsberg and Russo by offering him the directorship of the FBI while the trial was still in progress, that he failed to respond to warnings from his acting FBI director, Patrick Gray, who informed him of cover-up efforts by high-placed members of the White House staff, and that he himself had engaged in cover-up activities.

Nixon denied the charges made against him and there the matter might have stood: the President's word against those of several underlings. Most likely Nixon would have survived in office, albeit as a weakened President. But then it was discovered that tapes of all Oval Office conversations had been maintained, and these revealed that Nixon had known all along about the Watergate cover-up, had been engaging in cover-up activities and had been lying to the public. In August 1974, facing impeachment proceedings in the House of Representatives, Nixon resigned from office. Gerald Ford, the man he picked as Vice-President to replace Spiro Agnew (who had himself been forced to resign not long before), succeeded to the presidency and promptly pardoned Nixon.

Other high-placed persons found guilty in the Watergate affair, such as Herbert Kalmbach, Jeb Magruder and John Dean, were given sentences of four to six months.[39] Former Attorney General Richard Kleindienst, who committed perjury before a Senate committee regarding his role in related matters, was allowed to plead guilty to a misdemeanor count of "failing to testify fully,"

---

39. Tom Wicker in the *New York Times*, January 10, 1975.

was given a thirty-day suspended sentence and a $100 fine—and won praise from the judge for being an outstanding public servant.[40]

For some reason, not long after Nixon retired to his San Clemente estate with his presidential pardon and a yearly $55,000 pension, many opinion makers were announcing with satisfaction that "the system worked." Apparently they believed the tapes would be there again next time. But how did the system work? It was not only Nixon and his aides who attempted to limit the Watergate crisis to save their necks; Congress and even the press, which is credited with exposing the scandal, played a part in downplaying Watergate, first by not making any kind of investigation for half a year after the break-in,[41] then by emphasizing Nixon's personal role and defining the events in narrow ways. The press and Congress focused on Nixon's failure to pay his income taxes, his personal corruption in appropriating funds for his estate, his use of illegal campaign funds and his attempts at cover-up. Little attention was given to the President's repeated violations of the Constitution, his unlawful and genocidal bombing of Cambodia, his assassination of foreign leaders, his unlawful campaign to destroy radical groups, his use of political sabotage and denial of civil rights to leftists and others and the unlawful cover-up role played by the entire intelligence community including the FBI and CIA.[42]

In addition, Congress and the press used Watergate to legitimate the system by treating it as a unique and unprecedented instance of government lawlessness. In fact, there was very little that was unprecedented about it. For more than half a century the same illegal and clandestine tactics have been and continue to be employed against political heretics. What shocked the establishment politicians was that in this instance the crimes were committed against a segment of the establishment itself—specifically,

40. With the exception of E. Howard Hunt and G. Gordon Liddy, persons implicated served sentences ranging from several months to less than two years. See the *New York Times*, August 3, 1974.

41. It was probably only because of the persistent efforts of two cub reporters on the *Washington Post* that Watergate did not die a quiet death. For their own account see Bob Woodward and Carl Bernstein, *All the President's Men* (New York: Simon and Schuster, 1974). Critical analyses of Watergate and the Nixon administration are found in J. Anthony Lukas, *Nightmare: The Underside of the Nixon Years* (New York: Viking, 1975); and Jonathan Schell, *The Time of Illusion* (New York: Viking, 1976).

42. S. F. Bay Area Kapitalistate Group, "Watergate or the Eighteenth Brumaire of Richard Nixon," *Kapitalistate: Working Papers of the Capitalist State*, 3, Spring 1975, pp. 3–24; also Noam Chomsky, "Watergate and Other Crimes," *Ramparts*, June 1974.

the Democratic party and mass media newsmen. (The White House's use of such criminal activities was consistent with Nixon's claim that he had the "inherent executive power" under the Constitution to commit even unlawful acts when impelled by considerations of national security. And "national security" seemingly embraced every conceivable area of political activity.)

Rather than taking steps to prevent future Watergates, Congress and President Ford initiated measures to insure that a Watergate *exposure* would not happen again. Political leaders seemed to want not only to ignore the abuses of power that brought on the crisis but to ratify them into law. Thus Ford proposed, and Congress considered, bills that would make it a crime for anyone in government to give the public and the press access to classified information. The problem of the abuse of power is solved to the satisfaction of those in power by making sure no one ever again discovers the abuses. There will continue to be Watergates but no more Watergate scandals.

The Congress and the President have responded in a similar manner to the exposes about FBI and CIA crimes. Former CIA director Richard Helms was absolved of the crime of perjury even though he had lied under oath to a Senate committee when he denied that the CIA was involved in domestic spying and denied that it had taken part in overthrowing the democratic government in Chile. In March 1976 the White House decided against prosecuting those involved in assassination plots against foreign leaders, referring to the issue as a "deep hole." Neither the Senate nor House reports on the CIA offered a full account of the Agency's subversive and violent tactics abroad, nor a critique of why the CIA functions in the lawless manner it does. Rather the Agency's crimes were treated as "excesses" to be rectified by closer executive and legislative "oversight" and promises of restraint from the CIA itself.

Having seen the dangers of the police state loom with a new vividness during the Nixon administration, Congress busied itself codifying that police state into the S-1 bill, a product of the Mitchell-Kleindienst Justice Department. The bill threatened to remove many of the safeguards protecting political dissent and the right to assembly. It provided severe penalties for riots or the utterance of words that could be interpreted as incitement to riot. A "riot" was defined as involving as few as ten persons whose conduct "creates a grave danger of imminently causing" damage to property. The S-1 bill permitted conviction of defendants for crimes committed as a result of improper pressure from police agents—previously considered unlawful entrapment. It legalized wrongdoing by public officials when the crime was covered by "an official grant of express permission." (Under this provision the Watergate burglars would have gone free.) By 1976 public opposition to S–1 was so strong that congressional sponsors talked of amending and renaming the bill, then temporarily shelved it until after the presidential elections.

The response of congressional leaders to the attempted takeover of the nation by the executive branch has been to increase the power of the executive branch; their response to being completely deceived has been to increase government secrecy; and their response to the dangers of a secret police has been to issue the secret police a license for even wider action.[43] Unable and unwilling to stop police state crimes, Congress seemed prepared to make them legal.

Nor is the trend likely to reverse itself without a great deal of popular agitation and mass protest. As economic conditions worsen and popular discontent deepens, the necessity for tighter controls becomes more urgent. Unable to satisfy the needs of the people, the establishment must suppress or neutralize growing pressures for change. But it is difficult to have a "nice" repression. If it is the unenviable task of police to keep a lid on the anger and frustration of the victims of economic, racial and political oppression—a task assigned to them by those in power—then criminal acts by law officers inevitably occur. If it is the job of law officers to suppress radical political ideas and organizations and keep surveillance on every imagined political "troublemaker," then it is not long before the police, the FBI, the CIA, Army Intelligence and other such units begin to see the Constitution as little more than an obstacle to be circumvented or brushed aside. Before long, the state's security forces become a law unto themselves.

By now, it should be apparent that what is called "law and order" is a system of authority and interest that does not and usually *cannot* operate with equitable effect. The laws are themselves *political* rulings and judgments, the outcome of a legislative process that is most responsive to the pressures of the politically stronger, as we shall see. Rather than being neutral judgments, laws are the embodiment of past political victories and therefore favor the interests of the victors. The law is inevitably an out-

43. For a good statement on this see "Notes and Comment," *New Yorker,* April 26, 1976, p. 30.

growth of the established order which produced it, and by its nature it serves the established interests far better than the unestablished ones. When discussing law and order, then, it is imperative to ask *whose* law and *whose* order we are talking about. While the courts, the security forces and the lawmakers claim to be protecting order as such, they really are protecting a particular kind of order, one that sustains the self-appointed, self-perpetuating oligarchs who rule most of our economic, technological, educational and social institutions.

Psycho-controls for Law and Order

In their never-ending campaign to control behavior that is unacceptable to the existing order, authorities have moved beyond the clubs, bullets and eavesdropping devices of the police and are resorting to such things as electroshock, electrode implantations, mind-destroying drugs and psychosurgery. Since the established powers presume that the present social system is a virtuous one, it follows that those who are prone to violent or disruptive behavior, or who show themselves to be manifestly disturbed about the conditions under which they live, must be suffering from *inner* malfunctionings which can best be treated by various psycho-controls. Not only are political and social deviants defined as insane, but sanity itself has a political definition. The sane person is the obedient one who lives in peace and goes to war on cue from his leaders, is not too much troubled by the inhumanities committed against people, is capable of fitting himself into one of the mindless job slots in a profit-oriented hierarchical organization and does not challenge the established mores and conventional wisdom. If it happens that he actually has been victimized by class conditions—if, for instance, he has been raised in poverty, has received no education, has been repeatedly discriminated against because of his race, cannot find decent housing or employment and sees his children go hungry and his family and his life falling apart—then he must be able to handle these distresses without resorting to aggressive and troublesome behavior or other such "abnormalities." Most individuals treated by psycho-control methods are selected because of their socially deviant and "disturbed" (i.e., disturbing) attitudes and behavior.

What is called sanity or insanity, normal or abnormal, in many cases is a *political* judgment made by privileged medical professionals and other institutional authorities loyal to the status quo. Seldom do they manifest any awareness of the class, racial, sexual and political biases influencing their supposedly "scientific" diagnoses. Their eagerness to work with law enforcement authorities reflects the ideological presumption under which they operate. Since they accept the present politico-economic system as a good one, then anything that increases its ability to control dissident and unhappy persons—whose rebellion is rarely thought of as a justifiable response to an unjust social system—is also seen as good. One scientist financed by Washington, José Delgado, has proposed a billion-dollar government project to control minds through the use of electrode implants. Delgado already has experimented on human beings in mental institutions and has demonstrated his ability to produce placid, euphoric persons through electrical brain controls. His vision is of a "psycho-civilized society" in which disruptive emotions are done away with by electric controls.[44]

Among the psycho-control methods employed, probably the most inhumane is psychosurgery, a treatment that modifies behavior by destroying brain cells. About six hundred psychosurgical operations are performed each year, and the number is rising. In most cases, drastic personality changes result: individuals become placid and compliant; their emotions are greatly dulled; they become less able to cope with new situations, have disoriented reactions to things around them and suffer a marked deterioration in intelligence.[45] Dr. Walter Freeman, known as the "Dean of Lobotomies," admitted that men who receive psychosurgery find it difficult to get a decent paying job, and women find it easier to do housework and make good housekeepers.[46] Of the psychosurgery performed on the nonprison population, women make up the majority of cases.

After the Detroit ghetto rebellions in 1967, three doctors of the Harvard Medical School, leading proponents of psychosurgery, urged that "violent slum dwellers" be subjected to intensive clinical study and corrective "treatment." These same doctors eventually headed the Neuro-Research Foundation in Boston, funded in part

44. José M. Delgado, *Physical Control of the Mind: Toward a Psychocivilized Society* (New York: Harper and Row, 1969).
45. "Violence upon the Brain, Information on the New Lobotomists," unpublished monograph prepared by the Greater Boston Medical Committee for Human Rights, circa 1972. Although hailed as a new method for treating mental illness, psychosurgery is nothing more than the lobotomies of the 1930s and 1940s with some minor technical improvements and a new name.
46. *Liberation*, July/August 1976, p. 39.

by a $100,000 grant from the Law Enforcement Assistance Administration in the Justice Department. The foundation's function is to diagnose and treat persons who are "potentially violent offenders," both those with "brain diseases" and the "nondiseased."[47] It is interesting to note that among the victims of psychosurgery in recent years was a twenty-seven-year-old Black man who had been arrested in the very Detroit rebellion which so disturbed the Harvard lobotomists. He allegedly had threatened a policeman with a broken bottle. He was found mentally unfit for trial and committed to a mental hospital. But his psychiatrist at the hospital found that much of his mental trouble stemmed from head injuries suffered when police beat him after he was arrested.[48]

Prison inmates who are proponents of revolutionary or Black nationalist ideas or who have engaged in organizing protests among fellow inmates have been singled out for psycho-control programs. Prisoners like the socialist Stephen Kessler, charged with disrupting a federal penitentiary by "promoting racial unity, collectivizing the inmate population, attempting to secure legislative inquiries . . . into prison conditions and being involved with outside radical groups," are placed in "behavior modification" units to be subjected to mind-altering drugs, beatings, forced rectal searches, prolonged shackling, isolation and other tortures.[49] In the words of one Oklahoma prisoner: "As long as prisoners confine themselves to gambling, shooting dope, running loan rackets and killing each other, everything is fine. Let them pick up a book on Marx's theory of dialectical materialism and they are immediately branded a communist agitator and locked in solitary confinement."[50]

Behavior-modification programs use several approaches. One technique is to put the prisoner in solitary confinement under excruciating conditions of filth, cold, insufficient food and sensory deprivation and make piecemeal improvements in each of these conditions as a reward if he develops the kind of attitude and behavior patterns desired by the authorities. The conversion must be a "sincere" one and inmates are forced to make repeated and ever more heartfelt confessions of their "criminal and destructive attitudes." "Reformed" prisoners are then forced to harass, oversee

47. Quoted in "Violence upon the Brain . . ."
48. "Behavior Control: Psychosurgery Widespread," *Guardian*, April 28, 1976.
49. *New York Times*, February 20, 1974; *Guardian*, January 21, 1976.
50. Letter from Chuck Stotts, inmate in Oklahoma State Prison, *Liberation*, February 1975, p. 5.

and inform upon their fellow inmates and engage in marathon sessions to help break other prisoners. Those who refuse to cooperate are once more subjected to behavior modification torture themselves.[51]

Another method is "aversion therapy." By the use of electric shock, a prisoner is made to associate pain with whatever the authorities consider bad. In Vacaville, California, inmates accused of homosexuality are shown erotic gay films and shocked whenever a polygraph indicates the prisoner is sexually aroused. Drugs which induce a death panic by paralyzing one's breathing for a couple of minutes are sometimes used.[52] A group of prisoners in one behavior-modification program wrote: "Anyone who has spent any amount of time in [Dannemore State Hospital] must know at least one person who was sent for punishment, and returned with the mind of a vegetable or moron if he returned at all."[53] Eddie Sanchez, who became a socialist while in prison, wrote from the behavior-modification unit at the federal penitentiary in Marion, Illinois: "Since I've been confined here on and off since 1971, I've personally seen over two dozen men driven insane. . . . Others have been driven to suicide or attemps at suicide.[54]

"Hyperkinetic" children, guilty of "rebellious" behavior in schools, orphanages or reformatories, have been the victims of psychosurgery. More commonly, hyperactive children—many of whom come to school hungry, physically ill, and under emotional stress from growing up in impoverished, unhappy slum conditions—are treated with amphetamines and with drugs like Ritalin and Enterovioform, "whose safety has never been documented and whose efficacy has never been proved."[55] Among the ninety-nine symptoms of hyperactivity or "minimal brain dysfunction" listed by the "experts" are such vague and questionable categories as: general awkwardness, slowness in finishing work, foot-tapping, wriggling, insistent questioning, interest in sexual matters and "spotty or patchy" intellectual defects.[56] From 500,000 to 1 million

51. Mark Kleiman, "Drugs Replace Clubs in Nation's Prisons," *Guardian*, May 29, 1974.
52. Joel Meyers, "Electrode Torture and Starvation: Legal 'Therapy' in U.S. Prisons," *Workers World*, May 25, 1973, p. 6.
53. Letter by Dannemora inmates Chester Gibson, Isaac Richards, Felix Huerta, Che Avada, Juke Elmore, Makau-Chuh Champelle in *Workers World*, May 25, 1973, p. 15.
54. Letter to *Workers World*, November 15, 1974.
55. "Minimal Brain Dysfunction (MBD): Social Strategy or Disease?" unpublished report by the Medical Committee for Human Rights, New York, n. d.
56. Peter Schrag and Diane Divoky, *The Myth of the Hyperactive Child*

school children are being treated with drugs, at a yearly profit of many millions to the drug industry and with side effects like weight loss, growth retardation and acute psychosis.

All kinds of drugs are pushed onto the American public to keep people tranquillized and compliant. One of the worst is methadone. Given to addicts as a heroin substitute, it is even more difficult to stop using than heroin and just as damaging to the body and mind. The difference is that it is legal. As noted in an earlier chapter, doctors and businessmen have become millionaires by running methadone clinics. The government pays the costs, choosing methadone maintenance in preference to other programs, such as acupuncture, that can actually cure. Thus tens of thousands of low-income Blacks, Latins and Whites remain under state control and are forced to report regularly for their doses. For a time, Lincoln Detox, a community-operated program in New York City was making startling breakthroughs in the cure of addicts by using acupuncture and by getting addicts to see the social and political roots of their victimization. Then in 1974 the doctor in charge of that program, Richard Taft, an acupuncture expert, was found drugged to death and thrown in a closet. He had been on his way to a meeting with a top government drug program administrator, one Dr. Peter Bourne, a former Green Beret in Vietnam who returned to the United States, suddenly became active as a "radical" for a brief time, subsequently was appointed by then-Governor Jimmy Carter to head Georgia's methadone program and later served as number two man in Nixon's "war on drugs" campaign. Bourne was suspected by ex-addicts from Lincoln Detox of being an undercover agent and of involvement in Dr. Taft's murder. New York police never investigated Taft's death, ruling it a "suicide."[57] Lincoln Detox subsequently had its funds cut.

Other kinds of medical aggression are perpetrated against poor people, especially racial minorities. Frequently doctors perform sterilization on low-income women without their knowledge or consent. One out of every seven Native American women of childbearing age is sterilized. Some 35 percent of the women in Puerto Rico have been sterilized, many involuntarily. In parts of

(New York: Pantheon, 1975). Much hyperactivity in children has recently been traced to artificial flavorings and colorings in foods. Often hyperactivity diagnosed in school-aged children disappears miraculously when they leave school, suggesting that school is not just the setting but the cause of extreme nervousness in many children.

57. *Guardian*, May 19, 1976. This chilling story has received almost no exposure in the establishment press.

North Carolina and South Carolina, Black girls whose mothers are on welfare are routinely sterilized when they turn fifteen.[58] In Alabama two Black girls, aged twelve and fourteen, were sterilized after their illiterate mother put her "X" on a document she could not read, under the impression she was signing a permission slip for vaccination.[59]

Of the institutions devoted to repression and control, none is more pernicious than the mental hospital. There are almost four times more people in mental institutions than in prisons, and 90 percent of them are confined involuntarily. Like prisoners, they compose a population notably devoid of white middle-class Americans. Legal protections for mental patients are even less sound than those afforded ordinary criminals. In many instances commitment comes without the benefit of investigation, trial or other procedural safeguards, and is based on "medical" considerations that betray a marked class and racial bias.[60] A worker in a New York State mental hospital offers this testimony:

One Black woman was admitted . . . because she began screaming at the landlord who had come to evict her and her several children. . . . The Bureau of Child Welfare took her children. This upset her even more. She came to the Admissions Committee, crying, hysterical and angry. Obviously a "paranoid schizophrenic," as the racist officials would label her. The comfortable middle-class psychiatrist said so, and after all he knows. . . .

Patients [upon release] are often secured jobs working for companies which pay them considerably less than other workers. Social workers advise the patient not to join unions and "make trouble" or they will be returned to the hospital.[61]

When a Black woman GI, Babette Payton, protested the job assignments and work reports she was being given, she was committed by her commander, a psychiatrist, to an Army mental hos-

58. Claudia Dreifus, "Sterilizing the Poor," *Progressive*, December 1975, pp. 13–18; also Liberation News Service, "Welfare Ordered Sterilization," *Guardian*, June 11, 1975.

59. *New York Times*, June 28 and August 1, 1973.

60. See Bruce J. Ennis, "Mental Commitment," *Civil Liberties*, October 1969, p. 3; Thomas Szasz, *Law, Liberty and Psychiatry* (New York: Macmillan, 1963); Seymour Halleck, *The Politics of Therapy* (New York: Science House, 1971); Ronald Leifer, *In the Name of Mental Health* (New York: Science House, 1969).

61. "Mental Hospitals and the Poor," *Workers World*, December 25, 1970, p. 7. The author is identified only as a "woman worker" within the hospital.

pital for "chronic schizophrenia." Payton decided to go AWOL rather than submit to the order. "Having worked in an Army psychiatric clinic, I know that if you're not crazy when you go in, you're crazy when you come out," she said. Lawyers defending her intended to show that mental health facilities were often used to imprison dissidents.[62] Certainly such was the case with the Air Force sergeant who was placed in a psychiatric ward by his commanders after he said he wanted to file court-martial charges against President Nixon during the Watergate affair.[63]

As already noted, inmates in federal and state prisons are frequently transferred to mental hospitals for the "criminally insane" because of their political beliefs and rebellious ways, and they may end up staying many years after their prison terms expire. Others are brought in for having committed sexually deviant or other taboo acts, including using marijuana. Many are incarcerated on the testimony of hostile relatives, school authorities, social workers or police. In places like the Correctional Institution at Bridgewater, Mass., inmates are forced to live naked in barren cells without bed or toilet. Many are subjected to the sadistic sport of the guards. Some who are quite rational when they first arrive eventually begin to deteriorate.[64] Presumed insane (guilty) by virtue of their presence in the institution, they find it impossible to prove their sanity (innocence). The very protests they make against their oppression are taken as symptoms of illness. One reporter records these impressions of his visit to Bridgewater:

One could see a man walking in a small circle, round and round [in his cell]. "He doesn't talk to anyone any more," my guide said. "He just walks in circles now."

"And before?"

"I don't know just what he's supposed to have done. He used to be all right though. I remember when he came in, he was rational, could carry on a conversation, all that stuff. Then the doctor started telling him he'd be out of here soon. Every month or so they'd say he'd get out that month. Went on like that for two years. Then one day he stopped talking. No contact with anyone after that. He's been like that for years now."

62. *Guardian,* March 26, 1975.

63. Associated Press news release, Washington, D.C., September 10, 1973.

64. Frederic Wiseman did a prize-winning documentary film of Bridgewater entitled *Titicut Follies;* it is so devastating that authorities succeeded in having it banned in the state of Massachusetts. See the review by Robert Coles, "Stripped Bare at the Follies," *New Republic,* January 20, 1968, pp. 18, 28–30.

We walked on down the hall. The guide told me about one 60-year-old inmate who had been in since the age of 7. His offense: running away from home. . . . This was the section for killers, I had been told, so I asked what [one] thin man had done.

"He painted a horse. . . . It was in a field. A live horse. He was drunk and somebody bet him he couldn't make a horse look like a zebra, I think, so he painted it and they put him here. For being drunk, probably."

"How long has he been in?"

"Thirty-seven years. By the time they got around to letting him out he really was crazy. . . . For his own good we just can't let him go out of here."[65]

Police, judges, surveillance technicians, psycho-surgeons, drug-pushing school authorities, prison guards and the attendants in mental institutions all have one thing in common: they work to make the world safe for those on top by exercising arbitrary power over those below—all in the name of peace and security, normality and well-being, law and order.

65. Bruce Jackson, "Our Prisons Are Criminal," *New York Times Magazine*, September 22, 1973, pp. 54, 57.

The Mass Media: By the Few For the Many

10

THE FORCE OF LAW IS ONLY ONE OF the means used by the ruling elites to keep the populace in tow. There are the more subtle, powerful controls exercised over the very ideas and images in our heads. Most of the institutions of society propagate the values and myths of the established order, censoring out information that does not fit the accepted view of reality, while feeding us the notions and symbols which do.[1]

An important means of controlling what people think is through the mass media of newspapers, magazines, movies, radio and television. It is said that a free and independent press is a necessary condition for democracy, and it is frequently assumed that the United States is endowed with such a press. While the news in "totalitarian" nations is controlled, we Americans supposedly have access to a wide range of competing sources. In reality, the controls exerted over the media in the United States, while more subtle and less severe than in some other countries, leave us with a press that is far from "free" by any definition of the word.

The news media are important to any study of American politics. They select most of the information and misinformaton that help us define sociopolitical reality. Almost all the political life we experience is through the media. How

1. For an analysis of how people are socialized into the established political system and how institutions are agents of that socialization, see Michael Parenti, *Power and the Powerless* (forthcoming).

we view issues—indeed, what we even define as an "issue" or "event"—what we see and hear and what we do *not* see and hear are greatly determined by those who control mass media. By enlarging our vision through technology, we have actually surrendered control over much of our own sensory experience.[2]

It is argued that the media are not a crucial factor in political life: one can point to the many Democratic presidents who won elections despite the overwhelming endorsement of their Republican opponents by the press. But despite a low rate of editorial endorsement, Democratic candidates manage to buy political advertisements and receive coverage during their campaigns, unlike Socialist candidates, who receive almost no exposure and almost no votes. The argument also overlooks the subtler, more persistent role played by the media in defining the scope of respectable political discourse, channeling public attention in certain directions and determining—in ways that are essentially supportive of the existing socioeconomic structure—what is political reality.

He Who Pays the Piper

Who controls the mass media? Five New York banks (Chase Manhattan, Morgan Guaranty Trust, First National City, Bankers Trust and the Bank of New York) own controlling shares in the three national television and radio networks (NBC, CBS, ABC) and are powerful shareowners of the *New York Times, Time,* Columbia Pictures and Twentieth Century-Fox. These banks have representatives on the boards of the three networks and control all network fiduciary and debt financing functions. The networks themselves exercise a controlling interest over publishing houses, film companies and recording companies. They own television stations located in key urban areas, reaching a lion's share of the national audience.

Of the "independent" stations, 80 percent are network affiliates. Practically the only shows these "independents" produce are the local evening newscasts, the rest of their time being devoted to network programs. Most of the remaining "independents" are affiliated with NET, the "educational" network, which receives almost

2. Robert Cirino, *Don't Blame the People* (New York: Vintage, 1972), pp. 30–31. Cirino's book is a well-documented study of how the news media censor and distort the news. For a study of how the corporations control the media, see Herbert I. Schiller, *The Mind Managers* (Boston: Beacon Press, 1973).

all its money from the Ford Foundation (controlled largely by the Morgan and Rockefeller banks) and a few allied foundations. Ford Foundation picks NET's board of directors and reserves the right to inspect every program produced with Ford money.

Newspapers show the same pattern of ownership with most of the big circulation dailies being owned by chains like Hearst, Gannett and Copley. In the last twenty years some thirty-three dailies have disappeared. As of 1972, only 4 percent of American cities had competing newspapers under separate ownership. And in cities where there is a "choice," like Chicago with its four dailies, the newspapers are usually conservative in editorial policy. Most of the "independent" dailies rely on the wire services and big circulation papers for syndicated columnists and for national and international coverage. Like television stations, they are "independent" more in name than in content.[3]

Although declining in number, newspapers are doing quite well as business ventures. Through mergers, packaged news service and staff cutting, the larger conglomerates have paid off handsomely, grossing many billions in advertising revenues. The same is true of television. Despite recession, net sales of CBS rose 13 percent in 1974, and net income reached $108.5 million[4] In sum, the big media are big business, manifesting the same symptoms of high profits and centralized ownership. Like most of corporate America, control of the media is principally in the hands of the Morgan and Rockefeller financial empires. And like other businesses, the media corporations are diversified and multinational, controlling film, television and radio outlets throughout Latin America, Asia and the Middle East.[5]

The primary function of the media is not to keep the public informed but, like any business, to make money for their owners, a goal seldom coinciding with the need for a vigilant, democratic press. This is not to imply that those who control the media are indifferent to its political content. Quite the contrary: the influence of big-business ownership is reflected in its political content. The media are given over to trivialized "features" and gossip items. Coverage of national and local affairs is usually scant, superficial and oriented toward "events" and "personalities," consisting of a

---

3. See James Aronson, *Packaging the News, A Critical Survey of Press, Radio, TV* (New York: International Publishers, 1971).

4. *1974 Annual Report to the Shareholders of CBS Inc.*, p. 3.

5. Herbert Schiller, *Mass Communications and American Empire* (New York: Augustus M. Kelley, Publishers, 1969).

few short "headline" stories and a number of mildly conservative or simply banal commentaries and editorials. As one group of scholars noted after a study: "Protection against government is now not enough to guarantee that a [person] who has something to say shall have a chance to say it. The owners and managers of the press determine which person, which facts, which version of the facts, and which ideas shall reach the public."[6]

The business-owned media have little to say about the relationship of the capitalist system to pollution, bad housing, poverty and inflation; the relations between political and business leaders; and the role of the multinational corporations in shaping American interventionist policy abroad. No positive exposure is given to the socialist alternatives emerging throughout the Third World or the socialist critique of capitalism at home.

Many interesting documentaries made by independent film producers, dealing with racism, women's oppression, nuclear energy, conditions in prisons and mental hospitals, labor struggles, poverty, the FBI and U.S. imperialism, reveal a side of reality highly critical of the established order. Few of them have been shown in commercial movie houses or on the major television networks.[7]

Journalists, columnists and telecasters who occasionally report facts troublesome to the established interests have had their copy censored by superiors. Relying on institutional authorities for much of their information, newspersons are disinclined to be critical of these sources. A police reporter learns to see local crime from the perspective of the police and prosecution. News reports on business developments rely mostly on business and allow little space for the views of organized labor or consumers. Reports about State Department or Pentagon policies rely heavily on State Department and Pentagon releases. Media coverage of the space program uncritically accepts the government's claims about the program's de-

6. *A Free and Responsible Press* (Report by the Commission of Freedom of the Press, 1947), quoted in Cirino, *Don't Blame the People*, p. 47.

7. Andrew R. Horowitz, "Playing Monopoly with the News," *More*, March 1975, pp. 16–17 and 23. A few critical documentaries have been aired on public television stations, and in the last fifteen years two have been produced and shown by CBS: *Hunger in America* (1968) and *The Selling of the Pentagon* (1971). A documentary on the Vietnam war, *Hearts and Minds*, won international acclaim and an Academy Award, yet its producer, Columbia Pictures, refused to give it much distribution and its director, Peter Davis, has had trouble getting financial backing for another film. See Andrew Kopkind, "Hollywood Politics: Hearts, Minds and Money," *Ramparts*, August/September 1975, p. 46.

sirability and seldom gives exposure to the arguments made against such costly ventures. In general, most of what is reported as "news" is nothing more than the transmission of official views to an unsuspecting public.

Far from being vigilant critics, most newspersons share the counterrevolutionary, anti-Communist assumptions and vocabulary of the ruling class that employs them. For years the press has propagated support for cold war policies and attitudes, including hatred and fear of the Soviet Union and of socialism, and the domestic witch hunting and red-baiting that culminated in McCarthyism, loyalty oaths, the Korean war and U.S. involvement in Southeast Asia.[8]

Consider how the Vietnam war was covered. From 1945 to 1954 the United States spent several billions supporting a ruthless French colonialism in Vietnam, but the American public was never informed of this. In the following decade the United States assumed full responsibility for the maintenance of the South Vietnam dictatorship, but the public neither read nor heard a word of debate in the media about this major policy commitment. In 1965 the United States began a massive buildup of ground forces in Vietnam, but Americans were told that the troops were merely a small support force. The *New York Times* and other major news agencies knew the real nature of the buildup but felt it was in the "national interest" to keep this information from the public.[9] Reporters who covered the Vietnam war were expected to "get on the team," that is, to share the military's view of the war and its progress—and most of them did.[10] From at least 1965 on, American forces engaged in massive destruction of the Vietnamese countryside, resorting to indiscriminate saturation bombings, defoliation, free fire zones, and the wholesale killing of civilians. Yet is took years before these facts became widely known. Stories by journalists describing how American soldiers slaughtered hundreds of defenseless women, children and old people in the village of My Lai were turned down by the

8. James Aronson, *The Press and the Cold War* (Boston: Beacon Press, 1973); and Michael Parenti, *The Anti-Communist Impulse* (New York: Random House, 1970).

9. Robert Cirino, *Power to Persuade: Mass Media and the News* (New York: Bantam, 1974), p. 63.

10. The few reporters who challenged U.S. military operations in Vietnam, such as David Halberstam and Neil Sheehan, were not opposed to U.S. interventionism. They were quite committed to it but argued for a more flexible and more effective anti-communist policy in Southeast Asia. See Allen Young, "The Press: Theirs and Ours," *Liberation*, July/August 1973, pp. 55–57.

wire services, several national magazines and news weeklies, one network and major newspapers in New York and Boson.[11]

Throughout the Vietnam war, the insurgent forces were described as the "enemy," although it was never explained why they deserved to be so considered. Reporters who pride themselves on their "objectivity" saw cities "fall" to the "enemy" when they could have as easily viewed them as "liberated," or merely changing political hands.[12] Communists "nibbled" and "gobbled" territory and engaged in "terror" attacks, but the war of terror waged by U.S. forces was never labeled as such. During April 1975, as insurgent forces achieved a final victory in Vietnam, the U.S. public was bombarded with stories of refugees fleeing from the "invading communists." But a story buried in the back pages of the New York Times noted that most refugees reported they were fleeing because they feared the return of U.S. bombings or simply wanted to get away from the fighting. Almost none mentioned fear or hatred of communism as a cause for flight.[13] Yet the media continued to give the American public a contrary impression. During this period the press talked constantly of the impending "bloodbaths" that would supposedly occur when the communists took over in Vietnam, Cambodia and Laos. Subsequent reports by Westerners who remained in these countries revealed that the massacres never materialized. But this fact also was buried in the back pages of newspapers, if reported at all.[14]

Ten years before, there was a real bloodbath in Indonesia when right-wing military leaders, with the aid and guidance of the CIA, took power and slaughtered an estimated 250,000 to 500,000 peasants, workers, students, communists and progressives of all kinds, according to reports by Westerners who witnessed the events. The massacres continued for months, followed by mass arrests. Yet the U.S. media ignored this genocidal campaign and portrayed the military takeover as a move toward "stable" government and an improvement over the previous left-leaning regime.

---

11. More than a year and a half after My Lai, the story was finally broken by Dispatch News Service. See Cirino, Power to Persuade, p. 61–62.

12. Andrew Kopkind, "The Press at War," Ramparts, August/September 1975, p. 37.

13. New York Times, March 26, 1975.

14. See Newsweek, August 18, 1975; and Time, February 16, 1976. For an excellent treatment of how the Vietnam war was redefined in retrospect as a "mistake" and criticized by the press, as an "unsuccessful" venture, see Noam Chomsky, "The Remaking of History," Ramparts, August/September 1975, pp. 30–35, 49–53.

Generally, the U.S. press has defamed leftist movements and governments throughout the world and supported those "staunch" right-wing governments that are the allies of the multinational corporate system.[15] The view from the newsroom is essentially the view from the Pentagon and the CIA. As noted in the preceding chapter, at least forty overseas correspondents working for American news agencies are also in the pay of the CIA. Thus the "objective" news we get is often doctored to serve the ideological purposes of the cold warriors.

The workings of the capitalist political economy remain another area largely uncharted by the news media. The need to invest surplus capital; the falling rate of profit; the drive toward profit maximization; the tendency toward instability, recession, inflation and underemployment—these and other such problems are treated scantily, if at all, by newspersons and commentators who have neither the knowledge nor the permission to make critical analyses of multinational corporatism. Instead, economic adversity is ascribed to innocent and unavoidable causes such as "hard times." One television commentator put it this way: "Inflation is the culprit and in inflation everyone is guilty."[16]

There are few progressive and no socialist commentators in the mass media. In contrast, reactionaries, militarists and ultra-rightist elements have an estimated $14-million yearly propaganda budget donated by some 113 business firms and 25 public utilities, and each week across the country they make over ten thousand television and radio broadcasts—with much of the air time freely donated by sympathetic station owners.[17] In one three-week period the ultraconservative billionaire H. Ross Perot was able to present his viewpoints "supporting President Nixon's Vietnam policy in 300 newspapers with full-page advertisements and in a half hour television program. His qualifications? He had the $1 million it required."[18]

On the infrequent occasions when liberals muster enough money to buy broadcasting time or newspaper space, they still may be denied access to the media. Liberal commentators have

15. For a critique of how the U.S. press distorted the news about the leftist movement in Portugal, see Michael Parenti, "Portugal and the Press," *Progressive*, December 1975, pp. 43–45.

16. Garner Ted Armstrong, "Channel Nine News," Ithaca, N.Y., February 11, 1976.

17. Arnold Forster and Benjamin Epstein, *Danger on the Right* (New York: Vintage, 1964), p. 273.

18. Cirino, *Don't Blame the People*, p. 299.

been refused radio spots even when they had sponsors who would pay. A group of scientists, politicians and celebrities opposing the Pentagon's antiballistic missile program was denied a half hour on television by all three major networks despite the fact that they had the required $250,000 to buy time. On various occasions the *New York Times* would not sell space to citizens' groups that wanted to run advertisements against the war tax or against the purchase of war bonds. A *Times* executive turned down the advertisement against war bonds because he judged it not to be in the "best interests of the country."[19]

Denied access to the media, the political left has attempted to get its message across through local newspapers and magazines of its own, but this "undergound press" has suffered many financial difficulties and official harassments. In Cambridge, Mass., street vendors for the *Avatar* were arrested fifty-eight times within a short period on trumped-up charges, and newsstand owners, under threat of arrest, refused to carry the paper, thus causing a sharp decline in circulation. In Atlanta the radical newspaper *Great Speckled Bird* was subjected to repeated police harassments; its offices were then attacked by unknown persons three times and were finally destroyed by fire bombs. Police, of course, seemed unable to find a clue as to who did it. In San Diego the *Street Journal and San Diego Press* suffered bullets through its office windows, theft, destruction of equipment, fire bombings and repeated staff arrests on charges that were later thrown out of court. In Urbana, Ill., the editor of the *Walrus* was arrested for nonpossession of his draft card and imprisoned for three years. In the same city a radical printing cooperative was burglarized and destroyed by unknown persons. And in Peoria, Ill., another printer of radical publications had his press closed by authorities under a seldom enforced zoning law.[20]

The Politics of Entertainment

While the entertainment sector of the media, as opposed to the news sector, supposedly has nothing to do with politics, entertain-

19. *Ibid.*, pp. 90, 302.
20. Most of these incidents are reported in Aronson, *Packaging the News,* pp. 67–69. See also the *Guardian*, May 17, 1972, and the *Militant*, January 21, 1972. The information on Illinois is from my own observations.
21. Eric Barnouw, *The Television Writer* (New York: Hill and Wang, 1962), p. 27.

ment programs in fact undergo a rigorous political censorship. Shows that treat controversial antiestablishment subjects have trouble getting sponsors and network time.[21] In the late 1960s the "Smothers Brothers Comedy Hour," after being cut several times for introducing antiwar comments and other mildly liberal statements, was eventually removed from the air. Songs containing references to drugs, prison conditions, junk foods, the draft and opposition to the war have been cut from entertainment shows.[22] When Dick Cavett interviewed several New Leftists in 1974, his show was cut by ABC because it was "one-sided," a ruling never applied to progovernment and antiradical presentations. When David Susskind submitted five thousand names of people he wished to have appear on his talk show to the advertising agency that represented his sponsor, a third of the candidates were rejected because of their political viewpoints. The censorship code used by Proctor and Gamble for shows it sponsored stated in part: "Members of the armed forces must not be cast as villains. If there is any attack on American custom, it must be rebutted completely on the same show."[23]

While political critiques are censored out of entertainment shows, there is plenty of politics of another sort. In soap operas and situation comedies, adventure programs and detective stories, comic strips and children's cartoon shows, conventional American values are preached and practiced.[24] In the media world, adversities are caused by ill-willed individuals rather than by the economic and social system in which they live, and problems are solved by individual effort within the system rather than collective effort against it. Demonstrators, radicals, revolutionaries and foreign agents are seen as menacing our land and the military and police as protecting it. In an episode of "Kojak" on CBS, the tough cop was pitted against a terrorist Puerto Rican organization whose members were characterized as violent fanatics and assassins. The organization's name was "El Comite," the same as a Puerto Rican group founded in 1970 and committed to socialism. Shortly after the show was aired, the ever-alert FBI began a series of harassing raids on the homes of real-life members of El Comite.[25] Thus life imitates art.

22. See Cirino, *Don't Blame the People*, pp. 305–306, for various examples.
23. Murray Schumach, *The Face on the Cutting Room Floor*, quoted in *ibid.*, pp. 303–304.
24. See Rose Goldsen, *Television, The Product Is You* (New York: McGraw-Hill, 1977) for an excellent treatment.
25. " 'Kojak' Attacks El Comite on CBS," *New American Movement*, February 1975.

In the world of Hollywood and television, establishment figures like judges, businessmen, doctors and police are fair and competent—never on the take, never on the make, never corrupt, bigoted or oppressive. Or, if there *are* a few bad ones, they are soon set straight by their more principled colleagues. Various kinds of aggressive behavior are indulged in and even glorified. Conflicts are resolved by generous applications of violence. Nefarious violence is met with righteous violence, although it is often difficult to distinguish the two. The brutal and often criminal behavior of law officers is portrayed sympathetically, as one of those gutsy realities of life. One study of "cop and crime" shows found that police actions habitually violate the constitutional rights of individuals. ". . . The message communicated is that evil may be subdued by state-sponsored illegality."[26] The profound importance of the concept of due process is lost as TV police carry out illegal searches and break-ins, coerce suspects into confessing, and regularly use homicidal violence against criminals in shoot-em-up endings. Violence on television and in Hollywood films is omnipresent, often linked to sex, money, dominance, self-aggrandizement and other attributes that represent "manliness" in the male-chauvinist, capitalist American culture.[27]

In the media, women appear primarily in supportive roles as housewives, secretaries and girl friends. They usually are incapable of initiating actions of their own; they get into difficulties from which they must be extricated by their men. When not treated as weak and scatter-brained, women are likely to be portrayed as devious, dehumanized sex objects, the ornaments of male egoism. In media advertisements women seem exclusively concerned with getting a fluffy glow shampooed into their hair, waxing "their"

26. Ethan Katsh and Stephen Arons, "Television, the Law and the Police," *Wall Street Journal,* July 22, 1975; also Jerome L. Singer and Dorothy G. Singer, "A Member of the Family," *Yale Alumni Magazine,* March 1975, pp. 10–16. In 1976 "cop and crime" shows constituted 30 percent of prime time television.

27. The typical hour of TV network programing contains 7.43 violent episodes. Forty people are murdered every week; the wounded and assaulted are too numerous to contemplate. Saturday morning television, expressly designed for children, averages one violent act every three-and-a-half minutes. See Media Action Project findings reported in the *Guardian,* October 15, 1975; also *Liberation,* July/August 1976, p. 39; and Joseph J. Seldin, "The Saturday Morning Massacre," *Progressive,* September 1974, pp. 50–52. Studies show that adults become more belligerent after large doses of TV violence and more fearful of racial minorities, cities and criminal attack. See Richard Saltus, "The Research Shows Cop Shows Make Us Violent," *Leisure,* February 21, 1976, p. 22; and much of the work done by George Gerbner.

floors, making yummy coffee for hubby, getting Johnny's clothes snowy white, and in other ways serving as mindless, cheery handmaidens. Of late there have been a few programs featuring women as lawyers, police and other such lead characters, but even these women still play predominantly sexist roles, operating in an exclusively male-defined world devoid of feminist values and oblivious to the oppressions of women.

The mass media are also the White media. For years Blacks and other racial minorities were allowed no appearance on television or radio except in such shows as "Amos 'n' Andy," which specialized in Negro dialect stereotypes, or "Beulah," the Black maid in a White family "who looked as though she'd been taken off a package of pancake mix."[28] More recently, Blacks have been appearing in TV commercials living in make-believe integrated suburbs, in "superstud" detective movie roles and in comedy series like "Sandford and Son," an updated, slicker version of "Amos 'n' Andy." What is missing is any treatment of life as it is lived by the great mass of ordinary Black people in rural areas and urban ghettos. Most programs about Blacks are created by middle-class Whites who are guided by their own stereotyped notions of how Blacks live and feel.

As mentioned earlier, working-class people in general, be they White, Black, Chicano or whatever, have little representation in the entertainment media except as uncouth, ignorant persons, hoodlums, buffoons, servants and other such stock characters. The tribulations of working-class people in this society—their struggle to make ends meet, the specter of unemployment, the lack of decent recreational facilities, the machinations of unscrupulous merchants and landlords, the loss of pensions and seniority, the battles for unionization and union reform, the dirty, noisy, mindless, dangerous, alienating quality of industrial work, the abuses suffered at the hands of bosses, the lives wrecked and cut short by work-connected injury and disease—these realities and others relating to class struggle and class exploitation are not deemed worthy of dramatic treatment in the business-owned media.

One-fifth of all television time is taken up with commercials that characterize people as loudmouthed imbeciles whose problems are solved when they encounter the right medication, cosmetic, cleanser or gadget. In this way industry confines the social imagina-

28. Bob Ray Sanders, "Black Stereotypes on TV: 25 Years of 'Amos 'n' Andy'," *New American Movement*, February 1975, p. 9.

tion and cultural experience of millions, teaching people to define their needs and life-styles (and those of hubby, wifey and baby) according to the profit dictates of the commodity market.[29]

Not all air time is given to commercial gain. The Federal Communications Commission (FCC) requires that broadcasters set time aside for "public service announcements." The obligation is a vague one; the FCC has never denied any station its license for failing to live up to it, despite complaints from community groups. About 3 percent of air time, worth a half-billion dollars, is given to public service announcements. This free time, like the free space donated by newspapers and magazines, is monopolized by the Advertising Council, a group composed of representatives from the networks, the national magazines, the top advertising agencies and the big corporations. No public interest groups are represented on the Council's board.

While supposedly "nonpartisan" and "nonpolitical," the Council's "public service" commercials laud the blessings of free enterprise and urge viewers to buy U.S. Savings Bonds. The ads tell us that business is "doing its job" in hiring veterans, minorities and the poor. Workers are exhorted to take pride in their work and produce more for their employers—but nothing is said about employers paying more to their workers. The ads blame pollution on everyone (but not on industry) and define littering as the major pollution problem. Ecology and conservation are reduced to a fire prevention campaign led by Smokey Bear. Unemployment is a matter of better "job training." In general, social and political problems are reduced to individual failings or evaded altogether, and the air time that could be used by conservationists, labor, consumer and other public interest groups has been preempted by an Advertising Council which passes off its one-sided ads as noncontroversial.[30]

Repressing the Press

On those rare occasions when the news media expose the murky side of official doings, they are likely to encounter serious discour-

29. For a provocative study of how advertising has been used to create the kind of consumerism needed by capitalism, see Stuart Ewen, *Captains of Consciousness* (New York: McGraw-Hill, 1976).

30. Bruce Howard, "The Advertising Council: Selling Lies," *Ramparts*, December/January 1974–1975, pp. 25–32.

agements from public authorities. Government officeholders are inclined to treat news that places them in an unfavorable light as "slanted" and exert pressure on reporters to present the "accurate" and "objective" (that is, uncritical and supportive) viewpoint. Few political leaders have been more intolerant of the press than former President Nixon, who regarded all critical reporting of his administration as bordering on subversion. Despite the fact that 93 percent of the nation's newspapers had editorially endorsed him for President in 1972, and 99 percent had ignored the Watergate affair throughout the 1972 campaign, Nixon was convinced that the press was engaged in a personal vendetta against him especially when it began reporting about Watergate in 1973.

Nixon also professed little confidence in the people as such, observing that "the average American is just like the child in the family. . . . [If you] pamper him and cater to him too much, you are going to make him soft, spoiled and eventually a very weak individual."[31] Beset by such paternalistic concerns, the Nixon administration did its utmost to control the kind of information the childlike American was fed. Nixon's Vice-President, Spiro Agnew, repeatedly launched attacks upon the press. Agnew said nothing about the press' monopoly structure but criticized its occasional willingness to air facts and commentaries critical of the White House, a tendency that was certain evidence in his mind of a "liberal" bias and lack of "responsibility." This kind of attack by Agnew allowed the media to appear as liberal defenders of free speech against government censorship, instead of supporters of the established order as they more commonly have been.[32]

The Nixon administration used the FBI to harass and arrest newspersons who persisted in writing troublesome reports. The FBI approached various network executives concerning reporters who had done stories that displeased the President.[33] The White House tried to suppress publication of the Pentagon papers (which revealed how American intervention in Vietnam had been secretly shaped), and failing that, the administration carried out an un-

31. *New York Times*, November 10, 1972.
32. Cirino, *Don't Blame the People*, makes this point.
33. David Wise, "The President and the Press," *Atlantic*, April 1973, pp. 55–64. One reporter, Leslie Whitten, was arrested on trumped-up charges by the FBI after pursuing stories about ITT and CIA collusion in the Chile coup and ITT illegal contributions to the Nixon campaign. See Stephen Torgoff, "Press Freedom in Danger," *Guardian*, February 14, 1973. In 1974 the Justice Department subpoenaed the personal notes and records of a *New York Times* reporter who was investigating the IRS and the Nixon campaign fund.

successful prosecution of Daniel Ellsberg and Anthony Russo, former government employees who had released the papers. The Justice Department won a Supreme Court decision requiring reporters to disclose their information sources to grand jury investigators, in effect, reducing the press to an investigative arm of the courts and the prosecution—the very officialdom over whom it is supposed to act as a watchdog. Dozens of reporters have since been jailed or threatened with long prison terms on the basis of that decision.[34]

Nixon successfully exerted pressure on the Public Broadcasting System to cancel almost all news analysis programs that the White House disapproved of.[35] The administration doubled second-class postal rates, thereby placing a serious burden on the small, unprofitable journals which offered the kind of opposition viewpoints seldom heard in the mass media. While defending the increase as an economy measure, the government continued the heavy postal subsidy of the more than 12 billion pieces of junk mail sent out every year by business and advertising firms.

Much government pressure on the media occurs outside the public view. On repeated occasions the government has subpoenaed documents, films, tapes and other materials used by news media. Such interference imposes a "chilling effect" on the press, an inclination to think twice before reporting something, a propensity—already evident in news reports—to slide over the more troublesome and damning aspects of a story and censor oneself in order to avoid censorship by those in power. One might recall how the president of CBS offered to cooperate more closely on news stories about the White House in return for government assistance in quashing a congressional contempt citation against CBS for its mildly critical documentary about the Pentagon.[36]

Attempts to control or fabricate the news were not unique to the Nixon administration. Presidents like Eisenhower, Johnson,

34. *United States* v. *Caldwell,* 33 L. Ed. 2d 626 (1972). To cite one instance: four news reporters of the *Fresno Bee* were jailed for indeterminate sentences in 1976 for refusing to disclose the news sources for materials published concerning the bribery of a city official. *New York Times,* September 4, 1976. After being held a week or so, they were released.

35. *New York Times,* April 24, 1973; and "Mr. Nixon and the Media" ("Playboy Forum" report), *Playboy,* April 1973, p. 61.

36. *Ithaca* (N.Y.) *New Times,* January 18, 1976. The story was originally broken by *Variety,* the entertainment trade newspaper. CBS had refused to hand over the outtakes (film clips not included in the final showing) to a House subcommittee. The network has since made no other documentary critical of any government agency or policy.

Kennedy and Ford repeatedly won the cooperation of the press in killing "sensitive" stories and planting favorable ones. Members of the press knew that our government was flying U-2 planes over Soviet territory; they knew that our government was planning an invasion of Cuba at the Bay of Pigs; they knew that there were facts about the Tonkin Bay incident in Vietnam which differed from the official version; they knew that the United States was engaged in a massive, prolonged saturation bombing of Cambodia. But in each instance they chose to act "responsibly" by not informing the American public. More recently it was disclosed that a dozen news organizations, at the behest of the CIA, suppressed their knowledge of the Glomar project—the attempted raising of a sunken Soviet submarine by the CIA.

The appeal made by Presidents, governors, mayors and legislators, that the press be more "responsible" (i.e., self-censoring) in what it prints, usually achieves its intended purpose. Thus the Ford administration's campaign to suppress or discredit stories of the CIA's illegal domestic operations and picture the Agency as an erring but basically worthy victim of those who leak its vital secrets won the assistance of most news media.[37] Likewise, the White House's claims in the summer of 1976 that the economy was bettering itself were dutifully and uncritically reported by the press, while information indicating the contrary was downplayed. "The old blather about 'responsibility' to keep secrets instead of exposing abuses has begun to creep back into press parlance," Jack Anderson noted. "The old pre-Watergate, pre-Vietnam ideals of partnership with government, of cozy intimacy with the high and mighty, of a camaraderie of secrets shared by this peerage but kept from the public, begins to appeal once more to a press concerned that its abrasive successes have earned it a bad name and a hostile reception."[38] "Journalistic responsibility" should mean the unearthing and dissemination of true and significant information. But the "responsibility" demanded by government officials and often agreed to by the press is the opposite, to suppress some piece of information precisely because it is true and significant.[39]

From what has been said so far it should be clear that one

37. For some critical discussions see Anthony Lewis, "In Defense of Seymour Hersh," *New York Times*, July 10, 1975. For other critical discussions see Ben H. Bagdikian, "The Story Beneath the Non-Story," *New York Times*, September 2, 1975; and Tom Wicker, "Defending Dan Schorr," *New York Times*, February 24, 1976.

38. Quoted in *Ramparts*, July 1975, p. 8.

39. Bagdikian, "The Story Beneath the Non-Story," makes this point.

cannot talk about a "free press" apart from the economic and political realities that determine who owns and controls the media. Freedom of speech means not only the right to hear both sides of a story (Republican and Democratic) but the right to hear *all* sides. It means not only the right to *hear* but the right to *be heard*, to talk back to those in government and in the network offices and newsrooms, something few of us can do at present.

What also should be clear to anyone who understands human communication is that there is no such thing as unbiased news. All reports and analyses are selective and inferential to some inescapable degree—all the more reason to provide a wider ideological spectrum of opinions and not let one bias predominate. If in fact we do consider censorship to be a loathsome danger to our freedom, then we should not overlook the fact that the media are *already* heavily censored by those who own and control them. Creative, imaginative, progressive, socialist, antiimperialist, communalist, anarchist, radical feminist, Third World and working-class themes are consistently programmed out of the media, while violent, competitive, macho, authoritarian, trivial, tasteless, individuated, privatized, consumeristic, capitalist, racist, progovernment themes are programmed in. The very process of selection allows the cultural and political biases and class interests of the selector to operate as a censor. Some measure of ideological heterodoxy could be achieved if public law required all newspapers and broadcasting stations to allot substantial portions of space and time to a diverse array of political opinion, including the most radical and revolutionary. But knowing what we do about what interests the law serves, this is not a likely development.

Ultimately the only protection against monopoly control of the media is ownership by community people themselves, with legally enforceable provisions allowing for the maximum participation of conflicting views. As A. J. Liebling once said: freedom of the press is guaranteed only to those who own the presses. In Europe some suggestive developments have taken place: the staffs of various newspapers and magazines like *Der Stern* in Germany and *Le Figaro* in France have used strikes to achieve greater editorial control of the publications they help to produce. And *Le Monde's* management agreed to give its staff a 40 percent share in the profits and a large share in managerial decisions, including the right to block any future sale of the paper.[40]

40. Aronson, *Packaging the News*, p. 99.

While they point to alternative forms of property control, these developments are themselves not likely to transform the property relations of a capitalist society and its mass media. With few exceptions, those who own the newspapers and networks will not relinquish their hold over private investments and public information. Ordinary citizens will have no real access to the media until they come to exercise direct community control over the material resources that could give them such access, an achievement that would take a different kind of economic and social system than the one we have. In the meantime, Americans should have no illusions about the "free press" they are said to enjoy.

The Sound and
the Fury: Elections,
Parties and Voters

11

AS NOTED EARLIER, MOST INSTITUTIONS in America are ruled by self-appointed, self-perpetuating business elites who are answerable to no one. Presumably the same cannot be said of *government*, since a necessary condition of our political system is the provision for the regular election of those who govern, the purpose being to hold officeholders accountable to the people who elect them. Whether or not the electoral process keeps government responsive to public needs is a question to be treated here.

The Harvesting of Votes

The harvesting of votes is the task of the political parties. The job has gone to persons who have enjoyed a class and ethnic familiarity with the common voters and who have been sufficiently occupied by the pursuit of office and patronage to remain untroubled by questions of social justice. Alan Altshuler describes the machine politicians:

Though they distributed favors widely, they concentrated power tightly. Though their little favors went to little men, the big favors went to land speculators, public utility franchise holders, government contractors, illicit businessmen, and of course the leading members of the machines themselves. . . .

The bosses were entrepreneurs, not revolutionaries. They provided specific opportunities for individual representatives of deprived groups, but they never questioned the basic distribution of resources in society. Their methods of raising revenue tended toward regressivity. On the whole, the lower classes paid for their own favors. What they got was a *style* of government with which they could feel at home. What the more affluent classes got, though relatively few of them appreciated it, was a form of government which kept the newly enfranchised masses content without threatening the socio-economic status quo.[1]

Today, machine politicians still perform little favors for little men but seldom address themselves to the larger problems facing ordinary citizens. Party regulars take "the existing socio-economic structure . . . as given," Dahl notes. They assume "that the physical and economic features of the city are determined by forces beyond their control."[2]

These same politcians, however, are quite ready to serve those "forces beyond their control." "When Mayor Daley took office," reports Banfield in his study of Chicago, "he immediately wrote to three or four of the city's most prominent businessmen asking them to list the things they thought most needed doing. . . . He may be impressed by the intrinsic merit of a proposal . . . but he will be even more impressed at the prospect of being well-regarded by the highly respectable people whose proposal it is."[3] The machine depends on the sufferance and direct aid of urban capitalist interests.[4] Since their primary concern is to maintain their own positions of influence within society's established order, machine politicians, like most churchmen, union leaders and college administrators, generally take a conservative approach, showing little sympathy for new and potentially disruptive demands and little taste for the kind of dialogue and confrontation that one associates with the democratic process. "The man who raises new issues," observed Walter Lippmann more than a half-century ago, "has been distasteful to politicians."[5]

1. Alan A. Altshuler, *Community Control: The Black Demand for Participation in Large American Cities* (New York: Pegasus, 1970), pp. 74–75.
2. Robert Dahl, *Who Governs?* (New Haven: Yale University Press, 1961), p. 94.
3. Edward Banfield, *Political Influence* (New York: Free Press, 1961), p. 251. For a critical study of the Daley administration, see Milton R. Rakove, *Don't Make No Waves—Don't Back No Losers* (Bloomington, Ind.: Indiana University Press, 1976).
4. Gerald Pomper, "The First, New-Time Boss" *Transaction*, January 1972, p. 56.
5. Walter Lippmann, *A Preface to Politics* (Ann Arbor: University of Michigan Press, 1962), p. 195. Originally published in 1914.

"The rigidity of the two-party system is, I believe, disastrous," added Lippmann. "It ignores issues without settling them, dulls and wastes the energies of active groups, and chokes off the protests which should find a civilized expression in public life."[6] That scathing judgment has stood the test of time. Today the two parties are still more ready to blur than clarify political issues. Electoral contests, supposedly providing democratic heterodoxy, have generated a competition for orthodoxy. In politics, as in economics, competition is rarely a safeguard against monopoly and seldom a guarantee that the competitors will offer the consumer a substantive choice.

This is not to say there are no differences between (and within) the major parties or that one party is not preferred by some people over the other. Generally the racial minorities, union workers, lower-income urban groups and more liberally oriented professionals support the Democratic party, while the White Protestant, rural, upper-income groups, big and small businessmen and the more conservative elements of the electorate make their home in the Republican party. These differences are sometimes reflected in the voting records of Democratic and Republican legislators, albeit within a narrow range of policy alternatives.

When magnified by partisan rhetoric, the differences between the parties appear worrisome enough to induce many citizens to vote—if not *for* then *against* someone. While there is no great hope that the party of their choice will do much for them, there persists the fear that the other party might make things even worse. This lesser-of-two-evils approach is perhaps the most important inducement to voter participation.[7] It is not quite accurate to characterize the Republicans and Democrats as Tweedledee and Tweedledum. Were they exactly alike in image and posture, they would have even more difficulty than they do in maintaining the appearances of choice. Therefore, it is preferable that the parties be fraternal rather than identical twins.

From the perspective of those who advocate "a fundamental change in our national priorities," the question is not, "Are there differences between the parties?" but "Do the differences make a

6. *Ibid.*, p. 197.
7. See Murray Levin, *The Alienated Voter* (New York: Holt, Rinehart and Winston, 1960), pp. 37–39. A similar sentiment was expressed by many low-income voters in Newark and New Haven when explaining their somewhat reluctant preference for the Democratic party. See my "Power and Pluralism: A View from the Bottom," *Journal of Politics*, 32, August 1970, p. 515.

difference?" For the similarities between the parties in organization, funding, ideological commitment and policy loom so large as frequently to obscure the differences. The Democratic and Republican parties are both committed to the preservation of the private corporate economy; the use of subsidies, deficit spending and tax allowances for the bolstering of business profits; the funneling of public resources through private conduits, including whole new industries developed at public expense; the concoction of domestic programs, supposedly to assist the less fortunate segments of the population, which provide little assistance to anyone but private contractors; the use of repression against opponents of the existing class structure; the defense of the multinational corporate empire and forceful intervention against social revolutionary elements

abroad. In short, Republicans and Democrats are dedicated to strikingly similar definitions of the public interest, at great cost to the life chances of underprivileged people at home and abroad.

Disagreements between the two parties focus principally on which of them is better qualified to achieve commonly shared goals within a narrow range of means. For instance, Democrats seek to insure profit growth, limit unemployment and induce economic recovery by increasing consumer spending and government purchases. The Republican approach is to maintain profit growth and stabilize budgets by limiting wages and cutting nonmilitary spending, especially social services like food stamps and Medicaid. Yet even this pattern is not a fixed one, for Republicans frequently support greater deficit spending for economic growth and Democrats resort to cutbacks for budgetary stability—as when Democratic Governor Brown of California called on people in 1975 to "work more for less" and vetoed programs for emotionally disturbed children, and liberal Democratic Governor Dukakis of Massachusetts cut welfare payments and institutional care for the mentally handicapped.

The similarities between the parties do not prevent them from competing vigorously for the prizes of office, expending huge sums in the doing. The very absence of significant disagreement on fundamentals makes it all the more necessary to stress the personalized, stylistic features that differentiate oneself from one's opponent. As with industrial producers, the merchants of the political system have preferred to limit their competition to techniques of packaging and brand image. With campaign buttons and bumper stickers, television commercials and radio spots, sound trucks and billboards, with every gimmick and ballyhoo devoid of meaningful content, the candidate sells his image as he would a soap product to a public conditioned to such bombardments.[8] His family and his looks; his experience in office and devotion to public service; his sincerity, sagacity and fighting spirit; his military record, patriotism and ethnic background; his determination to limit taxes, stop inflation, improve wages and create new jobs by attracting industry into the area; his desire to help the workingman, the farmer, and the businessman, the young and the old, the rich and the poor and especially those in between; his eagerness to fight poverty but curb welfare spending while ending government waste and corruption and making the streets and the world itself safe by strengthening our laws, our courts and our defenses abroad, bringing us lasting peace and prosperity with honor and so forth—such are the inevitable appeals which like so many autumn leaves, or barn droppings, cover the land, only to be collected and carted away each November.

The Two-Party Monopoly

The two major parties cooperate in various strategems to maintain their monopoly over electoral politics and discourage the growth

8. On the methods of selling a candidate as one might sell a commodity, see Joe McGinnis, *The Selling of the President 1968* (New York: Simon and Schuster, 1970). For an earlier collection of case studies of mass media merchandising of political issues and candidates, see Stanley Kelley, Jr., *Professional Public Relations and Political Power* (Baltimore: Johns Hopkins Press, 1956).

of radically oriented third parties. "Each views with suspicion the third party movements in America," writes one Washington observer. "Each in effect is committed to the preservation of the other as its chief competitor."[9] Republicans and Democrats understand that neither will go "too far"; neither will move beyond a narrow range of goals and means; neither has much appetite for the risks of social change; each helps to make the world safe for the other.

All fifty states have laws, written and enforced by Republican and Democratic officials, regulating party representation on the ballot. Frequently the provisions are exacting enough to keep smaller parties from participating. In order to win a place on the ballot, minor parties are required to gather a large number of signatures on nominating petitions, an expensive, time-consuming task. In some states they must pay exorbitant filing fees ($5,000 in Louisiana for an independent candidate) and observe exacting deadlines when collecting and filing nominating petitions. In Pennsylvania, in 1972, third-party candidates for statewide office had to obtain the signatures of 36,000 registered voters within a three-week period. Sometimes a 5-percent requirement for signatures of registered voters has been interpreted to mean 5 percent of voters from every district within the state—an impossible task for a third party whose base might be confined to a few urban areas. Persons who sign nominating petitions for unpopular third parties sometimes find their names publicized by town clerks in an effort to embarrass them into withdrawing their names, as happened in Vermont in regard to Communist party petitions. In some states voters who are registered with the major parties are not allowed to sign or circulate minor-party nominating petitions. Petitions are often thrown out on technicalities arising from ambiguities in election laws, compelling the minor party to pursue costly court battles which, whether won or lost, usually are decided *after* the election. Sometimes during primary time, minor parties are raided by large numbers of voters from the major-party organizations who take over the third-party ticket—as was done in 1947 by the Democrats against the American Labor party in New York.

The system of representation itself limits the opportunities of third parties. The single-member district elections used throughout most of the United States tend to magnify the strength of the major parties and the weakness of the smaller ones, since the party that polls a plurality of the vote, be it 40, 50 or 60 percent, wins 100

9. Douglass Cater, *Power in Washington* (New York: Random House, 1964), p. 180.

percent of a district's representation with the election of its candidate, while smaller parties, regardless of their vote, receive zero representation. This is in contrast to a system of proportional representation that provides a party with legislative seats roughly in accordance with the percentage of votes it wins, assuring minor parties of some parliamentary presence. Duverger notes that under the winner-take-all system "the party placed third or fourth is under-represented compared with the others: its percentage of seats is lower than its percentage of votes, and the disparity remains constantly greater than for its rivals. By its very definition proportional representation eliminates this disparity for all parties: the party that was at the greatest disadvantage before is the one to benefit most from the reform."[10]

The winner-take-all, single-member-district system not only deprives the minority parties of representation but eventually of voters too, since not many citizens wish to "waste" their ballots on a party that seems incapable of achieving legislative representation. Some political scientists argue that proportional representation is undesirable because it encourages the proliferation of "splinter parties" and leads to legislative stalemate and instability. In contrast, the present two-party system muffles rather than sharpens ideological differences and allows for the development of a consensus politics devoid of fragmentation and polarization. But one might question why the present forms of "stability" and "consensus" are to be treated as sacred. Stability is often just another word for "keeping things as they are." Whose stability and whose consensus are we talking about? And one might wonder whether stalemate and fragmentation—with their consequent ill effects on the public interest—do not characterize the *present* political system in many policy areas. Above all, the muting effects of the two-party system so thoroughly limit the arena of political choice and dialogue as to manufacture a "stability" and "consensus" that fail to represent the needs of large segments of the populace.

If, despite rigged rules and official harassments, radical groups

10. Maurice Duverger, *Political Parties* (New York: Wiley and Sons, 1955), p. 248 and the discussion on pp. 245–255; also E. E. Schattschneider, *Party Government* (New York; Holt, Rinehart and Winston, 1960), pp. 74–84. Not long after World War II, Benjamin Davis, a Communist elected to the city council in New York, lost his seat when the city shifted from PR to single-member districts. The change was explicitly intended to get rid of Davis and limit the growth of other dissident parties. Proposals were introduced to abolish PR in local elections in Cambridge, Mass., in 1972 after victories by a few radically oriented candidates.

continue to prove viable, then authorities are likely to resort to more violently coercive measures. Almost every radical group that has ever managed to gain some grass-roots organizational strength, from the Populist movement in the last century to the Black Panther party of today, has become the object of official violence. The case of the American Socialist party is instructive. By 1918 the Socialist party held 1,200 offices in 340 cities including seventy-nine mayors in twenty-four different states, thirty-two legislators and a member of Congress.[11] In 1919, after having increased its vote dramatically in various locales, the Socialists suffered the combined attacks of state, local and federal authorities. Their headquarters in numerous cities were sacked by police, their funds confiscated, their leaders jailed, their immigrant members deported, their newspapers denied mailing privileges and their elected candidates denied their seats in various state legislatures and in Congress. Within a few years, the party was finished as a viable political force. While confining themselves to legal and peaceful forms of political competition, the Socialists discovered that their opponents were burdened by no similar compunctions. The guiding principle of the establishment was (and still is): *when change threatens to rule, then the rules are changed.*

The weeding out of political deviants is carried on *within* as well as outside the major parties. It begins long before the election campaign and involves social forces that extend beyond the party system. First, the acceptable candidate must be born or educated into the middle or upper class, displaying the linguistic and social styles of a bourgeois personage. This requirement effectively limits the selection to business and professional people. Then he must express opinions of a kind that win the support of essentially conservative community leaders, party bosses and other established interests. Finally the aspiring candidate must have large sums of money of his own or access to those who do. As one Senator remarked: "The fundamental problem is that the ability to raise money starts the screening-out process. If you can't get the money, you don't get the nomination."[12] On election day "the voters will have their choice between *two* such carefully chosen candidates. But the real election in which the candidates compete for the

11. James Weinstein, *The Decline of American Socialism* (New York: Monthly Review Press, 1967).
12. Senator Mathias quoted in Richard Harris, "Annals of Politics: A Fundamental Hoax," *New Yorker*, August 7, 1971, p. 54.

backing of business and of its representatives in the parties and the press, has already occurred."[13]

Money is the lifeblood of electoral politics, helping to determine the availability of manpower, organization, mobility and media visibility. Without money, the politician's days are numbered. Commenting on the plight of reformers in Congress. Representative Charles Vanik observed: "As things are now, the public-interest members here have no reward except personal satisfaction. In the long run most of them face defeat by the big-money people. Many of the best men who come here lose after one or two terms."[14]

The Democratic presidential candidate in 1972, Senator George McGovern, found himself abandoned in the early stages of his campaign by wealthy liberal financiers who opposed his proposals for tax reform and income redistribution.[15] McGovern quickly retreated from these positions, placing an advertisement in the *Wall Street Journal* to assure its readers of his faith in the private-enterprise system. In subsequent speeches he informed businessmen that if he were elected, profits would "be bigger than they are now under the Nixon Administration." McGovern eventually did receive some support from wealthy donors, although hardly as much as Nixon. In the 1976 presidential election, Jimmy Carter, former governor of Georgia, spent $35 million; a good part of this sum came from wealthy Georgians and other large contributors from banking and oil firms; the rest came from federal matching funds.[16]

Radical candidates face great difficulties. Besides severe money problems, they must try to develop a plausible image among a citizenry conditioned for more than a century to hate and fear "anarchists," "socialists," "communists," and "leftists." They find themselves dependent for exposure on mass media that are owned by the conservative interests they are attacking. They see that, along with the misrepresentations disseminated by a hostile press, the sheer paucity of information and haphazard reportage can make any meaningful campaign dialogue nearly impossible. The dissenters compete not only against well-financed opponents but against the media's many frivolous and stupefying distractions. Hoping to "educate the public to the issues," they discover that

13. John Coleman, "Elections Under Capitalism, Part 2," *Workers' Power,* September 1–14, 1972, p. 11.
14. Quoted in Harris, "Annals of Politics," p. 59.
15. "McGovern's Views Alarm Big Donors on Wall Street," *New York Times,* July 3, 1972.
16. *New York Times,* November 18, 1976, and *Workers World,* November 19, 1976.

the media allow little opportunity for the expositions needed to make their position comprehensible to voters who might be willing to listen.

Not all dissenters are starved for funds. Given the conservative interests they represent, right-wing critics and candidates have relatively little trouble getting money. In 1975, for instance, George Wallace emerged with one of the best-financed campaigns, having received $4.3 million in two years.[17]

On those infrequent occasions when progressive dissenters win office, they are often relegated to obscure legislative tasks and receive little cooperation from legislative leaders or bureaucratic heads. To achieve some effectiveness in a legislative institution whose forces can easily undercut him, the newly arrived representative frequently decides that "for now" he must make his peace with the powers that be, holding his fire until some future day when he can attack from higher ground. To get along he decides to go along; thus begins the insidious process that lets a person believe he is still opposing the ongoing arrangements when in fact he has become a functional part of them. There are less subtle instances of co-optation, as when reformers are bought off with promotions and favors by those who hold the key to their advancement. Once having won election, they may reverse their stands on fundamental issues and make common cause with established powers, to the dismay of their supporters. Those few reformers who persist in making a nuisance of themselves may subsequently find themselves redistricted out of existence, as happened during the 1970–1972 period in New York City to three of the more outspokenly liberal Democratic Congressmen and five of the more liberal Democratic state legislators.

In sum, of the various functions a political party might serve—(1) selecting candidates and waging election campaigns, (2) articulating and debating major issues, (3) formulating coherent and distinct programs, (4) implementing a national program when in office—our parties fulfill only the first with any devotion or success. The parties are loose conglomerations of local factions organized around one common purpose: the pursuit of office. For this reason, American parties have been characterized as "nonideological." And indeed they are—in the sense that their profound ideological commitment to capitalism at home and abroad and to the ongoing class structure is seldom made an explicit issue. But even as they evade

17. *News-Observer* (Raleigh, N.C.), July 10, 1975.

most important policy questions and refrain from commitment to distinct, coherent programs, the parties have a conservative effect on the consciousness of the electorate and on the performance of representative government. They operate from a commonly shared ideological perspective which is best served by the avoidance of certain ideas and the suppression or co-optation of dissenters.

Democratic Competition: Does It Exist?

According to democratic theory, electoral competition keeps political leaders accountable to their constituents: politicians who wish to remain in office must respond to voter preferences in order to avoid being replaced by their rivals at the next election. But, do the conditions of electoral competition actually exist? As noted earlier, a host of political, legal and economic forces so limit the range of alternatives as to raise serious questions about the meaning of popular participation.

Furthermore, with so much of electoral politics reduced to an issueless publicity contest, the advantages go to the incumbent, be he an ordinary Congressman or President of the United States. Obviously, the man who has won office already has built some kind of winning combination of money, organization and influence. But even if appointed as a replacement, he can use the resources of office to promote his own subsequent election, catering to the needs of important financial groups and performing favors that win him backing from special interests. He gets irrigation projects, bridges, harbors, post offices and various other government "pork barrel" projects for his home district, carries on a correspondence with thousands of voters and enjoys an access to the local newspapers and radio and television stations that helps establish him as a "brand name." He has at his disposal almost a quarter of a million dollars each year for staff and office expenses, "a major portion of which is used to help the home folks and keep his name in front of them in a favorable way."[18] The most important task facing any candidate for public office is getting his name known to the voters, and here the incumbent has a usually decisive advantage over the challenger.

The trend in Congress over the last century has been for members to serve for longer periods and to suffer fewer defeats

18. Milton Gwirtzman, "The Bloated Branch," *New York Times Magazine,* November 10, 1974, p. 102.

by challengers. In the 1870s about 50 percent of the Representatives in each new Congress were newcomers; in 1970 the number had dropped to 12 percent.[19] From 1924 to 1956, 90 percent of the Congressmen who stood for reelection were victorious. In 1970, 94 percent of those seeking reelection to the House were returned by the voters. (Three percent were defeated in primaries, and 3 percent lost in the election.)[20]

Over the last two decades there has been a noticeable breakup of one-party regions: Republicans are now winning victories in Mississippi and Democrats get elected in Maine. Yet one-party dominance is still the rule in a good many locales throughout the rural Northeast, Midwest and South and in many cities. In 1970 one out of every ten Representatives was elected to Congress with *no opposition in either the primary or the general election.* In some states, state and local officeholders often are elected to uncontested seats. One-party rule, considered the peculiar disease of "communist tyranny," is not an uncommon condition of American politics.

Death and voluntary retirement seem to be the important factors behind the turnover in representative assemblies. In this respect, legislative bodies bear a closer resemblance to the nonelective judiciary than we would imagine. One study of municipal governments found that upwards of half the city councilmen anticipated their own voluntary retirement after one term and about one-fourth held nonelective appointments to fill unexpired terms. Many of the councilmen admitted that they paid little heed to constituent complaints. They entered and left office "not at the whim of the electorate, but according to self-defined schedules," a procession of like-minded men of similar social background.[21]

The prevalence of victorious incumbents is both a cause and an effect of low voter participation. As voters become increasingly

19. Mark J. Green, James M. Fallows and David R. Zwick, *Who Runs Congress?* (New York: Bantam Books/Grossman, 1972), p. 229.

20. See David Leuthold, *Electioneering in a Democracy* (New York: Wiley and Sons, 1968), p. 127. For the breakdown on the 1970 election I am indebted to Garrison Nelson.

21. Kenneth Prewitt, "Political Ambitions, Volunteerism, and Electoral Accountability," *American Political Science Review,* 64, March 1970, p. 10. Prewitt presents data on eighty-two municipal governments. The noncompetitive leadership selection he found at the local level exists to a lesser extent in the more visible and prestigious U.S. Congress, but as Prewitt points out, the more than 35,000 municipalities, towns and townships and the equal number of school boards have a cumulative impact that may be more important than the influence exercised by the Congress or any of its special committees.

discouraged about the possibility of effecting meaningful change through the ballot box, they are less likely to mobilize or respond to reformist electoral movements, thus increasing the unassailability of the incumbents. As the incumbents show themselves unbeatable, their would-be challengers become fewer in number and weaker in spirit. This is not an iron law of politics and the cycle has sometimes been dramatically reversed; but the reversals are usually the notable exceptions. The predominant situation is one of officeholders who are largely unresponsive to voters and voters who are often cynical about officeholders.

Nonvoting as a Rational Response

Much has been written about the deficiencies of ordinary voters, their prejudices, lack of information and low civic involvement. More should be said about the deficiencies of the electoral-representative system that serves them. It has long been presumed that since the present political system represents the best of all worlds, those who show an unwillingness to vote must be manifesting some failing in themselves. Seldom is nonparticipation treated as a justifiable reaction to a politics that is meaningless in its electoral content and disappointing in its policy results.

In the United States during the nineteenth century, the small-town democratic system "was quite adequate, both in partisan organization and dissemination of political information, to the task of mobilizing voters," according to Walter Dean Burnham.[22] But by the turn of the century most of the political means for making important decisions had been captured by powerful industrial elites. Business interests perfected the arts of pressure politics, wielding a heavy influence over state legislatures, party organizations, governors and Congressmen. At the same time, the judiciary extended its property-serving controls over the national and state legislatures, imposing limitations on taxation powers and on regulatory efforts in the fields of commerce and labor. "Confronted with a narrowed scope of effective democratic options an increasingly large proportion of the eligible adult population either left, failed to enter or—as was the case with the Southern Negro . . . was systematically excluded from the American voting universe."[23]

22. Walter Dean Burnham, "The Changing Shape of the American Political Universe," *American Political Science Review*, 59, March 1965, p. 22.
23. *Ibid.*, p. 26.

Much of the blame for the diminishing popular participation, Burnham concludes, must rest with "the political system itself."

The percentage of nonvoters has climbed to impressive levels, running as high as 55 to 60 percent in congressional contests and 45 to 47 percent in recent presidential elections. Since 1960 an increasingly larger percentage of those who come of voting age have failed to go to the polls in presidential contests. In the presidential *primaries* of some states, the participation rate may be as low as 15 to 20 percent of the registered voters. In many local elections, voter participation is so low as to make it difficult to speak of "popular" representation in any real sense. Observing that in a municipality of 13,000 residents an average of 810 voters elected the city council, Prewitt comments:

> Such figures sharply question the validity of thinking that "mass electorates" hold elected officials accountable. For these councilmen, even if serving in relatively sizable cities, there are no "mass electorates"; rather there are the councilman's business associates, his friends at church, his acquaintances in the Rotary Club, and so forth which provide him the electoral support he needs to gain office.[24]

The political significance of low participation becomes apparent when we consider that nonvoters are disproportionately concentrated among the rural poor, the urban slum dwellers, the young, the elderly, the low-income and nonunion workers and the racial minorities. The entire voting process is dominated by middle-class styles and conditions which tend to discourage lower-class participation.[25] Among the reasons poor Whites in one city gave for not voting were the humiliating treatment they had received from poll attendants in previous elections, the intimidating nature of voting machines, the belief that they were not entitled to vote because they had failed to pay their poll tax (a misapprehension encouraged by unsympathetic town clerks), the feeling that they lacked education and information giving one the right to participate in the electoral process, and the conviction that elections are a farce and all politicians are ultimately out to "line their own pockets."[26] Residency requirements and the registration of voters

24. Kenneth Prewitt, "Political Ambitions, Volunteerism, and Electoral Accountability," *American Political Science Review*, 64, March 1970, p. 9.

25. Penn Kimball, *The Disconnected* (New York: Columbia University Press, 1972); Giuseppe Di Palma, *Apathy and Participation: Mass Politics in Western Societies* (New York: Free Press, 1970).

26. Opinions reported by McGovern campaign workers in Burlington, Vt., in 1972. I am indebted to Cheryl Smalley for gathering the information.

WARREN
LINN

at obscure locations during the political off-season discriminate against the less-established community elements, specifically the poor, the unemployed and transient laborers.[27]

Working long hours for low pay, deprived of the kind of services and material security that the well-to-do take for granted, made to feel personally incapable of acting effectively and living in fear of officialdom, low-income people frequently are reluctant to make political commitments of any kind. The entire social milieu of the poor militates against participation. As Kimball describes it:

Tenements, rooming houses, and housing projects—the dormitories of the ghetto electorate—provide . . . a shifting, changing human environment instead of the social reinforcements that encourage political involvement in more stable neighborhoods. And the immediate struggle for subsistence drains the reservoirs of emotional energy available for the distant and complex realms of politics. . . . Elections come and go, and the life of poverty goes on pretty much as before, neither dramatically better nor dramatically worse. The posturing of candidates and the promises of parties are simply irrelevant to the daily grind of marginal existence.[28]

Lower-strata groups are skeptical that any one candidate can change things. Their suspicions might be summarized as follows: (1) the reform-minded candidate is still a politician and therefore is as deceptive as any other; (2) even if he is sincere, the reformer is eventually "bought off" by the powers that be; (3) even if he is not bought off, the reformer can do little against those who run things. The conviction is that politics cannot deliver anything significant.[29]

It has been argued that if nonvoters tend to be among the less informed, less educated and more apathetic, then it is just as well they do not exercise their franchise. Since they are likely to be swayed by prejudice and demagogy, their activation would constitute a potential threat to our democratic system.[30] Behind this reasoning lurks the dubious presumption that the better-educated, upper-income people who vote are more rational, less compelled

27. See Charles E. Merriam and Harold F. Gosnell, *Non-voting, Causes and Methods of Control* (Chicago: University of Chicago Press, 1924), pp. 78 ff.; and Kimball, *The Disconnected*, p. 15.

28. Kimball, *The Disconnected*, p. 17.

29. Michael Parenti, "Power and Pluralism," p. 515; and Kimball, *The Disconnected*, pp. 61–62.

30. A typical example of this kind of thinking is found in Seymour M. Lipset, *Political Man* (Garden City, N.Y.: Doubleday, 1960), pp. 215–219.

by narrow self-interests, and less bound by racial and class prejudices, an impression which itself is one of those comfortable prejudices that upper-and middle-class people (including social scientists) have of themselves. As Kimball reminds us:

The level of information of the most informed voters is not very high by objective standards. The influence of ethnic background, family upbringing, and party inheritance is enormous in comparison to the flow of political debate. The choices in a given situation are rarely clearcut, and the decision to vote for particular candidates can be highly irrational, *even at the highest levels of education and experience*.[31]

Some writers argue that low voter turnout in the United States is symptomatic of a "politics of happiness": people do not bother to participate because they are fairly content with the way things are going.[32] But the 40 to 50 million adult Americans outside the voting universe are not among the more contented but among the less affluent and more alienated, displaying an unusual concentration of socially deprived characteristics.[33] The "politics of happiness" may be nothing more than a cover for the politics of discouragement. The nonparticipation of many people often represents a feeling of powerlessness, a conviction that it is useless to vote or demonstrate, useless to invest precious time, energy and hope, risking insult, eviction, arrest, loss of job and police assault—useless because nothing changes. For many ordinary citizens, nonparticipation is not the result of contentment or apathy or lack of civic virtue but an understandably negative response to the political realities they experience.[34]

31. Kimball, *The Disconnected*, p. 63. Italics added. Occasionally there is an admission by the well-to-do that voting should be limited not to protect democracy but to protect themselves. A letter to the *New York Times* (December 6, 1971) offered these revealing words: "If . . . everybody voted, I'm afraid we'd be in for a gigantic upheaval of American society—and we comfortable readers of the Times would certainly stand to lose much at the hands of the poor, faceless, previously quiet throngs. Wouldn't it be best to let sleeping dogs lie?"

32. Heinz Eulau, "The Politics of Happiness," *Antioch Review*, 16, 1956, pp. 259–264; Lipset, *Political Man*, pp. 179–219.

33. Burnham, "The Changing Shape of the American Political Universe," p. 27; and Kimball, *The Disconnected*.

34. A similar conclusion can be drawn from Studs Terkel, *Division Street: America* (New York: Pantheon, 1967); Kimball, *The Disconnected;* Levin, *The Alienated Voter;* Harold V. Savitch, "Powerlessness in an Urban Ghetto: The Case of Political Biases and Differential Access in New York City," *Polity*, 5, Fall 1972, pp. 17–56; Parenti, "Power and Pluralism"; Lewis Lipsitz, "On Political Belief: The Grievances of the Poor," in Philip Green and Sanford

With that in mind, we might question those public-opinion surveys which report that underprivileged persons are more apathetic than better-educated, upper-income citizens. If by *apathy* we mean the absence of affect and awareness, then the poor, the elderly, the young, the racial minorities and the industrial workers who have repeatedly voiced their outrage against oppressive social conditions can hardly be described as "apathetic." Apathy should not be confused with antipathy and alienation. Nor is it clear that these dissident groups are "less informed." What impresses the investigators who actually take the trouble to talk to low-income people is the extent to which they have a rather precise notion of what afflicts them. Certainly they have a better sense of the difficulties that beset their lives than the many middle-class officials who do not even recognize the legitimacy of their complaints.[35]

Voting as an Irrational Response

Civic leaders and educators usually characterize nonvoters as "slackers" and seldom as people who might be justifiably cynical about the electoral system. Conversely, they portray voters as conscientious citizens performing their civic responsibilities. Certainly many voters seem to agree, especially those who report that they vote primarily because of a "sense of citizenship duty"; often they believe their vote makes no difference and have little regard for the outcome of the election. Thus in the 1956 presidential campaign, 58 percent of those who described themselves as "not much interested" in the campaign voted anyway. Of those who "didn't care at all" about who won the election, 52 percent voted. Only 13 percent of the people with a "low sense of citizenship duty" voted, as opposed to 85 percent who had a "high" sense. The crucial variable in predicting turnout was "sense of citizenship duty" and not interest in substantive issues.[36] For many citizens, then, the vote seems to be more an exercise of civic virtue than civic power. This raises the interesting question of who really is the deadwood of democracy: the "apathetic" or the "civic minded," those who see no reason to vote or those who vote with no reason?

Levinson (eds.), *Power and Community* (New York: Pantheon, 1969), pp. 142–172.

35. See the citations in the previous footnote.

36. Angus Campbell et al., *The American Voter* (New York: Wiley and Sons, 1960), pp. 103–106.

There are, of course, other inducements to voting besides a sense of civic obligation. The tendency to vote for the lesser, or lesser known, of two evils has already been noted. The location of undesirable traits in one party suggests the relative absence of these traits in the other and sometimes becomes enough reason for partisan choice. Thus the suspicion that Democrats might favor Blacks and hippies leads some middle-class Whites to assume that the Republican party is devoted to their interests, a conclusion that may have no basis in the actual performance of Republican office-holders. Similarly, the identification of Republicans as "the party of big business" suggests to some working-class voters that, in contrast, the Democrats are *not* for business but for the "little man," a conclusion that may be equally unfounded. Like the masks worn in Greek drama, the party label gives distinct identities to otherwise indistinguishable and often undistinguished political actors, identifying some as villains and others as heroes. By acting as instigators of partisan spirit and partisan anxiety, the parties encourage participation, stabilize electoral loyalties and build reservoirs of trust and mistrust that survive the performances of particular candidates.

Recent data indicates that the events of the past decade have weakened party affiliations. Citizens are more inclined to cross party lines, identify themselves as "independents," and look with distrust on both political parties,[37] yet they continue to vote for major party candidates, even if in split-ticket fashion.

Some people vote because it is "the only thing the ordinary person can do."[38] Not to exercise one's franchise is to consign one-self to *total* political impotence, an uncomfortable condition for those who have been taught they are self-governing. The need to *feel* effective can lead to the mistaken notion that one *is* effective. A faith in the efficacy of voting also allows one to avoid the bother of other kinds of participation.

Voting not only induces a feeling of efficacy, it often *results* from such a feeling. Persons with a high sense of political efficacy are the more likely to vote. High efficacy is related to a citizen's educational and class level: better-educated people of comfortable income who feel most efficacious in general also tend to feel more

37. Norman H. Nie, Sidney Verba and John R. Petrocik, *The Changing American Voter* (Cambridge, Mass.: Harvard University Press, 1976).
38. Robert Lane, *Political Ideology* (New York: Free Press, 1962), p. 166; Gabriel Almond and Sidney Verba, *The Civic Culture* (Boston: Little, Brown, 1963), p. 131.

politically efficacious than lower-income persons.[39] But while many studies relate sense of political efficacy to voting, there is almost nothing relating sense of political efficacy to actual efficacy. In fact there may be little relationship between the two.[40]

The argument is sometimes made that if deprived groups have been unable to win their demands from the political system, it is because they are numerically weak compared to White middle-class America. In a system that responds to the democratic power of numbers, a minority poor cannot hope to have its way. The representative principle works well enough, but the poor are not strong enough nor numerous enough. Therefore, the deficiency is in the limited numbers of persons advocating change and not in the representative system, which operates according to majoritarian principles. What is curious about this argument is that it is never applied to more select minority interests—for instance, oilmen. Now oilmen are far less numerous than the poor, yet the deficiency of their numbers, or of the numbers of other tiny minorities like bankers, industrialists and millionaire investors, does not result in any lack of government responsiveness to their wants. On most important matters government policy is determined less by the majoritarian principle and more by the economic strength of private interests. The fact that government does little for the minority poor, and even shares in the middle-class hostility toward the poor, does not mean that it is devoted to the interests of the great bulk of belabored "middle Americans" nor that it operates according to majoritarian principles.

To summarize some of the observations offered in this chapter: important structural and material factors so predetermine the range of electoral issues and choices as to raise a serious question about the representative quality of the political system. Mass politics requires mass resources. Being enormously expensive affairs, elections are best utilized by those interests endowed with the resources necessary to take advantage of them. Politics has always been largely "a rich man's game." Ironically enough, the one institutional arrangement that is ostensibly designed to register the will of the many serves to legitimize the rule of the privileged few. The

39. See Robert R. Alford and Harry M. Scoble, "Sources of Local Political Involvement," *American Political Science Review*, 62, December 1968, pp. 1192–1206.

40. See Alan Wertheimer, "In Defense of Compulsory Voting," in J. Roland Pennock and John Chapman (eds.), *NOMOS XVI: Participation in Politics* (New York: Lieber-Atherton, 1975).

way people respond to political reality depends on the way that reality is presented to them. If people have become apathetic and cynical, including many of those who vote, it is at least partly because the electoral system and the major party organizations resist the kind of creative involvement that democracy is supposed to nurture. It is one thing to say that people tend to be uninvolved, ill-informed and given to impoverished and stereotyped notions about political .life. It is quite another to maintain a system that propagates these tendencies with every known distraction and discouragement. Elections, then, might better be considered a symbol of democratic governance than a guarantee of it, and voting often seems to be less an exercise than a surrender of sovereignty.

Who Governs?
Leaders and
Lobbyists

12 IT WAS TOCQUEVILLE WHO ONCE SAID that the wealthy have little interest in governing the working people, they simply want to use them.[1] Yet members of the propertied class seldom have been slow in assuming the burdens of public office. The political party, said Secretary of State Seward in 1865, using an image that fit his class experience, is "a joint stock association, in which those who contribute most direct the action and management of the concern."[2] The same might be said of government itself.

"Those Who Own the Country Ought to Govern It"

While the less glorious tasks of vote herding have fallen to persons of modest class and ethnic origins, the top state and federal offices and party leadership positions, to this day, have remained largely in the hands of White, Protestant, middle-aged, upper-income males of conventional political opinion, drawn from the top ranks of corporate management, from the prominent law and banking firms of Wall Street and

1. Alexis de Tocqueville, *Democracy in America*, vol. 2 (New York: Vintage, 1945), p. 171.
2. Quoted in Matthew Josephson, *The Politicos, 1865–1896* (New York: Harcourt, Brace, 1938), p. 13.

less frequently from the elite universities, foundations and the scientific establishment.[3]

From the beginning of the American Republic to modern times, the great majority of those who have occupied the top political offices of the nation—including the presidency and vice-presidency, the cabinet and Supreme Court—have been from wealthy families (the upper 5 or 6 percent of the population) and most of the remainder have been from well-off, middle-class origins (moderately successful businessmen, farmers, professionals). Of those who went to college, more than one-third attended the elite Ivy League schools.[4] Of the 125 top government appointments made by the liberal President Harry Truman in 1945–1947, forty-nine were bankers and industrialists, thirty-one were military men, and seventeen were lawyers, mostly with corporate connections, a situation that caused one newsman to observe: "The effective focus of government seemed to shift from Washington to some place equidistant between Wall Street and West Point."[5] Of the fifty or more top appointments in the first Eisenhower administration, three-fourths were linked with industry, finance and corporate law firms, while the remainder might be classified as government administrators or professional party politicians. The men who ran the nation's defense establishment between 1940 and 1967, according to Richard Barnet, "were so like one another in occupation, religion, style and social status that, apart from a few Washington lawyers, Texans, and mavericks, it was possible to locate the offices of all of them within fifteen city blocks in New York, Boston and Detroit."[6]

The wealthy and wellborn carry into public life many of the same class values, interests and presumptions that shape their private lives. Be they of "old families" or newly arrived, "reform-

---

3. As of 1977 in Congress there were seventeen Blacks and sixteen women (several of whom are also counted among the seventeen Blacks); no Black or woman has ever served as president or vice-president; a few have been in the cabinet; and only one Black and no women have been on the Supreme Court.

4. See the data in C. Wright Mills, The Power Elite (New York: Oxford University Press, 1956), pp. 400–402, fn., and passim; also Harold Lasswell et al., The Comparative Study of Elites (Stanford, Calif.: Stanford University Press, 1952), p. 30; G. William Domhoff, Who Rules America? (Englewood Cliffs, N.J.: Prentice-Hall, 1967), especially Chapters 3 and 4; G. William Domhoff, The Higher Circles: The Governing Class in America (New York: Vintage, 1970); Richard J. Barnet, Roots of War (New York: Atheneum, 1972); John C. Donovan, The Cold Warriors (Lexington, Mass.: D.C. Heath, 1973); George W. Pierson, The Education of American Leaders (New York: Praeger, 1972).

5. Howard K. Smith, The State of Europe (New York: Knopf, 1949), p. 83.

6. Barnet, Roots of War, pp. 48–49.

minded" or conservative, the rich are not known to advocate the demolition of the economic system under which they prosper. They do not support changes that might work against their class interests. Likewise, political leaders of relatively modest class origins, like Lyndon Johnson, Richard Nixon and Spiro Agnew, are unlikely to retain a strong identity with the low and humble throughout their ascension. As already noted, one of the preconditions of the rise of such persons is their willingness to accommodate themselves at a fairly early point in their careers to the interests of those privileged circles whose ranks they aspire to join.

Government and business elites are linked by organizational, financial and social ties, and move easily from public to private leadership posts. For instance, the Council on Foreign Relations, a nonofficial advisory group that plays a crucial role in shaping American foreign and domestic policies, is composed of international bankers, corporate heads, military chiefs, cabinet members, White House advisors, members of Congress, top bureaucrats, publishers, news commentators and academics. In 1974 the major oil companies had thirty of their top executives on the Council. Its members included the Rockefeller brothers, DuPonts and Morgans and various acolytes of theirs like Henry Kissinger, John McCloy and Elliot Richardson. Within five months, President Ford appointed fourteen Council members to cabinet, ambassadorial and other positions of responsibility in his administration.

Not every member of the ruling class is born rich but most are. Not all wealthy persons are engaged in ruling, some preferring to concentrate on making money or on living a life of ease. "The ruling class contains what could be called the politicized members of the upper class," writes Alan Wolfe.

They are all either businessmen or descendants of businessmen. They are born to power and grow up in an atmosphere that cultivates power. . . . They are chairmen, directors, trustees, vice-presidents, consultants, partners, secretaries, advisers, presidents, members and relatives. They, in other words, are the "they" that people (with acute perception) blame for their troubles. And the blame is deserved, for they have taken the responsibility of shaping the society in their interest. They are conscious of that responsibility . . . For amusement, they read books (often written with support from their foundations) which "prove" that no ruling class exists in the United States.[7]

7. Alan Wolfe, *The Seamy Side of Democracy* (New York: McKay, 1973), pp. 66–67.

The policies they pursue in office frequently are connected directly to the corporate interests they represent in their private lives. Thus the decision-makers involved in the U.S. armed intervention against the worker-student uprising in the Dominican Republic in 1965 consisted of Abe Fortas, A. A. Berle, Jr., Ellsworth Bunker, Averell Harriman and a half-dozen others who were stockholders, directors or counsels for large sugar companies that depended on Dominican sugar and molasses for their operations. "Even without these direct economic interests, it would be difficult for these gentlemen in their 'neutral' decision-making roles to escape the assumptions, inclinations and priorities inculcated by their economic and social milieu."[8]

Within the lower echelons of government, recruitment is less selective in regard to class background, but public employees are subjected to "security" checks to weed out the "risks." However, "the notion of what constitutes a 'security risk' is an elastic one," easily stretched to include anyone whose political opinions depart from the prevailing conservative consensus.[9]

Campaign Contributions:
What Money Can Buy

The way campaigns are funded is a reflection of the way wealth is distributed in the society. A small number of big donors pay the bulk of campaign expenses. In the 1968 election eighty-nine persons contributed more than $6.8 million.[10] It cost an estimated $100 million to elect a President that year, including all expenditures from the first primary to election day; some 85 percent of this money came from businessmen and their families.[11] In 1972

8. Fred Goff and Michael Locker, *The Violence of Domination: U.S. Power and the Dominican Republic* (New York: North American Congress on Latin America, n.d.), cited in James Petras, "U.S. Business and Foreign Policy," *New Politics*, 6, Fall 1967, p. 76.

9. Ralph Miliband, *The State in Capitalist Society* (New York: Basic Books, 1969), p. 124. In 1976 the Civil Service Commission eliminated all political loyalty questions on standard application forms. The Commission noted, however, that it would continue to be responsible for the loyalty of applicants or employees in sensitive jobs, all of whom are subjected to a full field investigation. *New York Times*, September 9, 1976.

10. *New York Times*, November 14, 1971.

11. Herbert Alexander, *Financing the 1968 Election* (Lexington, Mass.: D. C. Heath, 1971); a good study on this subject is David Nichols, *Financing Elections: The Politics of an American Ruling Class* (New York: Franklin Watts, 1974); see also Herbert Alexander, *Money in Politics* (Washington,

ninety-five persons donated $47.5 million to the Nixon campaign, approximately half of the President's election fund. Two years later, congressional races cost $74 million.[12] In national and state elections money remained the most crucial factor. "Despite the Watergate-induced flurry of concern about campaign financing," observed a *New York Times* reporter, "there was the usual overwhelming correlation between big spenders and big winners."[13]

While politicians insist that campaign contributions do not influence them, few are inclined to go against those who support them financially. A former assistant to two prominent Democratic Senators made the following observation:

Any member of Congress who says donations don't influence him is lying. All of them are corrupt. The only question is the degree of corruption. One reason members of Congress insist that money doesn't influence them is that they . . . often become convinced of the rightness of their backers' causes without admitting it even to themselves. In time, they come to really believe that the guy who gives the big dough is the best guy and that helping him is in the public interest. But campaign money *has* to influence even the most incorruptible men here, because most people don't give away large sums of money for nothing.[14]

Republicans generally receive from three to five times more from big corporate donors than do Democrats, although Democratic lawmakers with strategic committee positions have little difficulty in being funded. Thus both Democratic and Republican members of the House Ways and Means Committee have received heavy campaign contributions from the oil and gas industry, the real estate business, private utilities, large banks and several other interests seeking to preserve the favored treatment they receive under the tax laws.[15] In 1974 billionaire H. Ross Perot contributed $88,000 to Democratic and Republican members of congressional committees that had jurisdiction over programs of special interest to him. Most of the money was given after the election and much of it to persons who ran unopposed.[16] Some thirty House members

D.C.: Public Affairs Press, 1972); C. William Domhoff, *Fat Cats and Democrats* (Englewood Cliffs, N.J.: Prentice-Hall, 1972).

12. *New York Times*, April 11, 1975.
13. *New York Times*, November 7, 1974.
14. Quoted in Richard Harris, "Annals of Politics: A Fundamental Hoax," *New Yorker*, August 7, 1971, p. 54.
15. *New York Times*, September 20, 1974.
16. CBS television evening news report, May 22, 1975. Using two dummy committees, Perot funneled $100,000 into the 1972 presidential campaign effort

and nine Senators, including liberal Democrats, received campaign donations totaling about $1 million from the dairy industry, while another half-million or more went to President Nixon's campaign fund. In return, the dairy companies were granted federal milk price supports netting them some $500 million in added revenues.[17] Over a ten-year period forty-five Senators and Representatives of both parties received a total of $8 million in illegal payments from four oil companies.[18] In one election year, a group of bankers contributed more than $200,000 to some forty members of both parties who were on banking and finance committees.[19] The chairman of one of these committees, Wright Patman, observed: "It is an open secret on Capitol Hill that many campaign chests are swelled by contributions from the banks. . . . Today's economy which has the highest interest rates in the nation's history is largely the result of the banking and monetary policy written by the special interests for special interests."[20]

A $400,000 contribution from ITT to the Republican convention in 1972 was followed by the Justice Department's dropping an antitrust suit against ITT for its merger with the Hartford Insurance Co., a move that brought ITT a $2-billion property.[21] A $250,000 contribution by the president of McDonald's hamburger chain was followed by Nixon's veto of a minimum wage bill that would have directly benefited almost all of McDonald's young employees. A secret donation of $200,000 to the Nixon campaign fund by Robert Vesco allegedly bought him the services of former Attorney General John Mitchell and former Commerce Secretary Maurice Stans in obstructing an investigation into Vesco's looting of $224 million from a mutual fund complex.[22]

of Rep. Wilbur Mills (D.–Ark.), then-chairman of the powerful House Ways and Means Committee. *Rutland* (Vt.) *Daily Herald*, August 2, 1974.

17. Frank Wright, "The Dairy Lobby Buys the Cream of the Congress," *Washington Monthly*, May 1971, pp. 17–21; also *New York Times*, January 11, 1973. For making illegal contributions to the Nixon campaign, a group of milk producers were fined the grand sum of $5,000; *New York Times*, May 7, 1974.

18. According to investigators of the Securities and Exchange Commission documents. See Jack Anderson and Les Whitten, "The Corporate Payoff Story," *Ithaca* (N.Y.) *Journal*, March 22, 1976; and *New York Times*, September 9, 1976.

19. Harris, "Annals of Politics," p. 51.

20. Robert Cirino, *Don't Blame the People* (New York: Vintage, 1972), p. 144.

21. White House involvement in the ITT affair was confirmed in testimony given by Charles Colson, former Special Counsel to the White House. See *New York Times*, June 15, 1973.

22. For a detailed and documented account of the use of money and influence in the White House during the Nixon administration, see the entire

The career of Nelson Rockefeller provides us with an impressive example of the use of money in politics. The Rockefeller family spent $10 to $12 million on Nelson's campaign for governor of New York and another $12 million on his tries for the presidency in 1964 and 1968.[23] Rockefeller spent large sums to surround himself with a highly paid staff of lawyers, intellectuals, writers and public relations experts. He promoted himself through two costly commissions on "national goals" and "critical choices" designed to keep him in the public eye as a national statesman. At the time he was being considered for appointment to the vice-presidency, it was discovered that he had been buying not only political celebrity but political security. Rockefeller admitted to having given nearly $1.8 million in gifts and loans to eighteen public officials since 1957, including $50,000 to Henry Kissinger (who had worked for Rockefeller for fifteen years) three days before Kissinger became special advisor to President Nixon, and $625,000 to the chairman of the Port Authority of New York. (David Rockefeller's Chase Manhattan Bank has large bond holdings in the Port Authority.) Various associates received outright cash gifts from Rockefeller or had loans settled while they held state jobs—despite the fact that New York State law prohibits public employees from accepting any gift larger than $25. Judson Morhouse received $100,000, was later convicted of bribery charges in a liquor-licensing case, then had his sentence commuted by Governor Rockefeller. At a Senate hearing, Rockefeller insisted that these gifts were simply manifestations of his affection and esteem for the recipients. "Sharing has always been part of my upbringing," he told the Senators, none of whom doubled over with laughter.[24]

Neither the House nor Senate committees investigating his nomination to the vice-presidency questioned Rockefeller about the influence he gained from the gifts. No one wondered aloud whether a "gift" to officials in public agencies that make decisions affecting one's private fortune might not better be called by its more forthright name, a "bribe." Coming to Rockefeller's support, Rep. Shirley Chisholm (D.–N.Y.) made the revealing comment: "Who among us politicians in the House, indeed, in government today,

issue of NACLA's Latin America and Empire Report, November 1973, entitled: "The Money Behind Nixon . . . from Wall Street to Watergate." See also Eileen Shanahan, "3 More Corporations Tell About Illegal Aid to Nixon," New York Times, November 16, 1973.

23. See Alexander, Financing the 1968 Election.

24. Newsweek, October 21, 1974; New York Times, October 7, 1974.

is pure and above reproach?"[25] Who indeed? With only a few gingerly objections, Congress confirmed Nelson Rockefeller as Vice-President, thereby maintaining its impermeability to the "post-Watergate morality."

Rockefeller had been labeled an "Eastern liberal" by ultra-conservative members of his party. Yet in almost fourteen years as governor of New York, he greatly increased the tax burden on low- and middle-income people while failing to impose a single new tax on big business. During his administration, manufacturing properties were exempt from taxation in New York. He put a sales tax on the consumer, then increased it. He quadrupled the cigarette tax, tripled the gasoline tax and extended the state income tax to include low-paid working people who had been previously exempted. As more people were made destitute by the recession, Rockefeller responded with heavy cuts in human services. As Vice-President he supported all of President Ford's conservative policies, including the high military budget and the vetoes against social legislation. Rockefeller supported global interventionist policies and for years was a hawk on Vietnam, albeit not an honestly outspoken one like Barry Goldwater.

The bipartisan influence of big business contributors is so pronounced as to move one Democratic Senator to remind his party colleagues that they were neglecting to keep up appearances as "the party of the people." In a speech on the Senate floor urging that the scientific patents of the $25-billion space program not be given away to private corporations but applied for public benefit, Russell Long made these candid remarks:

Many of these [corporate] people have much influence. I, like others, have importuned some of them for campaign contributions for my party and myself. Nevertheless, we owe it to the people, now and then, to save one or two votes for them. This is one such instance. If any Senator should suspect that he might lose his campaign contributors by voting with me today, I might assure him that I have been able to obtain contributions from some of those people, even though they knew I voted for the public interest as I see it on such issues as this. We Democrats can trade on the dubious assumption that we are protector of the public interest only so long if we permit things like these patent giveaways.[26]

In election financing, labor unions are seldom able to match

25. *Guardian*, December 11, 1974.
26. *Congressional Record*, vol. 112, part 9, June 2, 1966.

the contributions of industry. Senator Long observed: "Labor contributions have been greatly exaggerated. It would be my guess that about 95 percent of campaign funds at the congressional level are derived from businessmen."[27] In 1974 the contributions of just six business interests (oil, real estate, securities, banking, utilities and trucking) to House Ways and Means Committee members amounted to four times the total labor contributions.[28] To juxtapose Big Labor with Big Business in the manner of some American Government textbooks is to overlook the fact that the great bulk of the spending and lobbying is dominated by business groups. This is not to discount organized labor as an interest group, but to indicate the insufficiency of its political strength, especially when measured against the needs of the working class it claims to represent.

Federal laws that sought to limit the sums candidates could spend and individuals could contribute have always been easily circumvented by such devices as dummy campaign committees or contributions made in the name of friends and relatives. In 1976 the Supreme Court removed most of the limits on campaign spending by (a) allowing an individual to expend any amount in an "independent" effort to elect or defeat any candidate, and (b) allowing candidates themselves to spend as much as they desired of their personal or family fortunes on their own campaigns, a decision greatly favoring the wealthy. The Court reasoned that limitations on spending were an infringement of the First Amendment right to free speech.[29] In addition, the Court upheld the law's authorization of contributions from corporate "political action committees." Many such committees with names like "Lockheed Good Government Committee" and Sun Oil's "Responsible Citizenship Program" sprang up during the 1976 campaign. The Court also upheld the use of public money up to $5 million to match funds of presidential candidates who raise a minimum of $100,000 from each of at least twenty states.

Under the 1974 amendments to the Federal Election Campaign Act, the government pays the costs of the Democratic and Republican conventions and provides matching funds of many millions

27. Quoted in Mark J. Green, James Fallows and David Zwick, *Who Runs Congress?* (New York: Bantam Books, 1972), pp. 12–13.

28. *New York Times,* September 20, 1974. One consequence was that almost no aspect of the pending tax bill was acceptable to organized labor.

29. *New York Times,* January 31, 1976. The Court was joined in this reasoning by liberals in Common Cause and in the American Civil Liberties Union who hoped to benefit from big contributions by liberal millionaire Stewart Mott. See the *New York Times,* May 19, 1975.

for "major" party candidates. The law denies assistance to parties that polled less than 5 percent of the presidential vote in the preceding election, effectively depriving all dissenting third parties of public funds.[30]

Lobbyists and Their Ways

Lobbyists are persons hired by organized interest groups to influence legislative and administrative policies. Some political scientists see lobbying as essentially a "communication process." They argue that the officeholder's perception of a particular policy is influenced solely or primarily by the information reaching him. The lobbyist's role is one of providing that information. By this view, the techniques of the "modern" lobbyist consist mostly of disseminating data and "expert" information and making public appearances before legislative committees rather than the obsolete tactics of secret deals and bribes.[31] The students of lobbying who propagate this image of the influence system overestimate the changes that have occurred within it. *The development of new lobbying techniques does not mean that the older, cruder ones have been discarded.* Along with the slick brochures, expert testimonies and technical reports, corporate lobbyists still have the slush fund, the kickback, the stock award, the high-paying job offer in private industry, the lavish parties and prostitutes, the meals, transportation, housing and vacation accommodations and the many other hustling enticements of money. From the lowliest city councilman to the White House itself, officeholders accept money and favors from lobbyists in return for favored treatment. "Members of the House Banking and Currency Committee," complained its chairman, the late Wright Patman (D.–Tex.), "have been offered huge blocks of bank stocks free of charge and directorships on bank boards. Freshmen members have been approached within hours of their arrival in Wash-

---

30. For a concise analysis see Robert Walters, "Millions for Third Parties (Nice Work if They Can Get It)," *Ramparts*, July 1975, pp. 13–16. The Supreme Court upheld this provision of the law. *New York Times*, January 31, 1976.

31. Lester Milbrath, *The Washington Lobbyists* (Chicago: Rand McNally, 1963), p. 185 and *passim*. See also Douglass Cater's comparison of the "new" with the "old" NAM in his *Power in Washington* (New York: Random House, 1964), p. 208. For a good critique of the Milbrath view of lobbying, see Ernest Yanarella, "The Military-Industrial Complex, Lobbying and the ABM Decision: Some Notes on the Politics of Explanation," unpublished monograph.

ington and offered quick and immediate loans. In one instance that was reported to me, the bank told the member, 'Just write a check, we will honor it.' "[32] "Everyone has a price," Howard Hughes once told his associate Noah Dietrich, who later recalled that the billionaire handed out about $400,000 yearly to "councilmen and county supervisors, tax assessors, sheriffs, state senators and assemblymen, district attorneys, governors, congressmen and senators, judges—yes, and vice-presidents and presidents, too."[33]

Many large corporations have a special division dedicated to performing favors for officeholders. The services include everything from free Caribbean trips on private jet planes to loans, private contracts and illegal gifts. An employee at ITT's congressional liaison section publicly complained about the way Congressmen continually called her office for favors "on a big scale." This situation "shocked" her, she said, even though "very little in Washington would shock me."[34]

The case of Claude Wild, Jr., is instructive. As a vice-president for Gulf Oil and a lobbyist, Wild had the full-time job of passing out, over a twelve-year period, about $4.1 million of Gulf's money to politicians like Lyndon Johnson, Hubert Humphrey, Richard Nixon and Gerald Ford. The money was delivered to Wild from Gulf offices around the country in cash packets of $25,000 each, to be divided about equally among federal, state and local politicians.[35] Other oil companies made illegal contributions to public officeholders in return for special tax favors and protection against

32. Quoted in Cirino, *Don't Blame the People*, p. 144.
33. Howard Kohn, "The Hughes-Nixon-Lansky Connection: The Secret Alliances of the CIA from World War II to Watergate," *Rolling Stone*, May 20, 1976, p. 44. Hughes contributed heavily to Nixon's campaigns in 1968 and 1972 and, according to his close aides, Robert Maheu and John Meier, sought to have the Vietnam war prolonged until he had made sufficient profits on his helicopter program; *New York Times*, April 9, 1975. Hughes has been romanticized as a "cowboy capitalist" by some; I have a better name for him.
34. Quoted in the *New York Times*, March 31, 1972. For a fascinating eyewitness account of corruption and special influence in Washington by a former lobbyist, see Robert Winter-Berger, *The Washington Pay-Off* (New York: Dell, 1972). See also Drew Pearson and Jack Anderson, *The Case Against Congress* (New York: Simon and Schuster, 1968); Lawrence Gilson, *Money and Secrecy* (New York: Praeger, 1972); and *New York Times*, April 28, 1975. For a description of how local politicians are bought off by large corporations, see Jack Sheperd, "The Nuclear Threat Inside America," *Look*, December 15, 1970, pp. 24–25.
35. Since the contributions were illegal, the money was first laundered by Gulf through a Caribbean subsidiary and then a Canadian bank. See the *Wall Street Journal*, November 17, 1975; and *Philadelphia Evening Bulletin*, November 12, 1975.

the growing agitation to break up the monopolized oil industry. Airline companies, heavily dependent on federal regulations and subsidies, passed along large sums, as did companies that were major suppliers to the federal government. In addition to the millions contributed at home, the multinationals paid hundreds of millions in bribes and contributions to right-wing governments and militarists in countries like Iran, South Korea, Bolivia and Taiwan.[36]

The big-time Washington lobbyists are usually attorneys or business people who have proven themselves articulate spokespersons for their firms, or ex-legislators or former bureaucrats with good connections. Whatever their varied backgrounds, the one common resource lobbyists should have at their command in order to be effective is—money. Money buys what one House aide called that "basic ingredient of all lobbying"—*accessibility* to the officeholder[37] and, with that, the opportunity to shape his judgments with arguments of the lobbyist's own choosing. Accessibility, however, involves not merely winning an audience with a Congressman—since even ordinary citizens sometimes can get to see their Representatives and Senators—but winning his active support. In one of his more revealing moments, Woodrow Wilson pointed out:

Suppose you go to Washington and try to get at your Government. You will always find that while you are politely listened to, the men really consulted are the men who have the big stake—the big bankers, the big manufacturers, and the big masters of commerce. . . . The masters of the Government of the United States are the combined capitalists and manufacturers of the United States.[38]

Much the same can be said for state and local governments. The idea (popular among political scientists in the 1950s) that strong party leadership would be an effective bulwark against such pressure groups appears to be without foundation. Individual legis-

36. *Workers World,* March 5, 1976, has a summary of some of these expenditures. Lockheed admitted to having paid $22 million in overseas bribes, including $7 million to the leader of an ultra-right militarist political faction in Japan. *New York Times,* February 5, 1976. Boeing admitted to $70 million in bribes during a five-year period. Gulf paid $4 million to the South Korean dictatorship in 1966, and Exxon made secret payments of $51 million to conservative leaders in Italy over an eight-year period. See Anthony Sampson, "How the Oil Companies Help the Arabs to Keep Prices High," *New York,* September 22, 1975, p. 48.
37. Quoted in Harris, "Annals of Politics," p. 55. Winter-Berger emphasizes this in *The Washington Pay-Off.*
38. Quoted in D. Gilbarg, "United States Imperialism," in Bill Slate (ed.), *Power to the People* (New York: Tower, 1970), p. 67.

lators vote as their party leaders want, but these leaders, in turn, are heavily influenced by business lobbyists. The influence exercised on state legislatures by big-money interests "is so widespread in this country it appears endemic."[39] The state legislatures are "the willing instrumentalities of an array of private corporate entities."[40] While most of the public has no idea what their state representatives are doing, the banks, loan companies, gambling interests, big franchise holders, insurance firms, utilities, manufacturers, oil and gas companies and Farm Bureau lobbyists carry on a regular liaison with them, showering them with campaign contributions, legal retainers, liquor, paid vacations, free entertainment, special-term "loans," business tips and opportunities to participate in growing investment areas. Subservience to business is so pervasive as to make it almost impossible to tell the lawmakers from the lobbyists. State legislators usually work only part-time at their tasks, devoting the better part of their days to their private law practices, insurance firms, realty agencies and other enterprises, which often benefit from their legislative efforts. About half the New York legislators are attorneys who service businesses with direct interests in state laws. A sizable number of the legislators are trustees or directors of banks.[41]

Surveying the organized pressure groups in America, E. E. Schattschneider notes: *The system is very small. The range of organized, identifiable, known groups is amazingly narrow; there is nothing remotely universal about it.*"[42] The pressure system, he concludes, is largely dominated by business groups, the majority of citizens belonging to no organization that is effectively engaged in pressure politics. Almost all organized groups, even nonbusiness ones such as community, religious, educational and professional associations, "reflect an upper-class tendency";[43] low-income people

39. Martin Waldron, "Shadow on the Alamo," *New York Times Book Review*, July 10, 1972, p. 2.
40. "The Sick State of the State Legislatures," *Newsweek*, April 19, 1965, p. 31. Six legislators from Massachusetts took the extraordinary step of publicly protesting the "unhealthy relationship" between big contributors, mostly business interests, and the legislative leadership, calling for the legislators to turn their backs on "those who would use political contributions to gain unfair advantage in the legislative process"; *Boston Globe*, September 8, 1976. In New York a prominent banking official was quoted as saying: "I don't buy legislators dinners, I buy legislators"; *Times-Union* (Albany), January 19, 1974.
41. *Times-Union* (Albany), January 19, 1974.
42. E. E. Schattschneider, *The Semi-Sovereign People* (New York: Holt, Rinehart and Winston, 1960), p. 31. Italics in the original.
43. *Ibid.*, pp. 33–34, and the studies cited therein.

rarely have the time, money or expectation level that would enable them to participate.

The pressure system is "small" and "narrow" only in that it represents a highly select portion of the public. In relation to government itself, the system is a vast operation. "Most of the office space in Washington that is not occupied by government workers is occupied by special-interest lobbyists, who put in millions of hours each year trying to get special legislation enacted for the benefit of their clients," writes Richard Harris. "And they succeed on a scale that is undreamed of by most ordinary citizens."[44] A favorable adjustment in rates for interstate carriers, a new tax write-off for industry, a special tax benefit for a family oil trust, a high-interest bond issue for big investors, a special charter for a bank, a tariff protection for auto producers, the leasing of some public lands to a lumber company, emergency funding for a faltering aeronautics plant, a lenient occupational health code for employers, a postal subsidy for advertising firms, a soil bank for agribusiness, the easing of safety standards for a food processor, the easing of pollution controls for a chemical company, an investment guarantee to a housing developer, a lease guarantee to a construction contractor—all these hundreds of bills and their thousands of special amendments and the tens of thousands of administrative rulings which mean so much to particular interests and arouse the sympathetic efforts of legislators and bureaucrats will go largely unnoticed by a public that pays the monetary and human costs, and has not the organization, information and means to make its case—or even discover that it has a case.

Public interest groups, professing to speak for the great unorganized populace, make many demands for reform but have few of the resources that could move officeholders in a reformist direction. In any case, most public interest groups accept the capitalist system as a given, hence the kinds of "within-the-system" changes they advocate are usually of a cosmetic nature or, at best, offer only marginal improvements: thus the advocacy of seat belts and pollution devices for automobiles rather than a nonprofit, publicly owned mass transportation system; better labeling of commercial products rather than an attack on the waste and abuses of commercialized consumerism; the elimination of no-deposit throwaway beverage bottles rather than the elimination of the profit system and its war against the environment; public exposure of lobbying

44. Harris, "Annals of Politics," p. 56.

spending rather than an end to the concentration and use of private wealth for public power.

In limiting their critiques, most public interest groups betray the limitations of their liberal politics and their commitment to the very system which creates the problems they deplore. A "people's lobby" like John Gardner's Common Cause, for instance, while supposedly designed as a counterbalance to corporate influence, accepts the corporate system as one to be "improved" and is closely associated with leading capitalists. For years Gardner has been one of the few nonfamily trustees of the Rockefeller Brothers Fund, a fact omitted from his lengthy official biographies. Furthermore, Common Cause received most of its original funding, some $70,000, from various members of the Rockefeller family and the Chase Manhattan Bank.[45]

Pressure group activities are directed not only at officeholders but encompass entire segments of the public itself. Grant McConnell offers one description of this "grass-roots lobbying":

The electric companies, organized in the National Electric Light Association, had not only directly influenced Congressmen and Senators on a large scale, but had also conducted a massive campaign to control the substance of teaching in the nation's schools. Teachers in high schools and grammar schools were inundated with materials. . . . Each pamphlet included carefully planted disparagement of public ownership of utilities. The Association took very active, if inconspicuous, measures to insure that textbooks that were doctrinally impure on this issue were withdrawn from use and that more favorable substitutes were produced and used. College professors . . . were given supplemental incomes by the Association and, in return, not infrequently taught about the utility industry with greater sympathy than before. . . . Public libraries, ministers, and civic leaders of all kinds were subjected to the propagandistic efforts of the electric companies.[46]

The purpose of grass-roots lobbying is to build a climate of opinion favorable to the corporate giants rather than to push a particular piece of legislation. The steel, oil and electronics companies do not advertise for public support on behalf of the latest tax depreciation bill—if anything, they would prefer that citizens not trouble themselves with thoughts on the subject—but they do "educate" the public, telling of the many jobs the companies create,

45. Richard Reeves, "The City Politic," *New York*, December 2, 1974, p. 12.
46. Grant McConnell, *Private Power and American Democracy* (New York: Knopf, 1966), p. 19.

the progress and services they provide, the loving care they give to the environment, etc. This kind of "institutional advertising" attempts to place the desires of the giant firms above politics and above controversy—a goal that is itself highly political.

Corruption as an American Way of Life

In recent years there have been reports on corruption involving federal, state and local officials in every state of the Union. In Congress, "Corruption is so endemic that it's scandalous. Even the honest men are corrupted—usually by and for the major economic-interest groups and the wealthy individuals who together largely dominate campaign financing."[47] "In some states—Louisiana, for instance—scandals are so prolific that exposure of them has absolutely no impact," reports one observer.[48] A Republican member of the Illinois state legislature estimated that one-third of his legislative colleagues accepted payoffs.[49] In 1970–1971, officials in seven of New Jersey's eleven urban counties were indicted or convicted for graft and corruption, along with the mayors of the two largest cities, the minority leader of the state assembly, the former speaker of the state assembly, a prominent state senator, a state prosecutor, a former secretary of state, and a Port Authority commissioner.[50] At about the same time, major scandals were occurring in Texas, Illinois, West Virginia, Maryland and New York. In New York City alone half the Police Department was reported by the Knapp Commission to be accepting payoffs. In 1974 widespread corruption was found in the police forces of Chicago, Philadelphia, Indianapolis, Cleveland, Houston, Denver and New York, involving gambling, prostitution, narcotics and stolen goods.[51] In Albany, N.Y., according to a state commission, policemen in every precinct of the city were involved in one or more of the following practices:

47. George Agree, director of the National Committee for an Effective Congress, quoted in Harris, "Annals of Politics," p. 62.
48. Waldron, "Shadow on the Alamo," p. 2. See also Peter Cowen, "Graft Held Fact of Life in Boston," *Boston Globe*, October 2, 1972.
49. Paul Simon, "The Illinois State Legislature," *Harper's*, September 1964, p. 74.
50. For revealing accounts of corruption in states like West Virginia, Maryland and New Jersey, see the articles by John Rothchild, Mary Walton, Thomas B. Edsall and Michael Rappeport published together under the title "Revenue Sharing with the Rich and the Crooked," *Washington Monthly*, February 1972, pp. 8–38.
51. *Time*, May 6, 1974; *New York Times*, March 11, 1974.

burglarizing stores (or covering up burglaries), looting parking meters, accepting bribes, protecting narcotics dealers, shaking down prostitutes and intimidating witnesses who attempted to testify against police crime. In 1976 it was revealed that FBI leaders had used Bureau funds for personal purposes and that FBI agents routinely accepted unsecured loans at preferred rates of interest from a bank in New Jersey.[52] Municipal and federal narcotics agents were found "to be some of the mob's most successful pushers."[53] Doctors were cheating the government out of "a billion dollars a year and all their patients much more," reported health officials, by falsifying health insurance claims, padding bills, participating in kickbacks and overcharging for often unnecessary laboratory tests by as much as 100 to 400 percent.[54]

On a still grander scale in Washington, the Nixon administration was implicated in major scandals involving the sale of wheat, an out-of-court settlement with ITT, price supports for dairy producers, corruption in the Federal Housing Administration, stock market manipulations, and political espionage—the Watergate Affair. And Vice-President Spiro Agnew resigned from office because of charges of bribery, extortion and corruption.[55]

Campaigning for President in 1976, Jimmy Carter made a plea for honesty in government at a $100-a-plate dinner in Miami while beside him on the dais sat a mayor recently imprisoned for tax evasion, a couple of Florida state senators who had just pleaded guilty to conflict of interest, a commissioner facing trial for bribery, and three other commissioners charged with fraud.[56]

Corruption in America is so widespread that, as Lincoln Steffens pointed out long ago, throwing the rascals out only means bringing more rascals in. Through all this, the public looks on with growing cynicism, uttering jokes about the habits of politicians

52. *New York Times,* April 13 and September 10, 1976.

53. Brooklyn District Attorney Eugene Gold, quoted in Nicholas Pileggi, *The Mafia at War* (New York: New York Magazine, Inc., 1972), p. 85. Gold testified that 70 percent of Brooklyn's detectives were taking graft. For a personal account of corruption in the police department, see Peter Maas, *Serpico* (New York: Viking, 1973).

54. *Buffalo Evening News,* July 27, 1976; *Seattle Post-Intelligencer,* August 1, 1976; *New York Times,* January 11, 1973.

55. Agnew pleaded guilty to income-tax evasion, . . . was fined $10,000 and given three years probation. In return for his guilty plea and resignation from the vice-presidency, the Justice Department dropped the other charges. Regarding the influence peddling and criminal behavior of the Nixon people, see Howard Kohn, "The Hughes-Nixon-Lansky Connection . . ." pp. 40–90.

56. *Workers World,* May 7, 1976.

and sometimes failing to appreciate how the corrupt officeholder is part of the same individuated acquisitive system that includes the plundering corporate manager, the lying advertiser, the rent-gouging landlord, the price-fixing merchant, the cheating lawyer, the fee-gouging doctor and, at a more modest level, the pilfering automechanic and television repairman.

Congress:
The Pocketing
of Power

13

AS WAS NOTED IN CHAPTER FOUR, THE Founding Fathers fashioned a Constitution with the intent of deflecting what they considered to be a tempestuous popular will. In order to guard against democratic "excesses" and ensure the rule of the more prudent elements of society, i.e., themselves and other men of their class and convictions, they separated the powers of state into executive, legislative and judicial branches and installed a system of checks and balances designed to forestall action and make fundamental class changes most unlikely. They understood what some theorists today seem to have forgotten: that the *diffusion* of power among the various segments of government does not necessarily mean its *democratization* but more likely the opposite. Diffusion leads to the pocketing of power by entrenched groups which can resist popular desires. Power that is elaborately fragmented is more accessible to specialized, well-organized interests and less responsive to the mass public.

Looking specifically at the United States Congress, one is struck by how effectively the diffusion of power has operated for undemocratic purposes. The deficiencies of Congress have been documented by journalists, political scientists and Congressmen themselves.[1] Without

1. The best of recent works is Mark J. Green, James M. Fallows and David R. Zwick, *Who Runs Congress?*

hoping to cover everything that might be said about the legislative branch, let us consider some of the more important points.

Rule by Special Interest

Power in Congress rests largely with the twenty or so standing committees in each house which determine the destiny of all bills —rewriting some, giving affirmative action to a few and burying most. For many years these committees were dominated, and to a large extent still are, by chairpersons who rise to their positions by seniority—that is, by being repeatedly reelected, usually from more conservative districts or states not known for their two-party competition or high electoral participation. The commitment to seniority has been a pervasive unwritten norm of Congress, determining not only the choosing of chairpersons but the assigning of members to committees and the selection of subcommittee chairpersons.[2] However, seniority is readily ignored by senior members when it is in their interest to do so. Former Senator Joseph Clark notes that during one session of the Senate the seniority rule was violated when filling vacancies to eight important standing committees, to the advantage of conservative Senators and the disadvantage of the already underrepresented Senate liberals.[3] Over the years, Clark himself was repeatedly denied appointment to the Foreign Relations Committee, sometimes because of lack of seniority and sometimes in violation of seniority.

The party with a majority, be it in the House or Senate, is the one that controls the chairmanships of that house. Since World War II, except for brief interludes, control of Congress has been in the hands of the Democrats or, more specifically, the senior members of the Democratic party, who for a long time were mostly Southern conservatives. Some of the aging Southern committee chairpersons in both the House and the Senate have been suc-

(New York: Bantam Books/Grossman, 1972). See also Joseph S. Clark, *Congress: The Sapless Branch* (New York: Harper and Row, 1964); Joseph C. Clark and Other Senators, *The Senate Establishment* (New York: Hill and Wang, 1963); Drew Pearson and Jack Anderson, *The Case Against Congress* (New York: Simon and Schuster, 1968); and Richard Billing, *House Out of Order* (New York: E. P. Dutton, 1965).

2. George Goodwin, "The Seniority System in Congress," *American Political Science Review*, 53, June 1959, p. 412.

3. Clark, *The Senate Establishment*, pp. 40 ff.

ceeded by non-Southerners who generally have been less conservative. By 1976 only six of the Senate chairpersons were from the Old South, and four of these were in their seventies. In the House, chairmanships have been moving away from rural districts toward somewhat less conservative urban and surburban ones.[4]

In the 94th Congress seniority remained the rule in both houses, although the House Democratic Caucus removed three chairpersons, replacing them with committee members who were next in line.[5] The role played by junior members of the Caucus signified a departure from rule by gerontocracy, but it hardly represented the "revolution" it was said to be. Seniority was now bypassed occasionally, according to criteria that were not always clear or consistent, but it was not abolished.

The House Democratic Caucus instituted changes to weaken the hold of committee chairpersons by expanding the role of subcommittees and allowing more participation by committee members. The Caucus successfully diminished the enormous power of the Rules Committee and the Ways and Means Committee,[6] and it strengthened the powers of the House Speaker and party whips in an attempt to facilitate cohesive party actions that might better reflect the legislative desires of the presumably liberal Democratic majority.

But as of the end of the 94th Congress in 1976, these structural reforms had brought forth relatively few substantive outputs.[7] The "New Congress" of 1974–1976, with its infusion of seventy-five freshmen Democrats in the House, bore a fairly close resemblance to the old Congress. The reforms and "gains" it made were extremely modest, while the problems remaining untouched were

4. *New York Times*, February 10, 1976.
5. The Democratic Caucus is the meeting of all House Democrats. Its function is to discuss strategies and issues. Composed of the majority—and therefore the governing—party of the House, the Caucus has recently come to play a revitalized role in shaping the rules under which the Democrats and, in effect, the House itself operates.
6. Previously, the Rules Committee, which controls the House calendar, could specify the conditions under which the rest of the House might consider a bill—if at all. By invariably imposing a closed rule on all tax bills and preventing members from offering amendments, it gave the erstwhile chairperson of the Ways and Means Committee, Wilbur Mills, a conservative from a rural one-party district in Arkansas, virtual one-man control over all such measures. Now, on petition by fifty members, the Caucus can instruct and bind Democratic members of the Rules Committee to allow Ways and Means legislation to be amended from the House floor.
7. See the reports by Larry Dodd, Catherine Rudder and Bruce Oppenheimer in *DEA News*, Summer 1976.

enormous. The 94th Congress abolished oil depletion allowances for large producers and tightened a few of the many tax loopholes enjoyed by the wealthy while broadening other business loopholes. It granted business firms an extra two years in which they could deduct past losses from future profits; it granted corporations a four-year extension of the investment tax credit, a tax break of many billions, and it almost tripled the amount of tax-free money that can be left to heirs, thereby giving upper-income people a new $2-billion tax break. In addition, the 94th Congress passed emergency job-fund programs,extended unemployment benefits by thirteen weeks and increased Social Security payments by 8 percent —not enough to compensate for inflation. It voted to continue the meager school lunch and breakfast programs for children and other social services, and it legislated funds for occupational safety and health enforcement.

Like every other Congress before it, the 94th Congress satisfied itself with band-aid spending programs for problems that required major structural changes in class and power. It accepted the continued existence of inflation, unemployment and high profits, and an economy run by and for the giant corporations. For all its supposedly "reform-minded" inclinations, the Congress at no time entertained any notion about moving toward nonprofit forms of production for social use rather than production for private profit. The entire system of big business subsidies, grants, investment write-offs, leases and giveaways remained intact. And by 1976 Congress was contemplating the abolition of federal protections against pollution and was threatening to turn the federal sewage-treatment program for cities into a giant bonanza for private developers and give the gas companies a free hand in setting gas prices.[8] And, as noted earlier, this same "New Congress" busied itself with new repressive legislation against political dissenters.

To its credit, the 94th Congress did turn down President Ford's request for funds to keep the war going in Vietnam in 1975 and refused to plunge into the Angola war the following year. At the same time, it voted the largest military budget in history, refused to halt development of the supersonic B-1 bomber or make reductions in the half-million U.S. troops stationed in foreign countries, and planned new strategic nuclear programs and weapon

8. David Zwick, "Clean Water Down the Drain," *Nation,* August 14, 1976, pp. 115–116, 123; also Alexander Cockburn and James Ridgeway, "Surplus Value," *Village Voice,* June 16, 1975.

systems that would dramatically increase the rate of military spending in the years ahead.[9]

Not surprisingly, the more powerful committees in both houses are those related to taxes and spending: House Ways and Means, House Appropriations, Senate Finance and Senate Appropriations. The committees are broken down into numerous subcommittees, most working with staffs of their own under the directorship of subcommittee chairpersons. "More than mere specialization, the subcommittee permits development of tight little cadres of special interest legislators and gives them great leverage."[10] In agriculture, for instance, cotton, corn, wheat, peanut, tobacco and rice producers compete for federal support programs; each interest is represented on the various subcommittees of the Senate and House Agricultural Committees by Senators and Representatives ready to do battle on their behalf. The fragmentation of power within the subcommittees simplifies the lobbyist's task of controlling legislation. *It offers the special-interest group its own special-interest subcommittee.* To atomize power in this way is *not* to democratize it.[11] The separate structures of power tend to monopolize decisions in specific areas for the benefit of specific groups. Into the interstices of these substructures fall the interests of large segments of the unorganized public.

On those rare occasions when public opinion *is* aroused about some particular issue like auto safety, pollution, or unsafe foods, Congress might move with noticeable velocity. Yet even then the final bill usually will be sufficiently diluted to accommodate producer groups. One of Congress' more predictable ploys is to respond to an aroused public by producing legislation that gives every *appearance* of dealing with the problem but which is usually wanting in *substance:* thus we have a lobbyist registration act that does little to control lobbying practices, a campaign financing act that is easily circumvented, a civil rights act that is seldom enforced, a public housing act that creates mostly private profits, and

---

9. *New York Times,* June 25, 1975, and May 14, 1976. In the wake of revolutionary victories in Indochina, Congress seemed gripped by spasms of jingoism. Even congressional "doves" were voicing their support of U.S. global commitments and support of right-wing dictatorships in South Korea, Spain and elsewhere. See *New York Times,* May 6, 1975.

10. Douglass Cater, *Power in Washington* (New York: Random House, 1964), p. 158.

11. See Grant McConnell, *Private Power and American Democracy* (New York: Knopf, 1966), p. 193 and *passim.*

an environmental protection act that fails to protect the environment.

Given the demands made on his or her time by job and family, and the superficial and often misleading coverage of events by the media, the average wage earner has little opportunity to give sustained informed attention to more than a few broad issues, if that. But throughout the legislative process the organized interests remain alert and actively engaged in shaping the substantive details of bills.

Somtimes, even in the face of an aroused public and sustained media exposure, Congress will make no positive response. After several years of intensive and massive public demonstrations against the Vietnam intervention and with polls indicating that a majority of the people favored withdrawal from Vietnam, Congress was still voting huge appropriations for the war by lopsided majorities, and large numbers of Senators and Representatives—a majority in the House—still adhered to a "hawk" position.[12] In April 1973, in the face of a nationwide meat boycott, demonstrations and a deluge of letters and telephone calls protesting inflation, Congress voted down all proposals for price freezes and price rollbacks. Opposing the proposals were "cattlemen, banking and business interests and food merchants."[13] The consumer and citizens' groups lost; the cattlemen, bankers and businessmen won.

Congress is inclined to remove itself from scrutiny whenever the public gets too interested in its affairs. The Senate Armed Services Committee responded to the public's growing concern about military spending by increasing its percentage of secret hearings from 56 percent in 1969 to 79 percent in 1971. The House Appropriations Committee held 92 percent of its meetings behind closed doors that same year. Most other committees held at least one-third of their sessions in secret.[14] Business interests enjoy a ready access to committee reports while newspersons and public-interest advocates are kept in the dark. "The thing that really makes me mad is the dual standard," complained a staff member of one key Senate committee. "It's perfectly acceptable to turn over information about what's going on in committee to the auto industry or the utilities but not to the public."[15]

12. See Garrison Nelson's excellent analysis: "Nixon's Silent House of Hawks," *Progressive*, August 1970, pp. 13–20.

13. The Associated Press report carried in the *Schnectady Gazette*, April 17, 1973.

14. See the *Washington Monthly*, September 1972, p. 17.

15. Green et al., *Who Runs Congress?*, p. 56.

Sometimes secrecy envelops the entire lawmaking process: a bill cutting corporate taxes by $7.3 billion was (a) drawn up by the House Ways and Means Committee in three days of secret sessions, (b) passed by the House under a closed rule after only one hour of debate with (c) about thirty members of the House present for the (d) non-roll-call vote.[16] Under such conditions even the highly motivated muckraker, experienced journalist, or academic specialist has difficulty ascertaining what is going on.

The addiction to secrecy is nowhere more evident than in Congress' campaign to keep the Central Intelligence Agency free from public scrutiny. Despite disclosures of widespread, covert, unlawful and dangerous activities by the CIA, Congress rejected moves to publicize the Agency's budget.[17] When Representative Michael Harrington (D.–Mass.) released classified information on the CIA's role in the overthrow of a democratic government in Chile, the House Armed Services Committee voted to deny him further access to classified materials about the Agency.[18] The House Select Committee on Intelligence wrote a report that was highly critical of CIA activities, but the House voted to withhold it from the public until it had been censored by the President, who could delete any information that might "adversely affect . . . intelligence activities."[19] White House incantations about "national security," repeatedly used during Watergate days to cover up crimes, were accepted by the House as reason enough to deny the American public information about the CIA. When the House report was leaked to CBS news reporter Daniel Schorr, who passed it on to the *Village Voice*, which published most of it, the House ordered its Ethics Committee to make a full investigation of the leak.[20]

16. See the observations of Thomas H. Stanton reported in the *Washington Monthly*, April 1972, p. 18.

17. *New York Times*, October 2, 1975.

18. *New York Times*, June 20, 1975. The secret testimony of then-CIA director William Colby, which Harrington made public, directly contradicted previous public testimony by former CIA director Richard Helms and public statements by Henry Kissinger and other officials who had repeatedly lied to Congress and the public.

19. *New York Times*, January 30 and February 2, 1976. The Select Committee that wrote the report, under the chairmanship of Rep. Otis Pike (D.–N.Y.), did not think it was harmful to national security and had voted to make it public.

20. *New York Times*, March 30, 1976. Schorr argued that to be forced to reveal one's sources would make independent reporting impossible and was therefore a violation of the First Amendment. The House Ethics Committee left off the investigation, after spending $150,000, without citing Schorr for contempt and without discovering the leak. See *New York Times*, September 19, 1976.

Neither Congress nor the President indicated what items in the report were damaging to national security. Apparently exposure of CIA crimes and abuses weakened the Agency's effectiveness and thereby posed a danger to our security. By this view, intelligence agencies should be free to do pretty much anything they want without being subjected to public scrutiny—a state of affairs which itself poses serious dangers to our security.

The American humorist Will Rogers once observed: "Congress is the best money can buy." Congressmen not only respond to monied lobbyists, many allow their offices to be used as bases of operation for lobbying activities. One influential lobbyist, Nathan Voloshen, regularly worked out of Speaker John McCormack's office, paying McCormack a substantial "rent" along with a percentage of the take in return for use of the Speaker's name and influence on behalf of Voloshen's business clients.[21] According to Winter-Berger, the lobbyist's main job is to circumvent existing laws and get preferential treatment "for clients who have no legal rights to them." To achieve this, he pays cash to "one or more members of Congress—the more influential they are, the fewer he needs," who make the contacts with the executive agency handling the matter. "Most lobbying is underground, because more than opinions are exchanged. Money is exchanged: money for favors, money for deals, money for government contracts, money for government jobs."[22] It is "a very common occurrence" for Congressmen to telephone or write the Justice Department on behalf of business interests, according to former Attorney General Richard Kleindienst, who added: "We have a responsibility to permit that kind of thing to occur."[23]

Frequently members of Congress act without benefit of prodding by any pressure group, either because they are so well attuned to its interests or because they have lucrative holdings of their own in the same industry. Thus Representative Clarence Brown of Ohio owned a broadcasting station and sat on the House subcommittee that regulated broadcasting. The late Representative Robert Wat-

21. See Robert Winter-Berger, *The Washington Pay-Off* (New York: Dell, 1972). Winter-Berger was a lobbyist who worked closely with Voloshen and McCormack. He offers a good deal of astonishing eyewitness testimony in his book. Voloshen was eventually convicted of fraud and given a suspended sentence. At his trial, McCormack professed to be ignorant of Voloshen's doings and everyone believed him.

22. *Ibid.*, pp. 14, 38.

23. Quoted in Martin Gellen, "ITT: The Tentacles of Power," *Guardian*, March 29, 1972, p. 3.

kins of Pennsylvania was chairperson of a trucking firm whose profits depended on rules passed by Watkins's Commerce Committee. Certain members of Congress, like Senator James Eastland (D.-Miss.), who are owners of large farm holdings, sit on committees that shape the farm subsidy programs that directly enrich them. Former Senator James Buckley (C.-N.Y.) and Senator Russel Long (D.-La.) have substantial holdings in oil and gas and regularly voted for oil depletion allowances and against price controls on fuels. Long is chairperson of the Senate Finance Committee, which controls tax bills affecting the oil industry. The late Senator Robert Kerr (D.-Okla.) exercised direct control over legislation affecting gas, uranium, oil and other natural resources. By 1960 he owned numerous oil wells, 25 percent of America's uranium mines and 75 percent of the world's richest helium pool. Much of his wealth was accumulated after he was elected to the Senate. Senator Jacob Javits (R.-N.Y.), who owns stock in First National City Bank and was a member of a law firm that did millions of dollars of business for the bank, has been a strong and persistent advocate for banking interests, enough to make him known as "the Senator from Wall Street."[24] What is called "conflict of interest" in regard to the judiciary is defined as "expertise" in Congress. What we have are persons who use their public mandate to legislate for their private interests. That they seldom see any conflict in these roles itself shows how readily they define the public good in terms compatible with their own fortunes.

Plutocracy—rule *by* the rich *for* the rich—prevails in Congress. In the Senate in 1976, at least twenty-five members were millionaires and another eighteen disclosed holdings of upward to a half-million dollars.[25] Ninety House members had substantial financial investments in banks and savings and loan associations. Included were twelve members of the House Banking Committee and six on the Ways and Means Committee, both of which pass on legislation for the banking industry. In the 92nd Congress, forty out of one hundred Senators were either on the boards of national banks or among the top stockholders. Most were investors in state banks and loan associations. The 535 members of Congress in 1970 in-

24. Charlie McCollum, "Jacob Javits: The Senator from Wall Street," *Village Voice*, August 29, 1974, pp. 3, 27–28.
25. Many Senators, including some of the richer ones, failed to report their entire holdings. See "Buckley Discloses Some Finances—Not All," AP story in the *Ithaca* (N.Y.) *Journal*, December 19, 1975. Twenty-two refused to make any public disclosure at all. The actual number of millionaires in the Senate is unknown, but it is likely higher than twenty-five.

cluded (with some overlap) 184 from banking and business, 310 lawyers, 50 farmers (mostly large successful ones) and others from various professions such as teaching, medicine and journalism.[26] The great bulk of the American population belongs to occupations and income levels that have no direct representation in Congress.

Congressmen pilfer from the public treasure. Among their bad habits the most common are: (1) junketing—traveling for fun at government expense under the guise of conducting overseas committee investigations; (2) having relatives on the payroll and pocketing their salaries; (3) taking salary kickbacks from other staff members; (4) keeping unspent travel allocations for personal use; (5) double billing—charging both the government and a private client for the same expense; (6) using their franking privilege for mailing campaign literature; (7) using committee staff workers for personal campaign purposes;[27] (8) keeping persons on the staff payroll whose major function is to perform sexual favors.[28]

Venality takes more serious forms. From 1968 to 1972 eight members of Congress or their aides were convicted of bribery, influence peddling or perjury. And these were only the few clumsy enough to get caught. Between 1973 and 1976 at least another thirteen House members faced charges of bribery, fraud and theft, campaign-spending violations, influence peddling or moral turpitude.[29] One of them, Rep. Robert Sikes (D.–Fla.) was charged with influencing government decisions on realty leases, bank charters and defense contracts involving firms in which he owned unreported stock.[30] The House voted to reprimand Sikes for "financial misconduct," the reprimand being the lightest sanction possible.[31] Sikes was allowed to keep his seat, his seniority and his chairmanship. In 1975–1976 at least nineteen Senators were implicated in a multimillion-dollar corporate slush fund, including then-

26. *New York Times Encyclopedic Almanac,* 1970.
27. Green et al., *Who Runs Congress?,* pp. 131–159.
28. A well-publicized case was that of Rep. Wayne Hays and Elizabeth Ray; the latter maintained that her job was to make herself sexually available to Hays; *New York Times,* May 26, 1976. Colleen Gardner charged that she and other women on the staff of Rep. John Young (D.–Tex.) were pressured into providing him with sex and that some men on Capitol staffs told her their jobs required homosexual activities with Congressmen. See *New York Post,* June 14, 1976.
29. *Boston Globe,* August 18, 1976; *New York Times,* September 4, 1976.
30. See the detailed account in the *New York Times,* June 20, 1975; also *New York Times,* July 3, 1976.
31. *New York Times,* July 30, 1976. Living in their own glass houses, Sike's colleagues threw only a few pebbles at him.

Senate minority leader Hugh Scott (R.–Pa.). Officials of Gulf Oil testified before the Securities and Exchange Commission that Scott had accepted and actively solicited illegal contributions from Gulf of $10,000 a year. These charges were widely publicized in the press, but instead of moving to clean house, the Senate reacted very much as had the Nixon administration to Watergate. Half the members of the Senate Ethics Committee declined to reply to inquiries about the Scott case and the other half observed that an investigation would be "premature." The committee had not investigated a Senator's ethics in almost ten years. Scott, a millionaire, suddenly decided to retire from the Senate in 1976.[32] The Ethics Committee finally initiated an investigation of Scott and two dozen other Senators which it decided to drop a short time later without calling any corporate witnesses (including Gulf lobbyists who were willing to name names). The committee refused to open Scott's financial papers or turn them over to the Internal Revenue Service.[33]

The Legislative Labyrinth

The very constitutional structure of Congress operates with conservative effect—as the Founding Fathers intended. The staggered terms of the Senate (only one-third selected every two years) makes any sweeping turnover impossible, even if there were a mass sentiment among voters for a thorough change. The division of the Congress into two separate houses makes legislative action all the more difficult. Reform legislation passed by the House, like the 1969 Patman bill to restrict the powers of bank holding companies or the 1975 bill to a eliminate certain tax shelters, often is not acted upon by the Senate. And humanitarian bills passed by the Senate, like the one to allow free food stamps for families with monthly incomes of less than $60, have perished in the House.

A typical bill before Congress might go the following route. After being introduced into, say, the House, it is (1) committed to

32. *Progressive*, March 1976, p. 11. Among Scott's other accomplishments was the way he lied for Nixon about Watergate, claiming that the Oval Office tapes exonerated the President when, in fact, the tapes did just the opposite, as was later discovered when they were released.

33. *Boston Globe*, September 22, 1976. The chairman of the Ethics Committee was Howard Cannon (D.–Nev.), who himself was said to be the recipient of illegal gifts from Northrup Corporation. See *The American Sentinel*, July 1, 1975, p. 3.

a committee where it is most likely summarily ignored, pigeonholed or gutted by the chairperson, or (2) parceled out to various subcommittees for extensive hearings where it might then meet its demise or (3) reported out of subcommittee to full committee, greatly diluted or completely rewritten to suit influential lobbyists and their clients, some of whom sit on the committees as members of Congress. In the unlikely event that it is reported out of the full committee, the bill (4) goes to the Rules Committee where it might be buried forever or subjected to further mutilation or replaced entirely by a bill of the Rules Committee's own preference. Upon reaching the floor of the House (5) it might be further amended during debate or voted down or referred back to committee for further study. If passed, *it must repeat essentially the same process in the Senate,* assuming the Senate has time and interest for it.[34]

If the bill does not make it through both houses before the next congressional election, it must be reintroduced and the entire process begins anew. Not surprisingly, the House and Senate frequently fail to pass the same version of a bill; differences then have to be ironed out in ad hoc conference committees composed of several senior members from each house. More than one conference committee has rewritten a bill to better suit special interests.

The bill that survives the legislative labyrinth and escapes an executive veto to become an *act* of Congress, and the law of the land, may be only an *authorization* act—that is, it simply brings some program into existence. Congress then must vote *appropriations* to finance the authorized policy; hence, *the entire legislative process must be repeated for the appropriations bill.* Not infrequently legislation authorizing the government to spend a certain amount for a particular program is passed, but no appropriations are subsequently voted to finance it.

Congress' task is made no easier by the duplication of bills and overlapping committee jurisdictions. In one session seventy bills were introduced to change the date of Veterans Day back to the traditional November 11. As of 1976 there were twenty-two House committees and subcommittees dealing—none of them very success-

---

34. There were 13,591 bills introduced in the 94th Congress, of which 232 became law. The actual numerical output of laws is no measure of Congress' productivity or worth. Along with some worthwhile measures, many worthless and frivolous bills are eliminated, and of the ones that become law many run counter to the public interest and *should* have been eliminated.

fully—with the problems of the aged. Yet for all their activity, the 435 members of the House and one hundred members of the Senate seem to have neither the time nor the staff to inform themselves in any depth about the many problems of the nation or the many doings of the executive. The Defense Department has more people preparing its budget than Congress has for all its functions combined (which tells us not only how understaffed is Congress but how immense is Defense). Congress does not have the ability to produce a comprehensive national program. For almost all its technical information and legislative initiatives it relies on the executive departments or on lobbyists from private industry, who often write the bills that friendly Congressmen later introduce as legislation.

The bulk of a Congressman's time is taken up performing services for constituents, making calls to public agencies on behalf of businessmen and interested parties back home, introducing private bills to permit alien relatives of constituents to enter or remain in the country and answering the huge quantity of mail that comes in. In the time he has left for legislative tasks, the Congressman devotes himself to several specialized subcommittees, trying to build up some expertise in limited areas, in effect making himself that much more of a special-interest representative who defines the legislative task in terms of distinct "problems" (e.g., trade, defense, forestry) and who focuses little attention on the interrelatedness and *systemic* nature of politico-economic problems. On matters that are outside his domain he defers to his other special-interest colleagues.

Congress is not just bicameral. With its quasi-independent committee potentates and minority pockets of power, it is almost "multicameral." These special-interest congressional factions achieve working majorities through various trade-offs and mutual accommodations, a "log-rolling" process that is not the same as compromise. Rather than checking one another as in compromise situations, and thus blunting the selfish demands of each—possibly with some benefit to the general public—interest groups end up supporting one another's claims, at the expense of those who are without power in the pressure system. Thus the oil lobby will back farm supports in exchange for farm bloc support of oil leases. In both cases the ordinary consumers and taxpayers bear the costs. *Log-rolling is the method by which the various haves reconcile their differences, usually at the expense of the have-nots.* The net effect is not a *check* on competing claims but a *compounding* of claims against the interests of the unorganized public.

Congress: A Product of Its Environment

While Congress is a body supposedly dedicated to a government of laws, not of men, its procedures "are founded all too much on unwritten, unspoken, and largely unnoticed informal agreements among men."[35] The norms and customs that are so much a part of life in the House and Senate are generally conservative in their effect. The emphasis on elaborate forms of courtesy and on avoiding public remarks that might be construed as personally critical of colleagues discourages a good deal of discussion of things that are deserving of criticism.[36] The tendency to minimize differences usually works to the advantage of those who prefer to keep things quiet and against the kind of confrontation needed to effect change. The unlimited debate in the Senate allows a small but determined number of Senators to filibuster a bill to death or kill it by exercising the *threat* of filibuster.[37] The quorum call stops all legislative business until enough members are rounded up and a roll call is taken. These kinds of parliamentary devices make it easier for minorities to thwart action.

The freshman legislator is socialized into a world of cronyism that makes the mobilization of legislative majorities around broad issue-oriented programs difficult to achieve. He learns not to give too much attention to issue politics—since issues can be divisive—but to develop personal loyalties to senior members, defer to their judgments, avoid exacerbating debates and become a reliable member of the club. The longer he stays in Congress the more his commitment to issues seems to blur.[38] He soon realizes that oppor-

35. Clark, *The Senate Establishment*, p. 15. Senator Clark was referring specifically to the Senate, but his observation applies to both houses.
36. A college student who worked as a congressional intern observed: "The Senate is unbelievable—the biggest mutual admiration society in history. . . . How heated can a debate get when every four seconds you're referring to your so-called rival as 'the honored gentleman from Illinois'? And that's not just a game; it's the whole spirit of the place." Quoted in Melvin Eli, "Most Interns Find D.C. Insulated and Elitist," *Valley Advocate* (Mass.), September 15, 1976.
37. Over the years the filibuster has been used mostly by Southern Senators against civil rights bills and to a lesser degree by conservatives against measures that were deemed harmful to big business; thus in 1974 a bill to establish an Agency for Consumer Advocacy was filibustered to death by Senators with the backing of the National Association of Manufacturers and the U.S. Chamber of Commerce. The agency would have been without regulatory powers and would merely have presented a "consumer viewpoint," but even this was too much for the filibusters.
38. Garrison Nelson gave me some helpful insights concerning the conservative functions and effects of personalism and leadership selection within the

tunities for choice committee assignments and other favors are extended to him by leaders in accordance with his willingness to go along with things.[39]

Although conservative bills sometimes get caught in the congressional log jam, generally when conservatives want action, they get it. As Senator Clark was not the first or last to complain, progressive bills are treated by congressional leaders with painfully slow deliberateness, if at all, while bills which interest them are expeditiously acted upon.[40] Without hesitation, Congress voted $6.75 million for a market news service to furnish timely reports on major agricultural commodities to enable agribusiness to better determine when to sell and how to price its products. But this same Congress debated at great length the passage of a minor pilot project supplying breakfast in school for hungry children, a program that would reach only a tiny number of the millions of malnourished American children.[41] In almost everything Congress does, the pattern remains the same. Multibillion-dollar tax breaks for big business are passed in a matter of days with little debate, while reform bills languish in committee. Multibillion-dollar defense bills are passed in a matter of hours, while pitifully inadequate welfare measures are haggled over with that kind of ungracious stinginess the haves so frequently display toward the have-nots.

Yet it is not quite accurate to call the legislature "unrepresentative." In a way, Congress is precisely and faithfully representative of the power distributions of the wider society. As Ralph Nader observes, "Power goes to those senior legislators who service powerful interests, while isolation goes to those who merely represent powerless people."[42] And as long as Congress reflects the distribution of economic power in the wider society, it is not likely to change much even if liberals in both houses manage to gain control of the major committees, and even if the cloture rule is changed to enable the Senate to rid itself of the filibuster, and even if the

House. See also his *Party Control Periods in the U.S. House of Representatives and the Recruitment of its Leaders, 1789–1971*, Ph.D. dissertation (University of Iowa, Iowa City, Iowa, 1973).

39. For one Congressman's confession of frustration, see Richard Madden, "Pike Tells of Futility in House," *New York Times*, July 1, 1972.

40. Clark, *The Senate Establishment*, p. 77.

41. *Hunger, U.S.A.*, a report by the Citizens' Board of Inquiry into Hunger and Malnutrition in the United States (Boston: Beacon Press, 1968), p. 80.

42. Ralph Nader, "Making Congress Work," *New Republic*, August 21 and 28, 1971, p. 19.

Rules Committee is deprived of all its arbitrary powers, and even if seniority is done away with. For what remains is the entire system of organized corporate power with its hold over the economic life of the nation and the material resources of the society, its control of the media and mass propaganda, its dominance of most cultural and social institutions, its organized pressure groups, high-paid lobbyists and influence-peddling lawyers, big money contributions and bribes—all of which operate with such telling effect on legislators, including most of the professedly liberal ones.[43]

To be sure, a representative system *should* be a pressure system, enabling constituents to exercise control over their lawmakers. But what is usually missing from the lawmaker's own view is any real appreciation of the one-sidedness of the pressure system. For many in the state legislatures, as in Congress, the existing pressure system *is* the representative system; that is to say, those groups having the money, organization, visibility and expertise to *take* an interest in legislative affairs are presumed to be the only ones that *have* an actual interest. The muted levels of society are left pretty much out of the picture.

43. The situation within the various state legislatures is comparable to that in Congress except that state lawmakers seem to be even less visible, less accountable and possibly even more corrupt than their national counterparts. See the discussion in Chapter Twelve.

The Special - Interest President

14

MUCH HAS BEEN MADE OF THE "UNIQUE-ness" and "sanctity" of the presidency. More should be said about how its occupants have operated within the same system of power and interest as other politicians. Our task here is not to join those who would mystify the presidency but to take a nonworshipful look at the office.

Guardian of Capitalism

While Congressmen are the captives of the "special interests," the President, occupying the highest office and elected by the entire country, tends to be less vulnerable to the monied pressure groups and more responsive to the needs of the unorganized public—at least this is what political scientists taught after years of observing Presidents like Roosevelt, Truman and Kennedy tussling with conservatives in Congress. Actually, our various Presidents resemble the average pressure politician much more than we were taught to believe.

The presidency is often described as a composite of many roles. The President, we are told, is not only the chief executive, he is "chief legislator," commander-in-chief, head of state and leader of his party. Seldom mentioned is his role as guardian and spokesman of capitalism. Far from being an opponent of the special interests, the President is the embodiment of the political system that serves them, playing an active part in fortifying modern capitalism at home and abroad. Whether a Democrat or a Republican, a liberal or a conservative, the President treats capitalist interests as representative of the interests of all Americans. He will describe the overseas investments of giant corporations as "*United States* investments abroad," part of "*America's* interests in the world," to be defended at all costs—or certainly at great cost. He will speak of "our" oil in the Middle East and "our" markets in Latin America and "our" raw materials in Southeast Asia (to be defended by *our* sons) when what he is referring to are the holdings of a small, powerful segment of the population. Presidents have presented their multibillion-dollar spending programs on behalf of private industry as necessary for "*America's* growing needs" and have greeted the expansion of big business and big profits as manifestations of "a healthy *national* economy" and as good for the "*national* interest."

As authoritative figures whose opinions are widely publicized, Presidents have played an active role indoctrinating the American people into the business ideology of the ruling class, publicly praising businessmen for their allegedly great contributions to American life. "You men . . . are the leaders of this community," President Lyndon Johnson once announced to a group of corporation heads, "and through your industries the leaders of the United States."[1] In the last century all Presidents have brought businessmen into key administrative posts and have relied heavily on the judgments of corporate leaders. Many Presidents themselves enter the White House after an extended period of professional and personal ties with banking and business firms. Since World War II, most of the men who have run as presidential candidates on the Democratic and Republican tickets have been millionaires either at the time they first campaigned for the office or by the time they departed from it. All of them have drawn their economic and foreign policy advisors mainly from industry, banking and the foundations.

Every modern President has had occasion to warn the citizenry of the wiles of radicalism, the regimentations of socialism and the tyrannies of communism. All have accepted and praised something called "the free enterprise system." One Washington correspondent describes President Ford:

1. From the *Public Papers of the Presidents, Lyndon B. Johnson, 1963–1964,* vol. 2, pp. 1, 147–151, reprinted in Marvin Gettleman and David Mermelstein (eds.), *The Failure of American Liberalism* (New York: Vintage, 1971), pp. 124–128.

Ford follows the judgment of the major international oil companies on oil problems in the same way that he amiably heeds the advice of other big businesses on the problems that interest them. . . . He is . . . a solid believer in the business ideology of rugged individualism, free markets and price competition—virtues that exist more clearly in his mind than they do in the practices of the international oil industry.[2]

In the 1976 campaign President Jimmy Carter identified himself as "an engineer, a planner and a businessman," who understood "the value of a strong system of free enterprise" with "minimal intrusion of government in our free economic system."[3] Carter was a member of the Trilateral Commission, organized by David Rockefeller and composed of corporate, political and other institutional leaders. Many of his advisors on economics, defense and foreign affairs, along with his vice-presidential running mate, Senator Walter Mondale, were members or key staff persons of the commission.[4]

Presidents have made a show of concern for public causes, using slogans and images intended to enhance their popular appeal; thus Teddy Roosevelt had his "Square Deal," Woodrow Wilson his "New Freedom," Franklin Roosevelt his "New Deal," Harry Truman his "Fair Deal," John Kennedy his "New Frontier," and Lyndon Johnson his "Great Society." Behind the fine sounding labels, one discovers much the same record of service to the powerful and neglect of the needy. Consider John Kennedy, a liberal President widely celebrated for his devotion to the underdog and his desire to "get America moving." In foreign affairs, Kennedy spoke of international peace and self-determination for all peoples, yet he invaded Cuba after Castro nationalized U.S. corporate holdings. He delivered an ultimatum during the Cuban missile crisis that brought us to the brink of nuclear war. He drastically increased military expenditures, instituted counterinsurgency programs throughout the Third World, and sent troops into Vietnam. Kennedy set up aid programs in underdeveloped nations that mostly benefited American investors. He envisioned major land reforms in these countries—supposedly to be carried out volun-

2. William V. Shannon in the New York Times, July 22, 1975.
3. Carter's acceptance speech at the 1976 Democratic National convention. Seattle Post-Intelligencer, July 16, 1976.
4. See the discussion in Kenneth M. Dolbeare "Alternatives to the New Fascism" (Paper given at the 1976 Annual Meeting of the American Political Science Association, September 1976), p. 12. Dolbeare points out that Carter spoke of his indebtedness to the Trilateral Commission in influencing his political views. See Jimmy Carter, Why Not the Best? (New York: Bantam, 1976), p. 146.

tarily by the landlords and the corporations—yet he sent vast quantities of arms to bolster the reactionary generals who ruled most of the "Free World." In all, his foreign policy was dedicated to ensuring the predominance of multinational corporations and to the pursuit of a militaristic, anti-Communist cold war.

In domestic matters Kennedy presented himself as a champion of civil rights, yet he did little to create new job opportunities for Black people; he refrained from taking legal action to support antidiscrimination cases in housing; he appointed conservative, racist judges in the South; and in the face of repeated atrocities against civil rights organizers in that region, his Justice Department was unable to bring a single murderer or arsonist to justice—although it did prosecute eight civil rights workers in Albany, Georgia, on charges of perjury and obstructing justice, leading to sentences ranging up to five years.

Kennedy talked as if he were the special friend of the working people. Yet he imposed wage restraints on unions at a time when the buying power of many wage earners was stagnant or declining. He strongly opposed introduction of the thirty-five-hour week, accepted a 5.5 percent unemployment rate as normal and instituted regressive income tax programs—including a 7 percent investment tax credit which netted billions for big busness. He pursued deficit spending policies that carried business profit rates to all-time highs without reducing unemployment. Kennedy discovered that millions of Americans still lived below the poverty level, but he never initiated a comprehensive program to deal with poverty, nor with the crises in transportation, housing and health care. Bernard Nossiter notes that the image of John Kennedy as antibusiness was an undeserved one: "In fact, in every significant area—wage policy, tax policy, international trade and finance, federal spending—the president showed a keen understanding and ready response to the essential corporate program."[5]

Through his youth, vigor, intelligence and public rhetoric Kennedy gave every appearance of being the liberal activist; actually, he chose a course of "pragmatic politics," working cautiously within the special-interest system instead of attempting to challenge or change it. He did nothing to mobilize new political strengths and mass movements among workers, Blacks, the young and the poor. If anything, he tended to distrust and discourage popular activism. He even opposed the peaceful and moderate civil rights

5. Bernard Nossiter, *The Mythmakers* (Boston: Beacon Press, 1964), p. 40.

March on Washington in 1963, going so far as to invite various Black leaders to the White House to urge them, without success, to call it off.[6]

Conservative Presidents, like Richard Nixon and Gerald Ford, have manifested the same tendency to *talk* for the people and *work* for the corporate elites. In January 1970, President Nixon pledged an all-out effort for conservation, but a month later he threw his weight behind the Timber Supply bill, which opened new national forest lands for commercial exploitation, and he vetoed the water pollution bill that passed Congress by a nearly unanimous vote. In March 1973, Nixon spoke of his administration's dedication to the returning Vietnam veteran. Yet just the month before, he had proposed cuts in benefits to disabled Vietnam veterans. In 1971, through his White House Conference on Aging, Nixon gave lip service to "the plight of the elderly," yet in 1972 he opposed an increase in Social Security retirement benefits. The following year he increased Medicare costs and stopped housing construction for the elderly.[7]

In the 1976 presidential campaign, President Ford presented himself as a champion of the middle-income taxpayer, yet his tax proposals from the previous year provided relief—some $10 billion— mostly for the very highest income groups. In addition he pushed for a 12 percent investment tax credit amounting to an estimated $4-billion windfall for business. While reviling the "big spenders" in Congress, Ford spent so freely on big business and the military as to create a $65-billion deficit in fiscal 1975. He talked about an energy policy to meet "the needs of America," then proposed the establishment of a public authority whose income would be used by big oil firms for investment purposes.[8]

6. My discussion of Kennedy draws heavily from the excellent article by Ian McMahan, "The Kennedy Myth," *New Politics*, 3, Winter 1964, pp. 40–48. Also Richard J. Walton, *Cold War and Counter-Revolution: The Foreign Policy of John F. Kennedy* (Baltimore: Penguin Books, 1972); Bruce Miroff, *Pragmatic Illusions* (New York: McKay, 1976). For a treatment of the disparity between Lyndon Johnson's liberal rhetoric and his conservative policies, see Gettleman and Mermelstein, *The Failure of American Liberalism;* also Robert Sherrill, *The Accidental President* (New York: Grossman, 1967), Chapters 3, 5, 6 and *passim*.

7. *New York Times*, June 8, 1973.

8. This proposal to use an estimated $100 billion in public funds for the private profit of the Rockefeller-dominated oil industry came to Ford directly from Nelson Rockefeller's "Commission on Critical Choices." See T. Mitchell, "Ford Asks $100 Billion Giveaway for Oil Giants," *Workers World*, October 3, 1975.

President Ford usually showed himself remarkably indifferent to the miseries of the unemployed, vetoing bills that would have created almost 2 million jobs in housing, public service and youth and college work programs. But whenever Congress threatened to impose environmental protections, he developed a sudden passion for the jobless, arguing that such programs would limit production and employment. Ford spoke about protecting the environment but twice vetoed mild bills to regulate strip mining. He opened more public land to the timber industry, allowing excessive logging quotas and "clear cutting" which wreaked havoc on national forests; he supported commercial developers on the land use bill, cattlemen on control of the southwestern wildlife refuge and the oil companies on planning the future of Alaska and much of the world.[9]

Ford talked about restoring morality in public life and fighting crime, then issued a "full, free and absolute" pardon to Nixon for criminal acts committed during his tenure in office, both those known and those yet to be discovered.[10] He described himself as a representative of "all the people" but sought to increase the cost of food stamps and scale down cost-of-living increases due to the aged on Social Security. He vetoed bills intended to provide stronger antitrust penalties, education funds for Vietnam veterans, and school lunch, child day care and child nutrition programs.[11] While agribusiness made $150 billion from food sales in 1975, and a million children suffered brain damage from malnutrition, Ford vetoed a bill providing food supplements to pregnant women and infants living below the poverty line. He vetoed rehabilitation bills for the physically and mentally handicapped, rural water and sewer grants, disaster aid and a minimum wage increase. Like the various Democratic and Republican Presidents who preceded him, Ford portrayed himself as a devotee of the people but was a staunch— and usually blatant—defender of the interests of Wall Street and the Pentagon.

9. William V. Shannon in the New York Times, July 10, 1975.

10. When his nomination for the vice-presidency was under consideration, Ford indicated his opposition to a pardon saying, "The American people will never stand for it." There is a likely possibility that Nixon's selection of Ford as Vice-President was contingent upon receiving a pardon from Ford when the latter became President. See I. F. Stone, "Mr. Ford's Deceptions," New York Review of Books, November 14, 1974, pp. 3–12.

11. See, for instance, the New York Times, September 11 and October 8, 1975.

The Pressure Politician

Like other politicians, the men who run for President must procure vast sums from the rich in order to pay their campaign costs. Big contributors disclaim any intention of trying to buy influence with their gifts, insisting that they give freely because they "believe" in the candidate and think he will make the best President—certainly the best that money can buy. They believe he will pursue policies that are the most beneficial to the national interest. That they view the national interest from the elevated positions they occupy in the social structure and that it is often indistinguishable from their own financial interests does not make their support hypocritical but all the more sincere. The contribution is not necessarily for a better personal deal but for a better America—this image encompasses the sum of the wealthy contributor's class experiences and life values.

If it should happen, however, that the man elected (or reelected) President wishes to express his gratitude by performing a favor for a big donor, the donor usually accepts without fear that he will thereby sully the selfless motives that originally inspired the contribution. Furthermore, if at any time in the four years after the election the contributor should find himself or his firm burdened by a problem that only the White House can handle, he sees no reason why he shouldn't be allowed to exercise his democratic rights like any other citizen and ask his elected representative, who in this case happens to be his friend, the President of the United States, for a little help. Such requests are a common practice. Large donors to President Nixon's campaign, including certain insurance moguls, dairymen, bankers, carpet manufacturers, coal mine owners, railroad tycoons, hamburger restaurant-chain owners and managers of giant conglomerates like ITT, benefited many times over from White House intercessions on their behalf. In the case of ITT, the Nixon administration helped settle a multibillion-dollar antitrust suit against that corporation in return for a promised $400,000 donation.[12] Nixon's former White House counsel, John

12. White House involvement in the ITT affair was publicly confirmed in testimony given to a congressional committee by Charles Colson, former Special Counsel to the White House. See *New York Times*, June 15, 1973; see also Anthony Sampson, *The Sovereign State of I.T.T.* (New York: Stein and Day, 1973). For other evidence of White House efforts on behalf of large contributors see James Ridgeway, "Republican Campaign Contributions (4), 'We Deserve a Break Today,'" *Village Voice*, October 20, 1972, pp. 13ff.; Ben A. Franklin, "Milk Aide Says a Lawyer for Nixon Sought Funds," *New York Times*, January 11, 1973: and the statement published by the Democratic party: "The Nixon Administration Peddles Special Favors to the Super-Rich," *New York Times*, October 25, 1972.

W. Dean, testified that on occasion the President requested the Internal Revenue Service to stop auditing the incomes of close friends.[13]

Some big contributors are awarded ambassadorships. Every four years the White House "auctions off its embassies in Western Europe and in a few other agreeable areas to the highest bidders. The cash goes not to the United States Treasury but to the Republicans or Democrats, whichever party is in power."[14] Arthur K. Watson donated $371,000 to various Nixon campaigns and was appointed ambassador to France in 1970. To become ambassador to Austria in 1968, John Humes gave $43,000; he renewed his tenure in 1972 with another $103,500. The embassy in cold, snowy Finland went to John Krehbiel for the cut-rate price of $5,500 in 1968 and $12,500 four years later, while beautiful sunny Jamaica went to Vincent de Roulet for $44,500 in 1968 and $32,000 in 1972. Ruth Farkas contributed $300,000 to Nixon's campaign in 1972 and was awarded the embassy in Luxembourg, an overpriced bid. Walter Annenberg renewed his lease on London with $254,000. All the aforementioned persons had several things in common: they were rich contributors; they were conservatives; and they had no professional diplomatic experience.[15]

There is a view—made popular about the time Harry Truman became President—that the greatness of the office lends greatness to its occupants; even those persons of mediocre talent and stature supposedly grow in response to the presidency's great responsibilities and powers. Closer examination shows that most White House occupants have been just as readily corrupted as ennobled by the power of the office, inclined toward self-righteous assertion, compelled to demonstrate their macho toughness and decisiveness, intolerant of, and irritated by, public criticism and not above using their power in unlawful ways against political opponents. Thus at least six Presidents employed illegal FBI wiretaps to gather incriminating information on rival political figures. The White House tapes revealed Richard Nixon as a petty, vindictive, bigoted man who manifested a shallowness of spirit and mind which the ma-

13. *New York Times,* June 21, 1973; also June 22, 1973, for other reports of intervention on behalf of White House friends.

14. *New York Times* editorial, April 4, 1973.

15. Nixon's personal lawyer, Herbert W. Kalmbach, pleaded guilty to selling an ambassadorship for a $100,000 campaign contribution. Earlier, with a characteristic feeling for the truth, President Nixon asserted at a press conference: "Ambassadorships have not been for sale." *New York Times,* February 26 and June 28, 1974.

jestic office could cloak but could not transform. In 1973 official audits revealed that Nixon had spent $10 million of the taxpayer's money on improvement of his private estates and that he had made illegal tax deductions of around a half-million dollars.[16] And President Ford had engaged in realty business deals with a developer who saved $100 million when Ford vetoed a strip mining bill.[17]

The success any group enjoys in winning the intervention of the President has less to do with the justice of its cause than with the position it occupies in the class structure. If a large group of migrant workers and a small group of aerospace executives both sought the President's assistance, it would not be too difficult to predict which of them would be more likely to win it. Witness these events of April 1971:

(1) Some 80,000 to 90,000 migrant farm workers in Florida, out of work for much of the season because of crop failures and explicitly exempted from unemployment compensation, were left without means of feeding themselves and their families. Welfare agencies supplied some surplus foods that were "almost pure starch, usually unpalatable, and cause diarrhea to children." Faced with the prospect of seeing their children starve, the workers demonstrated in large numbers outside President Nixon's Key Biscayne vacation residence in Florida. The peaceful gathering was an attempt to attract public attention to their desperate plight and to get the White House to intercede. The workers succeeded in attracting only the attention of the police, who dispersed them, charging their lines with swinging clubs. The demonstration was reported in a few small-circulation radical newspapers and ignored by most of the establishment news media.

There was no evidence that the farm workers' message ever intruded upon the President's attention although information about their condition did reach several lower-level federal agencies. Subsequent appeals to Washington brought no response. Eventually the Florida farm counties were declared disaster areas not because of the misery of the migrants but because of the crop losses sustained by the commercial farms. Since the migrant workers had no state residence, they did not qualify for relief. Most of the government emergency relief money ended in the hands of the big growers, who worked with state agencies in distributing it. The workers were "summarily left out of the decisions."[18]

16. *New York Times,* June 25, 1973, and April 4, 1974.
17. *New York Times,* December 19, 1974.
18. Tom Foltz, "Florida Farmworkers Face Disaster," *Guardian,* April 3, 1971, p. 4.

(2) During the very week the farm workers were being clubbed in Key Biscayne, leaders of the aerospace industry placed a few telephone calls to the right people in Washington and, without benefit of demonstration or agitation, were invited to meet quietly with the President to discuss their companies' job problems. Later that day the White House announced a $42-million authorization to the aerospace industry to assist 75,000 to 100,000 of its top administrators, scientists and technicians. The spending plan, an industry creation accepted by the government without prior study, provided $5 million for a "job search" program, $25 million for industry personnel retraining, $10 million to assist the companies in relocating personnel, $2 million for something called a "skill conversion fund," supposedly enabling the industry's scientists to "explore" ways of providing technical help for "traditional areas of the economy."[19]

Contrasting the treatment accorded the farm workers with that provided the aerospace industrialists, or big farm owners, or big dairymen, or representatives of Standard Oil, U.S. Steel, ITT, etc., we might ask: Is the President responding to a "national interest" or a "special interest" when he helps the giant firms? Much depends upon how the labels are applied. Those who believe the national interest necessitates taking every possible measure to maintain the profits and strength of the industrial and military establishment, of which the aerospace industry is a part, might say the President is not responding to a special interest but to the needs of national security. Certainly almost every President in modern times might have agreed and acted accordingly. Industry is said to be the muscle and sinews of the nation. In contrast, a regional group of farm workers represents a marginal interest. Without making light of the suffering of the migrants, it is enough to say that a President's first responsibility is to tend to our industrial economy. In fact, the argument goes, when workers act to disrupt and weaken the sinews of industry, as have striking coal miners, railroad operators and steel workers, the President may see fit to deal summarily with them.

Other people would argue that the national interest is not served when giant industries receive favored treatment at the expense of the taxpayers, consumers and workers and to the lasting neglect of millions like the farm workers. That the corporations have holdings which are national and often multinational in scope does not mean they represent the interests of the nation's populace.

19. *New York Times,* April 2, 1971.

The "national interest" or "public interest" should encompass the ordinary working public rather than the big commercial farm owners, corporate elites and their well-paid technicians and managers. Contrary to an established myth, the public monies distributed to these favored few do not "trickle down" to the mass of working people at the bottom—as the hungry farm workers would testify.

Whichever position one takes, it becomes clear that there is no *neutral* way of defining the "national interest." Whichever policy the President pursues, he is helping some class interests rather than others, and it is a matter of historical record that Presidents, whether Democrats or Republicans, liberals or conservatives, have rather consistently chosen a definition of the national interest that serves the giant conglomerates. It is also clear, whether we consider it essential or deplorable, that the President, as the most powerful officeholder in the land, is most readily available to the most powerful interests in the land and rather inaccessible to us lesser mortals.

The President versus Congress: Who Has the Power?

Since the turn of the century, the burdens of government have grown enormously at the municipal, state and federal levels and in the executive, legislative and judicial branches. But as industrial capitalism expanded at home and abroad, the task of serving and protecting its vast interests and dealing with the problems it has caused has fallen disproportionately on that level of government which is national and international in scope—the federal—and on that branch which is suited for carrying out the necessary technical, organizational and military tasks—the executive.[20] The powers of the executive have increased so much that today there is no such thing as a "weak" President, for even Eisenhower, who preferred to exercise as little initiative as possible in most affairs, found himself proposing huge budgets and participating in decisions of far greater scope than anything handled by a "strong" President a half century before.

The growth of the presidency has been so great as to have brought a *relative* decline in the powers of Congress (even though the scope of legislative activity itself has greatly increased over the

20. Today the federal government spends more in one day (about a billion dollars) than it spent in the first sixty years of its existence.

years). This is especially true in international affairs. Congressional influence over foreign policy has been exercised largely by withholding funds, passing resolutions, ratifying treaties, confirming ambassadors and other such means; but in recent times Presidents increasingly have bypassed Congress or confronted it with faits accomplis, making covert military commitments, ignoring legislative amendments in international matters, circumventing the Senate's power to ratify treaties by resorting to "executive agreements," and placing White House policy-makers beyond the reach of congressional interrogation by claiming "executive privilege" for them. Although "executive privilege" is nowhere mentioned in the Constitution, it has been used to withhold information on everything from undeclared wars to illegal campaign funds and burglaries. In 1976 Ford invoked it when refusing to supply a House committee with information on the CIA.[21] The net effect of the growth in presidential power has been to move important and potentially unpopular monetary and foreign policy decisions out of public view and into the secrecy of the executive office.

The legislative branch is often no better informed than the public it represents. For a number of years Congress unknowingly funded CIA operations in Laos and Thailand that were in violation of congressional prohibitions. Most of the members of the Senate who were questioned by Senator Proxmire had never heard of the automated battlefield program for which they had voted secret appropriations.[22] Congress ordered a halt to further expansion of a controversial naval base on an island in the Indian Ocean, only to discover subsequently that construction was continuing and air activities had steadily increased at the base.[23] A report from two House Foreign Affairs subcommittees complained of the White House's habits of secrecy and deviousness when dealing with Con-

21. "Executive privilege" was given a legal peg by the Nixon-appointed Supreme Court, which, while ruling that the concept did not apply to criminal cases (the release of the White House tapes in the Watergate affair), did declare that a "presumptive privilege" for withholding information belonged to the President. See *U.S.* v. *Nixon* 418 U.S. 683 (1974). Most certainly "presumptive" since it has no existence in the Constitution or in any law.

22. Paul Dickson and John Rothchild, "The Electronic Battlefield: Wiring Down the War," *Washington Monthly*, May 1971, pp. 6–14. If the Pentagon Papers reveal anything, it is the secretive, unaccountable nature of executive policy. See the latter portion of Richard J. Barnet's *Roots of War* (New York: Atheneum, 1972) for an account of the ways public opinion is manipulated by officialdom; also John C. Donovan, *The Cold Warriors: A Policy Elite* (Lexington, Mass.: D.C. Heath, 1973).

23. UPI dispatch in *Workers World*, January 2, 1976.

gress and the "unwillingness of the executive branch to acknowledge major decisions and to subject them to public scrutiny and discussion."[24]

In many instances, whether in foreign or domestic matters, it is not that the President acts without Congress but that he commands levers of power which leave the legislature no option but to move in a direction predetermined by him. The executive's control of crucial information, its system of management and budgeting and its vast network of specialized administrators and staff workers enables it to play a greater role in shaping the legislative agenda than the understaffed, overworked and often ill-informed legislators. In recent years approximately 80 percent of the major laws enacted have originated in the executive branch.

Congress itself has been compliant about the usurpation of its power. Since 1790 the legislature has granted each President, and a widening list of executive agencies, confidential funds for which no detailed invoices are required. The statute that created the CIA permitted its billions to be expended without regard to the provisions of law regulating government appropriations and spending and without the knowledge of Congress.[25] Congress has preferred to pass on to the President the task of handling crises and making troublesome and unpopular policy choices on behalf of the corporate system at home and abroad. In the last forty years, three Presidents have declared states of "national emergency" which have never been terminated, emergencies to win support for war, break strikes, freeze wages and stop bank failures. There exist at least 470 statutes passed by Congress which extend potentially dictatorial emergency powers to the President. A special Senate Committee warned:

Under the powers delegated by these statutes the President may seize properties, mobilize production, seize commodities, institute martial law, seize control of all transportation, regulate private capital, restrict travel and in a host of particular ways control the activities of all American citizens.

While danger of a dictatorship arising through legal means may seem remote to us today, recent history records that Hitler seized con-

24. The subcommittees' statement is quoted in Graham Hovey, "Making Foreign Policy," *New York Times*, January 22, 1973, p. 31. Yet as noted in the previous two chapters, Congress seems willing enough to go along with most of the executive's secret practices and has a number of its own.

25. Louis Fisher, *Presidential Spending Power* (Princeton, N.J.: Princeton University Press, 1975).

trol through the use of emergency powers contained in the laws of the Weimar Republic.[26]

Under the guise of limiting presidential power, Congress sometimes expands it. Thus the War Powers Act of 1973, placing the President under obligation to seek congressional approval within sixty days for any war he has launched, actually expands his warmaking powers, since the Constitution does not grant the President power to engage in warfare without prior congressional approval.

The peculiar danger of executive power is that it executes. Presidents have repeatedly engaged in acts of warfare for instance, without congressional knowledge or approval because they have had at their command the military forces to do so. If the legislature proposes, it is the executive that disposes (usually the executive does both), hence having the final word on what and how things get done, acting with the force of state, exercising daily initiatives of its own on a scale so massive and detailed, so secretive and closely linked to its military and security forces as to be held unaccountable more often than not. Indeed, the growth of the presidency has been a growth in its unaccountable and unilateral powers. The crimes of Richard Nixon, then, were not an anomaly but a fulfillment of the growing capacity for abuse and evil that inheres in the office.

Commanding the kind of media exposure that most politicians can only dream of, the President is able to direct attention to his program, be it for defense spending, taxes, wage controls, foreign trade, oil imports or international conflicts; and once he succeeds in defining his program as crucial to the "national interest" and himself as the key purveyor of that interest, Congress usually votes the necessary funds and enabling powers, contenting itself with making marginal modifications and inserting special amendments for special friends of its own. This is particularly the case if the President is not attempting anything of a radically deviant nature but much less true if he is hoping to initiate a program of a seemingly progressive kind.

One recalls that liberals frequently complained about the way Congress managed to thwart the desires of liberal Presidents like Truman and Kennedy. They concluded from this that Congress

26. Joint statement by Sen. Frank Church (D.–Ida.) and Sen. Charles Mathias (R.–Md.) for the Senate Committee on the Termination of the National Emergency, quoted in the *Guardian*, January 23, 1974.

had too much power and the President needed more. But having witnessed a conservative President like Richard Nixon regularly effect his will over a Democratic Congress, some of these same liberals then concluded that the President had too much power and Congress not enough. Actually, there is something more to these respective complaints than partisan inconsistency. In the first situation liberals are talking about the President's insufficient ability to effect measures that might benefit the many millions toward the bottom of the social ladder. And in the second instance liberals are talking about the President's seemingly limitless ability to make overseas military commitments and to thwart social welfare legislation at home.

What underlies the ostensibly inconsistent liberal complaint is the fact that *the relative powers of the executive and legislative branches depend in part on the interests being served,* and that regardless of who is in what office the political system operates more efficiently to realize conservative goals than reformist ones, both the executive and legislative branches being more responsive to the corporate powers than to economically deprived social groups. Furthermore, as the Founding Fathers intended, the system of separation of powers and checks and balances is designed to give the high ground to those who would resist social change, be they Presidents or Congressmen. Neither the executive nor the legislature can single-handedly initiate reform, which means that conservatives need to control only one or the other branch to thwart domestic actions (or in the case of Congress, key committees in one or the other house) while liberals must control both houses and both branches.

Small wonder that conservative and liberal Presidents have different kinds of experiences with Congress. Since a conservative President generally wants very little from Congress in the way of liberal domestic legislation and, with a few well-placed allies in the legislature, can often squelch what little Congress attempts to produce in that direction, he is less beholden to that body than a liberal President. Should Congress insist upon passing bills that incur his displeasure, the conservative President need control only one-third plus one of either the House or the Senate to sustain his vetoes. If bills are passed over his veto, he can still undermine legislative intent by delaying enforcement, impounding funds, re-programming or freezing funds under various pretexts relating to timing, efficiency and other operational contingencies. The Supreme Court has long been aware that its decisions have the force of law only if other agencies of government choose to carry them out. In recent years Congress has been coming to the same realization, developing a new appreciation of the executive's power to command in a direct and palpable way the people, materials and programs needed for carrying out decisions.

Monies which Congress allocated for pollution control, education and the food-stamp program were impounded by President Nixon in 1972 with the explanation that the sums could not be spent until there was a proper executive "development of approved plans and specifications"—which did not seem forthcoming. The Office of Management and Budget, under the President's direction, does not publicize these impoundings until the following year, when the new budget is presented.[27] Nixon vetoed twelve major social spending bills passed by Congress, while approving a defense budget of close to $80 billion—thus demonstrating that a President of the minority party can successfully promote major programs ("defense") or destroy them ("human services"); in either case the goal is essentially conservative.

The techniques of veto, impoundment, decoy and delay used by a conservative President to dismantle or hamstring already weak domestic programs are of little help to a liberal President who might claim a genuine interest in widespread social change, for the immense social problems he faces cannot be solved by executive sleight-of-hand. What minor efforts liberal Presidents make in the field of "social reform" legislation are frequently thwarted or greatly diluted by entrenched conservative powers in Congress. It is in these confrontations that the Congress gives every appearance of being able to frustrate presidential initiatives.

Change from the Top?

The ability of even a well-intentioned executive to generate policies for the benefit of relatively powerless constituents is, to say the least, quite limited. Not only Presidents but mayors and governors have complained of the difficulties of moving in new directions. The Black mayor of Gary, Indiana, Richard Hatcher, one of the more dedicated and socially conscious persons to achieve public office, offered this observation:

27. See "Expendables," *New Republic,* December 2, 1972, p. 9; also Fisher, *Presidential Spending Power.*

I am mayor of a city of roughly 90,000 Black people but we do not control the possibilities of jobs for them, or money for their schools, or state-funded social services. These things are in the hands of the U.S. Steel Corporation, and the County Department of Welfare, the State of Indiana. . . . For not a moment do I fool myself that Black political control of Gary or of Cleveland or of any other city in and of itself can solve the problems of the wretched of this nation. The resources are not available to the cities to do the job that needs doing.[28]

Hatcher's statement is not unique. "The speeches of mayors and governors," writes Richard Goodwin, "are filled with exculpatory claims that the problems are too big, that there is not enough power or enough money to cope with them, and our commentators sympathize, readily agreeing that this city or that state is really ungovernable."[29]

When Presidents, governors and mayors contend that the problems they confront are of a magnitude far greater than the resources they command, we can suspect them of telling the truth. Most of the resources are preempted by vested interests. The executive leader who begins his term with the promise of getting things moving is less likely to change the political-corporate-class system than be absorbed by it. Once in office, he finds himself staggered by the vast array of entrenched powers working within and without government. He is confronted with a recalcitrant legislature and an intractable bureaucracy. He is constantly distracted by issues and operational problems that seem to take him from his intended course, and he is unable to move in certain directions without incurring the hostility of those who control the economy and its institutional auxiliaries. So he begins to talk about being "realistic" and working with what is at hand, now tacking against the wind, now taking one step back in the often unrealized hope of taking two steps forward, until his public begins to complain that his administration bears a dismaying resemblance to the less dynamic, less energetic ones that came before. In the hope of maintaining his efficacy, he begins to settle for the *appearance* of efficacy, until appearances are all he is left struggling with. It is this tugging and hauling and whirling about in a tight circle of options and ploys that is celebrated by some as "the give-and-take of democratic group-interest politics." To less enchanted observers the failure of

28. From a speech delivered by Hatcher to an NAACP meeting, reprinted in the *Old Mole* (Boston), October 5, 1968.
29. Richard Goodwin, "Reflections: Sources of the Public Unhappiness," *New Yorker*, January 4, 1969, p. 41.

reform-minded leaders to deliver on their promises is another demonstration of the impossibility of working for major changes within a politico-economic system that is structured to resist change.

The Politics of Bureaucracy

15

AS EVERYONE COMPLAINS, BUREAUC-
racy is beset by inertia, evasion and unaccountability, but there are reasons why bureaucrats
behave as they do, and many of these reasons
are profoundly political, being less a peculiarity
of bureaucrats than a reflection of the wider
system of power and interest in which they
operate.

Government by Secrecy and Deception

The first line of defense for any bureaucracy,
Max Weber once wrote, is the withholding of
information. Actually, it is the first line of defense of any person in authority who wishes to
keep himself as much beyond public criticism
as possible. Officials who lie or who resort to
secrecy do so not only to maintain a free hand in
the pursuit of their interests (or the interests
they serve) but because they distrust the
public's ability to judge correctly. These two
sentiments strengthen each other, as when officeholders do their best to keep the public ignorant
and then use this ignorance as justification for
not inviting public criticism.

Chief executives have repeatedly misled
Congress and the public about U.S. overseas
interventions and then claimed a special knowledge or expertise in foreign affairs. Thus the
Eisenhower administration lied about its role in
overthrowing a democratic reform government

in Guatemala. It lied about its intervention in the Congo against Lumumba, and about the hand it took in the overthrow of Mossadegh in Iran, and about its part in the abortive coup against Sukarno in Indonesia in 1958. It lied about the CIA's use of U-2 spy planes over the Soviet Union until the Russians produced a live American U-2 pilot who had been shot down over their territory. The Kennedy administration lied about American involvement in the Bay of Pigs invasion of Cuba, about involvement in the Portuguese colonial war in Africa and about the extent of our intervention in Vietnam. The Johnson administration lied about its role in the successful overthrow of Sukarno in 1965 and the subsequent bloodbath in Indonesia. It lied repeatedly about growing U.S. involvement in Indochina and the nature of our intervention in the Dominican Republic and much of Latin America. The Nixon administration lied about attempts to subvert the Chilean election of a Marxist president. It lied about the presence of American military personnel in Laos and Cambodia and the role they played. And it repeatedly lied to keep secret some 3,630 B-52 raids that took place in Cambodia in 1969–1970.[1]

After a review of its secret files, the Defense Department declassified 710 documents and destroyed 355,300. The director of the CIA in 1973 destroyed all tape recordings of his calls over a six-year period. When President Ford took office, he refused to keep tapes and memoranda or even a log of his daily activities, so sensitive was he to how such record keeping had led to the downfall of his predecessor. He vetoed a bill that would have made government-held information more accessible to the public, tried to suppress informaton about the U.S. role in the overthrow of the democratic government of Chile and was able to keep secret the CIA's role in such places as Angola, Portugal and Jamaica.[2] Senate investigators estimated that the United States had as many as 400 to 600 secret agreements with other countries which the White House refused to deliver to Congress, including aid agreements with the fascist government of Chile and trade agreements with the Soviet Union.[3]

The White House and various executive agencies frequently cooperate more closely with private business than with Congress,

---

1. See David Wise, *The Politics of Lying* (New York: Random House, 1973) for more examples of government deception and secrecy.

2. Wise, *The Politics of Lying; New York Times*, October 18, 1974, March 2 and 26, 1976; *Guardian*, September 29, 1976.

3. *Charlotte* (N.C.) *Observer*, July 11, 1975.

especially when it comes to keeping things secret. Government regulation of prices charged by utilities and gas companies and government leasing of offshore drilling tracts to oil companies are based on data supplied by the interested corporations; this information is not available to Congress or the public. The FAA refuses to make public its reports on airline accidents and mechanical defects, distributing them only to the airline industry. The Social Security Administration has declined to publicize its report on Medicare operations and the way Blue Cross has carried out the program, despite growing public criticism of rising costs and curtailed benefits. While the Internal Revenue Service freely hands out tax records to agencies like the FBI, it refused to disclose to Congress its highly questionable ruling on a capital gains tax allowing ITT to take over a big Hartford insurance company.[4] And in the departments of Agriculture, Interior, Commerce and Defense, the doings of government and industry are frequently known only to select groups of bureaucrats and corporate leaders, leaving the rest of us to guess whether these policies are economically or socially beneficial.[5]

The government has repeatedly repressed information concerning health and safety problems. As early as 1954 the Food and Drug Administration was warned that the cyclamates put in many drinks and foods were linked to cancer. Yet five years later the FDA listed the cyclamates as safe, and it was not until 1969 that it removed them from beverages (it still allows them in certain foods). The Atomic Energy Commission has repeatedly suppressed information about the highly hazardous features of nuclear reactors. Although a study commissioned by the Department of Health, Education and Welfare showed that herbicides used in heavy

4. In covering up its dealings with ITT, the IRS was extending to tax rulings the statutory requirement that tax returns be kept confidential, despite a U.S. District Court decision under the Freedom of Information Act that rulings were not part of returns "but documents generated by the agency." *New York Times*, February 26, 1974.

5. James Ridgeway, "How Government and Industry Keep Secrets from the People," *New Republic*, August 21 and 28, 1971, pp. 17–19. Those who break the code of secrecy to inform the public of its interests are punished by their superiors. When a weapons-cost analyst, A. Ernest Fitzgerald, revealed the true cost of the C5A transport plane, the Air Force revoked his tenure, investigated his private life, then fired him. See Fitzgerald's account of how secrecy is used to hide waste and profiteering in the Pentagon: "Lockheed: The High Cost of Dying," *Ramparts*, June 1974, pp. 22–24, 57–58. The U.S. General Services Administration, on two separate occasions, fired its own internal criminal investigators for providing the press with evidence concerning wrongdoing inside the agency's own offices. *Boston Globe*, October 11, 1976.

amounts as defoliants in Vietnam and as weed killer in the United States produced birth deformities at low exposure levels, for three years this information was suppressed. Meanwhile one-eighth of the acreage in South Vietnam was sprayed with these chemicals, and a drastic increase in deformed births was reported. Investigations into these and other incidents caused two Stanford University scientists to report:

We believe, as a result of our studies, that . . . the executive decision-making process too often sacrifices the safety and welfare of the public to the short-term interests of the government bureaucracy and the large industrial interest to which it has become allied. . . . In these cases, where the facts and the best expert advice did not support the current administration policy, the primary interest of the Executive in the facts was to suppress them—even while stressing in public that its policies had a sound technical foundation.[6]

It is senseless to urge people to work for change "within the system" when they cannot find out what the system is doing.[7] This is not to say that government does not communicate with the public, indeed the public is subjected to a continual barrage of propaganda from official sources. Many millions of dollars are spent yearly by federal agencies and departments, of which the Pentagon is the most prolific, in the form of hundreds of magazine articles and motion pictures, thousands of radio scripts and tens of thousands of press releases and planted news stories.[8]

Bureaucratic Action and Inaction

The rulings of bureaucratic agencies are published daily in the *Federal Register*, a volume as imposing in size as the *Congressional Record* itself. Many of these rulings are as significant as major pieces of legislation, and in the absence of precise guidelines from Congress, they often take the place of legislation. In 1972, for instance, without a single law being passed and without a word of

6. Portions of the Stanford report are summarized and quoted in Bernard H. Gould, "Government Suppressed Scientists' Warnings of Dangers to the Health and Safety of Public," *National Enquirer*, February 21, 1971. The report's authors are Dr. Frank von Hippel and Dr. Joel Primack.

7. A point made by Lee Metcalf and Vic Reinemer, "Who Owns the Private Governments?" *Nation*, June 12, 1972, p. 745.

8. For instance see J. William Fulbright, *The Pentagon Propaganda Machine* (New York: Vintage, 1971).

public debate, the Price Commission approved more than $2 billion in rate increases for 110 telephone, gas and electric companies, thereby imposing upon the public by administrative fiat an expenditure far greater than what is contained in most of the bills passed by Congress.[9] Even when legislation does exist, it usually allows for leeway in application. Which laws are applied fully and which are ignored, what interpretations are made to suit what interests, what supplementary regulations are formulated—these matters, of keen concern to lobbyists, are almost unknown to the general public.

To treat public administration as a "neutral" "nonpartisan" function is grossly misleading.[10] *The political process does not end with the passage of a bill but continues with equal or even greater intensity at the administrative level, albeit in more covert fashion.* The administrative process becomes part of the pressure-group process and frequently has the effect of changing or subverting the intent of the law. This kind of development moved Theodore Lowi to call for more explicit articulation of the law by Congress and "the enunciation of decisions that are clear enough to guide administrators," so as to avoid passing "the application of these laws to lower and lower levels where there is less and less visibility."[11] But even in the face of rather explicit directives, executive agencies continually try to convert statutory mandates into discretionary guidelines. Consider what happens to environmental laws: (1) Sometimes the words of a law will be changed in violation of its purpose, as when the Forest Service decided that the "mark and designate" technique required by law to avoid clear cutting of forests really meant "mark *or* designate" which allowed widespread clear cutting. (2) An agency will engage in actions that violate a statute and will conclude that the statute has been "repealed by implication." Thus, although Congress expressly forbids damage to national parklands in developments on the Colorado River, the

9. See the statement by Senator Lee Metcalf reported in *Ramparts*, November 1972, p. 24.

10. The myth of administrative "neutrality" is encouraged by such things as the Hatch Act, a law prohibiting political activities by federal employees, presumably to preserve them from corrupt or biased influence. The act accomplishes no such thing. What it does is prevent millions of Americans from organizing in the defense of their own beliefs and interests, while leaving them fully exposed to the politics of bureaucracy. The constitutionality of the Act was upheld by the Supreme Court in 1973 by a 6–3 decision, in *U.S. Civil Service Commission* v. *National Association of Letter Carriers*.

11. Theodore Lowi, *The Politics of Disorder* (New York: Basic Books, 1971), p. 57.

Bureau of Reclamation flooded parkland terrain arguing that it was "authorized" to do so by implication because of its failure to get money for a dam. (3) Administrators will ignore statutory deadlines and delay carrying out the law. Thus a congressional act requiring commercial fishermen to use certain netting techniques to protect endangered species like porpoises remained unenforced because fishing interests found it too costly and burdensome.[12]

Sometimes when the funding is in the form of a block grant, supposedly to give greater flexibility to local administrators, the money ends up being spent for purposes not designated by law. Hence there is growing evidence that the "New Federalism" intended to decentralize spending programs for the inner-city needy has given "power to the powerful and peanuts to the poor."[13] Funds normally spent on community-development programs and Model Cities were used for such things as a tennis complex in an affluent neighborhood in Little Rock, Ark., a convention hall and downtown parking garage in Spartanburg, S.C., and a golf course in Alhambra, Calif.[14]

People who bemoan the "inaction" within municipal, state and federal administrations and who insist that things don't get done because that's simply the nature of the bureaucratic beast, seem to forget that only certain kinds of things don't get done—other things are accomplished all too well. A law establishing a "community development" program for the ghetto, passed by a reluctant Congress in response to the urgings of liberal spokesmen and the pressure of demonstrations and urban riots, is legally the same as a law enacted to develop a multibillion-dollar, high-profit weapons system, the latter supported by giant industrial contractors, well-placed persons within the military, scientific and university establishments and numerous Congressmen whose patriotism is matched only by their desire to bring the defense bacon home to their districts and keep their campaign coffers filled by appreciative donors. If anything, the weapons program is of vastly greater administrative complexity than the smaller, modestly funded ghetto program. Yet the latter is more likely to suffer from inaction and ineffectiveness, the important difference between the two programs

12. See the criticisms made by environmental lawyer James Moorman as reported in the New York Times, February 12, 1974.
13. Ian Menzies, "Money for Poor Going to Suburbs," Boston Globe, September 29, 1976.
14. Ibid.

being not bureaucratic but political. *The effectiveness of the law depends on the power of the groups supporting it.* Laws that serve powerful interests are likely to enjoy a vigorous life while laws that have only the powerless to nurture them are often stillborn.

Thus Congress discovered that under a law which was to have taken effect in 1969 making some 13 million children and youths eligible for medical examinations and treatment, almost 85 percent of the children were left unexamined, causing, in the words of a House subcommittee report, "unnecessary crippling, retardation, or even death of thousands of children." The report blamed HEW for its laxity in properly enforcing the program and failing to penalize laggard states.[15] The question is whether such a performance of nonenforcement is tolerated when the client interests are not powerless children but powerful industrialists, military contractors, oil companies or bankers.

Bureaucracies grow and grow, mostly in response to the needs of big business and the military, but also because bureaucrats themselves, in order to justify their existence and advance their careers, spawn new programs and consume more funds. In time the sheer vastness of the bureaucracy lends itself to waste and duplication. The National Science Foundation made a study of automotive fuel and another of mass transportation only to discover that the Army and the Department of Transportation had already conducted similar studies. There are thirteen different advisory committees on cancer, four on air pollution and three on alcoholism. Seventeen agencies deal with "consumer concerns," none of them very well. There are five water research agencies. Although there has been no draft since 1973, the Selective Service continues to spend $45 million a year. Federal agencies of one kind or another spend $67 million a year on "fire prevention." One of these, the Federal Fire Council, has done nothing for more than seven years except occasionally mail out some publications containing pictures of fires, yet it automatically receives its yearly budget of $70,000. About $14 million annually goes to maintaining 300 military golf courses around the world and millions more to provide free face-lifts, breast enlargements and other cosmetic operations for wives of American military personnel.[16]

With all the waste and duplication, important public needs remain improperly regulated or completely neglected, such as:

15. UPI dispatch in the *Collegian* (Amherst, Mass.), October 8, 1976.
16. *Syracuse Herald American*, August 31, 1975; *National Enquirer*, May 6, 1975, and January 6, 1976.

antitrust enforcement, occupational safety, transportation safety, community health, consumer protection (including regulation of cosmetics and drugs), environmental protection and welfare services. Millions of people staff the gargantuan federal bureaucracy, but relatively few perform the services most needed by ordinary citizens. Service goes to those who have the power to command it. The size of an agency, in any case, is a less significant determinant of its performance than the political influences bearing upon it. With a limited budget of only $3 million in 1949, the Food and Drug Administration proceeded against thousands of violators. In 1976, with a $200-million budget, FDA did not take court action against a single major drug company.[17]

With the right political support bureaucracies are capable of carrying out policies of momentous scope. "The feat of landing men on the moon," Duane Lockard reminds us, "was not only a scientific achievement but a bureaucratic one as well."[18] The same might be said of the Vietnam war, the U.S. counterinsurgency effort in Latin America, the exploits of the Internal Revenue Service and the farm, highway, housing and defense programs. These endeavors represent the mobilization and coordination of stupendous amounts of energy, skill and material resources by complex, centralized systems of command—i.e., bureaucracies. What is impressive about the federal housing program, for instance, is not how little has been done but how much, yet with so little benefit to low-income people: how many public agencies established, billions spent, millions of work hours expended, millions of tons of materials utilized, and hundreds of thousands of structures built and subsidized at such profit to realty speculators, manufacturers, big merchants, banks and public officials and at such cost to the taxpayers—a stupendous bureaucratic effort. Bureaucracy's failure to serve the unorganized and needy public has led some observers to the mistaken notion that it serves no one. But as we have seen in previous chapters, for some groups the government has been anything but idle.[19]

The same can be said of Congress. As already noted, the complaint that Congress can't get things done is incorrect. While

17. Paul Murphy and Rene Care Murphy, "Consumer Beware," *Village Voice*, April 12, 1976, p. 12.
18. Duane Lockard, *The Perverted Priorities of American Politics* (New York: Macmillan, 1971), p. 282.
19. See Orion F. White, Jr., "The Dialectical Organization: An Alternative to Bureaucracy," *Public Administration Review*, 19, January–February 1969, pp. 32–41.

unable to accomplish certain things, especially in regard to low-income housing, hunger, medical care, unemployment and mass transportation, it is capable of extraordinary achievements. The space, defense, highway, agricultural and tax programs are not only bureaucratic feats, they are legislative ones. The question is not, "Why can't administrators and legislators act?" but "Why are they able to act so forcefully and successfully in some ways and not at all in other ways?" The first question invites us to throw up our hands in befuddlement; the second requires that we investigate the realities of power and interest.

Why are reform-minded administrative bodies rarely able to operate with any effectiveness? Consider the fate of the agency set up to regulate some area of industry on behalf of consumers and workers. In its youth, it may possess a zeal for reform, but before long the public concern that gave it impetus begins to fade. The business-owned news media either turn their attention to more topical events or present an unsympathetic or superficial picture of the agency's doings. The President, if he was originally sympathetic to the agency's mission, is now occupied with more pressing matters, as are its few articulate but not very influential friends in Congress. But the industry that is supposed to be brought under control remains keenly interested and by now is well alerted and ready to oppose government intrusions. First, it may decide to challenge the agency's jurisdiction or even the legality of its existence in court, thus preventing any serious regulatory actions until a legal determination is made.[20] If the agency survives this attack, there begins a series of encounters between its investigators and representatives from the industry. The industry is able to counter the agency's moves with a barrage of arguments and technical information, not all truthful but sufficiently impressive to win the respectful attention of the agency's investigators. The investigators begin to develop a new appreciation of industry's side of the story and of the problems it faces in maintaining profitable operations. Indeed, for extended periods it is the only side administrators may be exposed to, and in time they begin to adopt industry's perspective.

If the agency persists in making unfavorable rulings, businessmen appeal to their elected representatives, or to a higher administrative official or, if they have the pull, to the President himself. In its youthful days after World War I, the Federal Trade Com-

20. See the discussion in Grant McConnell, *Private Power and American Democracy* (New York: Knopf, 1966), p. 288.

mission moved vigorously against big business, but representatives of industry prevailed upon the President to replace "some of the commissioners by others more sympathetic with business practices: this resulted in the dismissal of many complaints which had been made against corporations."[21]

Frequently members of Congress demand to know why an agency is bothering their constituents. Administrators who are more interested in building congressional support than making congressional enemies are likely to apply the law in ways that satisfy influential legislators. "If the bureaucrats are to escape criticism, unfavorable publicity, or a cut in their appropriations, they must be discreet in their relations with the legislative body."[22] Some administrative bodies, like the Army Corps of Engineers, so successfully cultivate support among powerful Congressmen and big business clientele as to become relatively free of supervisory control from department heads or the White House. "Fierce rivalries for funds and functions go on ceaselessly among the departments and between the agencies," reports Cater. "A cunning bureau chief learns to negotiate alliances on Capitol Hill [Congress] that bypass the central authority of the White House."[23] In the executive branch, as in Congress, the fragmentation of power is hardly indicative of its democratization. Rather it represents little more than a distribution among entrenched special interests.

Administrators are immobilized not only by "bureaucratic in-fighting" but by pressures bearing upon them from the wider politico-economic system. Given a desire to survive and advance, the bureaucrat tends to equivocate in the face of controversial decisions, moving away from dangerous areas and toward positions favored by the strongest of the pressures working on him. With time, the reform-minded agency loses its crusading spirit and settles down to standard operations, increasingly serving the needs of the industry it is supposed to regulate. The more public-spirited staff members either grow weary of the struggle and make their peace with the corporations, or leave, to be replaced by personnel who are "acceptable to, if not indeed the nominees of, the industry."[24]

21. Edwin Sutherland, *White Collar Crime* (New York: Holt, Rinehart and Winston, 1949), p. 232.

22. E. Pendleton Herring, "The Balance of Social Forces in the Administration of the Food and Drug Law," *Social Forces*, 13, March 1935, p. 364.

23. Douglass Cater, *Power in Washington* (New York: Random House, 1964), p. 10–11.

24. McConnell, *Private Power and American Democracy*, p. 288. For an interesting and well-edited selection of readings on the politics of bureaucracy see Francis E. Rourke (ed.), *Bureaucratic Power in National Politics* (Boston: Little, Brown, 1965).

Frequently administrative personnel are drawn from the very industry they are charged with regulating, their business background being taken as proof of their "expertise." They often return to higher positions in the same industry after serving their terms in office. Likewise, many career administrators eventually leave government service to accept higher paying jobs in companies whose interests they favored while in office. This promise of a lucrative post with a private firm can exercise a considerable influence on the judgments of the ambitious public administrator.

Little Administrators and Big Businessmen

Most administrative bodies fall under the command of department heads and the President. But the independent regulatory commissions operate outside the executive branch, making quasi-judicial rulings that can be appealed only to the courts.[25] Congress created the regulatory commissions to be independent of the normal administrative departments in the hope of keeping them free of the politics that permeated other executive bodies. The hope was an unrealistic one. For all the reasons discussed in this chapter, they are no more independent of special influences and they perform much the same as the regular departmental agencies—the niceties of structure counting for less than the realities of power and interest. The regulatory agencies "set up to protect the consumer from giant companies have become instead agents of the industries, granting fixed prices favorable to them, granting them monopolies, costing the public an estimated 16 to 24 billion a year more for what it buys."[26] Industry needs to be regulated but for whose benefit?

25. The major independent regulatory commissions are the Civil Aeronautics Board, Federal Communications Commission, Federal Power Commission, Federal Trade Commission, Interstate Commerce Commission, National Labor Relations Board, Securities and Exchange Commission, Consumer Product Safety Commission. While the commissions report directly to Congress, their personnel are appointed by the President, with Senate confirmation. See Louis Kohlmeier, *The Regulators: Watchdog Agencies and the Public Interest* (New York: Harper and Row, 1969) Kohlmeier finds that regulation has resulted in diminished competition, producer-controlled markets, restricted consumer choice and higher prices.

26. ABC news commentator Howard K. Smith, quoted in the *New York Post*, August 6, 1976. A two-year congressional investigation concluded that regulatory agencies are committed "to the special interests of regulated industry and lack . . . sufficient concern for underrepresented interests" of the public. *New York Times*, October 3, 1976.

As long as production is for the purpose of private profit rather than social use, regulation for the public interest is an improbable goal. On those rare occasions when government agencies succeed in enforcing a regulation on behalf of the unorganized citizenry, the accomplishment requires enormous time and effort and usually has only a minimal effect, if any, on the politico-economy. Thus it took the Federal Trade Commission twelve years of court orders and negotiations to get the manufacturers of Geritol, a vitamin and iron preparation, to stop claiming that their product fights something called "tired blood."[27] It took the FTC ten years to stop Crowell Collier from conducting fraudulent door-to-door encyclopedia sales, and another sixteen years to get the makers of Carter's Little Liver Pills to stop selling their laxative as an effective treatment for sluggish liver function.[28] And after more than twelve years the federal government was still involved in an enforcement conference with the state of New Jersey concerning pollution in the Raritan Bay.[29]

Administrators run into difficulties with the powers that be if they show themselves to be insufficiently understanding of "the needs of industry." The General Accounting Office (GAO) created by Congress to check on how government monies are used, did a series of studies on profiteering and waste in the defense industry. The probe incurred the displeasure of the Pentagon and big defense contractors who prevailed upon the House Government Operations Committee to investigate the GAO and instruct it to be more "constructive."[30] In its subsequent study of military spending, the GAO operated in more circumspect ways: it revealed that seventy-seven weapon systems would cost $28.7 billion more than estimated and that the average profit was a staggering 56 percent, but this time it sent the report to defense firms before releasing it and then incorporated many of their alibis into the report and toned down its own charges.[31]

Troublesome administrators do not enjoy a high survival rate. Consider John O'Leary, a career government administrator who was appointed director of the Bureau of Mines in 1968. Press

27. *New York Times*, July 5, 1969.
28. Philip A. Hart, "Swindling and Knavery, Inc.," *Playboy*, August 1972, p. 160.
29. *Hard Times*, no. 51, November 3–10, 1969.
30. This account is taken from Mark J. Green, James M. Fallows and David R. Zwick, *Who Runs Congress?* (New York: Bantam Books/Grossman, 1972), p. 127, including Holifield's comment.
31. *Ibid.*

reports and protests were being directed at the unsafe conditions in the mines and the failure of the Bureau to enforce safety regulations—in the wake of an underground explosion that had taken the lives of seventy-eight miners. Encouraged by the public concern, O'Leary ordered the Bureau's inspectors to make unannounced spot checks of safety conditions, a step involving an element of surprise that had been rarely tried before, although required by law. In one month O'Leary's men made 600 spot checks, almost four times the number for the entire previous year, and ordered workers out of more than 200 unsafe mines. O'Leary urged his inspectors to still greater efforts and publicly charged that the coal mining industry was "designed for production economy and not for human economy, and there's going to have to be a change of attitudes on that."[32] The change came—but it was not the one hoped for. The mine companies made known to the White House their strong desire to be rid of the troublesome Bureau director. After lasting only four months, O'Leary was removed from office. His successor, a former CIA employee, reestablished more cooperative relations with the mine owners, making personal appearances at corporate gatherings, riding in company planes and avoiding "get tough" policies.[33]

People like O'Leary are the exception. In most instances public bureaucrats are, and must be, faithful servants of private industry. The Civil Aeronautics Board, for instance, holds secret meetings with airline presidents to set air fares at an estimated 40 to 100 percent higher than open competition would allow.[34] The GAO discovered that the Federal Power Commission violated its own regulations and granted natural gas producers repeated and unjustified price-rise extensions, costing customers several billion dollars in a three-year period.[35] The probusiness bias affects all departments: the Defense Department came to the rescue of large

32. *New York Times*, February 17, 1969; also "Mine Safety Case Hit," *Christian Science Monitor*, April 8, 1970.

33. Jack Anderson, "Mine Officials Got Free Air Travel," *Times-Union* (Albany), June 17, 1973. The Bureau's deputy director accepted various gratuities including free football tickets and plane rides from firms under the Bureau's jurisdiction, Anderson reported.

34. *New York Times*, March 30 and June 30, 1975; also James Ridgeway, "The Antipopulists," *Ramparts*, December 1971, p. 6.

35. *New York Times*, September 15, 1974. The same kind of problem exists on the state level. A consumer-activist group charged that the Department of Public Utilities in Massachusetts was allowing the telephone company to overcharge Massachusetts residents $100 million a year. *The Boston Globe*, September 29, 1976.

commercial farms hurt by the farmworkers' grape boycott by increasing its orders for grapes by 350 percent. Several years later, the Pentagon tried to break the lettuce boycott by increasing its orders for nonunion lettuce.[36] A meat company faced with labor conflicts was awarded the bulk of the federal school lunch program's beef contract. And a trucking company that was losing sales because of a strike was bailed out by a $1.6-million government contract, illegally extended beyond the expiration date.[37]

And so it goes. The Highway Safety Bureau and the entire Department of Transportation defer to the oil-highway-automotive combine; the Agriculture Department promotes the policies and products of giant farming corporations; the Interstate Commerce Commission continues its long devotion to the trucking and railroad companies; the Federal Communications Commission serves the monopolistic interests of the telephone and telegraph companies and the media networks; the Securities and Exchange Commission regulates the stock market mostly for the benefit of the large investors and to the detriment of small ones; the Federal Power Commission pursues a permissive policy on behalf of the private utilities; the Army Corps of Engineers continues to mutilate the natural environment on behalf of agricultural corporations, utilities, and land developers; various bureaus within the Department of Interior serve the oil, gas, mining and timber companies;[38] and one need not speculate on the many billions distributed every year by the

36. The 16-million pounds of scab grapes bought by the Pentagon in 1969 were shipped to Vietnam, where the bulk of them rotted on the docks. The Pentagon's largest lettuce contract went to the nonunion producer Bud Antle, an affiliate of Dow Chemical, the company that made napalm for the government. See *About Face!* (U.S. Servicemen's Fund Newsletter) December 1972.

37. *Workers World*, October 25, 1974.

38. There is an ample literature documenting how administrative bodies serve the interests of the industries they are supposed to regulate. See Kohlmeier, *The Regulators;* Anthony Lewis, "To Regulate the Regulators," *New York Times Magazine,* February 22, 1959; Bernard Schwartz, *The Professor and the Commissions* (New York: Knopf, 1958); Walter S. Adams and Horace Gray, *Monopoly in America* (New York: Macmillan, 1955); The Ralph Nader Study Group Report, *The Interstate Commerce Omission: The Public Interest and the ICC* (New York: Grossman, 1970), Robert C. Fellmeth, project director; James Ridgeway, "The Antipopulists," *Ramparts,* December 1971, pp. 6–8; Richard Ney, *The Wall Street Jungle* (New York: Grove Press, 1970); William O. Douglas, "The Corps of Engineers; The Public Be Damned," *Playboy,* July 1969, reprinted in Walt Anderson (ed.), *Politics and Environment* (Pacific Palisades, Calif.: Goodyear, 1970), pp. 268–284; Arthur Maass, *Muddy Waters* (Cambridge, Mass.: Harvard University Press, 1951); Ross Macdonald, "Life with the Blob," in Anderson, *Politics and Environment,* pp. 130–131; Henning Sjöström and Robert Nilsson, *Thalidomide and the Power of the Drug Companies* (New York: Basic Books, 1973).

Department of Defense to pay the bloated profits and costs of favored manufacturers.[39]

It is often difficult to tell the regulators from the regulated. More than 50 percent of the appointments to regulatory jobs during 1972–1976 were persons who had previously been employed by the regulated industry.[40] The General Counsel of the National Labor Relations Board, Peter Nash, who sought a nationwide injunction against the lettuce boycott organized by Cesar Chavez's United Farmworkers (UFW), had previously served as counsel to agribusiness firms like Del Monte. Before his appointment as chief counsel for the Food and Drug Administration, Peter Hutt defended drug companies for a leading Washington law firm.[41] In 1974 the Federal Communcations Commission was composed of five high-ranking corporate executives, including one from the media industry and one former FBI man. In 1972 the Undersecretary of Agriculture, responsible for enforcing meat inspection, was Philip Cambell, a former state inspector with close ties to the meat industry, who had actively opposed the very federal meat inspecton laws he now was to enforce.[42] In 1976 the Secretary of the Interior was Stanley Hathaway, former governor of Wyoming, who had consistently opposed conservation programs that were now under his administration.[43] A Deputy Assistant Secretary in charge of water development had previously served as a paid lobbyist against water pollution legislation.[44] In 1970 a sixty-three-person National Industrial Pollution Control Council (with salaries and expenses of $475,000 a year paid by the government) was set up to advise the President on pollution reforms. All the members were businessmen from industries that, according to Senator Lee Metcalf, "contribute most to environmental pollution." Not a single conservation or public-interest group was represented. Federal housing programs have been supervised by conservative businessmen who were openly hostile to low-income public housing. The occupational safety program has been administered by business and government officials who were originally opposed to occupational safety legis-

39. See the section in Chapter Six entitled "The Pentagon: Billions for Big Brother."
40. New York Times, October 3, 1976.
41. Murphy and Murphy, "Consumer Beware," p. 13.
42. I. F. Stone's Weekly, January 27, 1969.
43. New York Times, April 28, 1975.
44. Lockard, Perverted Priorities of American Politics, p. 280. Of the first two men nominated by President Ford to the Federal Energy Administration, one was a top executive of Exxon and the other was president of an oil transport company. New York Times, August 31 and November 7, 1974.

lation. The head of the federal energy office in 1976 was an opponent of price controls on natural gas. And the chairperson of the Federal Power Commission, a Rockefeller associate, described himself as favoring less regulation of industry.[45] The head of the Arms Control and Disarmanent Agency was a former executive from the defense industry and an advocate of stronger military power. The ACDA staff, in general, was "dominated by military men, conservatives and Wall Street types."[46]

The opportunties for corruption and conflict of interest within the executive branch are plentiful. Officials have received illegal favors and gratuities from companies under their jurisdiction.[47] One Postmaster General had authorized hundreds of thousands of dollars worth of contract work to a friend, without soliciting a single bid from other firms.[48] Congressional auditors found that more than 150 officials of the FDA had violated federal rules by owning stock in pharmaceutical, food and cosmetic companies that FDA regulates. And the GAO discovered that at least nineteen officials of the Federal Power Commission owned securities of companies they regulated.[49]

It is not enough to bemoan the fact that government agencies end up serving interests they are supposed to regulate;[50] rather we should understand how this situation is an inescapable outcome of the politico-economic realities in which the administrators operate. Most agencies have the inherently contradictory function of both regulating a particular industry—supposedly for the public interest—and promoting the industry's economic health and viability. But to promote the interests of the industry in a profit system is to violate the interests of consumers and workers. Regulation, then, becomes a way to rig prices at artificially high levels, monopolize markets for a few large producers, secure high profits, evade safety and environmental standards, limit the ability of consumer and labor groups to effect competing demands, and allow private corporations more direct and covert access to public authority.

45. New York Times, September 11, 1975.

46. Sidney Lens, "The Doomsday Strategy," Progressive, February 1976, p. 28.

47. For instance see the cases of Robert Timm formerly of the CAB and Isabel Burgess formerly of the National Transportation Safety Board. New York Times, March 1 and November 16, 1975.

48. New York Post, May 4, 1974. Similarly, the GSA spent millions in high-priced contracts to a few favored companies, then covered up these violations. Boston Globe, October 11, 1976.

49. New York Times, September 15, 1974, and January 20, 1976.

50. See New York Times, October 3, 1967, for a report on federal regulatory commissions.

Public Authority in Private Hands

The ultimate submergence of public power to private interest comes when government gives, along with its funds and services, its very *authority* to business. Grant McConnell has documented how state authority is taken over by private groups in such areas as agriculture, grazing, medicine, industry and trade.[51] Thus Western ranches not only enjoy the use of federal land and water, they also have been granted the public authority that goes with the task of administering such resources. Control of land and water has been handed over to local "home-rule" boards dominated by the large ranchers, who thereby successfully transform their economic power "into a working approximation of publicly sanctioned authority."[52] Large agricultural producers exercise a similar authority in the administration of farm programs. Theodore Lowi commented: "Agriculture has become neither public nor private enterprise. It is a system of self-government in which each leading farm interest controls a segment of agriculture through a delegation of national sovereignty. Agriculture has emerged as a largely self-governing federal estate," enjoying a power that has extended "through a line unbroken by personality or party in the White House."[53]

One congressional committee, investigating relations between government and industry, complained of "a virtual abdication of administrative responsibility" on the part of officials in the Department of Commerce, their actions in many instances being "but the automatic approval of decisions already made outside the Government in business and industry."[54] In every significant line of industry, advisory committees staffed by representatives of leading firms work closely with government agencies, making most of the important recommendations. In trying to assess their roles it is "difficult to determine where the distinction between advice and the making of policy lies."[55] There are 3,200 committees and boards advising the executive branch and Congress, costing the government $65 million a year to finance. The most influential are composed exclusively of big businessmen and deal with banking,

---

51. See McConnell, *Private Power and American Democracy*. Another interesting work that picks up on McConnell's analysis and offers some additional evidence is Theodore Lowi, *The End of Liberalism* (New York: W. W. Norton, 1969).

52. McConnell, *Private Power and American Democracy*, p. 210.

53. Lowi, *The End of Liberalism*, pp. 103–104.

54. From a congressional report cited in McConnell, *Private Power and American Democracy*, p. 271.

55. McConnell, *Private Power and American Democracy*, p. 275.

chemicals, communications, pollution control, commercial farming, natural gas, oil, utilities, railroads, taxation, etc. They meet regularly with administrative leaders to formulate policies. Their reports become the basis for administrative actions and new legislation. These business advisers have unparalleled occasion to monopolize informational inputs, defining "industry's needs" from the vantage point of their own interests. With the coercive power of the state backing their decisions, they secure advantages over smaller competitors, workers and consumers of a kind less easily gained in open competition.

When the government first began to gather information for legislation on water pollution, it consulted the Advisory Council on Federal Reports, a private body which describes itself as the official business consultant to the Budget Bureau; it also considers itself responsible only to the business community. The Advisory Council, in cooperation with the Budget Bureau, set up a committee on pollution which included representatives of DuPont, the Manufacturing Chemists Association and the American Paper Institute. The committee opposed the policy advocated by Congress, which was to set up an inventory on water pollutants.[56] In deference to industry's wishes the government decided that the inventory would be provided by companies only on a voluntary basis, in effect approving industry's claim that the poisons and chemical wastes it unleashed into the public waters were a trade secret and a property right. The meetings of these business advisory committees are not open to the press or public.

The advisory committees have flourished under Democratic as well as Republican administrations. The Business Advisory Council was set up during Franklin Roosevelt's reign; the National Petroleum Council was established under Truman; and the Pentagon's Industry Advisory Council, "through which the nation's top defense contractors tone down General Accounting Office reports on exces. profits," was established by the Kennedy administration.[57]

In many state and municipal governments, as in the federal government, business associations, dominated by the biggest firms in the area, are accorded the power to nominate their own personnel to licensing boards, production boards and other administrative bodies. The transfer of public authority to private hands frequently

56. Robert W. Dietsch, "The Invisible Bureaucracy," *New Republic*, February 20, 1971, p. 19.
57. Vic Reinemer, "Corporate Government in Action," *Progressive*, November 1971, p. 30.

comes at the initiative of large companies. But sometimes the government will make the first overtures, organizing private associations, then handing them the powers of the state, thereby supposedly moving toward "voluntaristic" and "decentralized" forms of policy making. In fact, these measures transfer public power to favored producers without their being held democratically accountable for the sovereign authority they exercise.

There exists, then, unbeknownst to most Americans, a large number of decision-makers who are with the government but not quite within it, who exercise public authority without having to answer to the public and who determine official policy while considering their first interest and obligation to be their private businesses. They belong to what I would call the "public-private authority." Included in this category are the various quasipublic corporations, institutions, foundations, boards, councils, "authorities" and associations, the most powerful being the Federal Reserve Board. The "Fed," as it is called, determines the interest rate and the money supply. Its decisions affect the entire economy. Beholden to the banks and run mostly by bankers, the Fed favors tight money policies. At least two Presidents, Harry Truman and Lyndon Johnson, complained that the Fed had pursued policies that undermined the economic policies set by the White House and Congress. The Fed's members are appointed to staggered fourteen-year terms by the President, who can make only two appointments during his four-year term. Once appointed, the Board members answer to no one. The Fed operates without even the pretense of democratic accountability, working in total secrecy, refusing to have Congress or the White House audit its books. Its most powerful component, the Federal Open Market Committee, makes the overall monetary policy for the United States and is composed of seven Board members and the presidents of five regional Federal Reserve Banks, who are selected by local bankers. In sum, private bankers pick their own people to sit on a public agency and make public policy that is backed by the powers of government but is not accountable to government. In the words of one investigator, the Fed is "an intensely arrogant government agency, one that is mired in secrecy, often inept, responsible to no one . . . and dedicated to helping powerful, entrenched interests rather than the public."[58]

Another public-private entity is the Port Authority of New York, a "public corporation" created by interstate compact for the

58. Lee Berton, "Don't Bank on It," *Penthouse*, October 1976, p. 56; also "What Is the Federal Reserve?" *Dollars and Sense*, March 1976, p. 14.

purpose of running the bridges and tunnels between New York and New Jersey and the various metropolitan airports. Its bonds are sold to large financial and corporate institutions and rich individuals. It is answerable to none of the governing bodies in the region—not to the mayors, nor the city councils, nor the state legislators, nor the governors of New York and New Jersey, nor the U.S. Congress, but it can condemn property and construct tax-exempt developments. The profits from its commercial ventures ($12 million annually from the JFK Airport restaurants alone) are distributed as *tax-free returns to private investors*. Millions in surpluses which could be used to salvage New York's decaying mass-transit system are kept in reserve by the Port Authority, "not for the people of New York City, but for bondholders. Thus does public authority and private power come together in a massive fusion of wealth that leaves the ordinary taxpaying New Yorkers as its victim."[59]

There are numerous "public authorities" at the federal, state and local levels carrying out a widely varied range of activities. They all have several things in common: they are authorized by state legislatures or Congress to function outside the regular structure of government, and because of their autonomous corporate attributes, they are seldom subjected to public scrutiny and accountability. In 1972 the public authorities in New York State alone had an outstanding debt (bonds owned by banks and rich investors) of $8.9 billion, more than twice the state's debt. To meet their obligations, the public authorities float new bond issues, none of which are passed upon by the voters, and make demands on future tax revenues. Thus they are creatures that have the best of both worlds, feeding off the state treasure while accountable only to themselves.[60]

The public-private authority extends into overseas endeavors. When the Peruvian generals nationalized the holdings of private American oil companies, the President sent a special envoy to protest the move and negotiate for reacquisition. The U.S. Information Agency publishes, at the taxpayers' expense, pamphlets extolling

59. When the Port Authority had trouble renting space in its ugly World Trade Center, a predicament that could have meant a loss for its bondholders, then-Governor Rockefeller came to the rescue by renting fifty-eight floors for state government offices. One of the biggest Port Authority bondholders is the Rockefeller-controlled Chase Manhattan Bank. More recently the Port Authority has had some difficulty selling its bonds and has not been making money on some of its big investments. *New York Times,* November 10, 1974.
60. *New York Times,* December 27, 1972.

the benefits of private oil exploration for distribution in Ecuador. Agents of ITT and the CIA jointly consider ways of preventing a democratically elected Socialist from taking office in Chile.[61] The private interests do not merely benefit from public policy; they often *make* policy, selecting the key officials, using public funds or channeling funds of their own through public agents, directing World Bank loans and foreign aid investments, offering recommendations that are treated as policy guidelines—in sum, pursuing their interests abroad with all the formal authority and might of the United States government behind them.

The corporate interests exert an influence that cuts across particular administrative departments. Within a government whose power is highly fragmented, they form cohesive, though sometimes overlapping, blocs around major producer interests like oil, steel, banking, drugs, transportation and armaments; these blocs are composed of bureaucrats at all levels, regulatory commissioners, senior Congressmen, lobbyists, newspaper publishers, trade associations and business firms, operating with all the autonomy and unaccountability of princely states within the American polity.

Government "Meddling"

If government is capitalism's provider and protector at home and abroad, and if government and business are so intermingled as to be often indistinguishable, then why are businessmen so critical of "government meddling in the economy"? There are a number of explanations. First, as previously noted, businessmen are not opposed to government activity as long as it is favorable to them. Since the beginning of the Republic, state intervention in the economy usually has been at the behest of leading producers. "Whether we like it or not, the federal government is a partner in every business in the country," announced Lammot duPont Copeland, president of DuPont Chemicals. "As businessmen we need the understanding and cooperation of government in our effort to throw the economic machine into high gear."[62] When business leaders denounce government "meddling" they are referring to

61. See Tad Szulc, "I.T.T.: A Private Little Foreign Policy," *New York Times,* March 26, 1972.
62. Quoted in David Bazelon, "Big Business and the Democrats," in Marvin Gettleman and David Mermelstein (eds.), *The Failure of American Liberalism* (New York: Vintage, 1971), pp. 145–146.

those infrequent occasions when public agencies attempt to impose environmental protections, antitrust laws or worker and consumer safety regulations. When business criticizes "excessive government spending" they have in mind those modest programs which appear to benefit lower-income people. The business community has always been fearful that government might become unduly responsive to popular sentiments, arousing mass expectations and eventually succumbing to demands that could seriously challenge the existing distribution of income and wealth and perhaps even upset the class structure. The business critique is not against existing arrangements of government, most of which have served industry well, but against government activities that might mobilize new constituencies, introducing unsettling elements into policy areas now firmly under control of entrenched business groups. As McConnell explains:

The avowed hostility of business toward government may or may not be genuine. It is genuine where governmental action seems to threaten the autonomy and the system of rule established by a unit of business; it is false where a government agency is responsible purely to that unit. Hence, the railroad industry is largely content with regulation by the Interstate Commerce Commission, the securities trade is pleased to see extension of Securities and Exchange Commission policy, and the oil industry is happy to cooperate in the operation of the National Petroleum Council. Few industries or businesses, however, approve of any aggressive operation by the Anti-Trust Division, although this agency is the true protector of the avowed ideology.[63]

Second, attacks on government officials are a means of bringing them closer into line with industry's desires. Despite the controls exercised in the selection and advancement of government personnel, some public servants forget their commitment to the business community and entertain sympathies toward a wider constituency. Pressure must be applied to remind them of the vulnerabilities of their agencies and careers. Third, many of the complaints lodged against government are from firms least favored by government policies. Business is not without its interior divisions: policies frequently benefit the wealthier firms at the expense of smaller ones. The howls of pain emanating from these weaker competitors are more likely to be heard by us than the quiet satisfaction of the giant victors.

63. McConnell, *Private Power and American Democracy*, p. 295.

Finally, I would suggest that much of the verbal opposition to government is a manifestation of the businessman's adherence to the business ideology, his belief in the virtues of rugged individualism, private enterprise and private competition.[64] That he might violate this creed in his own corporate affairs does not mean his devotion to it is consciously hypocritical. One should not underestimate the human capacity to indulge in selective perceptions and rationales. These rationales are no less sincerely felt because they are self-serving; quite the contrary, it is a creed's congruity with a favorable self-image and self-interest that makes it so compelling. Many businessmen, including those who have benefited in almost every way from government contracts, subsidies and tax laws, *believe* the advantages they enjoy are the result of their own self-reliance, efforts and talents in a highly competitive "private" market. They believe that everyone *except* them goes running to the government for a handout.

64. See Francis X. Sutton et al., *The American Business Creed* (New York: Schocken Books, 1962).

The Supremely Political Court

16

ALL THREE BRANCHES OF GOVERNMENT are sworn to uphold the Constitution, but the Supreme Court alone has the power of reviewing the constitutionality of the actions of the other two branches and having its judgments treated as the final word, at least in regard to cases brought before it by others. While there is nothing in the Constitution giving the Court this power, the proceedings of the Constitutional Convention reveal that many of the delegates expected the federal judiciary to declare null and void laws it deemed inconsistent with the Constitution.[1] Of even greater significance than its constitutional adjudications is the Court's power to interpret the intent and scope of laws as they are applied in actual situations. This power of review is also limited to cases brought to the Court. Our main concern here is with trying to understand the *political* role the Court has played over the years.

Who Judges?

Some Americans like to think of their Constitution as a vital force, having an animation of its own. At the same time they expect Supreme

1. Max Farrand, *The Framing of the Constitution of the United States* (New Haven: Yale University Press, 1913), pp. 156–157. See Chief Justice John Marshall's argument for judicial review in the landmark case of *Marbury* v. *Madison*.

Court Justices to be above the normal prejudices of other persons. Thus they envision "a living Constitution" and an insentient Court. But a moment's reflection should remind us that it is the other way around. The Supreme Court is deeply engaged in the political process. If the Constitution is, as they say, an "elastic instrument," then much of the stretching has been done by the nine men who sit on the Court, and the directions in which they pull are largely determined by their own ideological predilections.

Some Supreme Court Justices have insisted otherwise, contending that the Court is involved in judgments that allow little room for personal prejudice. Justice Roberts provided the classic utterance of this viewpoint:

When an act of Congress is appropriately challenged in the Courts as not conforming to the constitutional mandate the judiciary branch of the government has only one duty—to lay the Article of the Constitution which is invoked beside the statute which is challenged and to decide whether the latter squares with the former. All that the Court does, or can do, is to announce its considered judgment upon the question.[2]

This image of the Constitution as a measuring stick and the Justice as measurer has been challenged by critics of the Court and even by some Justices. No less a member than Chief Justice Hughes pointedly observed, "We are under a constitution but the constitution is what the judges say it is."[3]

By class background, professional training and political selection, Supreme Court Justices over the generations have usually been inclined to identify with the landed interests rather than the landless, the slave owners rather than the slaves, the industrialists rather than the workers, the exponents of Herbert Spencer rather than the proponents of Karl Marx, the established social elites rather than unemployed Blacks, underpaid migrants or illiterate immigrants. Approximately a century ago Justice Miller, a Lincoln appointee to the Court, made note of the class biases of the judiciary:

It is vain to contend with judges who have been at the bar, the advocates for forty years of railroad companies, and all the forms of associated capital, when they are called upon to decide cases where such interests

2. *United States* v. *Butler,* 297 U.S. 1 (1936).
3. Dexter Perkins, *Charles Evans Hughes* (Boston: Little, Brown, 1956), p. 16.

are in contest. All their training, all their feelings are from the start in favor of those who need no such influence.[4]

Nor is the situation much different today. One study shows that the people who enjoy life-tenure positions on federal courts, whether appointed by Democratic or Republican Presidents, are drawn preponderantly from highly privileged Ivy League and private-school backgrounds.[5] The Nixon appointee Justice Louis Franklin Powell, Jr., is not an exceptional case: at the time of his accession to the Court, Powell disclosed personal holdings amounting to $1 million worth of stocks in over thirty major corporations. He had held directorships on the boards of a score of utilities, gas companies and banks. One study finds that the American Bar Association's quasiofficial Federal Judiciary Committee, whose task is to pass on the qualifications of prospective judges, favors those whose orientation is strongly conservative and supportive of corporate interests.[6] Few mavericks, reformers or populists ever come close to appointment to the federal bench. As one U.S. District Court judge puts it: "Who are we after all? The average judge, if he ever was a youth, is no longer. If he was ever a firebrand, he is not discernibly an ember now. If he ever wanted to lick the Establishment, he has long since joined it."[7]

Playing with the Constitution

There is an old saying that the devil himself can quote the Bible for his own purposes. The Constitution is not unlike the Bible in this respect, and over the generations Supreme Court Justices have shown an infernal agility in finding constitutional justifications for the continuation of almost every inequity and iniquity, be it slavery or segregation, child labor or the sixteen-hour day, state sedition laws or federal assaults on the First Amendment. Consider the Court's decisions in the area of political economy. Justice Felix Frankfurter once observed:

4. Quoted in Felix Frankfurter, *Mr. Justice Holmes and the Supreme Court* (New York: Atheneum, 1965), p. 54.
5. Sheldon Goldman, "Johnson and Nixon Appointees to the Lower Federal Courts: Some Socio-Political Perspectives," *Journal of Politics*, 34, August 1972, pp. 934–942.
6. See Joel B. Grossman, *Lawyers and Judges: The ABA and the Politics of Judicial Selection* (New York: Wiley, 1965).
7. Marvin E. Frankel, "An Opinion by One of Those Softheaded Judges," *New York Times Magazine*, May 13, 1973, p. 41.

The raw material of modern government is business. Taxation, utility regulation, agricultural control, labor relations, housing, banking and finance, control of the security market—all our major domestic issues—are phases of a single central problem, namely, the interplay of economic enterprise and government. These are the issues which for more than a generation have dominated the calendar of the Court.[8]

Throughout most of its history the Court was a bastion of conservative economics. Whether the government was judged to be improperly interfering with the economy depended on which social groups benefited. If the federal government wanted to establish national banks, or give away half the country to private speculators, or subsidize industries, or set up commissions and boards that fixed prices and interest rates on behalf of manufacturers, railroads and banks, or send Marines to secure corporate investments in Central America, such activities were as perfectly acceptable to the majority of the Court as to the majority of the business community. But if the federal or state governments sought to limit work-day hours, or outlaw child labor, or establish minimum wages, or guarantee the rights of collective bargaining, or in other ways impose some kind of limitation on the privileges of the business community, then the Court ruled that government could not tamper with the natural processes of the private market nor interfere with the principle of laissez-faire by depriving owner and worker of "liberty of contract" and "substantive due process."[9]

The concept of substantive due process illustrates as well as any other judicial doctrine the way the Court manufactures new constitutional meanings under the guise of interpreting old ones. By about 1890, after years of pressure from corporate lawyers and American Bar Association spokesmen, the Court decided that due process referred not only to procedural matters, such as safeguards against arbitrary arrest, right to counsel and a fair and speedy public trial, but to the *substance* of the legislation—that is, not only to the way the law had been made and applied but to its very content.[10] Having determined that there was such a thing as "substantive due process," which ordinarily might have been considered a

8. Frankfurter, *Mr. Justice Holmes* p. 41. Frankfurter made this comment in 1938, a year before he was appointed to the Court.

9. See for instance *Allgeyer* v. *Louisiana*, 165 U.S. 578 (1897); *Lochner* v. *New York*, 198 U.S. 45 (1905); and *Adair* v. *United States*, 208 U.S. 161 (1908).

10. The pressures of business lawyers and the Bar Association are described in Arthur A. North, S. J., *The Supreme Court, Judicial Process and Judicial Politics* (New York: Appleton-Century-Crofts, 1966), pp. 40–43.

contradiction in terms, the Court then could review every kind of legislation passed by the states brought before it by business plaintiffs. When Congress enacted social welfare legislation outlawing child labor, the Court would find it to be a violation of "substantive due process" under the Fifth Amendment and an unconstitutional usurpation of the reserved powers of the states under the Tenth Amendment.[11] When the states passed social welfare legislation, the Court would find it in violation of "substantive due process" under the Fourteenth Amendment.[12] Thus while prohibiting Congress from supposedly encroaching on the reserved powers of the states, the Court prevented the states from using their reserved powers.

The Fourteenth Amendment, adopted in 1868 ostensibly to establish full citizenship for Blacks, states that "No State shall make or enforce any law which shall abridge the privileges or immunities of citizens of the United States; nor shall any State deprive any person of life, liberty, or property, without due process of law; nor deny to any person within its jurisdiction the equal protection of the laws." The Court decided that the word "person" included corporations and that the Fourteenth Amendment was intended not only to uphold the civil rights of Blacks—which it seldom did—but to protect business conglomerations from the vexatious regulations of the states.

Perhaps encouraged by the loose construction given to the word "person" or more likely convinced that they really were persons despite the treatment accorded them by a male-dominated society, feminist advocates began to argue that the Fourteenth Amendment and the Fifth Amendment applied to women and that the voting restrictions imposed on them by state and federal government should be abolished. A test case reached the Supreme Court in 1894 and the Justices decided that they could not give such a daring reading to the Constitution.[13] The Court seemingly had made up its mind that "privileges and immunities of citizens" and "equal protection of the laws" applied to corporate institutions and not to women and Blacks.

By the late 1930s the Court was sufficiently reconstructed with

---

11. See *Hammer v. Dagenhart*, 247 U.S. 251 (1918). The Tenth Amendment reads: "The powers not delegated to the United States by this Constitution, nor prohibited by it to the States, are reserved to the States respectively or to the people." See also *Carter v. Carter Coal Co.*, 298 U.S. 238 (1936).

12. *Morehead v. New York*, 298 U.S. 587 (1936).

13. *Minor v. Happersett*, 88 U.S. 162 (1894).

new members to allow government to break out of the straitjacket imposed on "reform" legislation.[14] It is highly doubtful that New Deal legislation had the salutary reforming effects that liberals claimed and conservatives feared (a matter discussed in Chapter Five), but it does seem that from about 1937 onward, the Court became unwilling to impose an ultraconservative, laissez-faire interpretation on legislation and gave the state pretty much a free hand in servicing and rationalizing the corporate economy.

Nibbling Away at the First Amendment

While opposing restrictions on economic power, the Court seldom has opposed restraints on free speech. The same conservatism that feared experimentation in economics also feared expression of the heretical and radical ideas which espoused such changes.[15] The First Amendment says "Congress shall make no law . . . abridging the freedom of speech, or of the press." This would seem to leave little room for doubt as to the freedom of *all* speech.[16] Yet ever since the Alien and Sedition Acts of 1798, Congress and the state legislatures have found repeated occasion to pass laws penalizing the expression of heretical ideas. Over the years many who expressed opposition to government policy and to the established politico-economic system were deemed guilty of "subversion" or "sedition."[17] During the First World War, Congress passed the Espionage Act, under which almost two thousand successful prosecutions were carried out against persons, usually socialists, who expressed opposition to the war. One William Powell, who in private conversation in a relative's home voiced his dissatisfaction with U.S. policy and opined that the conflict in Europe was a rich

14. The Hughes Court voted down much of the New Deal program by 5–4 majorities until 1937, when Justice Roberts left the conservatives and began voting with the liberals in the aftermath of Roosevelt's attempt to pack the Court by expanding its membership. From then on, New Deal laws challenged in the Court were usually *upheld* by 5–4 decisions. It was known as "the switch in time that saved nine."

15. See Frankfurter's comments in *Mr. Justice Holmes*, p. 85.

16. Even the staunchest proponents of free speech allow that libel and slander might be restricted by law, although here, too, such speech when directed against public figures has been treated as protected under the First Amendment. See *New York Times Co.* v. *Sullivan*, 376 U.S. 254 (1964) and *Time, Inc.* v. *Hill* 385 U.S. 374 (1967).

17. *Sedition* is defined in Webster's Dictionary as "excitement of discontent against the government or resistance to lawful authority."

man's war, was convicted, fined $5,000 and sentenced to twenty years in prison.[18]

The High Court's attitude toward the First Amendment was best expressed by Justice Holmes in the *Schenck* case. Schenck was charged with attempting to cause insubordination among U.S. military forces and obstructing recruitment, both violations of the Esponage Act of 1917. What he had done was distribute a leaflet that condemned the war as a wrong against humanity perpetrated by Wall Street; it also urged people to exercise their right to oppose the draft but confined itself to advocating peaceful measures such as a petition for the repeal of the draft law. The leaflet was sent, Holmes contended, with the intention of influencing persons to obstruct the draft. The function of speech, especially of political advocacy, is to induce actions. In ordinary times such speech is amply protected by the First Amendment, but "the question in every case," Holmes reasoned, "is whether the words used are used in such circumstances and are of such a nature as to create a clear and present danger that they will bring about the substantive evils that Congress has a right to prevent."[19] Holmes never established why obstruction of the draft was a substantive evil except to assume that prosecution of the war was a substantive good (the very idea that Schenck was trying to challenge) and therefore actions hampering the war effort were evil and Congress could stop them.

Free speech, Holmes argued, "does not protect a man in falsely shouting fire in a crowded theatre and causing a panic." Maybe not, but the analogy is a farfetched one: Schenck was not in a theater but was seeking a forum in order to voice political ideas and urge nonviolent opposition to policies Holmes treated as above challenge. "When a nation is at war," Holmes continued, "many things that might be said in time of peace are such a hindrance to its efforts that their utterance will not be endured so long as men fight and that no Court could regard them as protected by any constitutional right." Behind the tempered prose Holmes was summoning the same argument paraded by every ruler who has sought to abrogate a people's freedom: these are not normal times; there is a grave menace within or just outside our gates; extraordinary

18. Hearings before a Subcommittee of the Senate Judiciary Committee, *Amnesty and Pardon for Political Prisoners* (Washington, D.C.: Government Printing Office, 1927), p. 54. See also Charles Goodell, *Political Prisoners in America* (New York: Random House, 1973), Chapter Four.

19. *Schenck* v. *United States*, 249 U.S. 47 (1919); also Holmes' decision in *Debs* v. *United States*, 249 U.S. 211 (1919).

measures are necessary and the democratic rules must be suspended for our nation's security.

At no time was it established that Schenck had actually obstructed anything. He was convicted of *conspiracy* to obstruct.[20] The allegedly wrongful *intent* of his action, regardless of its success, constituted sufficient reason to declare his leaflet a "clear and present danger" to the survival of the Republic.[21]

More than once the Court would treat the allegedly pernicious quality of an idea as certain evidence of its lethal efficacy and as justification for its suppression. This was especially true if the purveyors of the idea were thought to be radicals and revolutionaries. In 1940 Congress passed the Smith Act, making it a felony to teach and advocate the violent overthrow of the government. Soon after, a group of socialists were convicted under the act and sent to prison. Ten years later the Justice Department indicted the top leadership of the Communist party on charges of conspiring to organize to teach and advocate the violent overthrow of the government, specifically by forming the Communist party and teaching its members the ideas of Marxism-Leninism. The defendants were convicted but took their case to the Supreme Court. In a 6–2 decision in *Dennis et al.* v. *United States*,[22] the Court upheld the Smith Act and the convictions.

A look at the Court's reasoning in this case shows how, during witch-hunting times, most Justices are able to bend the First Amendment one way or another:

20. Under the law, "conspiracy" is said to be an agreement by two or more people to commit an unlawful act, or to commit a lawful act by unlawful means. In some cases, it has been argued by prosecutors and some judges that likemindedness or working for a common purpose, even without actual planning sessions or cooperative actions, is sufficient evidence of conspiracy. Thus, some of the Chicago Eight brought to trial for conspiracy to incite riot had not met each other until the time of the trial. The conspiracy doctrine has been described by Judge Learned Hand as the prosecutor's "darling"; it can make a crime out of the most amorphous political rally and out of the thoughts in people's heads even when these are expressed openly and promulgated by lawful means. For a discussion of the conspiracy doctrine, see Jessica Mitford, *The Trial of Dr. Spock* (New York: Knopf, 1969); also Thomas I. Emerson, *The System of Freedom of Expression* (New York: Vintage, 1971).

21. Holmes was considered one of the more liberal Justices of his day. And in subsequent cases he did place himself against the Court's majority and on the side of the First Amendment, earning the title of the "Great Dissenter." See his dissents in *Abrams* v. *United States,* 250 U.S. 616 (1919), and *Gitlow* v. *New York,* 268 U.S. 652 (1925).

22. 341 U.S. 494 (1951). Only eight Justices participated; the ninth, Tom Clark, excused himself from the decision because he had been Attorney General at the time the case was being handled by the Justice Department. Clark participated in subsequent cases of a similar nature and took the side of the prosecution.

(1) Chief Justice Vinson, with three other Justices concurring, reasoned that in the face of a Communist Menace the government need not wait until a putsch was about to be executed. There was no freedom under the Constitution for revolutionaries. Not only the clear and present quality of the danger but also its "gravity" and "probability" had to be taken into account.

(2) In a concurring opinion, Justice Frankfurter argued that free speech was not an absolute value but one of a number of competing values and that the priorities placed on these various interests were a question of public policy, a legislative matter best settled by the people's representatives in Congress. The Court was not a legislative body and should not place itself above the judgment of the Congress that had passed the Smith Act. Furthermore, "not every type of speech occupies the same position on the scale of values." The lewd and the libelous have no unqualified protection under the First Amendment, and certainly language that advocates violent overthrow of the government should rank low.

(3) Justce Jackson concurred, warning that the Communists sought to infiltrate every institution in American life. "Through these placements in positions of power [the Communist party] seeks a leverage over society that will make up in power of coercion what it lacks in power of persuasion. The Communists have no scruples against sabotage, terrorism, assassination or mob disorder. . . ." Clear and present danger was too ambiguous a rule to apply; suffice it to say that Communists were part of a well-organized conspiracy directed toward unlawful ends that enjoyed no protection under the Constitution.

(4) Dissenting from the majority view was Justice Black, who observed that the petitioners had not been charged with any overt acts nor even with saying anything about violent revolution. They were indicted for conspiring to organize the Communist party and at some future time publish things which would teach and advocate violent revolution. A restriction at the present time was nothing but prior censorship and a violation of the First Amendment. In any case, the First Amendment did not permit us to sustain laws suppressing free speech on the basis of Congress' or our own notion of "reasonableness" but was designed to protect those very ideas we might find heretical. Safe and orthodox views rarely needed the protection of the Constitution.

(5) Also dissenting was Justice Douglas, who reminded the Court that no evidence was introduced at the Dennis trial demonstrating that the petitioners were teaching or even planning to

teach the methods of terror and violence. What was being con-demned was the teaching of the classic works of Marx, Engels and Lenin. If communist beliefs were to be defeated, let it be in the marketplace of ideas. The attack should be against the ideas and not against those who hold them. "Full and free discussion," Doug-las concluded, "even of the ideas we hate encourages the testing of our own prejudices and preconceptions."

Six years after Dennis and the other top leaders of the Com-munist party were jailed, fourteen more party leaders were indicted and convicted under the same Smith Act. This time a majority of the Court made a distinction between "advocacy of abstract doc-trine and advocacy directed at promoting unlawful action" and decided that the Smith Act had intended to outlaw only the latter.[23] Thus, without declaring the act unconstitutional, the Court overthrew the conviction, arguing that the law had not been applied correctly. Justice Black, concurring in the decision, did enter a "dissent in part," along with Justice Douglas, expressing the opinion that the Smith Act itself should be declared a violation of the First Amendment. "I believe," Black stated unequivocally, that the First Amendment forbids Congress to punish people for talking about public affairs, whether or not such discussion incites to action, legal or illegal."

Needless to say, Black's postulate remains the minority opinion among the directors, trustees and owners of our public and private institutions and even among many who fancy themselves to be civil libertarians. They argue that revolutionaries should not be allowed to take advantage of the very liberties they seek to destroy. Revolutionary advocacy constitutes an abuse of freedom by urging us to violate the democratic rules of the game.[24] Hence, the argu-ment goes, in order to preserve our political freedom, we may find it necessary to deprive some people of theirs. Several rejoinders might be made to this position.

First, as a point of historical fact, the threat of revolution in

23. *Yates et al.* v. *United States*, 354 U.S. 298 (1957).
24. For samples of this kind of thinking see the Vinson and Jackson opinions in the *Dennis* case briefly summarized above; also Sidney Hook, *Political Power and Personal Freedom* (New York: Criterion Books, 1959); Carl A. Auerbach, "The Communist Control Act of 1954: A Proposed Legal-Political Theory of Free Speech," *The University of Chicago Law Review*, 23, Winter 1956, reproduced in edited form in Samuel Hendel (ed.), *Basic Issues of American Democracy*, 8th ed. (Englewood Cliffs, N.J.: Prentice-Hall, 1976), pp. 59–63; and Frederick Bernays Wiener, " 'Freedom for the Thought That We Hate': Is It a Principle of the Constitution?" *American Bar Association Journal*, 37, March 1951.

the United States has never been as real or harmful to "our liberties" as the measures allegedly taken to protect us from revolutionary ideas. History repeatedly demonstrates the expansive quality of repression: first, revolutionary advocacy is suppressed, then proponents of certain doctrines and theories, then "inciting" words, then "irresponsible" news reports and public utterances that are not "balanced" or "constructive," then any kind of dissent which those in power might find intolerable.

Second, the suppression is conducted by political elites who, in protecting us from what they consider "harmful" thoughts, deprive us of the opportunity of hearing and debating revolutionary advocates, and try to make up our minds for us. An exchange is forbidden because the advocate has been silenced.[25]

Third, it is a debatable point whether socialist, communist and other radical revolutionaries are dedicated to the destruction of freedom. Most revolutionaries would argue that freedom is one of the things lacking in the *present* society. The millions who are crushed by poverty and hunger and the millions more who are stupefied by the business-owned mass media are hardly as free as we might think. Revolutionaries argue that the constructing of new social alternatives and new modes of communal organization brings an *increase* in freedom, including freedom from poverty and hunger, freedom to share in making the decisions that govern one's work conditions, education, community and life, freedom to experiment with new forms of social organization and production. Admittedly some freedoms enjoyed today would be lost in a revolutionary society—for instance, the freedom to exploit other people and get rich from their labor, the freedom to squander human and natural resources and treat the environment as a septic tank, the freedom to monopolize information and use technical and professional skills primarily for personal gain and the freedom to exercise unaccountable power. In many countries throughout the world, successful social revolutionary movements have brought a net increase in the freedom of individuals, revolutionaries point out, by advancing the conditions necessary for the preservation of health and human life, by providing jobs and education for the unemployed and illiterate, by using economic resources for social

25. The classic statement on this position is John Stuart Mill, *On Liberty*, published more than a century ago. See also Alexander Meiklejohn, *Free Speech and Its Relation to Self-Government* (New York: Harper and Brothers, 1948), selections reproduced in Hendel, *Basic Issues of American Democracy*, pp. 64–67.

development rather than for private corporate profit and by over-throwing repressive reactionary regimes and ending foreign exploitation and involving large sectors of the populace in the task of socialist reconstruction. Revolutions have extended a number of real freedoms without destroying those that never existed for the common people. The repression in America is here and now, while the hope for a better life lies ahead. The argument can be debated but not if it is suppressed.

Far from being a bulwark against government suppression, the Court has usually gone along with it. When the Southern states imposed the tyranny of racial segregation on Black people and other non-Whites after Emancipation, the Court, in *Plessy* v. *Ferguson,* obligingly formulated the doctrine of "separate but equal" to give constitutional justification to segregation.[26] And when the government decided to uproot 112,000 law-abiding Japanese-Americans from the West Coast at the onset of World War II, forcing them to relinquish their homes, businesses, farms and other possessions and herding them into concentration camps for the duration of the war on the incredible notion that they might pose a threat to our West Coast defenses, the Supreme Court found that, given the exigencies of war, the government was acting within the limits of the Constitution.[27]

The Court Today

The Supreme Court's record in the area of personal liberties is gravely wanting, yet it is not totally devoid of merit. "Let us give the Court its due; it is little enough," Robert Dahl reminds us.[28] Over the years the Court has extended the protection of the First

26. 163 U.S. 537 (1896).

27. *Hirabayashi* v. *United States,* 320 U.S. 81 (1943), *Korematsu* v. *United States,* 323 U.S. 214 (1944) and *Ex parte Endo,* 323 U.S. 283 (1944). These decisions were rendered by the "liberal" Stone Court. As with many other shady aspects of American history, students are taught little about this. Implicit in the Japanese relocation was the assumption that the *race* likeness between Japanese here and in Japan would lead to treachery and disloyalty. The same reasoning was not applied to White "enemy ethnics" like the German-Americans and Italian-Americans. For a long time the Japanese-Americans had been an object of resentment because of their successful farming and social mobility on the West Coast. The relocation left many of them destitute, and almost all their land was grabbed by Whites.

28. Robert A. Dahl, "Decision-Making in a Democracy: The Role of the Supreme Court as a National Policy-Maker," *Journal of Public Law,* 6, no. 2, 1958, p. 292.

Amendment and other portions of the Bill of Rights to cover not only the federal government but state government (via the Fourteenth Amendment). Attempts by the states to censor publications,[29] deny individuals the right to peaceful assembly[30] and weaken the separation between church and state[31] were overturned. During the 1960s, the Court under Chief Justice Earl Warren took some important steps to strengthen the defendant's rights in criminal justice proceedings. In a 1963 decision the Court held that "the right of an indigent defendant in a [state] criminal trial to have the assistance of counsel is a fundamental right essential to a fair trial and . . . conviction wthout the assistance of counsel violated the Fourteenth Amendment."[32] In the *Escobedo* and *Miranda* cases the defendant's right to counsel was extended to include the onset of interrogation, one purpose being to diminish the likelihood of police beatings and forced confessions.[33]

The malapportionment and "rotten boroughs" of many state and congressional legislative districts were struck down when the Warren Court ruled that district lines had to be redrawn in accordance with population distribution. In some states less than a third of the population elected more than half the legislators. Voters in the overpopulated districts, the Court reasoned, were being denied equal protection under the law and, in effect, losing their right to suffrage because of the "debasement" and "dilution" of their votes.[34] The Court also gave every indication of taking the disestablishment clause in the First Amendment seriously by ruling that prayers in the public school were a violation of separation of church and state.[35]

29. *Near* v. *Minnesota*, 283 U.S. 697 (1931).
30. *DeJonge* v. *Oregon*, 299 U.S. 353 (1937).
31. *McCollum* v. *Board of Education*, 333 U.S. 203 (1948).
32. See *Gideon* v. *Wainright*, 372 U.S. 335 (1963).
33. *Escobedo* v. *Illinois*, 378 U.S. 478 (1964) and *Miranda* v. *Arizona*, 384 U.S. 436 (1966).
34. See *Baker* v. *Carr*, 369 U.S. 186 (1962) and *Reynolds* v. *Sims*, 377 U.S. 533 (1964). A similar decision was made in regard to congressional districts in *Wesberry* v. *Sanders*, 376 U.S. 1 (1964). It was anticipated that reapportionment would have all sorts of liberalizing effects on both state legislatures and Congress by shifting power from the overrepresented conservative rural areas to the supposedly more progressive and now more numerous urban and suburban districts. However, in the decade since the reapportionment decisions, there seems to have been no discernible change in the business-oriented propensities of state and national legislatures. See *supra*, Chapters twelve and thirteen.
35. See *Engles* v. *Vitale*, 370 U.S. 421 (1962), and *School District of Abington* v. *Schempp*, 374 U.S. 203 (1963). The First Amendment reads: "Congress shall make no law respecting an establishment of religion, or prohibiting the free exercise thereof."

The Warren Court handed down a number of decisions aimed at abolishing segregation in public facilities, transportation and education. The most widely celebrated was that in *Brown* v. *Board of Education*,[36] which unanimously ruled that "separate educational facilities are inherently unequal" because of the inescapable imputation of inferiority cast upon the segregated minority group, an imputation that is all the greater when it has the sanction of law. This decision overruled the "separate but equal" doctrine enunciated in 1896 in the *Plessy* case.[37] A few years later the Warren Court unanimously nullified the bans imposed by various states against interracial marriage, arguing that "there can be no doubt that restricting the freedom to marry solely because of racial classifications violates the central meaning of the equal protection clause."[38]

The direction the Court takes depends largely on the political composition of its majority. Refortified with four Nixon-appointed Justices and a Ford-appointed one, the Court under Chief Justice Burger has taken a decidedly conservative turn. In the area of criminal justice, for instance, the Burger Court decided that it was no longer necessary to have a unanimous jury verdict for conviction—a decision that, in effect, abolished the need for having a jury agree that the prosecution has proven guilt beyond a reasonable doubt.[39] In another decision the Burger Court ruled that police may stop and frisk people almost at their own discretion, thus making it easier for them to intimidate dissenters, demonstrators, Blacks and other "troublesome" elements.[40]

In *Rizzo* v. *Goode,* the Court overruled a lower court order which directed the Philadelphia Police Department to improve its procedures for acting on citizen complaints of police brutality. The evidence indicated a pattern of police department indifference to complaints. But the majority opinion, written by Justice Rehnquist, argued that "the evidence did not establish the existence of any [police] policy to disregard constitutional rights."[41] Appar-

36. 347 U.S. 483 (1954).
37. *Plessy* v. *Ferguson* 163 U.S. 537 (1896).
38. *Loving* v. *Virginia*, 388 U.S. 1 (1967).
39. *Johnson* v. *Louisiana*, 32 L. Ed. 2d 152 (1972) and *Apodaca* v. *Oregon*, 32 L. Ed. 2d 184 (1972).
40. In this instance, *Adams* v. *Williams*, the Burger Court was expanding on a policy set down by the Warren Court in *Terry* v. *Ohio*, 392 U.S. 1 (1968); see also *United States* v. *Robinson*, 414 U.S. 218 (1973).
41. See the discussion of *Rizzo* v. *Goode* in the *Progressive*, March 76, p. 9.

ently police departments are to be immune unless they explicitly declare their opposition to the Constitution. The Court also ruled that a police officer might make an arrest without a warrant in a public place even though there was adequate time to obtain a warrant.[42] The *Miranda* decision, which forbade the use of police torture in obtaining confessions, was weakened by the Burger Court, as was the right of Black defendants to have prospective jurors questioned about their possible racial prejudices.[43]

The Burger Court has handed down decisions undermining the right against self-incrimination and denying reporters a right to confidential news sources.[44] The Court let stand a lower court ruling allowing the Federal Communications Commission to require broadcasters to censor themselves.[45]

The Burger Court let stand a lower court order requiring that a former CIA employee submit all his future writings about the CIA to the Agency for prepublication censorship.[46] The Court ruled that military posts may ban speeches and demonstrations of a "partisan" political nature and may prohibit distribution of political literature.[47] In *Laird* v. *Tatum*,[48] the Burger Court was asked to rule on the constitutionality of Army surveillance of lawful civilian political activities. It dismissed the case by a 5–4 vote, refusing to impose any limitation on government surveillance. The passionate dissent by Justice Douglas is worth quoting from:

This case is a cancer in our body politic. . . . Army surveillance, like Army regimentation, is at war with the principles of the First Amendment. Those who already walk submissively will say there is no cause for alarm. But submissiveness is not our heritage. . . . The Bill of Rights was designed to keep agents of Government and official eavesdroppers away from assemblies of people. The aim was to allow [people] to be free and independent and to assert their rights against Government.

42. *United States* v. *Watson;* see the *New York Times,* January 27, 1976.
43. See *Michigan* v. *Mosley,* 46 L. Ed. 2d 313 (1975), and *Ristaino* v. *Ross,* 47 L. Ed. 258 (1976). In 1976 the Burger Court, in a 7–2 decision, declared the death penalty to be constitutional and not in violation of the Eighth Amendment's prohibition against "cruel and unusual punishment." *New York Times,* July 3, 1976.
44. *United States* v. *Caldwell,* 33 L. Ed. 626 (1972).
45. Specifically, to censor song lyrics that are played on the air. *Yale Broadcasting Co.* v. *FCC,* 414 U.S. 914 (1973).
46. *New York Times,* May 28, 1975. The ex-CIA employee was Victor Marchetti, coauthor, with John D. Marks, of *The CIA and the Cult of Intelligence* (New York: Knopf, 1974).
47. *Greer* v. *Spock,* 47 L. Ed. 2d 505 (1976).
48. 408 U.S. 1 (1972).

In most decisions in which individual rights have been pitted against the coercive powers of the state, the conservative Burger Court has sided with the latter.⁴⁹ Similarly, in most decisions involving disputes between workers and owners, the Burger Court has sided with the owners. Thus the Court decided that workers do not have the right to strike over safety issues if there are contract provisions for arbitration. Chief Justice Burger held that arbitration was a substitute for "industrial strife" and, in any case, it was in the national interest to avoid strikes.⁵⁰ (The case involved a wildcat strike by miners who had discovered that foremen were falsifying reports on underground airflow and combustion conditions in order to keep production going.) The Court also ruled that striking union members had no right to picket in a public shopping center.⁵¹

The Burger Court's dedication to social inequality was manifested with exceptional clarity in its decision to prevent school districts with low property values from having as much money spent on education as those with higher property values. The Court decided, with Justice Powell writing the opinion, that a state may constitutionally vary the quality of education which it offers its children in accordance with the amount of taxable wealth located in the districts in which they reside.⁵² The Court seemed to be saying, there could be any degree of inequality short of absolute deprivation; as long as the Chicano children had *some* kind of school to go to, this would satisfy the equal-protection clause of the Fourteenth Amendment. The decision hardly lived up to the principles enunciated in the 1954 *Brown* case, as Justice Marshall pointed out in a dissent.

In keeping with its support of social inequality and its defense of privilege, the Burger Court decided that the principle of "one-man, one-vote" need not be observed in elections for special-purpose governmental bodies like water districts. Since the expenses of the water district are met by the landowners, the majority reasoned, then landowners alone should have the vote.⁵³ In his dissent Justice Douglas pointed out that four corporations owned nearly 85 percent of the 193,000 acres in the district while 189 landowners had less

49. For a critique of the Burger Court, see Leonard W. Levy, *The Nixon Court and Criminal Justice* (New York: Harper and Row, 1975).

50. *Gateway Coal Co.* v. *United Mine Workers*, 414 U.S. 368 (1974).

51. *Hudgens* v. *NLRB*, 47 L. Ed. 2d 196 (1976).

52. *San Antonio Independent School District* v. *Rodriguez*, 36 L. Ed. 2d 16 (1973).

53. *Salyer Land Co.* v. *Tulare Lake Basin Water Storage District*, 35 L. Ed. 2d 675 (1973).

than 3 percent. Small owners, tenant farmers and sharecroppers all should have a say, he insisted, because irrigation, water storage, water usage and flood control "implicate the entire community." The ballot, he pointed out in a companion case, is restricted to the wealthy few who can violate "our environmental ethics" and in other ways do their will.[54]

In two other cases, the Court held, in 5–4 decisions, that indigents who could not afford court fees had no right to their day in court.[55] While not directly overruling certain Warren Court decisions, the Burger Court sometimes did its best to erode them. Finding no way to contravene the constitutionality of the earlier reapportionment cases, for instance, the Burger Court decided that the "one-man, one-vote" rule should be applied less rigorously to the state legislative districts than to congressional districts. In allowing for a population deviation as wide as 16.4 percent, the Court reasoned that state districts have indigenous qualities that ought sometimes to be preserved.[56]

Influence of the Court

It is easier to describe the blatantly political role played by the Court than to measure its actual political influence. But a few rough generalizations can be drawn. First, as a nonelective branch staffed by persons of elitist legal, corporate and political background, the Court has exercised a preponderately conservative influence. On matters of social welfare legislation, the Court wielded a strategic minority veto for about seventy years. Laws on workmen's compensation, child labor, unionization and other reform legislation of a kind that had been enacted in European countries a generation before were delayed ten to twenty-five years by the High Court. It prevented Congress from instituting income taxes, a decision that took eighteen years and a constitutional amendment to circumvent.[57]

But whatever our complaints about the "nine old men," we should remember that the Court's ability to impose its will on the nation is far from boundless. Presidents usually get the opportunity

54. *Associated Enterprise, Inc. v. Toltec Watershed Improvement District,* 35 L. Ed. 2d 675 (1973).
55. *Ortwein v. Schwab,* 35 L. Ed. 2d 572 (1973). Also *United States v. Kraus,* 34 L. Ed. 2d 626 (1973).
56. *Mahan v. Howell,* 35 L. Ed. 2d 320 (1973).
57. *Pollock v. Farmers' Loan & Trust Co.,* 157 U.S. H29 (1895).

to appoint two or more members to the Court and thus exert an influence over its makeup.[58] Furthermore, the Court cannot make rulings at will but must wait until a case is brought to it either on appeal from a lower court or, far less frequently, as a case of original jurisdiction. And the Court agrees to hear only a small portion of the cases on its docket, thus leaving the final word to the lower courts in most instances.

Political currents and changing climates of opinion do not leave the Justices untouched. Members of the Court have been aware that the efficacy of their decisions depends on the willingness of other agencies of government to carry them out. A Court that runs too glaringly against the tide risks being attacked. Its appellate jurisdiction might be circumscribed by Congress, its decisions ignored and itself subjected to ridicule and hostility. Some members of the Court such as Justices Harlan and Frankfurter have been so impressed by the limitations of its power and its vulnerability to the other branches as to counsel a doctrine of "judicial restraint," especially when the Court has tried to move innovatively.[59]

The Court is always operating in a climate of opinion shaped by political forces larger than itself. Its willingness to depart from the casuistry of *Plessy* v. *Ferguson* and take the Fourteenth Amendment seriously in *Brown* v. *Board of Education* depended in part on the changing climate of opinion concerning race relations and segregation between 1896 and 1954. At the same time the Court is not purely a dependent variable. That it had to accept segregation for more than half a century before upholding the Constitution is not certain. The arguments used on the eve of the *Brown* decision —that the Court should not push people, that hearts and minds had to change first, that you can't legislate morality, and that there would be vehement and violent opposition—were the same arguments used during the days of the *Plessy* case. In fact there was vehement and often violent opposition to the *Brown* decision. But there also was an acceleration of opinion in support of the Court's ruling, in part activated by that very ruling. (Just as there was an increase in *segregationist* practices after the *Plessy* case, from 1896 to 1914, probably in part encouraged by *Plessy* and decisions like it.) Hence, some of the Court's decisions have an important feedback effect. By playing a crucial role in defining what is legitimate

58. Dahl, "Decision-Making in a Democracy," p. 285.
59. For instance, see the dissents by Frankfurter and Harlan respectively in the apportionment cases: *Baker* v. *Carr*, 369 U.S. 186 (1962) and *Reynolds* v. *Sims*, 377 U.S. 533 (1964).

and constitutional, the Court gives encouraging cues to large sectors of the public. Unable to pass a civil rights act for seventy years, the Congress enacted three in the decade after the *Brown* case. And Blacks throughout the nation pressed harder in an attempt to make desegregation a reality. Organizing efforts for civil rights increased in both the North and the South, along with "Freedom Riders," sit-ins and mass demonstrations. The political consciousness of a generation was joined, and who is to say that the Warren Court did not play a part in that?[60]

The Supreme Court, then, probably has a real effect on political consciousness and public policy, albeit in limited ways and for limited durations. Progressive people have relied too heavily on the High Court and on courts in general. For anyone engaged in the struggle for justice, the courts may occasionally be a necessary evil, but they are not the friends of progressive and socialist causes. With the exception of a brief ten-year span under Chief Justice Warren, the Supreme Court has been the most conservative branch of government. The Court, like the very laws and Constitution it interprets, is limited to a frame of reference that accepts and defends the existing class and property relations.

60. For studies on the effects of High Court decisions, see Theodor Becker (ed.), *The Impact of Supreme Court Decisions: Empirical Studies* (New York: Oxford University Press, 1969).

Democracy for the Few

17

THE UNITED STATES IS SAID TO BE A pluralistic society, and indeed a glance at the social map of this country reveals a vast agglomeration of regional, occupational and ethnic groups and state, local and national governing agencies. If by pluralism we mean this multiplicity of private and public groups, then the United States is pluralistic. But then so is any society of size and complexity, including allegedly "totalitarian" ones like the Soviet Union with its multiplicity of regional, occupational and ethnic groups and its party, administrative, industrial and military factions and interests all jostling for position and power.[1]

But the proponents of pluralism presume to be saying something about how *power* is distributed and how *democracy* works. Specifically, pluralism means that (a) power is shared among representative sectors of the population; (b) the shaping of public policy involves inputs from a wide range of competing social groups; (c) no one group enjoys permanent dominance

1. See, for instance, Donald R. Kelly, "Interest Groups in the USSR: The Impact of Political Sensitivity on Group Influence," *Journal of Politics*, 34, August 1972, pp. 860–888; also H. Gordon Skilling and Franklyn Griffiths (eds.), *Interest Groups in Soviet Politics* (Princeton, N.J.: Princeton University Press, 1971). By the simple definition of pluralism offered above, even Nazi Germany might qualify as pluralistic. The Nazi state was a loose, often chaotic composite of fiercely competing groups. See Heinz Höne, *The Order of the Death's Head* (New York: Coward, McCann, and Geoghegan, 1970).

or suffers permanent defeat; and (d) the distribution of benefits is roughly equitable or certainly not consistently exploitative. Thus Ralf Dahrendorf writes: "Instead of a battlefield, the scene of group conflict has become a kind of market in which relatively autonomous forces contend according to certain rules of the game, by virtue of which nobody is a permanent winner or loser."[2] If there are elites in our society, the pluralists say, they are numerous and specialized, and they are checked in their demands by other elites. No group can press its advantages "too far" and any group that is interested in an issue can find a way within the political system to make its influence felt.[3] Business elites have the capacity to utilize the services of the government to further their interests, but, the pluralists argue, such interests are themselves varied and conflicting. The government does many different things for many different people; it is not controlled by a monolithic corporate elite that gets what it wants on every question. Government stands above any one particular influence but responds to many.

Pluralism for the Few

The evidence offered in the preceding chapters leaves us little reason to conclude that the United States is a "pluralistic democracy," as conceived by the pluralists. To summarize and expand upon some of the points previously made:

(1) Public policies, whether formulated by conservatives or liberals, Republicans or Democrats, fairly consistently favor the large corporate interests at a substantial cost to many millions of workers, small farmers, small producers, consumers, taxpayers, low-income people, urban slum dwellers, indigent elderly and rural poor. Those few benefits distributed to lower-income groups have proven gravely inadequate to their needs and have failed to reach

2. Ralf Dahrendorf, *Class and Class Conflict in Industrial Society* (Stanford, Calif.: Stanford University Press, 1959), p. 67.
3. One of the earliest pluralist statements is in Earl Latham, *The Group Basis of Politics* (Ithaca: Cornell University Press, 1952). See also Arnold M. Rose, *The Power Structure* (New York: Oxford University Press, 1967); Robert Dahl, *Who Governs?* (New Haven: Yale University Press, 1961); Edward Banfield, *Political Influence* (New York: Free Press, 1961); Nelson Polsby, *Community Power and Political Theory* (New Haven: Yale University Press, 1963). The criticisms of pluralism are many: the best collection of critiques can be found in Charles A. McCoy and John Playford (eds.), *Apolitical Politics* (New York: Crowell, 1967); see also Marvin Surkin and Alan Wolfe (eds.), *An End to Political Science: The Caucus Papers* (New York: Basic Books, 1970).

millions who might qualify for assistance. Government efforts in crucial areas of social need have rarely fulfilled even the minimal expectations of reform-minded advocates. There are more people living in poverty today than there were ten years ago, more substandard housing, more environmental pollution and devastation, more deficiencies in our schools, hospitals and systems of public transportation, more military dictatorships throughout the world feeding on the largesse and power of the Pentagon, more people—from Iran to Greece to the Philippines to Brazil to Mississippi—suffering the social oppression of an American-backed status quo, more unearned and corrupt profits going to the giant corporations, more glut in the private commodity market and more scarcity and want in public services.

(2) To think of government as nothing more than a broker or referee amidst a vast array of competing groups (these groups presumably representing all the important and "countervailing" interests of the populace) is to forget that government best serves those who can best serve themselves. That is not to say that political leaders are indifferent to popular sentiments. When those sentiments are aroused to a certain intensity, leaders will respond, either by making minor concessions or by evoking images of change and democratic responsiveness that are lacking in substance. Leaders are always "responding" to the public, but so often it is with distracting irrelevancies, dilatory and discouraging tactics, facile reassurances, unfulfilled promises, outright lies or token programs that offer nothing more than a cosmetic application to a deep social problem. The overall performance of our political system even in times of so-called social reform might best be characterized as giving *symbolic* allocations to public sentiment and *substantive* allocations to powerful private interests.

Indeed, one might better think of ours as a dual political system. First, there is the symbolic political system centering around electoral and representative activities including party conflicts, voter turnout, political personalities, public pronouncements, official role-playing and certain ambiguous presentations of some of the public issues which bestir Presidents, governors, mayors and their respective legislatures. Then there is the substantive political system, involving multibillion-dollar contracts, tax write-offs, protections, rebates, grants, loss compensations, subsidies, leases, giveaways and the whole vast process of budgeting, legislating, advising, regulating, protecting and servicing major producer interests, now bending or ignoring the law on behalf of the powerful, now applying it with full punitive vigor against heretics and "troublemakers." The symbolic system is highly visible, taught in the schools, dissected by academicians, gossiped about by newsmen. The substantive system is seldom heard of or accounted for.

(3) Far from the fluid interplay envisioned by the pluralists, the political efficacy of groups and individuals is largely determined by the resources of power available to them, of which wealth is the most crucial. Not everyone with money chooses to use it to exert political influence, and not everyone with money need bother to do so. But when they so desire, those who control the wealth of society enjoy a persistent and pervasive political advantage. Instead of being just another of many interests in the influence system, corporate business occupies a particularly strategic position. On the major issues which determine much of the development of society itself, business gets its way with Congress, the President, the courts and the bureaucracy because there exists no alternative way of organizing the economy within the existing capitalist structure. Because business controls the very economy of the nation, government perforce enters into a unique and intimate relationship with it. The health of the capitalist economy is treated by policymakers as a necessary condition for the health of the nation, and since it happens that the economy is in the hands of big companies, then presumably government's service to the public is best accomplished by service to these companies. The goals of business (rapid growth, high profits and secure markets) become the goals of government, and the "national interest" becomes identified with the dominant propertied interests. Since policy-makers must operate in and through the private economy, it is not long before they are operating *for* it.

(4) The pluralists make much of the fact that wealthy interests do not always operate with clear and deliberate purpose.[4] To be sure, elites, like everyone else, make mistakes and suffer confusions as to what might be the most advantageous tactics in any particular situation. But if they are not omniscient and infallible, neither are they habitual laggards and imbeciles. If they do not always calculate rationally in the pursuit of their class interests, they do so often and successfully enough.

It is also true that the business community is not monolithic and unanimous on all issues. The socialist economist Paul Sweezy has pointed out some of the fissures within the business world:

4. Dahl, *Who Governs?*, p. 272. Also see Robert A. Dahl, *Modern Political Analysis* (Englewood Cliffs, N.J.: Prentice-Hall, 1970).

there are regional differences (Eastern versus Southwestern capital), ideological ones (reactionary versus liberal capitalism) and corporate ones (Ford versus General Motors)—all of which add an element of conflict and indeterminancy to economic and political policies. But these are the conflicts of haves versus haves and they seldom include the interests of the unorganized public. Nor, as Sweezy reminds us, should we exaggerate the depths of these divisions:

Capitalists can and do fight among themselves to further individual or group interests, and they differ over the best way of coping with the problems which arise from their class position; but overshadowing all these divisions is their common interest in preserving and strengthening a system which guarantees their wealth and privileges. In the event of a real threat to the system, there are no longer class differences—only class traitors, and they are few and far between.[5]

(5) If American government is not ruled by one cohesive, conspiratorial elite, there is ample evidence of continual collusion between various corporate and governmental elites in every area of the political economy. Though there is no one grand power elite, there are many fairly large ones. And these elites often conspire with and seldom restrain each other. A look at the politico-economic system shows that many of the stronger ones tend to predominate in their particular spheres of activity more or less unmolested by other elites and unchecked by government.[6]

As we have seen, corporations are not merely beyond the reach of government; they incorporate public authority in their own undertakings. Government does play a crucial role in redirecting sectors of the corporate economy that tend to become disruptive of the system as a whole: hence Teddy Roosevelt's occasional trust-busting, Franklin Roosevelt's opposition to holding companies, and John Kennedy's attempt to force steel companies to hold back their prices. But such actions are usually limited in their range and are induced by a desire to protect the business economy *in toto*. Only in appearance is government a neutral mediator or defender of the public interest.

Most elitist conflicts, we noted, are resolved not by compromise but by log rolling and involve more *collusion* than competition.

5. Paul Sweezy, *The Present as History* (New York: Monthly Review Press, 1970), p. 138.
6. See Peter Bachrach, *The Theory of Democratic Elitism* (Boston: Little, Brown, 1967), p. 37.

These mutually satisfying arrangements among "competitors" leave out the interests of broad, unorganized sectors of the public. The demands of have-nots may be heard occasionally as a clamor outside the gate, and now and then some scant morsels are tossed to the unfortunates—especially if private suppliers can make money on it. But generally speaking, whether in times of conservative retrenchment or "progressive change," pluralist interest-group politics engages the interests of extremely limited portions of the population and operates within a field of political consensus largely shaped by the interests of corporate capitalism.

In addition, it is worth repeating: *the diffusion of power does not necessarily mean the democratization of power*. When decision-making power is parceled out, it goes to special public-private interest groups—quasiautonomous, entrenched minorities that use public authority for unaccountable private purposes of low visibility. The fragmentation of power is the pocketing of power, a way of insulating portions of the political process from the tides of popular sentiment. This purpose was embodied in the constitutional structure by the Founding Fathers and has been perpetuated by government decision-making arrangements ever since 1787.

The Myth of the Mixed Economy

The continued growth of government activity in the economy has led some observers to the mistaken notion that we are gradually moving toward a "post-capitalist" society, one that is neither capitalist nor socialist but a "mixed economy."[7] Proponents of this view avoid any consideration of what government does and whom it benefits when mixing itself with the economy. They fail to differentiate between federal regulation *of* business and federal regulation *for* business, and they assume that the power of government is neutral and socially beneficent.[8]

Both liberal and conservative theorists have treated the increasingly socialized *costs* of the public sector as evidence of increasingly socialized *benefits*, with liberals generally approving and conservatives disapproving of this trend. Conservatives attack the "welfare state" and liberals defend it; few in either camp ques-

7. See, for instance, Dahrendorf, *Class and Class Conflict in Industrial Society*.
8. Gabriel Kolko, *The Triumph of Conservatism* (Chicago: Quadrangle Books, 1967), p. 286.

tion whether we really have one. In reality, government involvement in the economy represents not a growth in socialism (as that term is normally understood by socialists) but a growth in state-supported capitalism, *not the communization of private wealth but the privatization of the commonwealth*. This development has brought a great deal of government planning, but it is not of the kind intended by socialism, which emphasizes the subordination of private profit and the reallocation of resources for new social priorities. As several English socialists have pointed out, in criticism of the policies of the British Labour party:

Planning now means better forecasting, better coordination of investment and expansion decisions, a more purposeful control over demand. This enables the more technologically equipped and organized units in the private sector to pursue their goals more efficiently, more "rationally." It also means more control over unions and over labor's power to bargain freely about wages. This involves another important transition. For in the course of this rationalization of capitalism, the gap between private industry and the State is narrowed.[9]

In Western industrial nations today, including the United States, government economic planning revolves around "the preservation and regulation of capitalism, not its demise."[10] The outcome is a more centralized blend of capitalist public-private powers. Under the notion of "rational planning" and the guise of insulating decision-making from selfish interest groups and corrupt politicians, corporate-political elites will push for more concentration of power in the higher reaches of the executive, gaining a tighter control over the political economy while bypassing the public, the trade unions and the Congress. "Herein lies the fallacy of the liberal hope that planning can achieve social justice."[11] For it is state planning *for* and *by* the corporate elites, offering only a more systematic exploitation of workers, consumers, taxpayers and environment. Its function is not social welfare or reform but the maintenance of capital profitability at home and abroad.

9. Stuart Hall, Raymond Williams and Edward Thompson, "The May Day Manifesto," excerpted in Carl Oglesby (ed.), *The New Left Reader* (New York: Grove Press, 1969), p. 115.

10. Stanley Aronowitz, "Modernizing Capitalism," *Social Policy*, May/June 1975, p. 20.

11. Aronowitz, "Modernizing Capitalism," p. 24. See also S. M. Miller, "Planning: Can It Make a Difference in Capitalist America?" *Social Policy*, September/October 1975, pp. 12–22.

Given the near monopoly they enjoy over society's productive capacity, the giant corporations remain the sole conduit for most public expenditures. Whether it be for schools or school lunches, sewers or space ships, submarines or airplanes, harbors or highways, government relies almost exclusively on private contractors and suppliers. These suppliers may be heavily subsidized or entirely funded from the public treasure, but they remain "private" in that a profit—usually a most generous risk-free one—accrues to them for whatever services they perform. The government is not a *producer* in competition with business, such rivalry not being appreciated in a capitalist economy, but a titanic *purchaser* or *consumer* of business products. Bound by this consumer role, government is dependent on business. This can be seen clearly during wars and cold wars, when intensified public spending brings greater governmental reliance on private industry. While some people bemoan the growth of government "interference" in business affairs, the reality is that big-business management has moved more deeply into public affairs with each new national mobilization, keeping public spending closely in line with industry's own profit interests.[12]

The commitment by government to mobilizing its industrial efforts primarily through private conduits in ways that do not compete with, and only serve to bolster, the private profit system marks one of the key differences between socialism and state-supported capitalism. Whether the difference is thought to be desirable or not, it first should be understood. The "mixed economy" as found in the United States has very little to do with socialism. Increases in spending may represent a growth in the public sector of the economy but not in the *publicly owned, public-serving* sector. The distinction between the "public" and "private," then, is a misleading one, since *the growth of the public sector represents little more than an increase in the risk-free, high-profit market of the private sector.* Sometimes the government will exercise direct ownership of a particular service, either to assist private industry—as with certain port facilities and technological research and training institutions—or to perform services which private capital no longer finds

12. See Walter LaFeber, *The New Empire: An Interpretation of American Expansion, 1860–1898* (Ithaca, N.Y.: Cornell University Press, 1963) for evidence of the growing interdependence of government and business as each expanded its activities. Also see Paul Koistinen, "The 'Industrial-Military Complex' in Historical Perspective: The Inter War Years," in Irwin Unger (ed.), *Beyond Liberalism: The New Left Views American History* (Waltham, Mass.: Xerox College Publishing, 1971), pp. 227–239; and David Horowitz (ed.), *Corporations and the Cold War* (New York: Monthly Review Press, 1969).

profitable to provide—as with nationalized coal mines in Great Britain or the bus and subway lines in many American cities. Private capital relinquishes its franchise and moves on to greener pastures, while the ownership, risks and losses are passed on to the public.[13]

There is the anticipation, common among some radicals, that as the problems of the economy deepen, modern capitalism will succumb to its own internal contradictions; as the economic "substructure" gives way, the "superstructure" of the capitalist state will be carried down with it and the opportunity for a humane, anti-imperialist, democratic, socialist society will be at hand. One difficulty with this position is that it underestimates the extent to which the political system can act with independent effect to preserve the capitalist class. The political system is more than a front for the economic interests it serves; it is the single most important force that corporate America has at its command. The power to use the police and the military, the power of eminent domain, the power to tax, spend and legislate, to use public funds for private profit, the power of limitless credit, the power to mobilize highly emotive symbols of loyalty and legitimacy—such resources of the state give corporate America a durability it could never provide for itself through the economy alone. The resilience of capitalism cannot be measured in isolated economic terms. Behind the corporation there stands the organized power of the state; "the stability and future of the economy is grounded, in the last analysis, on the power of the state to act to preserve it."[14] To maintain themselves, the corporations can call on the resources of the state to rationalize and subsidize their performance, maintain their profit levels, socialize costs by taxing the many and keep the malcontents under control through generous applications of official violence.

In sum, the merging of the public and private sectors is not merely a result of the growing complexity of technological society or a transition toward socialism; it is in large part the outcome of the realities of power and capitalist class interest.

13. Public ownership in this context is often only on paper. In the case of transit systems that are passed from private to public hands (discussed in Chapter Seven), the takeover really represents nothing more than a change from private stocks to public bonds—owned by the same wealthy class and banks that had owned the stocks. In addition the bonds are tax-free and offer a return guaranteed by the public treasure.

14. Kolko, *The Triumph of Conservatism*, p. 302.

Reform Within the System?

It is not quite accurate to presume that non-elites never win victories. The last century of intensive struggle between labor and management, continuing to this day and involving such groups as farm workers, hospital workers, teachers and white-collar employees, brought notable advances in the working conditions of millions.[15] But change, if not impossible within state-supported capitalism, is always limited by the overall imperatives of that system and is usually of a cosmetic or marginal nature. In most instances the acceptable changes prove to be supportive and even profitable to the larger capitalist interests. Hence, as already noted, most of the regulatory "reforms" benefited the giant producers at the expense of smaller producers and consumers.

Sometimes elites will initially oppose even these kinds of changes, not realizing the gains available to them. The auto industry was against safety features in automobiles until it realized that they could be installed as high-priced accessories which the customer was legally required to buy. And doctors vigorously opposed Medicare and Medicaid as steps toward "socialism" until they discovered gold in those programs. For with public funding available, the doctors and the hospitals now were able to double and triple their fees, charging their patients amounts they would not have dared impose had the patient been the sole payer. The result is that medical expenses zoomed upward without a commensurate improvement in medical care—although certainly some elderly people now have assistance they would not have had earlier. *To*

---

15. These advances have been exaggerated in the popular mind. Thus one hears complaints about plumbers and construction workers who make more than doctors, and sanitation workers who make more than college professors. Such complaints are unfounded. First, I am not sure why sanitation workers should not make more than college professors, since they work harder and at more unpleasant tasks. Second, as a matter of fact, they make substantially less. Even the well-paid "aristocracy of labor" in the construction field, given seasonal layoffs and assuming they can find work at all, earn about $10,000 in a good year. The average auto worker, backed by one of the stronger unions and operating in one of the better-paying labor markets, takes home less after years on the assembly line than the young college graduate who enters a management trainee program for the telephone company or the same auto industry. And income differences between managerial and professional occupations and working-class ones are widening rather than narrowing (see the *New York Times,* December 27, 1972). Furthermore, discussions on "how good labor has it" always focus on these better-paying jobs and ignore the 40 million or more workers who earn subsistence or poverty-level wages, like the farm workers who make $2,200 a year and who face high injury rates, job insecurity, and chronic indebtedness.

*pour more money into a service without a change in the market
relations enjoyed by the suppliers is merely to make more public
funds available to the suppliers without guaranteeing an improvement in the service.*

It is somewhat ironic to credit capitalism with the ability to
reform itself through gradual improvements when (a) most of the
reforms have been vehemently resisted by capitalist elites, (b)
most of the problems needing reform have been caused or intensified by capitalism and (c) most of the actual programs end up
primarily benefiting the capitalist producers.

Conservatives complain that we have thrown billions at our
socioeconomic problems with no results. From this correct observation they mistakenly conclude that since little can be done about
these problems within the *present* system, then the problems are
insoluble. For the elites who own this country, if wiping out widespread poverty and starvation entails changing the entire system
and jeopardizing elite class positions, then better to have poverty
and starvation.

Some of the more liberal elites believe our problems can be
solved within the present system of state-supported capitalism, it
being principally a matter of changing our "warped priorities." To
be sure the priorities are warped: by the end of the 1960s, upper-
income Americans were spending $2 billion a year on jewelry—
more than was spent on housing for the poor—and no less than
$3 billion on pleasure boating—a half billion more than what the
fifty states spend on welfare. Over the years greater sums have
been budgeted by the government for the development of the
Navy's submarine-rescue vehicle than for occupational safety, public libraries and day care centers, combined. The value of military
aircraft parts and components kept in storage ($9 billion in 1969)
exceeds the yearly federal outlays for elementary, secondary and
higher education, manpower training, old age assistance, and aid
to the blind and the permanently disabled. The Pentagon stores
more ammunition in its dumps ($10.4 billion worth) than the costs
of all natural resource programs including pollution control, conservation, community development, housing, occupational safety
and mass transportation. The total expenses of the legislative and
judiciary branches and all the regulatory commissions combined
constitute little more than one-half of 1 percent of the Pentagon's
budget. More public monies are given away every year to the
creditor class, the top 1 percent of the population, in interest payments on public bonds, than are spent in five years on services to
the bottom 20 percent.

The government has any number of policy options which might be pursued: it could end its costly overseas military interventions, drastically cut its military expenditures, cease its underground nuclear testing, phase out its expensive space programs,[16] eliminate the multibillion-dollar tax loopholes for corporations and rich individuals, increase taxes on industrial profits, cut taxes for lower- and middle-income groups, prosecute industries for pollution and for widespread monopolistic practices, end multibillion-dollar giveaways and legislate a guaranteed minimum income well above the poverty level. Government also could distribute to almost 2 million poor farmers the billions now received by rich agricultural producers, and it could engage in a concerted effort at conservation and enter directly into nonprofit production and ownership in the areas of health, housing, education and mass transportation.

Such measures have been urged, but in almost every instance government has pursued policies of an opposite kind. It is not enough to scold those who resist change as if they did so out of obstinance, perversity or ill-will; it is necessary to understand the dynamics of power and interest that make these policies persist in the face of all appeals and human needs to the contrary. Those who bemoan the "warped priorities" of our society assume that the present politico-economic system could produce a whole different set of effects. But the question is, *Why* have new and more humane priorities not been pursued? And the answer is twofold: first, because the realities of power do not allow for fundamental reform, and second, because the present politico-economic system could not sustain itself if such reforms were initiated. Let us take each of these in turn:

(1) Quite simply, those who have the interest in fundamental change have not the power, while those who have the power have not the interest. It is not that decision-makers have been unable to figure out the technical steps for change; it is that they oppose the things that change entails. The first intent of most politicians is not to fight for social change but to survive and prosper. Given this, they are inclined to respond positively not to group *needs* but to group *demands,* to those who have the resources to command their attention. In political life as in economic life, needs do not become marketable demands until they are backed by "buying power" or "exchange power" for only then is it in the "producer's" interest to respond. The problem for many unorganized citizens

16. The space shuttle program and the B-1 bomber together cost more than the entire Vietnam war.

and workers is that they have few political resources of their own to exchange. For the politician, as for most people, the compelling quality of any argument is determined less by its logic and evidence than by the strength of its advocates. And the advocate is strong if the resources he controls are desired and needed by the politician. The wants of the unorganized public seldom become demands —that is, they seldom become imperatives to which political officials find it in their own interest to respond, especially if the changes needed would put the official on a collision course with those who control the resources of the society and who see little wrong with the world as it is.

(2) Most of the demands for fundamental change in our priorities are impossible to effect within the present system if that system is to maintain itself. The reason our labor, skills, technology and natural resources are not used for social need and egalitarian redistribution is that they are used for corporate gain. The corporations cannot build low-rent houses and feed the poor because their interest is not in social reconstruction but in private profit. For the state to maintain whatever "prosperity" it can, it must do so within the ongoing system of corporate investments. To maintain investments, it must guarantee high-profit yields. To make fundamental changes in our priorities, the state would have to effect major redistributions in income and taxation, cut business subsidies, end deficit spending and interest payments to the rich, redirect capital investments toward nonprofit or low-profit goals and impose severe and sometimes crippling penalties for pollution and monopolistic practices. But if the state did all this, the investment incentives would be greatly diminished, the risks for private capital would be too high, many companies could not survive and unemployment would reach disastrous heights. State-supported capitalism cannot exist without state support, without passing its immense costs and inefficiencies on to the public. The only way the state could redirect the wealth of society toward egalitarian goals would be to exercise total control over capital investments and capital return, but that would mean, in effect, public ownership of the means of production—a giant step toward *socialism*.

It is understandable then why appeals to fair play and exhortations for change do not bring the fundamental reallocations needed: quite simply, the problem of change is no easier for the haves than for the have-nots. Contrary to the admonitions of liberal critics, it is neither stupidity nor opaqueness which prevents those who control the property and the institutions of this society from satisfying the demand for change. To be sure, elites suffer their share of self-righteous stubbornness, but more often than not, meaningful changes are not embarked upon because they would literally threaten the survival of privileged interests; like most other social groups the elites show little inclination to commit class suicide.

What is being argued here is that, contrary to the view of liberal critics, the nation's immense social problems are not irrational offshoots of a basically rational system, to be solved by replacing the existing corporate and political decision-makers with persons who would be better intentioned and more socially aware. Rather, the problems are rational outcomes of a basically irrational system, a system structured not for the satisfaction of human need but the multiplication of human greed. Within the imperatives of that system, well-intentioned reform-minded persons end up having either to obey the economic imperatives of that system or be removed from positions of responsibility. The reforms they manage to effect are the kind the system will allow, ones which do not tamper with the basic interests of class privilege, power and property.[17] As long as liberals proceed with an incorrect diagnosis, they will never come up with solutions. As long as we look for solutions within the very system that causes the problems, we will continue to produce cosmetic, band-aid programs. The end result is shameful public poverty and shameless private wealth.

Questioning the Status Quo

Defenders of the status quo are eager to point out that protest is a thing of the past and that today people are returning to the conventional, conservative values of the 1950s. Anyone who remembers the stupefying conformity of the fifties should find this difficult to believe. Social consciousness does not freeze in time nor does it revert to an earlier reality untouched by the experiences of twenty years. If the 1970s saw students return to careerist pursuits (and most of them had never left such pursuits, even during the height of the 1960s protest era), it is not with the same unquestioning

17. It is not that state-supported capitalism is the cause of every social ill in modern society but that capitalism and the capitalist state have no fundamental commitment to remedying social ills, despite their command over vast resources that might be directed toward such ends. And, from the evidence of past chapters, it might be argued that state-supported capitalism has been doing much to create, sustain and intensify the very conditions which breed social ills both at home and abroad.

belief in the "good life" of "affluent America" that characterized the 1950s. To be sure, the end of the Vietnam war brought an end to the antiwar movement with its teach-ins, mass demonstrations, sit-ins, draft resistance and acts of civil disobedience. Yet it would be a mistake to assume there no longer is any concern for the struggle for social justice in the United States. On campuses today, there is probably more critical analysis of the capitalist system than during the more activist antiwar days of the 1960s. In any case, college students are hardly the sole purveyors of political consciousness. Large numbers of women, working people, Blacks, Chicanos, Native Americans and other racial minorities are developing a critical perspective of the existing beliefs and practices of American society. In 1976 tens of thousands of people massed for a people's bicentennial demonstration in Philadelphia, demanding an end to American imperialism and capitalism—an event that was ignored by the business-owned press. Growing numbers of people were mobilizing against the proliferation of nuclear power plants. Environmentalist and public-interest groups continued to disseminate their views to increasingly sympathetic audiences. Repeatedly pronounced dead and gone, labor militancy among rank-and-file workers continued to erupt in the form of wildcat strikes against cutbacks, layoffs, forced overtime and unsafe working conditions. The struggles and protests of workers were more intense during the mid-1970s than during the late 1960s, but they were mostly ignored by the media. One thing is certain: it is a grossly misleading stereotype to portray workers as jingoistic, conservative, racist flag-wavers who are enamored of the status quo.[18]

Political consciousness changes sometimes visibly and noisily, sometimes deeply and quietly. The transition in Black consciousness offers an interesting case in point. It is probably no accident that the first challenges to the established ideology and to the image of "America, the beautiful" came from Black people. Forcibly brought to this country centuries ago as chattels for the sole purpose of economic exploitation, Blacks, after the Emancipation and over the generations, continued to suffer every exploitation, discrimination and violence to body and spirit that White America was capable of inflicting. By the 1960s Blacks were saying publicly

18. Andrew Levison, *The Working-Class Majority* (New York: Penguin Books, 1975), offers much evidence to debunk the Archie Bunker stereotype of workers. For excellent studies of radicalism and militancy in the American labor movement, see Jeremy Brecher, *Strike* (New York: Fawcett, 1974); and Richard O. Boyer and Herbert M. Morais, *Labor's Untold Story* (New York: United Electrical, Radio and Machine Workers, 1972).

what many of them had always felt privately: that there was no justice for Black people in White America, that Blacks did not share equally in the progress our country was allegedly enjoying and that they must develop their own identities and consciousness and mobilize against White bosses, unions, landlords, merchants, police, government officials and the White power system in general.

As the Black protest grew, other groups began getting the message, and by the early 1970s Chicano, Native American, Puerto Rican and women's liberation groups were voicing similar indictments about the social roles and social conditions imposed upon them. And just as the Black protest started with demands for integration into the established system only to develop serious questions about the desirability of that goal ("Who wants to integrate into a burning house?"), so did the other protest groups begin to wonder whether piecemeal entry into the established structure would bring them any closer to a resolution of widespread social ills. When a Black becomes a corporation vice-president or a woman becomes a Navy pilot it is a net loss for all oppressed people, they argued, since corporate executives and Navy officers, whether White males or Black females, serve the interests of those in power and not those in need.[19]

Today many Black leaders reject total integration as an unrealistic and even undesirable goal. Integration, they point out, usually means the selective absorption of talented Blacks into White-dominated institutions, with little substantive return to the Black masses. No ethnic group in the United States ever wanted total integration, Nathan Wright, Jr., notes: "All have asked simply for desegregation. Desegregation involves some integration as a means to an end but not as an end in itself."[20] Desegregation is an important step forward, leading to the removal of legal and de facto barriers that loom as instruments of racial insult and oppression. Ultimately, though, the betterment of the Black people will come,

19. For discussions of how the Black liberation struggle is tied to the class struggle, see the writings of James Boggs and Grace Boggs; see also Julius Lester, "The Current State of Black America," *New Politics*, 10 June 1973, pp. 4–13. For an earlier statement see my "Assimilation and Counter-Assimilation: From Civil Rights to Black Radicalism," in Philip Green and Sanford Levison (eds.), *Power and Communty* (New York: Pantheon, 1969), pp. 173–194. For statements on how the liberation of women is tied to the liberation of the working class, see Rosalyn Boxandall et al. (eds.), *America's Working Women: A Documentary History—1600 to the Present* (New York: Random House, 1976).

20. Nathan Wright, Jr., "The Crises Which Bred Black Power," in Floyd D. Barbow (ed.), *The Black Power Revolt* (Boston: Sargent, Porter, 1968), p. 117.

radical Blacks say, not through piecemeal absorption into the White establishment but through an upheaval of the entire exploitative politico-economic system and the deliverance of the resources of power into the hands of the poor and the working people of all races—what we call social revolution. Within the Black community today there is also a growing identification with the antiimperialist struggles of the Third World, especially those in Africa, and with this a deeper indictment of the corporate system at home.

Millions of Americans, of course, are still committed to the acquisitive, competitive values discussed in Chapter Three. Millions still live with a fear of equality and a scarcity psychology that pits each against the other. Much of this sentiment is reenforced by the simple fact that the system obliges us to compete against each other in order to survive and in order to live with any modicum of comfort and security. But despite these powerful conditioning forces, despite the secret actions and manipulations used by the state to maintain the status quo and despite elitist control over most of the resources of power and over the institutions and information of this society, the American people are not indifferent to the exploitative and unjust features of the existing system. As noted in Chapter Three, opinion surveys show that Americans have far more progressive positions than the leaders of both parties. The opinion polls note the marked decline in "faith" that the public, including many "middle Americans," feels for its political and economic institutions, a development troublesome enough to evoke alarmed comments from business leaders and their counterparts in government. Ordinary Americans are not as oblivious to their own needs as are their leaders. They justly feel victimized as wage earners, tenants, home owners, taxpayers, commuters and consumers.

Upward from Capitalism

More than half a century ago the great sociologist Max Weber wrote: "The question is: How are freedom and democracy in the long run at all possible under the domination of highly developed capitalism?"[21] That question is still with us. And the answer suggested in this book is that freedom and democracy have at best a tenuous, marginal existence in capitalist society.

21. *From Max Weber: Essays in Sociology* (New York: Oxford University Press, 1958), ed. H. H. Gerth and C. Wright Mills.

How can we speak of most government policies as being products of the democratic will? What democratic will demanded that Washington be honeycombed with high-paid lobbyists and corporate lawyers who would spend their time raiding the public treasury on behalf of rich clients? When was the public consulted on tideland oil leases, Alaskan oil leases, bloated defense contracts, agribusiness subsidies and tax write-offs? When did the American people insist on having unsafe, overpriced drugs and foods circulate unrestricted and an FDA that protects rather than punishes the companies marketing such products? When did they urge the government to help the gas, electric and telephone companies to overcharge the public? When did the voice of the people clamor for a multibillion-dollar space program that fattened corporate contractors and satisfied the curiosity of some astronomers and scientists while leaving the rest of us still more burdened by taxes and deprived of necessary services here on earth? What democratic will decreed that we destroy the Cambodian countryside between 1969 and 1971 in a bombing campaign conducted without the consent or even the knowledge of Congress and the public? And what large sector of public opinion demanded that the government intervene secretly in Laos with U.S. Marines in 1969 or financially sustain a war of Portuguese colonial oppression in Africa or subvert progressive governments in Chile, Indonesia, Iran, and elsewhere?

Far from giving their assent, ordinary people have had to struggle to find out what is going on. And to the extent that a popular will has been registered, it has been demonstrably in the opposite direction, against the worst abuses and most blatant privileges of plutocracy, against the spoilage of the environment and the plunder of the treasury, against the use of government power to serve corporate conglomerates, and against military intervention in other countries.

The political system will belong to the people only when the resources of power belong to them, enabling them to effect their democratic will at all levels of private and public institutional life. This will entail a struggle of momentous scope against the corporate elites that now control our labor and our politics. The purpose will be not to replace those at the top with others but to demonstrate that we do not need anyone *on top,* that there is no immutable need for gargantuan government and stratified, bureaucratized, authoritarian institutions and that those involved in the life activities of an institution and affected by its actions should have command of its resources. In a democratic socialist system, the factories, mills, mines, offices, educational institutions, newspapers, hospitals, etc., will not be privately owned for private gain but will be controlled by and for their clients and workers. That is the goal toward which our efforts should be directed.

What is important under socialism is not only whether something is publicly owned and financed but the *purpose* or goals toward which production is directed and the way priorities are set and decisions made. The commitment is, or should be, to communal, collective and responsible decision-making and toward the elimination of poverty and pollution, the end of imperialism, the equalization of life chances, the bettering of the lives of millions of needy working people.[22] Once the wealth, labor and creative energies of people are liberated from the irrational social purposes of a capitalist system, the potentialities for human advancement and individual initiative will be greatly increased, as has happened in a number of Third World countries that have liberated themselves from imperialism. Under the present system we are taught passivity, consumerism, spectatorism, isolation and incompetence. Our energies often are directed into overly specialized and mindless tasks for the production of a glut of gadgets and gimmicks that no one really asked for. We are taught that the controlling decisions over our lives must remain in the hands of those "above" us, those who claim to know better—or else "there will be chaos." There are people who insist that worker control of factories is "impracticable," yet worker-control systems have been set up in several countries with workers devising their own job assignments, rotating their tasks, teaching each other new skills, setting their own work paces, making managerial decisions, controlling budgets and production schedules, etc. The results have been remarkable for worker morale and production efficiency, but in capitalist nations such innovations are potentially dangerous to the owning class, for once workers realize they do not need management to command them, they may begin to question why the profits must

22. In the view of many socialists, especially those identified with the radical movement in America, public ownership of the means of production for the purpose of building an authoritarian, hierarchical society with substantial income inequalities, dominated by a bureaucratic elite as in the USSR, is not socialism, or, at best, it is a tragically misshaped form of socialism, one that might provide a fairly decent minimum standard of social services for all its citizens, including free education and good medical care, but which denies them the opportunities for personal initiative and cooperative control over the conditions of work, study, community and environment and over the products of their minds and their labor and over the larger policies of their nation.

go to the corporate owners, who contribute nothing to production.

There are people who cannot imagine an alternative university system and are frightened at the prospect of changing the present structure, which gives nearly total power to successful businessmen who serve as oligarchic trustees while the rest of us remain powerless dependents. Yet there already exist more democratically organized institutions of learning. There are people who cannot imagine that hospitals can be organized in any way that would diminish the elitist, authoritarian, money-making role of the head doctors and trustees, and allow staff and patients to play a real part in decision-making, openly criticizing mistakes and collectively working for improvements. Yet such hospitals, and quite good ones, exist in other parts of the world.[23] What a pathetic failure of the political imagination that some of our professional people cannot, or dare not, imagine more sensible, efficient and democratic ways of organizing our social, political and economic institutions. Out of a fear that their class and professional privileges might be challenged, some people resist all equalizing changes and commit themselves to living unexamined lives.

But those of us who have some feeling for social justice and liberation must educate ourselves about the nature of the politico-economic system we live in (hopefully this book has been a step in that direction). We must liberate our political imaginations and learn about alternative forms of social organization and alternative social values. We must confront and engage our peers in the kind of dialogue that heightens our awareness and helps us free ourselves and each other from the elitist, hierarchical values that imprison us, including the bigotry toward working-class people and the sexism, racism and fear of equality we have all been taught. We must, in our places of work and community, organize politically, learn to work cooperatively, engage in direct action, demonstrations, strikes, boycotts and in every way work against the manifold inhumanities of capitalism.

Finally, we must make the effort to educate not only ourselves but others, through the use of what limited political resources we have, to the unjust and undemocratic features of state-supported capitalism and to the possibilities for an alternative antiimperialist, antiracist, antisexist, democratic socialism. This last point is an important one. The wasteful, destructive effects of corporatism within our nation, the pressures of competition between capitalist nations,

23. See Joshua Horne, *Away with All Pests* (New York: Monthly Review Press, 1971) for a discussion of medical practices in China.

the growing discontent and oppression of the populace, the continual productive growth within socialist nations, the new revolutionary victories against Western imperialism in the Third World, all these things make objective conditions increasingly unfavorable for capitalism. Yet people will not discard the system that oppresses them until they see the feasibility of an alternative one. It is not that they think society *should* be this way but that it *must* be. It is not that they don't want things to change, but they don't believe things *can* change—or they fear that whatever changes might occur would more likely be for the worse.

What is needed is widespread organizing not only around particular issues but for a socialist movement that sees both the desirability of an alternative system and the *possibility* and indeed the great *necessity* for an alternative. Throughout the world and at home, forces for change are being unleashed. The survey data cited in Chapter Three show that Americans are well ahead of the existing political elites in their willingness to embrace new alternatives, including public ownership of the major corporations and worker control of production. With time and struggle, as the possibility and necessity for progressive change become more evident and the longing for a better social life grows stronger, people will become increasingly intolerant of the monumental injustices of the existing capitalist system and will move toward a profoundly revolutionary solution. Hopefully the day will come, as it came in social orders of the past, when those who seem invincible will be shaken from their pinnacles and a new, humane and truly democratic society will begin to emerge.

About the Author

MICHAEL PARENTI received his Ph.D. in political science from Yale University and has lectured and taught at various colleges and universities over the past twenty-two years. He also has been an active spokesperson for the antiwar movement and for other social reforms. Numerous articles of his on American politics, foreign policy and ethnic politics have appeared in academic journals and popular periodicals. Among his books are *The Anti-Communist Impulse, Trends and Tragedies in American Foreign Policy* (a book of edited readings), and the forthcoming *Power and the Powerless.*

Index